Beyond the National Divide

Regional Dimensions of Industrial Relations

Edited by
Mark Thompson
Joseph B. Rose
Anthony E. Smith

Published for the Canadian Industrial Relations Association /
Association canadienne des relations industrielles and the
School of Policy Studies, Queen's University
by McGill-Queen's University Press
Montreal & Kingston • London • Ithaca

National Library of Canada Cataloguing in Publication

Beyond the national divide : regional dimensions of industrial
relations / edited by Mark Thompson, Joseph B. Rose, Anthony E. Smith.

Includes some text in French.
Includes bibliographical references.
ISBN 0-88911-965-1 (bound).—ISBN 0-88911-963-5 (pbk.)

1. Industrial relations—Canada—Regional disparities.
I. Thompson, Mark, 1939-   II. Rose, Joseph B. III. Smith, Anthony E.
IV. Canadian Industrial Relations Association V. Queen's University
(Kingston, Ont.). School of Policy Studies

HD8106.5.B49 2003   331'.0971   C2003-903746-0

Beyond the National Divide

Regional Dimensions of Industrial Relations

SCHOOL OF
Policy Studies
QUEEN'S UNIVERSITY

The School of Policy Studies at Queen's University is a leading centre for advanced research and education in public policy. The School offers a multidisciplinary graduate degree, sponsors a number of research institutes and programs, and serves as a bridge between the world of academic research and the world of public affairs.

L'École des études en politiques publiques de l'Université Queen's est un centre de tout premier plan pour la recherche et les études de haut niveau dans le domaine des politiques publiques. L'École offre un diplôme d'études supérieures multidisciplinaires; elle parraine plusieurs instituts et programmes de recherche et sert de lien entre le monde de la recherche universitaire et celui des affaires publiques.

The Canadian Industrial Relations Association (CIRA) is the major academic and professional association concerned with work and employment in Canada. Through the journal *RI/IR – Relations industrielles-Industrial Relations*, an annual spring conference and refereed proceedings of the best papers, its research volumes and a network of local chapters, CIRA brings together researchers and practitioners in specialist areas such as labour relations, human resources management, labour law, labour studies, health and safety at work, work organization, and labour and employment policy. For further information on membership and forthcoming activities, please consult the CIRA Web site (http://www.cira-acri.ca/).

L'Association canadienne des relations industrielles (ACRI) est la principale association universitaire et professionnelle s'intéressant au travail et à l'emploi au Canada. Par la diffusion de la revue scientifique *RI/IR – Relations industrielles-Industrial Relations* à ses membres, par la tenue de son congrès annuel et la publication des actes arbitrés regroupant les meilleurs textes présentés lors de ce congrès, par la publication, en volumes, de ses recherches et par son réseau implanté de sections régionales, l'ACRI réunit les chercheurs et les personnes de la pratique professionnelle dans les champs spécialisés suivants : les relations du travail, la gestion des ressources humaines, le droit du travail, les études syndicales, la santé et la sécurité au travail, l'organisation du travail et les politiques publiques en matière de travail et d'emploi. Pour de plus amples renseignements sur la démarche à suivre pour devenir membre et les activités à venir, prière de consulter le site Web de l'ACRI (http://www.cira-acri.ca/).

Dedication

This book is dedicated to Anthony E. (Tony) Smith, 1942–1998.
He helped conceive this book and was co-editor until his untimely passing.
Tony was a valued friend and colleague of CIRA members.

TABLE OF CONTENTS

TABLES AND FIGURES

TABLES

FIGURES

FOREWORD

The Canadian Industrial Relations Association (CIRA-ACRI) is the major academic and professional association concerned with work and employment in Canada. As an open, interdisciplinary forum for researchers, practitioners and policymakers on issues of contemporary significance for the study of work and employment, it seeks to promote fruitful exchange and scholarly research on these issues. As a complement to our other activities, the CIRA executive initiated a policy of specially commissioned research volumes in order to cover important gaps in our knowledge about work and employment issues in Canada and to promote the publication of scholarly research of interest to our members and the wider community.

Beyond the National Divide: Regional Dimensions of Industrial Relations is the tangible result of this policy. Despite the fact that most labour and employment issues are in a provincial rather than a federal jurisdiction, there has not been any authoritative source on patterns of industrial relations in each province. Not only does this book do an admirable job in filling this gap, but the substantive and practical engagement of its authors with the complexities of employment relations in their particular province shines throughout its pages. This will make this volume an invaluable teaching and research tool for all those who seek to understand the regulation of work and employment in each province as well as the regional variations in patterns of industrial relations in Canada.

This project is the result of many different contributions. On behalf of the CIRA executive, I wish to take this opportunity to acknowledge them. First of all, special thanks are due to the editors and authors of this engaging work and, in particular, to Mark Thompson and Joe Rose for taking on extra responsibilities as the result of the death of the late Anthony Smith, who was the initial moving force behind this project. Second, thanks are due to the efforts of successive CIRA presidents, secretary-treasurers, and executive and research committee members for their work in the gestation and completion of this project — in particular, Renaud Paquet, Reynald Bourque, Yonaton Reshef, Gregor Murray, Frank

Reid, Colette Bernier and Sylvie Montreuil. Third, we wish to thank Keith Banting and his team of highly efficient publications staff at the School of Policy Studies at Queen's University for partnering CIRA in the publication of this research volume. Finally, and certainly not least, the publication of this volume would not be possible without the support of the CIRA members who pay a special research levy in order to support our research policy.

Gregor Murray
CIRA Past President

AVANT-PROPOS

L'Association canadienne des relations industrielles (ACRI-CIRA) est la principale association universitaire et professionnelle s'intéressant au travail et à l'emploi au Canada. En tant que forum interdisciplinaire portant sur des enjeux contemporains relatifs à l'étude du travail et de l'emploi, les travaux de l'ACRI s'adressent à la fois aux chercheurs, aux praticiens et aux personnes responsables de l'élaboration des politiques publiques; l'ACRI vise la promotion d'échanges fructueux et de la recherche scientifique portant sur ces enjeux. En complément à ses autres activités, l'exécutif de l'ACRI a adopté une politique de parrainage des volumes de recherche afin de combler des lacunes dans nos connaissances portant sur le travail et l'emploi au Canada d'une part, et afin d'assurer la publication de la recherche scientifique susceptible d'intéresser les membres de l'ACRI et la communauté élargie, d'autre part.

Beyond the National Divide: Regional Dimensions of Industrial Relations est le résultat tangible de cette initiative. Les questions portant sur le travail et l'emploi relèvent avant tout des compétences provinciales et jusqu'à ce jour, il n'y avait pas, au Canada, une œuvre de référence faisant le point sur les relations industrielles dans chaque province. Cet ouvrage remplit admirablement ce vide certes, mais il faut ajouter que chacune des pages de ce livre offre un éclairage soigné, attribuable à l'implication profonde et concrète de ses auteurs dans les rapports d'emploi dans leur province respective. Voici donc un outil d'enseignement et de recherche indispensable pour quiconque cherche à comprendre la régulation du travail et de l'emploi dans chaque province ainsi que les variations régionales des différents modèles de relations industrielles au Canada.

Ce projet est le fruit de contributions multiples. Au nom de l'exécutif de l'ACRI, nous tenons à leur exprimer notre gratitude. Au premier chef, il faut remercier les directeurs et les auteurs de cet ouvrage si intéressant. En particulier, Mark Thompson et Joseph Rose ont dû assumer des responsabilités additionnelles suite au décès du regretté Anthony Smith qui a été l'instigateur énergique de ce projet. Ensuite, notons les efforts des présidents, des secrétaires-trésorières et des membres de l'exécutif de l'ACRI et son comité de recherche — en particulier, Renaud Paquet, Reynald Bourque, Yonatan Reshef, Gregor Murray, Frank Reid, Colette Bernier et Sylvie Montreuil — qui ont œuvré pour mener ce projet à terme. Ensuite, nous tenons à remercier Keith Banting et son équipe d'édition de l'École des études en politiques publiques, Université Queen's, pour leur excellente collaboration en tant que partenaires dans l'édition de cet ouvrage. Enfin, il faut souligner que la publication de cet ouvrage n'aura été possible que grâce au supplément de cotisation assuré par les membres de l'ACRI, à titre d'appui concret à notre politique de recherche.

Gregor Murray
Président sortant de l'ACRI

PREFACE

This book was supported by the Canadian Industrial Relations Association (CIRA) as its first research volume on major issues in Canadian industrial relations. The selection of this topic recognizes that Canada is a nation of regions. The division of powers in the constitution, the shape of national politics, the structure of the economy, language, geography, and other factors reinforce the regional identity in Canadian life. Despite the importance of regionalism in Canada, previous industrial relations research has recognized region as a variable only for Quebec. CIRA sponsored the first book published in any country that addresses the influence of region on industrial relations explicitly.

The project was conceived by Mark Thompson and Anthony Smith. They prepared a proposal and outline for the chapters in the volume. Tony met with the CIRA executive and received their endorsement. Initially, the project was to include a separate chapter for each province, except Prince Edward Island, and a conclusion. PEI was omitted because of its size and the lack of an author to write a chapter. Tony Smith took the lead in producing a chapter for New Brunswick, the province where he had lived and taught for a number of years.

Tony's sudden death in 1998 affected all involved in the project. At the time of his death, he was the past-president of CIRA. Joseph Rose volunteered to become co-editor of the volume, in addition to writing a chapter on Ontario. The editors and CIRA executive were unsuccessful in finding a replacement for Tony Smith to write a chapter on New Brunswick. Joe Rose, who taught at the University of New Brunswick for several years, wrote a brief summary of industrial relations in the province for use in the concluding chapter.

1 INTRODUCTION

Mark Thompson
Joseph B. Rose

Résumé — Le Canada est un pays constitué de régions qui, toutes, expriment de nombreux aspects de la vie nationale. Toutefois, dans le présent livre, les relations industrielles ne sont pas examinées dans un contexte régional. Ce qui justifie cette approche est le fait que, d'une part, dans l'ensemble du traitement des relations industrielles canadiennes, le Québec exige un traitement à part en raison de la structure particulière de ses relations industrielles, et, d'autre part, les autres parties du pays sont plus ou moins homogènes à cet égard. La définition d'une « région » peut varier, mais ici chaque province est considérée comme une région distincte. Le droit constitutionnel qu'ont les provinces de régir leurs relations industrielles selon les contextes politique, économique et historique qui leur sont propres justifie cette distinction.

D'après la théorie des relations industrielles, les influences de la collectivité sont des variables dans le fonctionnement d'un régime de relations industrielles. Quelques travaux de recherche sur l'influence des facteurs régionaux sur les relations industrielles ont été effectués aux États-Unis, en Australie et au Royaume-Uni, mais la plus grande partie de ces travaux porte surtout sur des régions qui ne constituent pas une entité politique distincte et, par conséquent, la politique publique de ces entités n'est pas importante. De plus, la conclusion générale de ces travaux indique que les modèles régionaux de relations industrielles sont fonction de la structure industrielle. Or, l'étude comparative des relations industrielles tient toujours compte de l'influence des forces historiques, juridiques, politiques et sociales, en plus de la structure industrielle. En conséquence, l'incidence de tous ces facteurs sur les relations industrielles dans les provinces canadiennes est prise en compte dans ce livre.

Huit chapitres traitent respectivement d'une province. (L'Île-du-Prince-Édouard et le Nouveau-Brunswick n'y sont pas traités : la première, faute d'auteur; le second parce que l'auteur est décédé avant d'avoir achevé son étude.) Chaque auteur a reçu un aperçu du modèle de régime de relations industrielles élaboré par Dunlop, mais a été invité à aborder les relations industrielles de la province étudiée sous un thème qui les caractérisent.

Les réviseurs ont conclu que quatre provinces (le Québec, l'Ontario, le Manitoba et la Colombie-Britannique) ont un régime de relations industrielles reconnu, c'est-à-dire que les relations industrielles et la négociation collective constituent des institutions centrales dans la vie de la province. Les quatre autres (Terre-Neuve-et-Labrador, la Nouvelle-Écosse, la Saskatchewan et l'Alberta) ont un régime subordonné, c'est-à-dire que les questions liées au travail occupent tout au plus un second rang dans les affaires provinciales.

Les relations industrielles en Ontario sont considérées représenter le modèle de « régime canadien ». Malgré l'influence de sa taille et de son secteur industriel sur les autres provinces, l'Ontario a conservé un régime de relations industrielles solide au cours des décennies où le Parti conservateur a gouverné cette province. L'un après l'autre, les gouvernements de ce parti ont cherché à assurer la stabilité dans le monde du travail, car, à leurs yeux, elle constituait un avantage concurrentiel.

Les relations industrielles au Québec revêtent un certain nombre de traits distinctifs. Le taux de syndicalisation et le nombre de grèves y sont supérieurs à la moyenne nationale. Le Parti québécois a toujours entretenu des liens étroits avec les syndicats pendant qu'il était au pouvoir, et l'essor des relations industrielles est intimement lié à la Révolution tranquille des années 1960 et 1970. Dans les années 1990, le gouvernement, le milieu des affaires et les syndicats ont établi un réseau d'institutions consultatives qui ont stimulé la coopération patronale-syndicale dans le milieu de travail.

En Colombie-Britannique, les relations industrielles sont marquées par la présence de groupes bien organisés dans de vastes unités de négociation. Donnant le ton aux relations patronales-syndicales, les industries primaires influencent l'économie provinciale. Tant les syndicats que les associations d'employeurs sont en général mieux organisés dans cette province que dans les autres. La politique très partisane influe également sur les relations industrielles. La fréquence des grèves a diminué dans les années 1990, mais les conflits de travail dans le secteur public ont continué d'être nombreux.

Les relations patronales-syndicales au Manitoba sont uniques : elles reflètent la division des classes bien ancrée dans l'histoire de cette province, une économie fragile et un milieu des affaires de plus en plus isolé. Les nombreux conflits de travail qui ont marqué le début du XXe siècle et le radicalisme politique ont poussé le milieu des affaires à rechercher la paix sociale. Lorsque les gouvernements conservateurs ont tenté de rompre cet équilibre, le nombre de grèves a brusquement augmenté, et le Nouveau Parti Démocratique (NPD) en a profité au plan politique.

La Saskatchewan est l'une des provinces les moins industrialisées. Pourtant, le NPD (et avant lui la CCF dont il est issu) gouverne cette province depuis les années 1940. Durant les premières années de gouvernement de ce parti, une forte tradition d'action directe a influencé la législation et forcé le pays à accorder des droits aux travailleurs. Toutefois, le NPD étant un parti agrarien et favorable aux PME, les gouvernements de ce parti ont rompu avec leurs traditions réformistes en matière de relations de travail.

Terre-Neuve-et-Labrador dépend fortement des ressources naturelles, de la construction et des emplois dans le secteur public. Après l'entrée de cette province dans la Confédération, le premier ministre Joey Smallwood a pris les dispositions nécessaires pour protéger les droits des travailleurs, ce qui ne l'a pas empêché, en 1959, de mettre fin à une grève et d'expulser le syndicat de la province. Depuis, et malgré le taux de syndicalisation élevé, les gouvernements et les employeurs sont capables d'imposer leur volonté au mouvement syndical.

Les gouvernements qui, favorables à l'entreprise, ont cherché à attirer les investissements ont dominé la vie politique en Nouvelle-Écosse. Dans les années 1930, le militantisme syndical au Cap-Breton a poussé le gouvernement à adopter une législation plus favorable aux travailleurs que celle des autres provinces. Depuis, l'importance industrielle du Cap-Breton ayant diminué, les gouvernements provinciaux ont progressivement affaibli les mesures de protection des travailleurs.

L'Alberta représente, aux plans politique et social, la province la plus conservatrice du Canada. Ses politiques publiques sont moins favorables aux travailleurs que celles des autres provinces. L'absence d'un important secteur manufacturier et d'un NPD puissant, a affaibli le mouvement syndical. Les grèves y sont moins nombreuses qu'ailleurs au pays, mais l'industrie pétrolière favorise de bonnes conditions de travail et des salaires relativement élevés. L'institution de la négociation collective y est cependant bien établie, tant dans le secteur public que privé.

Le dernier chapitre traite des origines et de la définition des deux catégories de régimes de relations industrielles, soit le régime « reconnu » et le régime « subordonné ». Les provinces canadiennes affichent une variabilité considérable au sein du régime de relations industrielles canadien.

C anada is almost unique among industrialized nations in the degree of decentralization of its industrial relations system. In this group of countries, only Australia grants substantial authority to subnational units (states) to regulate industrial relations. Unlike Canada, the Australian national government can intercede in industrial relations at the initiative of either party (normally the union side). Other nations in Europe and the United States have a national legislative regime and a tradition of industrywide or national bargaining units, leaving little scope for regional variation.

Canadian constitutional arrangements give provinces the right to legislate over employment matters, and many industries (automobile manufacturing, for instance) have a strong provincial focus. These factors, combined with the strong regional influences over economic and political affairs in Canada raise the question of whether Canada has a "national" industrial relations system on the same terms as European countries or the United States. Most industrial relations scholars have assumed the existence of a single system, but contemporary political and economic thought have emphasized subnational factors. The editors of a recent volume on provincial politics called the "provincial state" "one of the most neglected areas in the study of Canadian history and politics" (Brownsey and Howlett 2001, 13). A major statement of the need to consider regional influences in industrial relations was Locke's (1992) theoretical challenge to national-level industrial relations.

Regionalism is a profound and fundamental feature of Canadian political and economic life. The nation emerged by absorbing existing colonies or by incorporating large territories with distinct identities when they achieved provincial status. Federal politics is often viewed in regional terms, as "western" political parties emerge, for instance. National parties in Parliament are judged by their ability (or failure) to elect members in all regions of the country. The special place of Quebec in Confederation is a central issue for national life. The Task Force on Canadian Unity reported in 1979 that regionalism was one of the two "lines of cleavage" in Canada (the other being language) (Task Force on Canadian Unity 1979). Provincial branches of national political parties often differ from their national leadership. Provincially based political parties have governed British Columbia, Alberta, and Quebec. National economic policy is examined for its impact on a particular region, especially the Atlantic and western provinces. Amending formulas for the constitution were debated in regional terms. Provincial economic performance is often compared, as are compensation and other indicators of living standards (see Cousineau and Vaillancourt 2000).

Surprisingly little attention has been devoted to explaining these economic or political differences. Occasional studies compare government policies, and a larger literature attempts to explain variations in living standards. Popular perception holds that cultural differences exist across regions, although few data are available other than comparisons of Quebec with the other provinces (Brodie 1990). Thus, no major theoretical literature supports any attempt to explain regional differences in industrial relations.

WHAT IS A "REGION"?

For all of the debate about regionalism, no consensus on the definition of a region in Canada (or in other nations) exists. Regions are both spatial and cultural, a dialectic between persons and space. Places are frames of social reference, the incubators of values. Well-identified regions usually operate through political structures and organizations of interest groups (Lomnitz-Adler 1992). Regions are essentially intellectual constructs, so they vary by discipline. Most geographers define regions by landscape or natural features, on the assumption that common geographical features promote common political, social, and cultural characteristics. Thus, physical boundaries, combined with internal hierarchies and spatial images can be important determinants of regions. Political scientists identify regions by political boundaries, as do economists. In Canada, economists usually disaggregate data into provincial units because data from smaller units are seldom available.

In Canada, the mere definition of regions has been controversial. Commonly, the larger provinces — Quebec, Ontario, and British Columbia — each constitute a "region," in the minds of most observers. Smaller provinces are combined into larger regions, such as the Atlantic or Prairie provinces. In debates over amending formulas for the constitution or other divisions of political power within Confederation, these distinctions are significant.

Quebec is the exception to this generalization. Apart from a boundary issue in Labrador, Quebec's identity as a region is unquestioned. Not only is the province defined by certain traditional physical boundaries, but its distinctive features are the product of historical experience, human organizations, and social interactions (Brodie 1990). Other jurisdictions, lacking that experience, have less defined status.

In theory, it is possible to define regions in similar terms outside the limits of provincial boundaries, for example, northern Ontario as opposed to the heavily populated areas in the southwestern part of the province. The Acadian area in New Brunswick has obvious links to Quebec, and northern Alberta and northern British Columbia have many common characteristics. Because political boundaries do not coincide with political divisions, tensions between economic (or cultural) and political units arise (Van Young 1992). Each of these sub-regions has a sense of grievance against the province in which it is located.

For purposes of Canadian industrial relations, the province is the logical unit for regional comparisons, as opposed to areas within a province or groups of provinces. The provinces have the political structures and organizations of interest groups that Lomnitz-Adler identified as necessary for a region. In the literature of industrial relations, Hyman defined a national industrial relations system as: "Institutional arrangements shaped by legislative frameworks, historical traditions, accumulated vested interests and learned patterns of behaviour" (1994, 2). Because the provinces have the constitutional authority to regulate industrial relations and employment in most industries, they attain the status of a state in this subject area. It is this feature of the Canadian industrial relations system that makes the province a logical variable for analysis. The chapters in this book will examine each of the other factors that Hyman identified.

REGIONALISM AND INDUSTRIAL RELATIONS

Regional differences in Canadian industrial relations have not been analyzed extensively, with the occasional exception of Quebec. The few general treatments of the subject (Thompson 1998; Craig and Solomon 1993; Gunderson, Ponak and Taras 2001) do not examine regional differences as such, apart from special notice of Quebec and brief discussions of provincial variation in labour legislation. In international comparisons, Canada is treated as a homogenous entity (see Rose and Chaison 1996). Survey occasionally divides data by province, although issues of the size of the sample preclude detailed analysis on this basis (see Betcherman *et al.* 1994). Legislative comparisons focus on the more controversial aspects of Canadian labour law, including certification procedures, restrictions on the use of strike replacements and essential services.

Since industrial relations in the public sector is regulated more closely than in the private sector, legislative differences are particularly important. For this reason, provinces have been treated individually. Variations are found in the right to strike, legislated bargaining structures, dispute-settlement procedures and the like (Ponak and Thompson 2001). Recent literature has identified several provinces for separate analysis (Swimmer 2001; Adell, Grant and Ponak 2001).

The most detailed discussions of a provincial experience are the differences between Quebec and the rest of Canada. This is often reflected by separate chapters on Quebec in leading industrial relations textbooks in Canada (Miller and Isbester 1971; Gunderson, Ponak and Taras 2001; and Swimmer and Thompson 1995). As well, the annual meetings of the Canadian Industrial Relations Association have occasionally featured sessions on industrial relations in the region where the meeting was being held. Further, given that provincial labour laws cover 90 percent of the workforce, reviews of labour legislation often focus on regional differences. The decentralized legal framework has taken on even greater importance over the past 30 years. Whereas the federal government established the direction of labour law reform for the first 75 years, the provinces now set the tone for labour policy changes (Weiler 1980).

The traditional focus of industrial relations research has been the level of a union or an industry. The work by Chaykowski and Verma (1992) contained 12 industry-level studies, for example. A research volume published by the Industrial Relations Research Association included 12 case studies of collective bargaining in individual American industries (Voos 1994). Each of these books produced insights about their respective national industrial relations systems which had not been previously available or had been treated tentatively in broader studies.

The lack of any geographic emphasis in industrial relations is notable theoretically. Dunlop (1958) examined the context of industrial relations, including the technological characteristics of the workplace and community, as well as the distribution of power in the larger community. Clearly, Dunlop included social as well as economic variables in his systems model. The 1968 Woods Task Force, relying on a paper written by Alton Craig, referred to the political, economic, and social environment of Canadian industrial relations, but the remainder of their analysis focused on national issues, except for provincial legislative differences. The traditional systems approach to industrial relations has emphasized the spatial or political aspects of industrial relations at the national level (see Bamber and Lansbury 1998), but seldom at the subnational or regional level. Perhaps by default, industrial relations scholars have concluded that the context of industrial relations is dominated by economic variables, that is, industrial structures or national institutions, including legislation, labour and employer organizations or bargaining structures.

If one analyzes industrial relations on a regional basis, the impact of industrial structures across regions clearly is significant. Regional economies dominated by heavy manufacturing or resources are expected to exhibit different industrial relations characteristics than those with light manufacturing, services or transportation. In other words, is region an independent variable in an industrial relations system, or are regions the collection of the dominant industry-specific or sectoral industrial relations systems? This mode of analysis neglects the social variables in the systems model and relies on economic factors as the major independent variables.

Non-economic variables in the Dunlop context have been identified, but not often analyzed. An American symposium on "comparative community influences on industrial relations" explicitly focused on non-economic variables. In his introductory essay, Seidman (1965) identified the labour force, union organizations, market structures, and industrial or bargaining structures as possible influences on industrial relations in a community. All of the essays in the series covering Los Angeles, Decatur, Illinois, Minneapolis/St. Paul and New York, identified industrial structure as a significant variable (Bernstein 1965; Derber 1965; Romer 1965; Cook and Gray 1966). Most pointed to the demographics of the labour force, that is, the geographic or ethnic origins of the labour force and the extent and structure of the labour movement, as being important. The history of labour relations in the communities was mentioned in passing.

In Los Angeles, for example, the lack of local traditions and ties of workers contributed to the fragmentation of labour relations, while the peaceful rise of industrial unionism in Decatur promoted relatively cooperative labour relations there. By contrast, a tradition of militant and left-wing unionism in Minneapolis/St. Paul helped establish a strong position for labour in the political and social life of the two cities. Ultimately, however, the symposium did not identify major differences among the cities examined, and the effort did not stimulate further research.

An important stream of "regional" industrial relations research in North America is the American South. For decades, southeastern states were notable for their low levels of union density compared to other regions of the country, despite the growth in heavy industry that occurred during and after World War II. This anomalous situation led to a number of studies, some impressionistic, others more analytical. The most common explanation for the low level of unionization in the South is the industrial structure of the region. Industrial firms, beginning with textile mills, first appeared in predominantly rural areas, where community mores, supported by the clergy and political elites, opposed collective bargaining. Early southern "industry" was concentrated in the supply of raw materials, with few links to manufacturing, undermining labour's bargaining power. Labour unions without organizational bases outside the South had difficulty overcoming strong employer opposition (Marshall 1967). Contrary to expectations that the South would accept unionization and collective bargaining, the effects of right-to-work laws (the single significant element of US labour law within state control) and employer hostility stunted the expansion of collective bargaining in the region (Bain and Spritzer 1981). Later work confirmed this analysis, but emphasized political and social factors, adding the observation that the alliance of business leaders, clergy, and law enforcement officials that combined to sustain a union-free environment in the South also enforced racial segregation (Zieger 1991).

An ambitious effort to distinguish at least part of an industrial relations system on a regional basis was a study of the labour movement in Illinois by Derber (1989). Derber emphasized the political strength of the labour movement, although its influence was often reactive. Labour was more successful at blocking employer political initiatives than accomplishing its own agenda. Thus, Illinois did not enact comprehensive public sector collective bargaining legislation until 1983. Labour's strength was based on the economy being dominated by heavy industry and transportation and a tradition of labour struggle. Some of the most notable strikes in the history of the American labour movement (the Haymarket Affair, the Pullman Strike and the Memorial Day Massacre) occurred in Illinois. The first collective agreement in the men's clothing industry was negotiated in Chicago in 1910–11. The thrust of the book was that economic forces shaped position of labour in Illinois.

A growing literature on regional differences in industrial relations exists in Australia (Pullin, Fastenau and Mortimer 1996). Most of these studies focus on regions defined by topography. Benson and Hince (1987) noted substantial differences in industrial relations between regions. The same authors (1996) reviewed a number of studies of industrial relations in specific industries concentrated in a geographic region and noted the influence of policy decisions taken by state governments. They argued for a multi-factor analysis of regional issues, including the social and political factors, the characteristics of the actors in a region and the characteristics of industrial relations processes.

Blain and Dufty (1989) examined industrial relations in the state of Western Australia. Their premise was that the physical and human characteristics of the state affected industrial relations. In particular, distance from the major centres of Australia gave shop stewards more power in the workplace. Blain and Dufty reviewed industrial relations in the state from a traditional Dunlop perspective, without really concluding that industrial relations in Western Australia could be distinguished from other states independently from the industry mix. Macdonald and Burgess (1998) examined industrial relations in the Hunter Valley of the state of New South Wales, on the premise that regional vitality and innovation was a response to globalization. They relied on European research on industrial districts and flexible specialization as a framework within which to examine the Hunter Region, once a centre of labour unrest in the coalfields. However, the lack of data on sub-state regions made it difficult to determine if industrial relations in the Hunter Valley was distinct from other parts of Australia. Workplace survey data were available for the Hunter Valley, and they revealed greater propensity to labour-management cooperation in export sectors than other areas of the country. However, no new patterns of enterprise growth or work organization existed, and evidence of a distinctive pattern of industrial relations in the region was mixed at most.

Australian scholars also used national workplace survey data to determine if employment relations in the Illawarra Valley, an industrialized region south of Sydney, were distinctive (Markey et al. 1999). The authors contributed to the debate on globalization and industrial districts as a local response to international economic trends. However, they found little evidence of flexible specialization in the Illawarra Valley. Instead, they concluded that employment relations there were based on the "old system," with a major role for unions and collective bargaining. A strong union base produced an important regional labour council, but strong links remained to the state system of New South Wales.

Mortimer's (1996) review of the literature suggested that a focus on employment relations could add depth to human resource management by incorporating the role of the external environment. Future studies should incorporate not only the historical variables, but also comparisons of empirical data across regions.

Industrial relations in the United Kingdom traditionally has a national focus, yet British observers believe there is a north-south divide in the country, with union density and collective bargaining in the north exceeding levels in the south. Beaumont and Harris (1998) attempted to test those observations. Their hypothesis was that variations were due to industrial structure. Indeed, the collective bargaining structure was correlated with industrial structure, although more for men than women.

Overall, the literature from other countries emphasizes the impact of economic organizations on industrial relations. In other words, the mix of industries in a region usually overwhelms any local, cultural, political or historical factors to explain regional differences in the practice of industrial relations.

The central issue addressed in this volume is whether those generalizations hold true for Canada. Apart from industrial structure, how much influence do historical, legal, political, and social forces have on industrial relations?

ORGANIZATION OF THE BOOK

The main purpose of this book is to profile industrial relations in eight provinces in the post-World War II period (PEI was excluded because of its size and New Brunswick because the author and editor of this volume, Professor Anthony Smith, died before completing the chapter). It offers an alternative to the traditional "national" focus by providing a detailed examination of the experience of different provinces. In doing so, it strives to develop a deeper understanding of the common patterns and regional variations on many aspects of Canadian industrial relations.

In order to capture the common and distinctive features of regional industrial relations, a standard framework was developed. Of primary importance was to gain an appreciation of the impact of the economic, political and legal context on industrial relations processes and outcomes. To that end, the authors were asked to include the following information in their analysis.

- The theme of industrial relations in the province.
- The economic structure.
- Patterns of political behaviour.
- The history of industrial relations in the province.
- The structure of the parties, including union density and structure, management organization, government agencies and consultative bodies.
- Labour legislation and public policy, including its development and distinctive features.
- Dispute patterns.
- The results of industrial relations processes, including such outcomes as collective-agreement provisions, arbitration jurisprudence, and workplace behaviour.
- Distinctive and common features of industrial relations in the province.

In addition, Human Resources Development Canada provided statistics on work stoppages and collective-agreement provisions for each of the provinces. Nevertheless, owing to differences in the size of the provinces and data limitations, the treatment of these issues, by necessity, varies among chapters.

OVERVIEW OF THE CHAPTERS

The chapters are organized according to their assessment of the strength of labour in the industrial and political life of each province, in two groups. Four provinces (Ontario, Quebec, British Columbia, and Manitoba) have "confirmed" industrial relations systems, where labour and collective bargaining are central to the life of the province. The remaining four provinces — Saskatchewan, Nova Scotia, Newfoundland and Labrador, and Alberta — fall into the "dependent" category, where labour issues are at most secondary to the provinces. The full implications of this division are discussed in the concluding chapter.

The confirmed provinces all have a combination of a significant primary and secondary industry mix and an active parliamentary voice for labour's concerns.

Industrial relations in Ontario was traditionally regarded as the "Canadian system." The province has the nation's largest and most geographically dispersed population. As described in Chapter 2 by Joseph Rose, the prominence of natural resources (mining) and manufacturing (automobiles and steel) has made the province the industrial heartland of Canada. It also spawned a strong and militant labour movement, particularly through the mid-1960s, and established the Canadian Autoworkers Union and the United Steelworkers of America as dominant voices for organized labour. Unlike other provinces, there is intense competition among three political parties: the Liberals, the Conservatives, and the NDP. Nevertheless, the Conservatives have dominated, holding power from 1943 to 1985 and since 1995. Pragmatism was the hallmark of Tory rule as a succession of governments recognized labour stability as a *quid pro quo* for attracting business investment.

The cultural and political context of Quebec created a number of distinctive industrial relations features. Industrial relations is characterized by union density and strike rates above the national average, a high level of employer organization and centralized bargaining, close ties between labour and the Parti Québécois (PQ) and innovative labour policies. In Chapter 3, Michel Grant argues that the three most important factors contributing to the evolution of industrial relations are: the modernization and transformation of nationalism commencing with the Quiet Revolution in the early 1960s; provincial government leadership in promoting economic and social development; and a greater degree of union pluralism and fragmentation. In addition to shaping the pattern of industrial relations, these factors have contributed to efforts to establish social contracts at the societal and firm level. With the election of the PQ in 1976, economic nationalism stressed building a consensus among representatives of business, labour, community groups and the cooperative movement. In the private sector, government-supported initiatives, such as labour investment funds and social contracts, reduced adversarial labour relations and increased labour-management cooperation and commitment to workplace change. As in other jurisdictions, restraint policies produced turbulent public sector industrial relations. In addition, the highly centralized and politicized nature of public sector negotiations in the province exacerbated the resolution of disputes over cutbacks.

As described by Mark Thompson and Brian Bemmels in Chapter 4, the economic and political climate exerts a profound effect on industrial relations in British Columbia. The economy is heavily dependent on natural resources, for example, forestry, mining and fishing, and the presence of two national railway systems and several large natural ports on the Pacific Coast. The economic structure has contributed to a union density rate well above the national rate and high levels of strike activity. In response to strong and militant unions, there is a high level of employer organization and industrywide bargaining structures. Highly partisan provincial politics have also influenced industrial relations, with the NDP drawing its support from the labour movement and the Social Credit Party receiving the backing of the business community. Labour policy often has been subject to pendulum shifts depending on which political party is in power. It has also sparked major labour protests in the 1980s over the Social Credit government proposals affecting public sector industrial relations, social welfare programs and revisions to the *Labour Code*. With the decline of primary and secondary industries over the past two decades, the province has experienced both a decline in union density and surrendered its position as the national wage leader.

In Chapter 5, John Godard argues that Manitoba's labour-management accord is unique, reflecting historical class divisions, a fragile economy, and an increasingly isolated business community. Such factors have contributed to labour unrest and radicalism dating to the Winnipeg General Strike in 1919. At the same time, labour unrest and radicalism have been tempered by the awareness of business and labour of the need to strive for industrial peace. Even though provincial politics has been dominated by strong "right-" and "left-"wing parties, a labour-management review committee system has been in place since 1960 to advise governments on labour policy. Overall strike activity in the province is below the national average, but conflict has been higher when labour felt it was under attack from conservative governments. This was particularly evident when the Filmon government aggravated class divisions by cutting social programs, adopting pro-development strategies, and passing anti-labour legislation. The neo-conservative policies may have created a more favourable investment climate for business, but it also led to more adversarial labour relations and contributed to the government's electoral defeat by the NDP in 1999.

Saskatchewan is one of the nation's smaller and least industrialized provinces. As described by Larry Haiven in Chapter 6, the economy is heavily dependent on agriculture and, to a lesser extent, natural resources. The political context is unique in that the CCF became the first socialist government in North America after World War II. Over the course of the postwar period, popular support has swung between strong right-of-centre (the Liberals and Conservatives) and left-of-centre (CCF-NDP) parties. Despite the greater success of social democratic parties in Saskatchewan than elsewhere in Canada and the unique and labour-friendly features of the *Trade Union Act* of 1944, the province's reputation in the postwar period has been more closely associated with progressive social policies such as medicare, than innovative labour policies. Indeed, although labour has consistently backed the NDP, its political influence has been limited by the party's need to reconcile the interests of a small working class with those of its strong agricultural and small business constituencies. In response to the province's staggering debt problem in the 1990s, the NDP adopted severe fiscal measures and pursued closer ties with the business community. The economic and political contexts have contributed to relatively modest levels of union density and strike activity.

The Atlantic provinces are characterized by economies that are less diversified and have relied on federal government support to promote economic development, and political systems dominated by right-of-centre political parties. In Chapter 7, Andrew Luchak observes that Newfoundland, Canada's most isolated province and the last to join Confederation, has depended economically on natural resources, notably the fishery, mega construction projects (e.g., Hibernia), and public employment. Its isolation, strong sense of community, economic structure, and employment instability have combined to give the province the highest union density rate in Canada and made it the most strike-prone province. In the early post-Confederation period, the Smallwood Liberal government supported unions and collective bargaining, but government relations with labour soured in the wake of the 1959 strike by the International Woodworkers of America. A succession of Liberal and Conservative governments emphasized pro-business policies they hoped would promote development rather than accommodating labour interests. Disaffection with the two right-of-centre parties coupled with a weak NDP presence has limited the political influence of organized labour. Although labour policy falls within the Canadian mainstream, reforms have typically followed changes initiated elsewhere. The introduction of public sector wage restraint and downsizing measures in the 1980s and 1990s led to some of the most intense labour disputes in Canada.

Like Newfoundland, industrial relations in Nova Scotia has been shaped by the dominance of Liberal and Conservative governments which have pursued a pro-business agenda of attracting investment and jobs. In Chapter 8, Terry Wagar argues that the influence of the labour movement has been relatively modest, reflecting both its size (union density is below the national average) and the absence of a strong NDP presence.

In 1962, the Joint Labour-Management Study Committee (JLMSC) was created to promote understanding and trust between labour and management, and advise the government on labour policy. Unfortunately, the high priority attached to investment ultimately led to the JLMSC's demise following adoption of the so-called Michelin Bill in 1979, which protected the French tire manufacturer against unionization. This bill was by no means an isolated attack on labour rights. In 1977, Nova Scotia became the first province to abandon card check certification in favour of mandatory certification votes. Economic uncertainty and political isolation have contributed to strike activity exceeding the national average (particularly illegal strikes) and, in the 1990s, government cutbacks were bitterly opposed by public sector unions. The government's failure to protect labour interests in the mining industry led to a fatal explosion at the Westray Mine.

Alberta is the most conservative and least "labour-friendly" province in Canada. It has the lowest union density rate in Canada, its employment and labour laws are less supportive of workers and trade unions, and right-of-centre parties have governed continuously leaving the NDP politically impotent. As described by Allen Ponak, Daphne G. Taras and Yonatan Reshef in Chapter 9, the economy is dominated by the oil and gas industry, which has historically relied on union substitution strategies stressing progressive and paternalistic human resource policies. The absence of a strong manufacturing base, restrictive labour laws and the inability to exert political leverage through the NDP, have left organized labour in a weak position. As a result, strike activity in the province is well below the national average. Union weakness was also evident following Premier Klein's massive budget cuts and restructuring initiatives in the mid-1990s. Taking note of the strong public support for Klein and substantial private sector layoffs, public sector unions acquiesced to wage rollbacks out of fear for job security.

In the concluding chapter, Mark Thompson and Joseph Rose examine the significance of regional patterns of industrial relations. Specifically, they identify common characteristics across regions and sources of regional differences. A theoretical model is developed based on the pattern of union growth and the institutionalization of industrial relations. They find that provincial industrial relations systems fall into the "confirmed" and "dependent" industrial relations systems. In the confirmed systems, early economic development was based on substantial natural resources and manufacturing sectors, strong and militant trade unions, and the incorporation of labour into the social, legal, and political life of the jurisdiction. Conversely, in "dependent" industrial relations systems, the economies are less industrialized and trade unions are numerically weaker and exert considerably less political influence. The findings demonstrate considerable regional variation within the Canadian industrial relations system.

REFERENCES

Adell, B., M. Grant and A. Ponak. 2001. *Strikes in Essential Services.* Kingston: IRC Press, Queen's University.

Bain, T. and A. Spritzer. 1981. "Industrial Relations in the South," *Labor Law Journal* 42 (8):536-45.

Bamber, G.J. and R.D. Lansbury. 1998. *International and Comparative Employment Relations: A Study of Industrial Market Economies.* St. Leonards, Australia: Allen & Unwin.

Beaumont, P.B. and R.I.D. Harris. 1998. "The Spatial Dimension in British Industrial Relations," *British Journal of Industrial Relations* 26 (3):397-408.

Benson, J. and K. Hince. 1987. "Understanding Regional Industrial Relations Systems," in *Australian Labour Relations Readings,* 4th ed., ed. G.W. Ford, J.M. Hearn and R.D. Lansbury. Melbourne: Macmillan, pp. 129-46.

—— 1996. "Understanding Regional Industrial Relations Systems," in *Regional Employment Relations,* ed. Pullin, Fastenau and Mortimer, pp. 35-44.

Bernstein, I. 1965. "Labor Relations in Los Angeles," *Industrial Relations: A Journal of Economy and Society* 4 (2):8-26.

Betcherman, G., K. McMullen, N. Leckie and C. Caron. 1994. *The Canadian Workplace in Transition.* Kingston: IRC Press, Queen's University.

Blain, N. and N. Dufty. 1989. "Industrial Relations in Western Australia," *Journal of Industrial Relations* 31 (4):552-78.

Brodie, J. 1990. *The Political Economy of Canadian Regionalism.* Toronto: Harcourt Brace Jovanovich.

Brownsey, K. and M. Howlett, eds. 2001. *The Provincial State in Canada.* Peterborough, ON: Broadview Press.

Chaykowski, R.P. and A. Verma, eds. 1992. *Industrial Relations in Canadian Industry.* Toronto: Holt, Rinehart and Winston of Canada Limited.

Clark, P., J.T. Delaney and A.C. Frost, eds. 2002. *Collective Bargaining in the Private Sector.* Champaign, IL: Industrial Relations Research Association.

Cook, A.H. and L.S. Gray. 1966. "Labor Relations in New York City," *Industrial Relations: A Journal of Economy & Society* 5 (3):86-104.

Cousineau, J.-M. and F. Vaillancourt. 2000. "Regional Disparities, Mobility and Labour Markets in Canada," in *Adapting Public Policy to a Labour Market in Transition,* ed. W.C. Riddell and F. St-Hilaire. Montreal: Institute for Research on Public Policy, pp. 143-76.

Craig, A.W.J. and N.A. Solomon. 1993. *The System of Industrial Relations in Canada,* 4th ed. Scarborough: Prentice-Hall Canada Inc.

Derber, M. 1965. "A Small Community's Impact on Labor Relations," *Industrial Relations: A Journal of Economy and Society* 4 (2):27-41.

—— 1989. *Labor in Illinois: The Affluent Years, 1945-1980.* Urbana: University of Illinois Press.

Dunlop, J.T. 1958. *Industrial Relations Systems*, rev. ed. Cambridge, MA: Harvard Business School Press.

Gunderson, M., A. Ponak and D.G. Taras, eds. 2001. *Union-Management Relations in Canada*, 4th ed. Don Mills: Addison-Wesley Longman.

Hyman, R. 1994. *New Frontiers in European Industrial Relations.* Oxford: Blackwell.

Locke, R.M. 1992. "The Decline of the National Union in Italy: Lessons for Comparative Industrial Relations Theory," *Industrial and Labour Relations Review* 45 (2):229-49.

Lomnitz-Adler, C. 1992. "Concepts for the Study of Regional Culture," in *Mexico's Regions: Comparative History and Development,* ed. E. Van Young. San Diego: Center for US-Mexican Studies, University of California, pp. 60-89.

Macdonald, D. and J. Burgess. 1998. "Globalization and Industrial Relations in the Hunter Region," *Journal of Industrial Relations* 40 (1):3-24.

Markey, R., A. Hodgkinson, M. Murray, T. Mylett, S. Pomfret and M. Zanko. 1999. "Employment Relations by Region: The Illawarra Regional Workplace Industrial Relations Survey." A paper presented to the Changes at Work Conference, Victoria University of Technology.

Marshall, R. 1967. *Labor in the South.* Cambridge, MA: Harvard University Press.

Miller, R.U. and F. Isbester, eds. 1971. *Canadian Labour in Transition.* Scarborough: Prentice-Hall of Canada.

Mortimer, D. 1996. "Regional Employment Relations Research: Where to From Here?" in *Regional Employment Relations,* ed. Pullin, Fastenau and Mortimer, pp. 249-54.

Ponak, A. and M. Thompson. 2001. "Public Sector Collective Bargaining," in *Union-Management Relations,* ed. Gunderson, Ponak and Taras, pp. 414-46.

Pullin, L., M. Fastenau and D. Mortimer, eds. 1996. *Regional Employment Relations: Contemporary Research.* Nepean, NSW: Centre for Employment Relations, University of Western Sydney.

Romer, S. 1965. "Twin Cities: National Patterns and Sibling Rivalry," *Industrial Relations: A Journal of Economy and Society* 4 (2):42-50.

Rose, J.B. and G.N. Chaison. 1996. "Linking Union Density and Union Effectiveness: the North American Experience," *Industrial Relations* 35 (1):78-105.

Seidman, J. 1965. "Community Influences on Industrial Relations," *Industrial Relations: A Journal of Economy and Society* 4 (2):1-7.

Swimmer, G., ed. 2001. *Public-Sector Labour Relations in an Era of Restraint and Restructuring.* Don Mills: Oxford University Press.

Swimmer, G. and M. Thompson, eds. 1995. *Public Sector Collective Bargaining in Canada.* Kingston: IRC Press, Queen's University.

Task Force on Canadian Unity. 1979. *A Future Together: Observations and Recommendations.* Ottawa: Supply and Services Canada.

Task Force on Labour Relations (Woods Task Force). 1968. *Canadian Industrial Relations: The Report of the Task Force on Labour Relations.* Ottawa: Privy Council Office.

Thompson, M. 1998. "Employment Relations in Canada," in *International and Comparative Employment Relations*, ed. Bamber and Lansbury, pp. 89-109.

Van Young, E. 1992. "Are Regions Good to Study?" in *Mexico's Regions: Comparative History and Development*, ed. E. Van Young. San Diego: Center for US-Mexican Studies, University of California, pp. 2-27.

Voos, P., ed. 1994. *Contemporary Collective Bargaining in the Private Sector.* Ithaca, NY: Industrial Relations Research Association.

Weiler, P. 1980. *Reconcilable Differences.* Toronto: Carswell.

Zieger, R.H. 1991. "Introduction," in *Organized Labor in the Twentieth-Century South.* Knoxville: The University of Tennessee Press, pp. 3-12.

2 ONTARIO: THE CONSERVATIVE HEGEMONY

Joseph B. Rose

Résumé — L'Ontario occupe le premier rang des provinces canadiennes du point de vue de la population, de l'urbanisation, de la diversité économique et de la prospérité. En raison de la taille, de la situation géographique centrale et des caractéristiques socioculturelles de leur province, les Ontariens sont les Canadiens les plus centrés sur la fédération : ils se considèrent avant tout comme Canadiens. Aux yeux des résidants des autres provinces, pour qui le régionalisme est central pour la vie économique et politique, cette attitude semble arrogante et incorrecte.

La domination du Parti progressif-conservateur a modelé les relations industrielles en Ontario durant l'après-guerre. Pendant plus de 40 ans (de 1942 à 1985), les Conservateurs ont détenu le pouvoir et mis l'accent sur le développement économique et la réforme sociale modérée. L'orientation idéologique progressiste, qui a permis tantôt d'innover en matière de politique sociale tantôt de s'attribuer des politiques adoptées à la suite de pressions exercées par les partis d'opposition, a été la clé de la longévité des torys. En gouvernant au centre, ils ont pu offrir quelque chose à tout le monde.

Reflétant en grande partie les changements adoptés dans les autres provinces, la politique ontarienne du travail a suivi une voie prudente et gradualiste. Les réformes du travail ont généralement fait suite à de vastes consultations de la collectivité des relations de travail. Les torys ont cru que la stabilité des relations de travail était essentielle pour attirer les investissements des entreprises. En conséquence, les gouvernements conservateurs ont, l'un après l'autre, entretenu des liens étroits avec les dirigeants syndicaux et favorisé les intérêts des travailleurs de façon pragmatique et opportuniste. Tandis que le mouvement syndical tissait des liens étroits avec le NPD et se faisait le défenseur d'un plan d'action en faveur de la démocratie sociale, il était le bénéficiaire de la bienveillance des torys.

Les malheurs financiers et les changements de cap politiques des années 1990 (d'abord vers la gauche, ensuite vers la droite) ont mené à une escalade des tensions entre le gouvernement et les travailleurs. Le gouvernement Rae s'est mis à dos les syndicats de la fonction publique en adoptant la *Loi de 1993 sur le contrat social* pour forcer les employeurs et les syndicats du secteur public à négocier des conventions collectives qui permettraient de réduire les dépenses de six milliards de dollars. Par l'élection du gouvernement Harris en 1995, la riche tradition ontarienne en matière de consensus et de compromis en vue d'attirer les investissements a fait place à un programme néoconservateur fondé sur la déréglementation, la baisse des impôts et la réduction des dépenses gouvernementales. Le gouvernement Harris était ouvertement favorable à l'entreprise et hostile au mouvement syndical. Il en a résulté des protestations dans toute la province, allant de fermetures de lieu de travail dans douze villes et de grandes manifestations de la part de groupes de travailleurs et de groupes communautaires (Journées d'action en Ontario) à des conflits de travail avec les employés de la Couronne et les enseignants.

L'exercice des relations de travail a également été façonné par la structure économique de la province, qui est axée sur l'industrie lourde, les exportations, les multinationales et les syndicats internationaux. Même si la province se vante d'avoir le plus grand nombre de syndiqués de toutes les provinces canadiennes son taux de syndicalisation a été inférieur à la moyenne nationale durant la plus grande partie de l'après-guerre. En outre, le déclin de l'emploi dans les industries primaire et manufacturière a contribué à une baisse générale du nombre de syndiqués. Néanmoins, grâce à l'importance des industries de l'automobile et de l'acier, les travailleurs de l'auto et les métallos du Canada continuent d'être la principale voix des syndicats du secteur privé. Réunis en deux syndicats, ces travailleurs ont été une force importante de négociation collective et d'action politique dans leur milieu et au sein de la Fédération du travail de l'Ontario. Comme c'est généralement le cas au Canada, c'est dans le secteur public que le nombre de syndiqués a le plus augmenté au cours des 30 dernières années en Ontario.

La négociation collective est très décentralisée en Ontario. Les associations d'employeurs ne négocient que dans quelques industries (p. ex., la construction et le transport routier) et cette négociation est beaucoup moins développée qu'en Colombie-Britannique et au Québec. Les types de conflits révèlent que, comparativement à sa part de la main-d'oeuvre nationale, l'Ontario a un nombre peu élevé de jours-personne perdus pour cause de grève. De même, l'envergure moyenne des grèves est légèrement inférieure à la moyenne nationale. Correspondant à la tendance nationale, les mouvements de grèves en Ontario ont augmenté dans les années 1960 et subi un déclin prononcé dans les années 1990. En même temps, la part ontarienne des mouvements de grève a diminué après 1970. Les grands conflits de travail entraînant la perte de 100 000 jours-personne ou plus ont été concentrés autour des cols bleus de l'industrie lourde. Dans le secteur public, il y a eu un accroissement des conflits de travail ces dernières années.

Dans le cadre des processus de relations de travail, les syndicats ontariens ont souvent réalisé des progrès décisifs dans leurs négociations (notamment les TCA-Canada) et maintenu la position de la province à titre de leader au plan salarial. À d'autres égards, les processus de négociation ont reflété les tendances d'ailleurs, entre autres, le déclin de la négociation type, une baisse des règlements salariaux et de l'importance de la sécurité d'emploi ainsi que la négociation de conventions collectives de plus longue durée.

Ontario, the largest Canadian province, is the "most diversi-fied province in terms of economy and population" and it "constitutes Canada's industrial heartland" (Dyck 1996, 299). Conse-quently, Ontario's industrial relations system is less distinctive than other provinces, Quebec and British Columbia, for instance, in terms of trade union and employer organization, political climate, and industrial con-flict. Put simply, Ontario does not "stand out" as a regional identity. For many Ontarians, the system and practice of industrial relations, like other facets of life, appears synonymous with the "Canadian system." As Dyck notes:

> Ontarians themselves have next to no provincial consciousness. Largely due to the province's central location, and perhaps because the province houses the national capital, Ontarians see themselves primarily as Cana-dians. Ontarians are the most federally oriented of all Canadians — 90 percent, according to *Maclean's* magazine — and, at least until recently, lacked a distinctive regional identity and were rather apathetic about provincial affairs (1996, 310).

This attitude appears arrogant and incorrect to other Canadians. From their perspective, regionalism is central to political and economic life.

This chapter examines Ontario industrial relations in the postwar period. Its theme is the domination of the Progressive Conservative Party. For over 40 years, the Conservatives held power and emphasized eco-nomic development and moderate social reform. For the most part, la-bour policy followed a careful and gradualist path. Labour reforms tended to follow the lead of other jurisdictions. Labour relations stability was seen as essential to attracting business investment. Accordingly, govern-ment nurtured close ties with union leaders and accommodated labour's interests in a context of pragmatism and political expediency. Whereas organized labour developed close ties with the New Democratic Party (NDP) and strongly supported a social democratic agenda, it often ben-efited from Tory benevolence.

GEOGRAPHIC AND ECONOMIC CONTEXT

The 2001 census reveals that over 11.4 million inhabitants or about 38 percent of Canada's population live in Ontario. It is Canada's most urbanized province; 21 municipalities have more than 100,000 in-habitants (www.statscan.ca./census01). The population is concentrated in southern Ontario, with approximately 40 percent located in the Toronto labour market. As such, Toronto is the province's "economic, political, and cultural core" (Dyck 1996, 300).

Ontario's broad economic base puts it at or near the top of a number of leading economic indicators. In terms of overall economic performance, Ontario's gross domestic product (GDP) in 2000 was about $429.5 billion or 40.6 percent of the Canadian total. The Ontario labour force represents nearly 39 percent of the Canadian total and its labour force participation rate of 67.5 percent is slightly above the national average (66.1 percent) (Statistics Canada 2002). The province's unemployment rate has been consistently below the national average since 1966 (Craig and Solomon 1996). Ontarians enjoy a high standard of living; income per person typically exceeds the national average and the industrial composite index of average weekly earnings is the highest in Canada (Statistics Canada 2002). This economic prosperity is partly due to the province having one of the highest levels of educational attainment (Dyck 1996, 305).

The course of economic development is distinguishable in Ontario. As one commentator put it: "The historical development and location of industry, commerce and agriculture in Ontario has resulted in a very different pattern of population concentration and urban growth than found in the western provinces" (Bertram 1968, 455). Originally, Ontario's economy was based on primary resources, notably agriculture, mining, and forestry. Today, primary resources account for "only 3.5 percent of the province's employment, the lowest proportion in the country" (Dyck 1996, 301). At the same time, Ontario "usually ranks first among the provinces in terms of the total value of agricultural production," ranks second to Alberta in the total value of mineral production (excluding oil and gas), and third nationally in forestry production (ibid.).

The provincial economy depends on branches of foreign-owned multinational firms as well as the manufacturing industry. Ontario is the manufacturing centre of Canada, representing about 55 percent of national production and 50 percent of employment. Manufacturing has located in Ontario for many reasons, including raw materials, abundant and inexpensive electricity, an ample supply of skilled labour, good transportation, and proximity to markets (Dyck 1996). Manufacturing employment, which declined sharply during the recession in the 1990s (by more than 13 percent), rebounded by adding more than 250,000 jobs by the end of the decade (Statistics Canada 2000).

The most important element of manufacturing is the automobile industry, which consists of three segments: assembly of cars, trucks, and vans; parts and accessories; and truck and bus bodies. Ontario accounts for 86 percent of employment in motor vehicle assembly and 95 percent in parts and accessories. The industry is highly unionized and collective bargaining coverage for hourly production workers is 99 percent in assembly manufacturing and 90 percent in the manufacture of parts and accessories (Kumar and Meltz 1992). The major producers include the Big Three North American manufacturers, plus Honda, Toyota, and Suzuki. The industry has benefited from the 1965 Canada-US Auto Pact, and approximately 80 percent of cars and trucks produced in Canada are exported to the United States (Craig and Solomon 1996). Indeed, the automobile sector is the province's largest source of exports. The province also accounts for 80 percent of Canada's steel production and is home to the nation's three largest steel producers (Verma and Warrian 1992). Other important manufacturing activities include chemicals and chemical products, pulp and paper products, food and beverages, and electrical and electronic products. Mining and forestry are important activities in northern Ontario.

Ontario is "Canada's exporting powerhouse," with exports to other countries and other provinces accounting for over 70 percent of provincial GDP (Little 1999). Foreign exports have soared under free trade. Between 1989 and 1999, foreign exports rose from 30 to 54 percent of provincial GDP. Leading the way were auto-related exports and impressive gains in telecommunications and computer exports (Ibbitson 2000).

More corporate head offices are in Ontario than in any other province. Nearly 40 percent of the 500 largest companies are headquartered in Toronto. Toronto is the financial capital of Canada and major banks, financial services, and insurance companies have their headquarters there, as do "more than 60 percent of the nation's largest legal, human resource, advertising and public accounting firms" (Ontario. Ministry of Finance 1994, 94). Ontario also has highly developed road, rail, and air transportation systems linking urban centres and facilitating trade with the United States. Public services are a major component of economic activity, with large numbers of provincial and federal public servants being employed in Toronto and Ottawa, respectively. In addition, municipalities, health, education, and Crown agencies and corporations figure prominently in the economy. For example, prior to its break-up in 1999, Ontario Hydro was the largest public utility in North America (Craig and Solomon 1996).

PATTERNS OF POLITICAL BEHAVIOUR IN THE POSTWAR PERIOD

The political culture or orientation of the province has several unique features. First, the Progressive Conservative Party has dominated provincial politics. The Tories won 12 consecutive elections and held power from 1942 to 1985 (including three minority governments) and again after the 1995 election. The ascendancy of the Tories can be traced to the pivotal role played by Liberal Premier Mitchell Hepburn in the 1937 General Motors strike in Oshawa. Prior to the strike, "Hepburn and the Liberals had a corner on the labour, progressive and left-wing vote in the province" (Abella 1974, 124). By aligning himself with General Motors in the dispute, Hepburn eventually lost the support of the labour movement and the moderate left to the Cooperative Commonwealth Federation (CCF). The decline of Liberalism gave control of the government to the Tories. Second, the province has had a vibrant three-party political system. Although the Liberals and CCF/NDP remained out of power for most of the postwar period, both parties consistently attracted a sizeable popular vote and wielded influence in their capacity as the official opposition and during minority governments. Further, each party elected majorities between 1987 and 1990.

A dominant theme of the Tories' political success in the post-World War II era was "a capacity to manage the affairs of the province in a businesslike way, and the ability to maintain an equitable balance among the principal interests of the province" (Dyck 1996, 315). The Tories' political longevity reflected the party's ability to maintain strong ties with the business community and to be flexible on social policy issues. This underlined its approach to labour policy. In the 1940s, the Tories sought to achieve satisfactory labour relations and to position themselves as a reform alternative to the CCF. The rise of Tory Ontario began with the minority government of George Drew. The Drew government initially embarked on ambitious strategies based on industrial development and social reform, including the establishment of a stable industrial relations system based on union recognition and collective bargaining under the aegis of the Ontario Labour Relations Board (OLRB) (Brownsey and Howlett 1992).

The economic development and social reform strategies initiated by Drew were important features of the "paternalism and pragmatism" adopted by successive Tory leaders, beginning with Leslie Frost, who governed from 1949 to 1961. The Tories were adept at understanding the nexus between demographic changes, economic development, and social reform. For example, Ontario passed the first equal pay for equal work law in Canada in 1951, the *Female Employees Fair Remuneration Act* (Weiner 1995). Ontario was also one of the first jurisdictions in North America to adopt comprehensive anti-discrimination legislation. This followed a large influx of non-British immigrants and recognized the importance of anti-discrimination legislation to labour market stability and uninterrupted economic development (Brownsey and Howlett 1992). Frost also employed Jacob Finkelman as labour advisor for the purpose of helping to stabilize labour relations and to keep the labour movement sufficiently happy so that the CCF would not benefit from union militancy. Finkelman, a strong proponent of collective bargaining, had been appointed the first Registrar of the Labour Court in 1943 and the first chair of the OLRB in 1944 (Willes 1979). At the request of Frost, he resumed the duties of chair of the OLRB between 1953 and 1967 (Roberts 1994).

This legacy continued into the 1960s and 1970s under the Robarts and Davis governments. "The wide-ranging agenda of the Conservative reformism is sometimes seen as evidence of 'Red Toryism' or creeping socialism" (Roberts 1994, 106). Davis was particularly adept at being pragmatic and evoked a mastery of conciliation, compromise, and consensus (Dyck 1996). As the electoral significance of the public sector expanded during the 1960s and 1970s, both Robarts and Davis were able to retain the allegiance of traditional Tory supporters and gain the support of a new middle class that benefited from the expansion of public services. This was especially evident in the expansion of the education sector and the support for Davis among teachers (Brownsey and Howlett 1992). Taking a page from Frost, in 1975, Davis recruited Tim Armstrong, law partner of the federal NDP leader, "to head the labour board and to take charge of the labour ministry as deputy" (Roberts 1994, 161). The moderately progressive ideological orientation of the Tories allowed them at times to introduce innovations in social policy and at other times to claim credit for policies they had been pressured to adopt by opposition parties. They had a knack for steering a middle course and appearing to provide something for everybody.

Arguably, the three major political parties operated in what Dyck calls a "fairly narrow progressive conservative ideological range" (1996, 318) until 1990. Indeed, the downfall in Tory rule was sealed when Frank Miller, who succeeded Davis, abandoned any pretence of running as a "progressive" candidate and the middle class, so carefully nurtured by his predecessors, abandoned the party. The Tory mantle was initially picked up by the Liberal-NDP Accord (1985–87) and followed by a Liberal majority government in 1987 headed by David Peterson. Overall extensive public spending and social reform marked the period 1985–90.

Prior to 1990, labour law reforms were approached with caution and care. As described in greater detail below, periodic revisions to the *Labour Relations Act* typically followed the establishment of inquiry commissions and consultation with the labour relations community. This approach served a number of useful purposes, notably it allowed the government to defuse difficult issues, it bought time, it demonstrated empathy for labour relations problems and signalled a commitment to study these matters and explore solutions to them.

Relations between government and trade union leaders extended beyond the formality of commissions and task forces. These relationships were often carefully nurtured. Premier Davis was a master at making political deals with top labour leaders.

> Premier Davis respected raw union muscle. He saw stable labour relations as the key to Ontario's ability to attract investment. He cultivated good relations with labour leaders in autos, mining and steel who could help him avoid B.C.-style polarization that might scare business off. He had appointed ... Tim Armstrong as deputy minister of labour to keep channels of communication open and relations on track (Roberts 1994, 203).

Political deals with public sector unions, especially OPSEU (the Ontario Public Service Employees' Union), were not considered of paramount importance to governing the province (Roberts 1994). Nevertheless, Davis demonstrated a capacity to consult with public sector unions when necessary. In 1982, he was sharply rebuked by public sector unions for following the lead of the federal government's "6 and 5" program when he introduced the *Inflation Restraint Act*. This law imposed wage restraints on public sector employees and suspended collective bargaining rights for one year. In an attempt to achieve a consensus on policy options, Davis and his Cabinet met with public sector unions to discuss a second stage of public sector wage controls. These discussions appear to have contributed to the decision to restore collective bargaining rights and access to interest arbitration, albeit within explicit fiscal guidelines, pursuant to the *Public Sector Prices and Compensation Review Act*.

During the 1990s, there was a transformation of the political landscape in Ontario. The "narrow progressive conservative ideological range," which dominated the postwar period, expanded with the election victories of the NDP in 1990 and the Tories in 1995 and 1999. During the

1990s, labour policy-making became increasingly partisan and attempts were made to discredit industrial relations institutions (Burkett 1998).

Both the NDP government of Bob Rae and the Harris government alienated the labour movement, albeit in different ways. Specifically, the pattern of consensus and compromise in government-labour relations has fallen by the wayside to be replaced by confrontation. This began with the attempt by the Rae government in 1993 to persuade public sector partners to enter into a social contract that would provide job security in exchange for $6 billion in expenditure cuts over three years. When it failed to achieve a consensus, the government passed the *Social Contract Act* as a means of coercing public sector employers and unions into negotiating agreements to achieve the expenditure targets. The Act imposed a deadline for achieving an agreement containing expenditure reductions. The sanctions for failing to do so included a three-year compensation freeze and up to 12 unpaid days annually for three years (known as "Rae" days) (Hebdon and Warrian 1999). Public sector unions considered this to be an attack on fundamental collective bargaining rights and withdrew their political support for the NDP, as did the Canadian Auto Workers (CAW). The entire affair contributed to the NDP's election defeat in 1995.

The Harris government was stridently pro-business and exhibited antipathy toward unions (labour was a "special interest group" and labour leaders were "union bosses"). The Tories steadfastly implemented the "Common Sense Revolution" by deregulating social policy and practice, reducing the budget deficit, cutting personal income taxes, and redressing the "imbalance" in the province's labour laws (Progressive Conservative Party of Ontario 1994). In response to the new agenda, there were workplace shutdowns in 12 cities and large demonstrations by labour and community groups (known as the "Ontario Days of Action") (Schenk 2000). The plan to restructure the Ontario Public Service led to a five-week strike by Crown employees in 1996. In subsequent years, there were numerous confrontations over government legislation restricting the bargaining rights of public sector employees. There was massive opposition by public sector unions, including police associations, over the manner in which Bill 136 proposed to modify collective bargaining and interest arbitration following the amalgamation of municipalities, hospitals, and school boards. The government made changes to the law in response to critics. Bill 160, which among other things, increased teacher workloads and removed class size as a subject of collective bargaining, sparked a two-week walkout by 126,000 teachers. Government-teacher hostilities persisted through 2001 (Rose 2002).

STRUCTURE OF THE INDUSTRIAL RELATIONS PARTIES

Trade Union Organizations

Union membership in Ontario has been consistently higher than in any other province and reached 1.3 million members in 2001 (Akyeampong 2001). Between 1946 and 1956, Ontario union membership growth was nearly twice as great as in Canada as a whole (115.5 percent and 65.5 percent, respectively). As a result, the Ontario share of total union membership reached 38 percent by the late 1950s. In subsequent years, its share declined marginally to 34.7 percent by 2001 (ibid.). The public sector has been the major source of union growth over the past 30 years. By 1991, a majority of union members were employed in the broader public sector (Rose 1995).

The union density rate in Ontario has been consistently below the national rate in the postwar period. Between 1946 and 1955, Ontario had the lowest density rate by region, but its relative position improved over the next decade (Ashagrie and Eaton 1970). In 1962, Ontario's union density rate of 32.7 percent exceeded the national rate (31.1 percent) and ranked second only to British Columbia (Coates, Arrowsmith and Couchene 1989). Since then, it has fallen to 26.1 percent in 2001, a figure that is below the national average (30 percent) and is lower than all other provinces except Alberta (Akyeampong 2001). Unionization rates in Ontario for most major industry groups (including the private and public sectors) and for female workers are also uniformly lower than the national average (Statistics Canada 1994).

Given the historical presence of strong unions in manufacturing and resource-based industries, and the close ties between labour and the NDP, Ontario's low union density rate is somewhat surprising. Meltz (1989) found that interprovincial differences in union density were not attributable to the distribution of employment by industry. Rather, private sector unionization had the most important impact on the overall density rate. For example, in 1982, Ontario would have had a density rate of 33 percent (its actual rate was 30.7 percent) if the industries in the province were unionized to the same extent as the national average. Whether that explanation is still valid is uncertain. Other factors may also contribute to the low density rate. Unlike Newfoundland, where a resource-based economy, a large public sector, and above average unemployment contribute to high union density, Ontario's low density rate may reflect a highly diversified economy, below average unemployment, and greater geographic dispersion of industry and population. Additionally, the electoral dominance of the Tories and their gradualist approach to labour law reform, may have produced a legal environment that was less supportive to union organizing.

A distinguishing feature of unionism in Ontario is that international unions are numerically more important in Ontario than in other regions. Whereas international union membership has fallen steadily in Canada since the mid-1960s, its decline has been less pronounced in Ontario, where American-based unions represent a larger share of total membership than in other provinces. A further indication of the prominence of international unions is that they are responsible for 55.4 percent of the collective agreements in the province, a figure well above the Canadian total (46.9 percent) (Statistics Canada 1994). It follows that national and independent unionism is less pronounced in Ontario than in Canada as a whole and in the larger provinces, notably Quebec and British Columbia.

The largest unions in the province are similar to the country's largest unions. The major public sector unions include the Canadian Union of Public Employees (CUPE), OPSEU, and the Public Service Alliance of Canada (PSAC). Reflecting the province's industrial base, the largest private sector unions are the CAW, the Steelworkers, and the United Food and Commercial Workers Union. Most major unions in Canada are headquartered in Ontario (usually Toronto or Ottawa) (Canada. HRDC 1996).

The peak labour organization in the province is the Ontario Federation of Labour (OFL). The OFL, which was established by the Canadian Congress of Labour in 1944, speaks for 650,000 workers in more than 1,500 affiliated local unions. It provides affiliates with a broad range of services, including education, legislation and political action, research, training, human rights and health and safety (OFL 1995).

Employer Organizations

Unlike the Employers' Council of British Columbia or the Conseil du patronat du Quebec, no umbrella employer's organization represents the Ontario business community or spearheads business-government relations. Instead, employers are represented by a number of provincial affiliates of national organizations such as the Chamber of Commerce, the Canadian Federation of Independent Business, and the Canadian Manufacturers' Association, as well as the Toronto Board of Trade and numerous industry groups, for example, in the mining, construction and automotive parts sectors. For the most part, these organizations have pursued their interests with respect to economic development, industrial relations, and government relations in an uncoordinated manner. A notable exception was in 1992 when the business community strongly opposed the NDP government's proposed amendments to the *Labour Relations Act*, including a ban on the use of strike replacements (Bill 40). These amendments were labelled "anti-business" and it was argued they would discourage job creation and economic investment (Jain and Muthuchidambaram 1995). Although the campaign to defeat Bill 40 was unsuccessful, the Harris government subsequently repealed the law.

On the collective bargaining front, employer association bargaining is the exception rather than the rule in the province and is far less developed than in British Columbia and Quebec. As is the case generally in Canada, employer association bargaining is found in industries such as construction, printing, clothing, and trucking (Craig and Solomon 1996). Multi-employer bargaining is highly developed in the construction industry, partly due to legislation in the 1970s requiring contractors to bargain through provincial associations (Rose 1986*a*). Although there are numerous employer organizations in the public sector, only the Ontario Hospital Association has a major role in collective bargaining. Other provincial groups — the Association of Municipalities of Ontario and the Association of Police Services Boards of Ontario — are not directly involved in collective bargaining nor have they assumed a major support role.

Joint Labour-Management Bodies

There have been two types of labour-management sectoral organizations established in Ontario. The first type was set up by government to act as an advisory body on sectoral policy development (Sharpe 1992). Ontario has relied on these advisory bodies to obtain input from experienced participants into ways of promoting better labour-management relations in selected industries. For example, the establishment of an industrial inquiry commission into bargaining structure in the construction industry in 1976 was the result of a recommendation from the Construction Industry Review Panel, "a joint labour-management advisory body which advises the Minister of Labour on matters relating to the construction industry" (Franks 1976, 1). This inquiry led to the adoption of mandatory provincewide bargaining in the construction industry.

During the 1980s, a second type of sectoral council emerged, largely in response to increasing international competition, technological change, and economic restructuring. These bodies are (i) engaged in developing programs and activities for individual workplaces or the entire sector and (ii) "act on an agenda jointly developed by labour while government plays a supportive role" (Sharpe 1992, 27). Although most of the councils have been funded by Human Resources Development Canada (HRDC), and are essentially national, many of the councils are particularly relevant to Ontario, for example, auto parts, steel, and electrical/electronics industries.

A prominent example is the Canadian Steel Trade and Employment Congress (CSTEC) which was formed by the United Steelworkers Union along with major steel companies in 1985. It lobbies government on trade and employment issues and, with financial assistance from the Department of Employment and Immigration, developed and implemented a number of labour market services. These included the joint development of labour adjustment programs and a broad range of services (e.g., counselling, training, and job referral).

Administrative Agencies Including Tripartite Consultative Bodies

Administrative Agencies: Labour Relations. The Ontario Labour Relations Board (OLRB) is a tripartite tribunal, which administers the *Labour Relations Act.* Its main duties include the certification of trade unions, the investigation of unfair labour practice complaints and determining the legality of strikes and lockouts. At various times, other tribunals have been responsible for administering public sector collective bargaining statutes (e.g., school teachers and Crown employees). The adjudication of rights disputes in the provincial public service is handled by the Grievance Settlement Board (Ontario 1995).

Ministry of Labour Services. The Labour-Management Services Division of the ministry performs three broad functions. The Office of Mediation assigns conciliation officers and mediators in interest disputes. The Office of Collective Bargaining Information collects and disseminates collective bargaining data. The Office of Arbitration maintains a roster of arbitrators and makes ministerial appointments of grievance and interest arbitrators. The Office of Arbitration is also responsible for the training and development of new arbitrators (www.gov.on.ca).

The Employment Standards Branch is responsible for administering the *Employment Standards Act* and regulations. Complaints are investigated and decided by employment standards officers. Employers and employees may appeal an officer's determination to the Ontario Labour Relations Board. Under the *Occupational Health and Safety Act*, inspectors are responsible for investigating health and safety complaints. Their findings can also be appealed to the Ontario Labour Relations Board. The Workplace Health and Safety Agency is a tripartite body with responsibilities for the certification of members of health and safety committees and development and delivery of education and training programs. As well, the Workplace Hazardous Materials Information system (WHMIS) is a product of federal and provincial legislation. It includes a tripartite appeal board to hear requests from employers for exemptions regarding information disclosure and the Ontario minister of labour nominates individuals to chair the appeal boards for the Ontario jurisdiction (Ontario 1995).

Other Administrative Bodies. There are a number of other important agencies and bodies situated within and outside the Ministry of Labour. The Ontario Human Rights Commission is responsible for the investigation of complaints involving employment discrimination and enforcement of the Human Rights Code. The Workplace Safety and Insurance Board in charge of administering the *Workplace Safety and Insurance Act* (formerly the *Workers' Compensation Act*). The Pay Equity Commission is divided into two independent bodies. The Pay Equity Office manages and administers program delivery and advises employers, employees, and bargaining agents on attaining pay equity. The Pay Equity Hearings Tribunal is a tripartite body that adjudicates complaints under the *Pay Equity Act*.

Other Advisory and Consultative Mechanisms. A number of tripartite bodies have been established over the years to advise government. For example, the Advisory Council on Occupational Health and Safety was created in 1977 to advise the minister of labour on government programs and other matters on workplace health and safety. Another example is the advisory body established under section 49 (10) of the *Labour Relations Act*. It provides that the minister may establish a labour-management advisory committee consisting of a chair, to be selected by the minister, and six members (with equal representation from employers and trade unions), to advise on all matters related to arbitration, including who is qualified to act as arbitrator (Ontario 1995). This advisory committee has been in existence since the 1960s and works with the Office of Arbitration to train new arbitrators and maintain the ministry's roster of approved arbitrators. The Premier's Council on Economic

Renewal, established by the Peterson government and adapted by the NDP, established the Ontario Training and Adjustment Board (OTAB). It provided unions, employers, and equity groups with a decision-making role in the development and administration of training programs (McBride 1996).

Since the 1960s there have been numerous commissions and task forces (individual and tripartite) appointed to study a broad range of employment issues ranging from collective bargaining and labour disputes (Rand 1968; Goldenberg 1962; Little 1999; and Johnston 1974) to workers' compensation (Weiler 1980) to hours of work and overtime (Donner 1987). As well, ad hoc committees have been established to study revisions to the *Labour Relations Act*, as was done in 1991 (Jain and Muthuchidambaram 1995).

LABOUR LEGISLATION/PUBLIC POLICY

The development of labour policy in Ontario has followed the general Canadian pattern of frequent modifications that generally strengthened trade unions. What has distinguished Ontario has been a labour reform process marked by caution, pragmatism, and a disinclination to innovate. The province typically has steered a middle course, responding to political interests within the province and interpreting the efficacy of labour policies elsewhere. As noted by Carter (1992, 6), Ontario was "never a leader in labour law reform." It preferred to let other jurisdictions experiment and then follow the lead where the results were favourable. In general, the institutionalization of a social democratic political party within a federalized parliamentary system has aided the cause of labour law reform (Bruce 1989). The viability of the NDP in Ontario gave it the political leverage to compel Tory governments to deal with labour policy issues. For example, in its role as the official opposition in the mid-1970s, the NDP was instrumental in the establishment of a royal commission to study health and safety in mining and to get the Workers' Compensation Board "to recognize asbestos as a cause of cancer" (Dyck 1996, 344).

The evolution of labour policy reveals that the most substantial labour policy initiatives occurred when the party in power (usually the Conservatives) either required the support of the NDP (or its predecessor, the CCF) or sought to undermine that party's electoral support. In 1944, the minority Conservative government (1943–45) introduced

collective bargaining legislation (*Labour Relations Board Act*) and established the Ontario Labour Relations Board (supplanting the Liberal government's *Collective Bargaining Act*, 1943 and the Ontario Labour Court).
The minority Tory governments of 1975–77 and 1977–81 (the official
opposition was the NDP and Liberals, respectively) enacted numerous
labour reforms, including strengthening the OLRB's powers, passage of
the *Occupational Safety and Health Act*, adoption of a statutory expedited grievance arbitration system in response to union complaints about
the cost and delay of arbitration and requiring collective agreements to
include a dues check-off provision where a union requests it. Labour reform under Premier Davis typically involved efforts to balance employer
and union interests by providing something for both sides, for example,
unions received dues check-off and employers were given the right to
request votes on the employer's last contract offer. Pursuant to the Liberal-NDP Accord (1985–87), there were improvements in health and safety
legislation, human rights legislation and a system of first contract arbitration was introduced. Generally, "unions rather than employers were the
main beneficiaries of these past reforms to the Labour Relations Act"
(Carter 1992, 7).

Changes in labour policy also represented reactions to specific
employer-union disputes or patterns of conflict. For example, compulsory dues check-off was enacted in the wake of bitter labour disputes at
Radio Shack and Fleck Manufacturing. These and other high-profile strikes
(e.g., the 1985 Eaton's strike) contributed to the adoption of the first
contract arbitration in 1986. As well, the widely reported links between
security firms and picket-line violence led to the ban on the use of professional strikebreakers by a Tory majority government in 1983. Labour policy
initiatives have often followed the appointment of special inquiry commissions to study politically sensitive labour disputes or to more broadly
consider the public interest in labour-management relations. There are
numerous examples of this practice: (i) the adoption of compulsory arbitration in hospitals followed strikes at Trenton Memorial Hospital and
Douglas Memorial Hospital (Hines 1972; Adams 1981); (ii) the introduction of employer accreditation (1971) and provincewide bargaining
(1977) in the construction industry was a response to unacceptably high
levels of strike activity and inflationary wage settlements (Rose 1986*a*);
and (iii) in response to union complaints that substantial amounts of overtime were being worked at a time when other workers (often at the same
establishment) were unemployed or laid off, the Liberals established the
Task Force on Hours and Work and Overtime in 1986 to determine

whether imposing restrictions on overtime would promote job creation (Donner 1987).

The evolution of public policy in the public sector can be distinguished from most other regions. One feature was the adoption of separate collective bargaining statutes for virtually every major employee group in the public sector. Additionally, with few exceptions, the province broadly embraced arbitration as an alternative to public sector strikes. Where the right to strike was granted, the applicable legislation typically provided for more elaborate non-binding dispute resolution procedures.

During the 1980s, labour policy evolved gradually under the Conservatives and their successors. The Davis government adopted a number of reforms, including legislation improving severance pay in the wake of high unemployment following plant closures and layoffs, reforming the Workers' Compensation Board and expanding the Human Rights Code by offering protection to the handicapped and with respect to sexual harassment. Under the Liberal-NDP Accord (1985–87), Workers' Compensation benefits were improved, enforcement mechanisms in occupational health and safety legislation were strengthened, and the scope of human rights legislation was expanded to include sexual orientation (Dyck 1996). The most notable labour policy initiative of the majority Liberal government of David Peterson (1987–90) was the introduction of pay equity legislation in 1988. It established a proactive pay equity system and it was the only one applicable to both the public and private sectors in Canada. This established Ontario as one of the more progressive jurisdictions respecting pay equity.

The process of developing balanced reforms through consultation and consensus has dissipated during the 1990s. The NDP government, although chastised by labour for the *Social Contract Act*, did adopt sweeping labour policy changes, including the establishment of a wage protection fund under the *Employment Standards Act* (an insurance scheme to assist employees collect unpaid wages), the extension of the right to strike to Crown employees, the alteration of the workers' compensation system and the adoption of the nation's most comprehensive employment equity legislation (ibid.). The most significant change was Bill 40. It provoked a negative and heated response from the business community because it was perceived as a departure from past practice, that is, from a practice of incremental and balanced legislative changes to one characterized by large pendulum swings more often associated with BC politics (Burkett 1998). Displeasure with NDP labour policy was not confined to employers. The *Social Contract Act* soured relations between the NDP government and organized labour and led to the withdrawal of financial and political support for the NDP by the Ontario Federation of Labour and many of its large affiliates.

In response to the lingering resentment of the business community over Bill 40, the Harris government repealed it with Bill 7 in 1995. Bill 7 marked a further shift in policy-making in Ontario, as the law was passed without consultation, and without any meaningful attempt at seeking a consensus. In addition, it went far beyond simply repealing Bill 40 (including the substitution of certification votes for card checks), removing the successor rights provisions from the *Crown Employees Collective Bargaining Act,* and changing the *Employment Standards Act* by deleting the successor employers' provisions and reducing compensation recoveries under the Employee Wage Protection Program. This marked the first of many government initiatives to deregulate labour policy and address the government's perceived need to restore a "balance" between management and labour (Yates 2000). These developments indicate that labour policy is increasingly being formulated according to political ideology rather than on the basis of consensus following extensive consultation with the labour relations community.

Summarizing, in most areas of labour policy, for example, collective bargaining, employment standards, and occupational health and safety, Ontario has occupied the middle ground rather than being an innovator. By the same token, the province has often taken the lead on human rights and equality issues — pay and employment equity.

DISPUTE PATTERNS

For the period 1946–2001, Ontario experienced nearly 10,000 strikes, involving about 3,700,000 workers and 71,000,000 person-days lost (see Table 1). The province accounted for 35.3 percent of Canadian strikes and 33.1 percent of person-days lost. Relative to its share of the labour force, person-days lost in Ontario are low. Ontario workers also represented about one-quarter of the total number of workers involved in stoppages. These figures indicate that the average size of disputes in Ontario is somewhat lower than the Canadian average. Overall, Ontario strikes were marginally longer than the national average (Workplace Information Directorate, various years).

Table 1 also divides strike activity into five-year averages (as well as for 1996–2001). It can be seen that strike frequency increased steadily

TABLE 1
STRIKE ACTIVITY IN CANADA, 1946–2001

Year	Strike Measures			Ontario as a Percentage of Canada		
	WS	WI	PDL	WS (%)	WI (%)	PDL (%)
1946–50	355	113,758	1,141,185	39.0	21.7	11.2
1951–55	493	203,309	3,931,470	50.2	52.9	47.4
1956–60	629	190,983	3,561,535	51.5	45.1	42.6
1961–65	973	254,305	3,523,460	54.8	48.2	46.7
1966–70	1,264	535,849	13,665,900	44.2	36.8	47.9
1971–75	1,289	499,795	10,944,550	30.1	20.9	30.0
1976–80	1,376	504,234	9,958,890	27.6	16.2	25.4
1981–85	1,169	346,041	7,872,210	29.8	23.3	30.3
1986–90	1,014	311,796	7,182,820	32.0	15.7	29.1
1991–95	600	161,237	2,367,460	30.8	21.9	25.3
1996–01	804	594,042	6,784,760	37.2	45.4	43.1
1946–70	3,714	1,298,204	25,823,550	47.9	39.1	41.1
1971–01	6,252	2,417,145	45,110,690	34.2	24.9	29.8
1946–01	9,966	3,715,349	70,934,240	35.3	25.9	33.1

Notes: WS – number of work stoppages; WI – workers involved in strikes; PDL – person-days lost due to strikes.

Source: Calculations based on special data requests from the Workplace Information Directorate.

through the 1976–80 period and then declined. The steepest increase in strike frequency occurred during the 1960s and the steepest decline took place in the 1990s. It is noteworthy that Ontario accounted for the majority of Canadian work stoppages between 1951 and 1965. In subsequent years, the Ontario share declined, averaging about 34 percent over the period 1971–2001. The Ontario share of workers involved in strikes and person-days lost was also substantially lower in the period 1971–2001 than it was between 1946 and 1970 (Workplace Information Directorate, various years).

What do these comparisons tell us about the contours of strike activity in Ontario? By and large, strike frequency in Ontario was broadly similar to the national pattern in most periods. This suggests the decision to call or take strikes was influenced by general economic conditions. In the immediate postwar period, there was an "unprecedented wave of large and protracted strikes" which "represented major 'tests of strength' between unions and employers, in industries in which, for the most part, unionism and collective bargaining on a significant scale were relatively new and unfamiliar phenomena" (Jamieson 1968, 301-02). Although Ontario had its share of these strikes, which centred on wages, shorter hours, and establishment of industry patterns — for example, the 1946 Stelco strike — the province's share of total strike activity was relatively modest in the immediate postwar period. Commencing in the 1950s and continuing through the mid-1960s, Ontario accounted for almost half of all strike activity. This reflected the "settling in" or adjustment period of bargaining in "heavy" industries, notably automobiles, iron and steel, non-ferrous mining and smelting, and chemicals. Bargaining in this decade focused on job and income security (e.g., pensions, health and welfare plans, and supplementary unemployment benefits) with industrial unions seeking to emulate the pace-setting agreements achieved by their parent organizations in the United States (Jamieson 1968).

Beginning in the 1960s, Ontario and the nation as a whole witnessed a rise in strike activity. The annual record for person-days lost in Ontario was set in 1969. Unlike the national trend and indeed the worldwide trend, the volume of strike activity in Ontario declined in the 1970s. Although strike activity in Canada has declined since the recession of the early 1980s and most dramatically during the 1990s (Gunderson, Hyatt and Ponak 2001), the decline has been somewhat greater in Ontario as the province's share of workers involved and person-days lost declined. The latter finding is partly attributable to the depth of the province's economic recession in the early 1990s, particularly its impact on manufacturing. However, the downward trend was interrupted by major public sector disputes involving Crown employees (1996) and teachers (1997). In these two years, Ontario accounted for nearly three-quarters of the workers involved in labour disputes and 55 percent of the person-days lost in Canada (Workplace Information Directorate, various years).

An earlier study of strikes between 1966 and 1975 (Jamieson 1979) reported that the strike profile in Ontario differed from the pattern in Quebec and British Columbia. With respect to average strike duration, strikes in Ontario and British Columbia were roughly twice as long (23.8 and 22.6 days, respectively) as stoppages in Quebec (12.9

days). On the other hand, the average size of strikes was much smaller in Ontario (422 workers) than in Quebec (768 workers) and British Columbia (588 workers).

These interprovincial differences in strike size and duration can be attributed to the industrial relations characteristics and industry mix of Ontario. In terms of workers involved, it would appear that Ontario's decentralized bargaining structures would account for the low incidence of participation in and mobilization for work stoppages. For the most part, Ontario bargaining is conducted on a "single employer-single local union-single establishment" basis and there is far less multi-employer or industry bargaining than is found in British Columbia and Quebec. Additionally, there is considerable fragmentation of bargaining in the public sector (e.g., education and municipalities). As well, in those parts of the public sector with large bargaining units, for example, the Ontario Public Service and hospitals, compulsory arbitration has been in place for most of the postwar period. As for Ontario's tendency to experience longer disputes, this is largely attributable to the concentration of major disputes in selected industries such as autos, mining, steel and construction, and attempts to establish or extend pattern bargaining. These major disputes are discussed in greater detail below.

The historical pattern of illegal strike activity in Ontario is consistent with the overall strike trend, that is, Ontario accounted for a disproportionately high level of illegal strike activity prior to 1970 and a disproportionately low level since 1970. Consistent with the national pattern, illegal strikes in Ontario as a proportion of all strikes have declined substantially over the past 20 years. Although the underlying reasons for this trend have not been fully explored, there is reason to believe that labour policy changes have contributed to the reduction of mid-contract disputes. The streamlining of conciliation procedures (removing the requirement for conciliation boards) has probably reduced strikes to protest delays in achieving renewal agreements and the adoption of statutory grievance mediation and expedited arbitration procedure appears to have lessened pressures to strike over excessive delays in processing grievances. Further, the widespread use of statutory expedited grievance arbitration appears to have contributed to the decline in illegal strike activity (Rose 1986b).

Major work stoppages, that is, disputes involving 100,000 or more person-days lost, reflect the industrial structure of the province. A majority of major disputes occurred in manufacturing, predominantly transportation equipment (notably the automobile industry), primary metals, electrical products, tires (prior to 1980), and pulp and paper (since 1970). The construction industry accounted for almost one-quarter of major disputes and metal mining accounted for just over 10 percent of the total. Major strikes between 1946 and 1959 were almost exclusively in manufacturing and mining. Commencing in 1960s, there was a diffusion of major strike activity. The construction industry became a strike-prone industry over the next four decades and accounted for 40 percent of major strikes between 1980 and 1995. Three of the five major strikes in the public sector took place between 1996 and 2002. The unions most heavily involved in major disputes have been the CAW and the Steelworkers. The employers most frequently involved in major disputes were the Big Three automakers, major aircraft manufacturers, Stelco, and Inco (Workplace Information Directortate, various years).

Since major strikes have been concentrated in a few industries, it follows that annual strike totals have been heavily influenced by a single dispute or bargaining in a single industry. For example, the 1997 teachers' dispute with the Harris government, the 1981 Stelco strike, the 1978–79 Inco strike and the 1955–56 General Motors strike accounted for 39 to 66 percent of the person-days lost in Ontario in those years (Workplace Information Directorate, various years). Additionally, some industries tend to be more strike prone than others. The construction industry, which represents about 7 percent of total employment in the province, often accounts for a much larger share of strike activity in those years when major bargaining rounds occur (Rose 1986*a*).

Seven labour disputes involved one million or more person-days lost. Four of these disputes involved Inco (twice), Stelco, and General Motors (Workplace Information Directorate, various years). In recent years, such disputes have been in response to public sector restructuring initiatives by the Harris government. These included the first two strikes by Crown employees against the Government of Ontario (1996 and 2002) and a massive walkout by teacher unions in 1997 to protest government efforts to increase teacher workloads.

RESULTS OF INDUSTRIAL RELATIONS PROCESSES

Given the predominance of decentralized bargaining, settlement outcomes typically have been tailored to the particular interests of the individual employer and the local union. Departures from the overall pattern occur under multi-employer bargaining in the private sector (e.g., construction and trucking) and centralized bargaining in the public sector (e.g., hospitals and community colleges). In a few instances, collective bargaining has been coordinated across provincial borders, including such prominent industries as automobiles, steel, meatpacking (until its dissolution in the 1980s), and construction (e.g., pipelines).

The CAW has often been cited as the most innovative union in collective bargaining. This reputation is based on a number of breakthrough settlements in the automobile industry. These achievements include the Rand Formula (based on the arbitration award ending the 1945 Ford Windsor strike), the cost-of-living adjustment clause (COLA), the annual improvement factor, paid personal holidays, income maintenance, and pension indexing for future retirees (Kumar and Meltz 1992). The breakthrough on pension indexing, achieved in 1987, was followed by settlements featuring pension indexing in the airline industry (Air Canada and the Machinists' Union in 1987), the mining industry in 1988 (between the Steelworkers and Inco and Mine Mill and Falconbridge), and at Stelco in 1990 (Chaykowski 1992; Verma and Warrian 1992).

In recent years, one finds evidence of the changing nature of collective bargaining. One change involves decentralization and disruptions to pattern bargaining in a number of jurisdictions, for example, West Coast forest products, construction, and the railways. Ontario has not escaped unscathed. In addition to the fallout created in industries such as meatpacking, there has been increased resistance to pattern bargaining in the pulp and paper industry and the breakup of chain bargaining at Stelco (Chaykowski 2001; Frost and Verma 1999). A second change involves longer term collective agreements. Consistent with the national pattern, the average length of collective agreements in Ontario rose from 24.7 to 32.2 months between 1990 and 2000. Some agreements are for five or six years (e.g., Maple Leaf Meats and Stelco) (Van Alphen 2001).

There has also been a downward trend in negotiated wage settlements in Canada since 1981, and average annual wage settlements in the mid-1990s reached an all-time low. As well, throughout most of the 1990s, settlements in the private sector outpaced the public sector. The same general pattern is found in Ontario. However, between 1982 and 2000, average annual increases in base wage rates in Ontario exceeded the national average in most years (Akyeampong 2001; Office of Collective Bargaining Information 2001). Using a wage index (1981=100), the Ontario index (186.2) exceeded the national index (181.8) in 2000. The difference is even more remarkable when one considers that the Ontario data are based on smaller bargaining units (200 or more employees) than the national figures (500 or more employees).

Another important development in Ontario and Canada as a whole has been a shift in bargaining priorities toward job-security issues, including provisions that minimize the impact of layoffs (e.g., severance pay or retraining) or reduce the need for layoffs (e.g., early retirement provisions) (Chaykowski 1992). For example, the 1990 Stelco-Steelworkers agreement, established among other things a joint labour-management committee to "examine all plans to subcontract work and to consider the possible alternatives" (including union access to Stelco's books), recall security and enhanced severance and early retirement plans (Verma and Warrian 1992). The 1999 GM-CAW agreement restricted outsourcing of work and required the creation of "a new job for every job lost to outsourcing" (Kumar 1999, 177).

There have also been innovative collective bargaining responses to globalization and competitiveness, some precipitated by crisis situations. The most publicized example is undoubtedly the agreement reached at Algoma Steel following multi-party negotiations between the Steelworkers, Dofasco, the Rae government, and lending institutions. These negotiations led to the creation of the largest employee-owned company in Canada and established a framework agreement to restore the company to profitability based on worker participation and joint decision-making. (Financial difficulties pushed the company to the brink of bankruptcy in 2001.) The 1990 Stelco-Steelworkers agreement introduced an income-sharing plan based on value-added as a means of rewarding "high-quality work during periods of high profitability" (Verma and Warrian 1992, 113). A notable example of collaborative labour relations is CAMI, the General Motors-Suzuki joint venture, which integrates collective bargaining and the Japanese production system (Frost 2001).

On balance, there has only been a modest union response to employer efforts to increase workplace flexibility in Ontario, a response similar to Canada as a whole. Some unions, the CAW, for example, have been indifferent to or have opposed management-initiated employee involvement programs (Chaykowski and Verma 1992). The Steelworkers at Stelco have exhibited a more supportive response to innovative employer initiatives on gain-sharing and employee involvement. It appears that "where change has occurred in unionized firms, the change and adaptation process has largely happened in the context of the traditional labour relations system" (Verma and Chaykowski 1999).

Bargaining outcomes in the public sector have exhibited two major changes over the 1990s. First, as noted above, wage settlements lagged behind the private sector in the 1990s. This resulted from government restraint measures, notably the *Social Contract Act* and the massive budget cuts instituted by the Harris government. Fiscal pressures led to a major shift in bargaining priorities and the adoption of innovative job-security arrangements. For example, the 1992 agreement for the Ontario public service (OPS) provided a comprehensive job-security package, including a guaranteed job offer to employees affected by contracting-out, divestment or relocation of an operation. Although the job-security provisions were weakened in the next bargaining round, which included a five-week strike by Crown employees in 1996, the government's privatization initiatives were impeded by the contractual obligation that it make "reasonable efforts" to find employment with successor employers for employees transferred out of the public service (Rose 2001; Leeb 2002). The 1992 OPS agreement became the model for central hospital arbitration awards issued between 1992 and 1995 (for service workers represented by CUPE and the Service Employees' Union). These awards provided for union involvement in restructuring plans and staff planning committees, six months notice of layoffs to the union and employees, improved bumping rights (increased in scope to 5 percent on either side of employee's job rate), and enhanced severance and early retirement plans. These changes paved the way for improvements in employment and income security in other parts of the public sector.

The grievance arbitration process in Ontario is broadly similar to other jurisdictions. In 1979, Ontario became an innovator in Canada by developing a statutory expedited grievance arbitration procedure. The procedure, which subsequently was adopted in Manitoba and British Columbia, allows either party to opt out of the collectively bargained procedure into the fast-track statutory procedure. It provided for grievance mediation (if both parties agreed), the appointment of single arbitrators by the minister of labour, and expedited hearings and awards. Since its inception the procedure has been widely used and has generated substantial time and cost savings. This has led to a transformation of the arbitration system, for example, less use of tripartite arbitration boards and greater use of grievance mediation to resolve disputes. (As a result of budget cuts, the government no longer provides grievance settlement officers.) In addition, the number of qualified arbitrators has increased as a result of a training and accreditation program for new arbitrators (Rose 1986*b*). In response to the demand for effective systems for resolving grievances, a number of private expedited arbitration procedures have been developed in Ontario and elsewhere (Burkett 2000).

CONCLUSIONS

At the outset of this chapter, it was noted that Ontario does not have a distinct regional identity like other regions. Owing to its size, central location and socio-cultural characteristics, Ontario residents perceive themselves as Canadians first. Although industrial relations in Ontario has occasionally been perceived as synonymous with the Canadian system, it has numerous distinct features that have been shaped by the province's political system and economic structure.

The most distinctive features of the political landscape have been the dominance of the Tories, a vibrant and competitive three-party system, and the tendency, until quite recently, of all three parties to operate within a narrow Progressive Conservative framework. This has allowed the Conservatives to develop economic investment strategies to satisfy business interests and initiate social reforms to accommodate labour interests. The development of labour policy has been marked by pragmatism and opportunism. With few exceptions, Ontario labour reforms followed the lead of other jurisdictions. From a substantive standpoint, Ontario labour law is situated comfortably in the Canadian mainstream. Because stable labour relations were deemed essential to attracting business investment, the Tories sought to maintain good relations with organized labour. Accordingly, a high priority was placed on maintaining close links with trade unions through various arrangements, including ministerial appointments (e.g., Finkelman and Armstrong), creation of consultative advisory committees and the institutionalization of tripartite administrative bodies.

The Harris government represented a significant departure from the past in three important respects. First, consultation with organized labour and the search for consensus have been abandoned. Second, accommodating organized labour is no longer deemed essential to attracting business investment. There has been a major shift in emphasis — labour relations stability is no longer considered the *quid pro quo* for attracting investment. The priority is now on fiscal conservatism and the deregulation of markets. Third, pragmatism has given way to a doctrinaire approach to labour reform and economic adjustment. It should be noted that the Harris government has not limited itself to reducing public expenditures and restructuring the broader public sector. A number of initiatives have rescinded union rights that have been in place for decades (e.g., card-based certification and successor rights). In the process, the province's rich tradition of promoting harmony and cooperation has been replaced by confrontation with organized labour. This pendulum shift has resulted in massive public protests and confrontations with public sector unions. It remains to be seen whether the resignation of Premier Harris in April 2002 and the ascension of Ernie Eves to the premier's position, will produce a shift back to the pragmatic centre and a more inclusive and consultative government (Urquhart 2002). Early indications suggest that the new premier is moving in that direction.

The province's economic structure, with its emphasis on heavy industry, multinational firms and international unions, has also shaped the practice of industrial relations in Ontario. Union density is below the national average and declining employment in the primary and manufacturing industries have contributed to an overall drop in union membership. As is generally the case in Canada, the largest gains in union membership have been in the public sector.

Dispute patterns reveal that relative to its share of the total labour force, person-days lost due to strikes in Ontario are low. As well, the average size of strikes in Ontario is smaller than the national average. Whereas these dimensions of strike activity reflect the overall pattern in the postwar period, more discrete patterns are found for selected periods. For example, consistent with the national trend, strike activity in Ontario increased in the 1960s and experienced a steep decline in the 1990s. At the same time, Ontario's share of strike activity declined after 1970. Major labour disputes involving 100,000 or more person-days lost were concentrated among blue-collar workers in heavy industry.

With respect to industrial relations processes, Ontario unions have often established significant bargaining breakthroughs (notably the CAW) and established the province as the national wage leader. In the public sector, the right to strike is restricted for selected employees. For these groups, compulsory arbitration is an important aspect of dispute settlement patterns and bargaining outcomes. The system of expedited grievance arbitration has been successful and has been adopted by other jurisdictions. In other respects, bargaining processes have mirrored trends elsewhere. These trends include the decline in pattern bargaining, a downward trend in wage settlements, the growing importance of job security, and the negotiation of longer collective agreements.

NOTE

The author wishes to acknowledge the financial assistance of the Arts Research Board, McMaster University, as well as the research assistance of Christine Manuel.

REFERENCES

Abella, I. 1974. "Oshawa 1937," in *On Strike: Six Key Labour Struggles in Canada 1919-1949*, ed. I. Abella. Toronto: James Lewis & Samuel Publishers, pp. 93-125.

Adams, G.W. 1981. "The Ontario Experience with Interest Arbitration: Problems Detecting Policy," in *Interest Arbitration*, ed. J. Weiler. Toronto: Carswell, pp. 133-74.

Akyeampong, E.B. 2001. "Fact-Sheet on Unionization," *Perspectives on Labour and Income* 13 (3):46-54.

Ashagrie, K. and J.K. Eaton. 1970. *Union Growth in Canada, 1921-1967*. Ottawa: Canada Department of Labour.

Bertram, G.W. 1968. "The Structure and Performance of Collective Bargaining Systems," in *Construction Labour Relations*, ed. H.C. Goldenberg and J.H.G. Crispo. Ottawa: Canadian Construction Association, pp. 416-519.

Brownsey, K. and M. Howlett, eds. 1992. *The Provincial State: Politics in Canada's Provinces and Territories*. Toronto: Copp Clark Pitman, pp. 147-74.

Bruce, P. 1989. "Political Parties and Labor Legislation in Canada and the United States," *Industrial Relations* 28 (Spring):115-41.

Burkett, K.M. 1998. "The Politicalization of the Ontario Labour Relations Framework in the 1990s," *Canadian Labour and Employment Law Journal* 6 (2):161-84.

—— 2000. "Cost and Delay in Labour Arbitration," in *Labour Arbitration Yearbook 1999-2000*, ed. K. Whitaker *et al.* Toronto: Lancaster House, pp. 317-25.

Canada. Human Resources Development Canada (HRDC). 1996. *Directory of Labour Organizations in Canada, 1996*. Ottawa: Human Resources Development Canada.

Carter, D. 1992. *Labour Law Reform: A Radical Departure or Natural Evolution?* Kingston: Industrial Relations Centre, Queen's University.

Chaykowski, R.P. 1992. "Industrial Relations in the Canadian Mining Industry: Transition Under Pressure," in *Industrial Relations in Canadian Industry*, ed. Chaykowski and Verma, pp. 141-86.

—— 2001. "Collective Bargaining: Structure, Process and Innovation," in *Union-Management Relations in Canada*, 4th ed., ed. M. Gunderson, A. Ponak and D.G. Taras. Toronto: Addison Wesley Longman, pp. 234-71.

Chaykowski, R.P. and A. Verma. 1992. "Canadian Industrial Relations in Transition," in *Industrial Relations in Canadian Industry*, ed. Chaykowski and Verma, pp. 448-74.

——, eds. 1992. *Industrial Relations in Canadian Industry*. Toronto: Holt, Rinehart and Winston of Canada Ltd.

Coates, M.L., D. Arrowsmith and M. Courchene. 1989. *The Labour Movement and Trade Unionism Reference Tables*. Kingston: Industrial Relations Centre, Queen's University.

Craig, A. and N. Solomon. 1996. *The System of Industrial Relations in Canada*, 5th ed. Scarborough: Prentice Hall Canada Inc.

Donner, A. (Chairman). 1987. *Working Times: The Report of the Ontario Task Force on Hours of Work and Overtime*. Toronto: Ontario Ministry of Labour.

Dyck, R. 1996. *Provincial Politics in Canada: Towards the Turn of the Century*, 3d ed. Scarborough: Prentice-Hall Canada Inc.

Franks, D. 1976. *Report of the Industrial Inquiry Commission into Bargaining Patterns in the Construction Industry in Ontario*. Toronto: Ontario Ministry of Labour.

Frost, A.C. 2001. "Creating and Sustaining Local Union Capabilities: The Role of the National Union," *Relations industrielles-Industrial Relations* 56 (2):307-35.

Frost, A.C. and A. Verma. 1999. "Restructuring in Canadian Steel: The Case of Stelco Inc.," in *Contract and Commitment: Employment Relations in the New Economy*, ed. Verma and Chaykowski, pp. 82-112.

Goldenberg, H.C. (Commissioner). 1962. *Report of the Royal Commission on Labour-Management Relations in the Construction Industry*. Toronto: Queen's Printer.

Gunderson, M., D. Hyatt and A. Ponak. 2001. "Strikes and Dispute Resolution," in *Union-Management Relations in Canada*, 4th ed., ed. M. Gunderson, A. Ponak and D.G. Taras. Don Mills: Addison-Wesley Longman, pp. 314-58.

Hebdon R. and P. Warrian. 1999. "Coercive Bargaining: Public Sector Restructuring Under the Ontario Social Contract, 1993-1996," *Industrial and Labor Relations Review* 52 (2):196-212.

Hines, R.J. 1972. "Mandatory Contract Arbitration: Is it a Viable Process?" *Industrial and Labor Relations Review* 25(4):533-44.

Ibbitson, J. 2000. "It's Proof that the Good Times Are Now," *The Globe and Mail*, 3 May, pp. A1, A13.

Jain, H.C. and S. Muthuchidambaram. 1995. *Ontario Labour Law Reform: A History and Evaluation of Bill 40*. Kingston: IRC Press, Queen's University.

Jamieson, S.M. 1968. *Times of Trouble: Labour Unrest and Industrial Conflict in Canada, 1900-66*, Task Force on Labour Relations, Study No. 22. Ottawa: Information Canada.

—— 1979. "Industrial Conflict in Canada, 1966-75," Discussion Paper No. 142. Ottawa: Economic Council of Canada.

Johnston, D.L. (Chairman). 1974. *Report of the Hospital Inquiry Commission*. Toronto: Ontario Ministry of Labour.

Kumar, P. 1999. "In Search of Competitive Efficiency: The General Motors of Canada Experience with Restructuring," in *Contract and Commitment: Employment Relations in the New Economy*, ed. Verma and Chaykowski, pp. 137-81.

Kumar, P. and N. Meltz. 1992. "Industrial Relations in the Canadian Automobile Industry," in *Industrial Relations in Canadian Industry*, ed. Chaykowski and Verma, pp. 39-86.

Leeb, G. 2002. "A Global Experience Up Close and Personal: Ontario Government Workers Resist Privatization," *Canadian Labour and Employment Law Journal* 9 (1):1-35.

Little, B. 1999. "Q: Who Supplies Canada's Trading Muscle? A: Ont ...." *The Globe and Mail*, 13 December, p. A16.

Little, W., Judge. 1969. *Collective Bargaining in the Ontario Government Service – A Report of the Special Adviser*. Toronto: Queen's Printer.

McBride, S. 1996. "The Continuing Crisis of Social Democracy: Ontario's Social Contract in Perspective," *Studies in Political Economy* 50 (Summer):65-93.

Meltz, N. 1989. "Interstate vs. Interprovincial Differences in Union Density," *Industrial Relations* 28 (2):142-58.

Ontario. Office of Collective Bargaining Information. 2001. Special data request.

Ontario. 1995. *Guide to Agencies, Boards and Commissions of the Government of Ontario*. Toronto: Queen's Printer for Ontario.

Ontario. Ministry of Finance. 1994. *1994 Ontario Economic Outlook*. Toronto: Queen's Printer.

Ontario Federation of Labour (OFL). 1995. "Historical Background: The Ontario Federation of Labour." Unpublished manuscript.

Progressive Conservative Party of Ontario. 1994. *The Common Sense Revolution*. Toronto: Progressive Conservative Party of Ontario.

Rand, I.C. 1968. *Report of the Royal Inquiry Commission into Labour Disputes*. Toronto: Queen's Printer.

Roberts, W. 1994. *Don't Call Me Servant*. Toronto: Ontario Public Service Employees Union.

Rose, J.B. 1986*a*. "Legislative Support for Multi-Employer Bargaining: The Canadian Experience," *Industrial and Labor Relations Review* 40 (1): 3-18.

—— 1986*b*, "Statutory Expedited Grievance Arbitration: The Case of Ontario," *The Arbitration Journal* 41 (4):30-45.

—— 1995. "The Evolution of Public Sector Unionism," in *Public Sector Collective Bargaining in Canada*, ed. G. Swimmer and M. Thompson. Kingston: IRC Press, Queen's University, pp. 20-52.

—— 2001. "From Softball to Hardball: The Transition in Labour-Management Relations in the Ontario Public Service," in *Public Sector Labour Relations in Transition in an Era of Restraint and Restructuring*, ed. G. Swimmer. Don Mills: Oxford University Press, pp. 66-95.

—— 2002. "The Assault on School Teacher Bargaining," *Relations industrielles-Industrial Relations* 57 (1):100-28.

Schenk, C.R. 2000. "Union Renewal – New Directions," *Workplace Gazette* 3 (3):96-106.

Sharpe, A. 1992. "The Role of Business-Labour Sectoral Initiatives in Economic Restructuring," *Quarterly Labour Market and Productivity Review*, Numbers 1-2. Ottawa: Canadian Labour Market and Productivity Centre.

Statistics Canada. 1994. *The Corporations and Labour Unions Returns Act Annual Report, Part II – Labour Unions 1992*. Ottawa: Statistics Canada.

—— 2000. *Historical Labour Force Statistics*. Cat. No. 71-201. Ottawa: Supply and Services Canada.

—— 2002. *Canadian Economic Observer: Historical Statistical Supplement 1997/98*. Cat. No. 11-010-XPB. Ottawa: Supply and Services Canada.

Urquhart, I. 2002. "Tory Pendulum Swings, But How Far?" *Toronto Star*, 13 April. At <www.thestar.com>.

Van Alphen, T. 2001. "Union Contracts Getting Longer," *Toronto Star*, 4 November, p. C3.

Verma, A. and P. Warrian. 1992. "Industrial Relations in the Canadian Steel Industry," in *Industrial Relations in Canadian Industry*, ed. Chaykowski and Verma, pp. 87-140.

Verma, A. and R.P. Chaykowski. 1999. "Employment and Employment Relations at the Crossroads," in *Contract and Commitment: Employment Relations in the New Economy*, ed. Verma and Chaykowski, pp. 1-20.

——, eds. 1999. *Contract and Commitment: Employment Relations in the New Economy*. Kingston: IRC Press, Queen's University.

Weiler, P. 1980. *Re-Shaping Workers' Compensation for Ontario*. Toronto: Ontario Ministry of Labour.

Weiner, N. 1995. "Workplace Equity," in *Public Sector Collective Bargaining in Canada*, ed. G. Swimmer and M. Thompson. Kingston: IRC Press, Queen's University, pp. 78-102.

Willes, J. 1979. *The Ontario Labour Court 1943-1944*. Kingston: Industrial Relations Centre, Queen's University.

Workplace Information Directorate. Various years. Special data requests.

Yates, C. 2000. "Staying the Decline in Union Membership: Union Organizing in Ontario," *Relations industrielles-Industrial Relations* 55 (4):640-74.

3 QUEBEC: TOWARD A NEW SOCIAL CONTRACT – FROM CONFRONTATION TO MUTUAL GAINS?

Michel Grant

Résumé — L'évolution des relations industrielles dans la province de Québec doit être analysée dans le contexte historique des transformations de la société québécoise, particulièrement depuis le déclenchement de la Révolution tranquille au début des années 1960. Sans se lancer dans le débat de l'existence ou des mérites d'un modèle québécois à l'échelle sociétale, le régime de relations industrielles présente un nombre suffisant de particularités historiques et institutionnelles pour dégager une configuration propre ou distincte à la province. En effet, le rôle actif de l'État comme agent de développement économique et social l'a conduit à construire un cadre plein de contrastes dans ses formes institutionnelles et juridiques de même que dans les pratiques des acteurs, entre autres lorsqu'on compare les modes de régulations et les structures de négociation dans les secteurs public et privé.

La Révolution tranquille comme moment pivot. Contrairement à certaines images reçues, la Révolution tranquille ne constitue pas un passage subit de la noirceur à la clarté! Elle exprime un processus de modernisation socio-économique dans lequel s'inscrivent les changements au cadre et aux pratiques de relations industrielles. La passage d'un nationalisme conservateur et frileux à un nationalisme plus ouvert et réformateur a favorisé la mise en place de conditions plus favorables aux organisations syndicales et à l'expansion de leur influence et de leurs droits. Ainsi, la présence étatique et les pratiques alliées à une conception et à une tradition plus interventionnistes développées depuis les années 1960 dans la vie économique, de même que la participation des organisations patronales et syndicales aux nombreux forums de concertation et de consultation, ont amené les acteurs à se compromettre à l'égard de certaines politiques publiques relatives par exemple à l'élimination des déficits budgétaires du gouvernement et de la création d'emplois. La récession économique importante du début des années 1980 a conduit dans cette foulée le gouvernement à mettre en place des programmes pour créer des emplois, particulièrement lors de la création du Fonds de solidarité de la FTQ.

Le mouvement syndical. Bien avant la Révolution tranquille, le mouvement syndical présentait un portrait diversifié à l'image des tensions et des contrastes qui traversaient son évolution et qui marquaient ses choix. Situé au confluent des influences d'un côté anglo-saxonnes et surtout protestantes, et de l'autre, des influences francophones et catholiques, le travailleur québécois avait à choisir entre des syndicats américains qui correspondaient plus à ses aspirations économiques et revendicatrices mais moins à ses caractéristiques culturelles, et des syndicats catholiques qui intégraient beaucoup mieux sa mentalité francophone et catholique mais dont les stratégies de négociation s'avéraient plus frileuses et moins agressives. On trouve donc au Québec les mêmes organisations syndicales qu'au Canada anglais, telles les Métallurgistes Unis d'Amérique ou le Syndicat Canadien de la Fonction publique, et qui se trouvent regroupées au sein de la Fédération des travailleurs du Québec (FTQ), mais aussi des organisations émanant de conditions historiques exclusivement québécoises, la Confédération des syndicats nationaux (CSN) dont s'est détaché un certain nombre de ses syndicats du secteur privé en 1972 pour créer la Centrale des Syndicats Démocratiques (CSD).

Les différences entre les organisations syndicales s'amenuisèrent progressivement au cours de la Révolution tranquille alors que la FTQ, organisme représentant les syndicats affiliés au Congrès du travail du Canada (CTC), affirmait de plus en plus sa spécificité québécoise tant au niveau sociétal qu'au sein de la structure syndicale canadienne, et que de son côté le changement de nom de la Confédération des travailleurs catholiques du Canada en Confédération des syndicats nationaux (CSN) officialisait son caractère non-confessionnel et sa transformation en organisation combative. Si la transformation et l'influence de la CSN furent plus marquantes avec le gouvernement du Parti Libéral au début de la Révolution tranquille, celles de la FTQ s'affirmèrent au moins autant avec l'appui de celle-ci au Parti Québécois, à son programme social-démocrate en 1976 et à l'appui de cette centrale au *Oui* lors des deux derniers référendums de 1980 et 1995.

Si les années 1960 sont celles de la modernisation des institutions, les années 1970 sont celles de la radicalisation du discours syndical et des affrontements majeurs tant dans le secteur privé que public. Toutefois l'élection du Parti Québécois et l'appui d'une bonne couche des syndiqués et des organisations syndicales, font ressortir des intérêts et des conceptions différents et même opposés, particulièrement entre la FTQ avec la majorité de ses effectifs dans le secteur privé, et la CSN dont la majorité des membres se retrouvent dans le secteur privé. Les premiers voient dans le gouvernement un arbitre ou un intermédiaire entre eux et le patronat, alors que les seconds y voient un employeur.

Le cadre juridique des relations du travail. Cet appui à un appui ou du moins les relations entre les syndicats et les gouvernements visaient la mise en place de politiques publiques favorables à la syndicalisation et à la négociation collective. Si les relations privilégiées de la CSN avec le parti au pouvoir au début des années 1960 a favorisé la syndicalisation et l'obtention du droit de grève dans les secteurs public et para-public, celui-ci a subi des restrictions majeures au fur et à mesure des lois spéciales et des amendements législatifs, particulièrement à l'égard du respect des services essentiels lors de grèves. La mise en place d'un régime d'encadrement juridique à trois paliers en 1969 a constitué pendant plus d'un quart de siècle une particularité du régime juridique québécois et a survécu jusqu'à tout récemment avec la mise en place d'une Commission de relations du travail semblable à celles qu'on retrouve dans les autres provinces canadiennes. L'avenir nous dira si la création de ce nouvel organisme contribuera à déjudiciariser les relations du travail.

Le Québec est la seule province, sauf pour le bref séjour du Nouveau Parti Démocratique en Ontario, à prévoir dans son Code du travail des mesures limitant de façon significative le droit d'un employeur de remplacer ses salariés pendant une grève ou un lock-out légal. Finalement, une autre particularité du régime juridique et institutionnel québécois concerne la *Loi sur les décrets de convention collective* dont l'objet consiste à étendre à tous les salariés d'un secteur d'activité les salaires et d'autres conditions de travail négociés par le syndicat. Cette loi existe depuis 1935, particulièrement dans des secteurs où on retrouve beaucoup de petites entreprises en concurrence entre elles, et veut éviter que cette compétition se fasse aux dépens des conditions de travail. Malgré que les secteurs d'activité couverts par décrets soient caractérisés par de bas salaires reflétant les conditions très concurrentielles du secteur, le législateur, sous l'influence d'un lobby patronal important et persistant, a abrogé d'importants décrets comme ceux du secteur du vêtement au nom de la libre concurrence!

Conclusion. Si on a pu déceler l'émergence au cours des années d'un nouveau contrat social dans le secteur privé des relations du travail, on ne peut pas dire de même pour les secteurs public et para-public. La paix industrielle observée depuis la dernière décennie reflète les conditions économiques et commerciales de l'époque. Syndicats et patrons envisagent respectivement le recours à la grève et au lock-out dans la mesure où ces actions s'avèrent efficaces eu égard aux objectifs recherchés. L'avenir nous dira dans quelle mesure les conditions permettront ou non la redéfinition de nouvelles pratiques dans les secteurs public et para-public. L'élection éventuelle d'un gouvernement dirigé par l'Action Démocratique du Québec pourrait remettre en question le modèle d'un État moins interventionniste et interpeller les organisations syndicales par rapport au modèle ou au contrat social hérité de la Révolution tranquille.

In March of 1996, Quebec's former premier, Lucien Bouchard, held his government's first economic summit and persuaded business, labour, and community leaders to endorse a zero-deficit target for the provincial budget by the year 2000. The premier used a threatened reduction of the province's credit rating to persuade labour leaders of the need to reassure financial markets (*The Globe and Mail*, 19 June 1997). This episode demonstrated the influence of the political and economic environment on labour relations and the role that institutional actors can sometimes play at the societal level in the "Quebec model" of industrial relations. A major impact of this consensus fell on public sector workers who, facing the threat of special legislation, agreed to re-open collective agreements and negotiate legislative amendments to their pension plans and to the earlier retirement for approximately 37,000 persons, an experience, when added to other public service cuts, left public sector union officials and members bitter and frustrated.

Labour's tactics in dealing with the Parti Québécois government reflect the dilemmas of leaders and members, confronted on the one hand by the province's economic difficulties and the impact of these factors on bargaining, and on the other hand by their duty to represent their members and protect their conditions of work. This dilemma is further complicated by labour's active support for Quebec sovereignty.

CONTEXT OF QUEBEC INDUSTRIAL RELATIONS

Quebec shares many characteristics of the North American industrial relations systems, including some institutional and legal features, but also the type of changes in the workplace. The province has experienced the shift from Fordism to more flexible production units, occurring elsewhere in the region. However, Quebec's cultural and political context has produced distinct adaptations in its industrial relations system.

Three factors stemming from Quebec cultural and historical attributes contribute to the development of its specific industrial relations system: the modernization and transformation of nationalism beginning with the Quiet Revolution in the early 1960s; the role of provincial government as a leading agent of change in economic and social development; and a higher degree of union pluralism and fragmentation (Déom and Boivin 2001). The combination of these three variables has influenced the broad pattern of industrial relations in the province while shedding light on the analysis of the new social contract emerging at both the societal and firm levels.

This chapter begins with a brief review of the conditions that shaped the role of the state as an instrument of economic and social growth. In spite of the worldwide winds of deregulation and privatization, the Quebec government maintained a relatively active and interventionist role. The present institutional framework also is fragmented and contrasting, particularly the differences in regulation and bargaining structures between the public and private sectors. The evolution of labour-management relations and unionism is examined through the transformations undergone in the structure and actions of unions. This section will underline the unusual features of the legal framework regulating labour-management relations. When examining the issues confronting managers and workers, one must look at the cultural features of Quebec to grasp the origins and diversity of labour organizations.

THE QUIET REVOLUTION AND ITS AFTERMATH: THE STATE AS AN AGENT OF SOCIO-ECONOMIC CHANGE

Despite its label, the Quiet Revolution initiated profound and not so quiet changes, even though the preceding decades had established institutional infrastructures, such as cooperatives in the banking sector, necessary for more substantial transformations at the societal and economic levels. This revolution, though highly important and profound, was not a passage from darkness to light (Paquet 1999), and Quebec's modernization had evolutionary aspects (Linteau 2000). Although the present relevancy of the "Quebec model" that developed in the 1960s is debated (Bélanger, Comeau and Métivier 2000), the impact of the Quiet Revolution was substantial and transformed or created major institutions. This revolution even reverberated in other provinces. For example, it stimulated governments to grant collective bargaining rights to most public sector workers (Panitch and Swartz 1993). The election of the reformist provincial Liberals in 1960 marked not only the end of an autocratic anti-union government, but also the beginning of a period of an accelerated modernization of Quebec institutions. From a traditional nationalism based on religious and rural values, a new nationalism emerged, based on economic and social development through assertive state intervention.

Prior to 1960, Catholic clergy controlled the education and health-care systems. After promising universal access to education and health care, the new Liberal government nationalized these sectors. Thus, tremendous growth in public sector employment occurred in the 1960s. The majority of the population identified with the state as an instrument of collective progress and "economic liberation" as expressed in the provincial Liberals' campaign slogan "masters in our own house" (*maîtres chez nous*). The objective was to create a wider and more significant economic power base for the French-speaking business class and to promote homegrown firms (Drache and Gertler 1991). During this period, union leaders met with company representatives and academics to urge employers to create a provincial body that could speak for all Quebec employers on public policy issues. These discussions resulted in the creation in 1969 of the most important and influential employer association in the province, the Conseil du patronat du Quebec (Dufour 1980, 2000). The role of employer associations was enhanced by a governmental approach based on tripartism and concerted action (Delorme, Fortin and Gosselin 1994). A form of corporatism emerged, in which through various channels such as economic summits, different interest groups can have an impact on the definition of public policies ranging from fiscal policy to labour-management legislation (Archibald 1983; Dufour 2000; Paquette 1998; Déom and Boivin 2001, 488; Gagnon 2001).

A strong role for the provincial government was at the heart of Quebec's new economic policies. Economic nationalism and the ideas of autonomy and control of their own future by the majority of French-speaking Quebecers drove the Liberal government. This government created a number of public enterprises between 1960 and 1966, beginning with the nationalization of private electric companies to form Hydro-Québec. It then formed an investment fund to promote industrial development by financing Quebec companies. In 1965, the Quebec Deposit and Investment Fund (Caisse de dépôt et placement du Québec) was created to manage the contributions of employers and employees to the Quebec pension plan and also those of several other bodies. It became the most important financial institution in the province. These organizations formed a network of state enterprises and acted as bankers, traders, investors and producers, competing with private companies in finance, forest products, steel, mining, oil and gas, and television broadcasting. By 1985, at the beginning of the privatization drive, they constituted the most important network of state enterprises in any Canadian province (Bernier 1995).

The 1976 election of the Parti Québécois (PQ) marked the second stage of economic nationalism. The PQ vigorously re-affirmed the need to foster economic development through government initiative. The PQ proposed a general development strategy that emphasized a high-level self-sufficiency, diversification, local processing of natural resources, and extension of ownership and control by Quebec interests. Simultaneously, the PQ promoted an open economy, based on comparative advantages and exports.

A few months after its election, the new government held a series of socio-economic summits aimed at establishing a permanent dialogue among representatives of management, unions, the cooperative movement, and community groups. This consensus-building operation marks a corporatist state, which seeks to integrate all functional social groups. The state acts as an arbitrator and engineers the establishment of participative schemes involving the principal interest groups (Archibald 1983).

These government initiatives consolidated the positions of firms controlled by French-speaking executives, and by the mid-1980s, the expression "Quebec Inc." was common parlance. The three pillars of this Quebec Inc. model were: Crown corporations (e.g., Hydro-Québec), cooperatives (such as Mouvement Caisses Desjardins, which is the largest private sector employer in the province and with a membership of over five million, and private firms (Bombardier, Cascades, Shermag, etc.). The cooperative movement, represented by Desjardins, expresses a long-standing tradition of cooperatism and social solidarity which has produced a brand of alternative, community-based economics. While the first two pillars are collectively owned, even private corporations controlled by French-speaking managers form part of a collective endeavor. Indeed, many of these companies still remain under local control with state support through the Caisse de depôt and other public institutions.

Labour organizations were directly involved in Quebec Inc. socio-economic summits. Their representatives served on the board of directors of the Caisse de dépôt. The weight of labour influence in this type of participation is controversial for some who consider that union participation and other tripartite arrangements only endorses the government decision-making without generating corresponding benefits for employees. Generally, labour organizations in Quebec believe that this participation allows them to be better informed and to convey perspectives that would be neglected without their presence; moreover, they gain public and political legitimacy.

For example, during the 1981–82 recession, the Fédération des travailleurs du Québec (FTQ), a Canadian Labour Congress (CLC) affiliate, sought measures to counter the massive layoffs its members were suffering. The socio-economic summit in 1982 led to a program called Corvée-Habitation. Its purpose was to stimulate job creation in the construction industry while facilitating home ownership for consumers through lower mortgage rates. Five partners were involved in financing the program: the provincial government, municipalities, financial institutions, employers, and unions. In three years the program generated 57,000 construction jobs and twice as many in related industries (Fournier 1991; Boivin and Déom 1995).

As the recession dragged on, the FTQ suggested a large investment fund to maintain and create jobs in Quebec, especially in small and medium-sized firms. The government passed legislation in 1983 to loan $10 million to enhance the FTQ's own fund. This was the first "labour-sponsored" investment fund in Canada. Several other provinces later adopted similar plans. The fund is managed as a separate unit from the

FTQ, but union officers from the federation control its board of directors. Contributions are open to both union members and the general public. Contributors enjoy the tax deferral advantages of both a Registered Retirement Savings Plan and Quebec's Equity Savings Plan, which means a tax deduction of 80 percent of the original investment (Boivin and Déom 1995; Déom and Boivin 2001). By 2001 almost 500,000 individuals had bought shares for $4.6 billion and had invested in 1,829 firms. The fund has been one of labour's best success stories of the last 20 years. It also contributed to shifting the climate of labour-management relations in the province toward greater cooperation while generating a new source of union power. More than ten years after it had expressed its opposition to this fund (Fournier 1991), the rival Confédération des Syndicats Nationaux (CSN) obtained legislation to create a similar fund with the same fiscal benefits. The legislation specifies that the CSN *Fondaction* must invest in firms promoting employee involvement and labour-management cooperation.

The election of the provincial Liberals at the end of 1985 did not produce major changes in the policies of "province-building" and union-management dialogue. Inspired by the research of Michael E. Porter of the Harvard Business School (1990), the strategy of industrial clustering put forward by the minister of industry, commerce, science and technology figured prominently in the dialogue among the various actors, notably in management-union relations. Hence, the committees and roundtables representing different industrial clusters brought employers and unions together. The ministry actively promoted two programs advocating union involvement in the firm. First, management and unions had to sign the social contracts in order to gain access to funding provided by the Industrial Development Corporation (Société de développement industriel), a state venture-capital firm. These social contracts had to include a long-term collective agreement and union and employee participation schemes at the workplace level (Quebec 1993). Clearly, the intention was to move from a traditional model based on confrontation to a mutual-gains model. Second, worker-shareholder cooperatives (WSC) enabled workers to own a block of shares jointly, between 10 and 30 percent, thereby giving employees representation on employers' boards of directors. WSC-promoted employer-employee partnerships and collective agreements included the shareholders' contract defining the rules governing this partnership (Grant and Lévesque 1997).

In the private sector, economic nationalism clearly encouraged partnership and dialogue between management and unions not only at the broader provincial level, but also in the workplace. In a private sector exposed to competitive challenges and pressures, unions and managers became more aware of the value of collaboration in the organization of work to achieve profitability, better working conditions, and better job protection. Private sector unions shifted their strategy from confrontational rhetoric and tactics to cooperation and dialogue (Grant and Lebeau 1994; Boucher 1994).

The Labour Movement Before the Quiet Revolution

The labour movement in Quebec is the most diversified and fragmented in Canada (Heron 1996) (see Table 1). Locals affiliated to American and Canadian unions represented by the FTQ face provincially based bodies

TABLE 1

DISTRIBUTION OF WORKERS (%) COVERED BY A
COLLECTIVE AGREEMENT BY UNION AFFILIATION AND
SECTOR (PUBLIC OR PRIVATE), 1996

Sector	Affiliation						Total
	CEQ	CSD	CSN	FTQ	Independents	Others	
Public	86,965	5,435	150,298	103,718	170,296	107	516,819
	(16.8)	(1.0)	(29.1)	(20.0)	(33.0)	(0.02)	
Private	2,450	29,130	80,640	250,705	55,952	11,538	430,415
	(0.6)	(6.8)	(18.7)	(58.2)	(13.0)	(2.7)	
Total	89,415	34,565	230,938	354,423	226,248	11,645	947,234
	(9.4)	(3.7)	(24.4)	(37.4)	(23.9)	(1.2)	

Note: These data do not cover construction workers and those under federal jurisdiction. Centrale de l'enseignement du Québec (CEQ) is the umbrella organization for the great majority of teachers at the elementary and high school level and for other categories of teachers and workers in the education and health sectors. Centrale des syndicats démocratiques (CSD) was created when a group of unions left the Confederation of National Trade Unions (CSN) in 1972 to create their own organization. CSN stands for Confédération des syndicats nationaux. The Fédération des travailleurs du Québec (FTQ) represents the CLC affiliates in the province. The category independents refers to any union not affiliated to one of the previous organizations. The category others represents groups not affiliated to one of the previous groups but affiliated to the AFL-CIO, the Confederation of Canadian Unions, the Canadian Labour Congress, the Canadian Federation of Labour or the Union des producteurs agricoles (farmers' union). Public sector covers civil service, health and education, Crown corporations, universities, public transit, and municipalities. Budget cuts at the Department of Labour have meant that we were unable to obtain more recent data.
Source: CRSMT (1997).

whose existence and development can only be explained by the distinct history and culture of the province. This fragmentation has not prevented Quebec from reaching the highest rate of unionization for comparable provinces.

Quebec workers historically have been able to choose between one type of unionism closer to their religious beliefs and ethnic characteristics, but less aggressive in promoting their economic interests (e.g., Catholic, French-speaking, and based in the province), and another type of unionism emphasizing improvement of their working conditions, but less sensitive to their cultural needs (e.g., religiously neutral, English-speaking, and mostly based in the United States) (Vadeboncoeur 1961). Quebec's history of labour strife and inter-union rivalry was a response to unique economic and cultural realities. By the end of the nineteenth century, international unions were already less dominant in Quebec than elsewhere in Canada because of the importance of national unions (Rouillard 1979). The influence of international unions in the province grew more important as transportation improved and labour mobility increased. They out-numbered the Catholic unions through the Quiet Revolution until 1973, when their numbers started to decline (Table 2), a trend experienced in other provinces (Fréchet and Simard 1990).

Though the Catholic hierarchy initially opposed unionization, it adapted to the reality of industrialization late in the nineteenth century. In Quebec (and some European countries) the Church established unions which were open only to Catholics. Elsewhere in North America,

TABLE 2
AFFILIATION OF LOCALS TO CATHOLIC AND
INTERNATIONAL UNIONS, 1931–1961

Year	International Unions		Catholic Unions	
	Number of Unions	% of Quebec Unions	Number of Unions	% of Quebec Unions
1931	286	58.2	121	24.6
1936	275	48.0	190	33.1
1940	306	43.8	239	34.2
1946	437	44.1	338	34.1
1951	459	40.7	439	39.0
1955	601	44.4	441	32.6
1961	725	45.1	469	29.2

Catholics joined secular, that is, non-religious, unions. Quebec clergy applied Church doctrines in a restrictive and conservative fashion by creating unions closed to non-Catholic workers (Boisvert 1970).

In contrast to international unions, which used collective bargaining to pressure management, Catholic unions, under the control of their chaplains, viewed labour-management relations differently. They insisted that workers and employers act on their mutual interests and resort to conciliation rather than to work stoppages in order to settle their differences (Rouillard 1979). The Confédération des travailleurs catholiques du Canada (CTCC) was founded in 1921 to represent Catholic unions and to provide workers with an institution imbued with their faith and opposed to Marxism. This organization retained its religious status until 1960, when it changed its name to Confédération des syndicats nationaux (CSN) and severed all ties with the Church.

Faced with large international unions emphasizing the protection of workers' interests, Catholic unions gradually had to adopt a similar collective bargaining approach. They gradually transformed into genuine labour unions, not only because they had to adjust to their members' needs arising from industrialization, but also in order to compete with the rival international unions in economic action.

The crucial event in this transformation was the 1949 Asbestos strike. The CTCC was involved in a major confrontation in the mining towns of Asbestos and Thetford Mines, not only against management, but also against the government. The Church hierarchy supported the workers against these interests, a struggle that helped launch the Quiet Revolution. When the CTCC abandoned its confessional status in 1960, it had already modernized its policies and was prepared to benefit from the Quiet Revolution. Ten years later, the parent body representing public school teachers' unions also abandoned its religious ties and professional status to become a conventional union, the Centrale de l'enseignement du Québec (CEQ). This organization recently changed its name to Centrale des syndicats du Québec (CSQ) to emphasize its goal of organizing workers outside education.[1]

International unions in Canada also experienced internal problems in Quebec. At the outset of the Quiet Revolution, craft unions represented the most conservative element in the Quebec labour movement, while those groups and the newer industrial unions had moved closer together through their common and more aggressive opposition to right-wing governments. Under pressure from their parent bodies at the American and Canadian levels, locals affiliated with the new CLC in Quebec merged. In 1957 the FTQ was created and soon became the biggest labour organization in the province.

The political and economic conditions prevailing at the outset of the Quiet Revolution favoured the CSN. The name change from CTCC to CSN was more than symbolic. This action showed how the organization had distanced itself from the Church and had become a genuinely independent labour organization, a leading opponent to the conservative regime of the Union Nationale Party, and one of the main actors for social and economic change in Quebec. The CSN presented a modern agenda while being based in the province and led by Quebecers close to the Liberal Party. Jean Marchand, president of the CSN during the height of the Quiet Revolution, later became a senior minister when Pierre Trudeau became prime minister. The opposition role that labour organizations had played during the previous regime lent substantial credibility to the labour movement at the outset of the Quiet Revolution and to the modernization process it stimulated. While the political activity of the Quebec labour movement was previously limited to the civil society, the new regime provided tripartite forums which would allow unions to act within the political system and achieve a degree of integration (Gagnon 1994).

The Quiet Revolution and Labour Relations: A Period of Catching-Up and Centralization

The Royal Commission on Bilingualism and Biculturalism found that French-speaking Quebecers ranked twelfth in income in the province, just above immigrants of Italian origin and the Aboriginal peoples. Unions were at the forefront of "the extensive process of political democratization, social development and redistributive justice that helped to define contemporary Quebec" (Denis and Denis 1995). Quebec moved toward a more complete and contemporary mass production, mass consumption, and collective bargaining model combined with Keynesian economic policies and the construction of a welfare state.

Between 1964 and 1976 a radicalization process occurred that reached its peak with the election of the Parti Québécois in 1976 (Grant 1990). Provincial and local public services had experienced many strikes immediately following the granting of the right to strike in 1964: Quebec Liquor Board (1964); engineers at Hydro-Québec (1964); public transit in Montreal (1965, 1967); hospitals (1966); professional groups in the civil service (1966); Canadian Union of Public Employees (CUPE) locals at Hydro-Québec (1967). Table 3 shows the evolution of the number of

TABLE 3

NUMBER OF WORK STOPPAGES AND PERSON-DAYS LOST, 1966–2001 (SELECTED YEARS): PRIVATE AND PUBLIC SECTORS (PROVINCIAL JURISDICTION)

Year	Number of Work Stoppages			Number of Person-Days Lost		
	Private	Public	Total	Private	Public	Total
1966	126	11	137	1,277,620	649,270	1,926,890
1968	123	5	128	680,670	322,770	1,003,440
1970	116	10	126	1,276,150	141,410	1,417,560
1972	136	11	147	835,450	1,993,860	2,829,310
1974	378	12	390	2,568,550	42,400	2,610,950
1976	286	7	293	4,938,955	1,394,159	6,333,114
1977	247	29	276	1,184,582	113,620	1,298,202
1980	302	42	344	2,570,356	1,438,303	4,008,659
1983	240	3	243	1,048,480	1,278,220	2,326,800
1986	252	16	268	2,115,509	115,396	2,230,905
1989	220	14	234	649,571	848,396	1,497,967
1993	161	3	164	476,388	12,166	488,554
1996	101	3	104	375,192	12,147	387,339
2001	90	18	108	432,121	28,247	460,368

Note: The category "public sector" covers civil service, health and education, and provincial Crown corporations. This table does not include workers under federal jurisdiction, but provides a breakdown along private and public sectors. Sources: Parent and Dompierre (1983, 55); Courchesne and Dompierre (1984, 63-63); Dompierre, Courchesne and Martel (1987, 78); Morin (2002, 6).

work stoppages and person-days lost for the public and private sector under provincial jurisdiction (Parent and Dompierre 1983; Courchesne and Dompierre 1984; Dompierre, Courchesne and Martel 1987; Dompierre 1997; Morin 2002). Even though the number of stoppages in the public sector is below the private sector, the provincial scope and number of workers involved in public sector conflicts created high levels of person-days lost.

Radicalism peaked in 1976. After the election of the PQ, less militant tendencies gained support. Gaining the right to strike fuelled unionization drives in the public services, a phenomenon not limited to Quebec. The conditions for unionization in Quebec were even more favourable than elsewhere. The close ties between the Liberals in power and union leaders, and the high degree of centralization of bargaining structures in the education and health-care sectors helped labour gain members. The labour movement's support gave legitimacy to government policies and generated pay-offs in an institutional and legal framework conducive to unionization and collective bargaining gains, particularly in the public sector. The recognition of the right to strike had a major impact on the industrial relations system, when issues connected to collective bargaining and conflicts in the public sector dominated the province's political agenda.

From 1960 to 1966, the unemployment rate in the province fell from 9.2 percent to 4.1 percent (see Table 4), conditions of work improved, but earnings remained at 20 percent below Ontario (CSN-CEQ 1984). This situation led a growing number of both workers and unions to question the regional distribution of wealth in Canada. Polarization on economic issues thus provided a new frame of reference for unions and workers in interpreting and transforming their nationalism (Hudon 1980).

The new PQ government (dominated by individuals with public sector backgrounds) acknowledged that public sector workers needed stronger collective bargaining rights in order to improve working conditions and recruit and retain qualified personnel, thus building a strong

TABLE 4

UNEMPLOYMENT RATES (%) FOR SELECTED YEARS
CANADA-QUEBEC-ONTARIO, 1960–2002

Year	Quebec	Ontario	Canada
1960	9.2	5.4	7.0
1966	4.1	2.6	3.4
1970	7.0	4.4	5.7
1975	8.1	6.3	6.9
1979	9.7	6.5	7.5
1982	13.9	9.7	11.0
1985	12.2	8.1	10.7
1989	9.6	5.1	7.5
1992	12.7	10.7	11.2
1997	11.4	8.4	9.1
2000	12.7	10.7	11.2
2002 (May)	8.3	7.0	7.7

Source: Statistics Canada. *Historical Labour Force Statistics*, Cat. No. 71-201 annual; Statistics Canada, *Labour Force Information*, Cat. No. 71-001-PIB, 7 June 2002.

infrastructure to promote social and economic development. The right to strike was nonetheless obtained in a context of union pressures and some illegal action, such as striking nurses in some Montreal hospitals in 1963 (Lemelin 1983). The general context of the Quiet Revolution and the more specific changes to labour legislation fuelled significant increases in union membership from 353,044 workers in 1961 to 662,778 workers in 1966, with the unionization rate climbing from 30.5 percent to 35.7 percent (see Table 5); these changes were even more beneficial to the CSN who saw its share grow from 25.7 percent to 30.5 percent, while the CLC locals represented by the FTQ dropped from 57 percent to 48.2 percent (Rouillard 1989). In the early 1960s, the FTQ lacked adequate tools and authority to compete with a more centralized and better organized CSN, which enjoyed a competitive advantage at the organizational and political levels (Grant 1990).

The image of the CSN's invincibility finally suffered a serious setback during a provincewide vote at Hydro-Québec in 1966 when the CUPE defeated the CSN to obtain the right to bargain for both blue-collar and

TABLE 5
UNION DENSITY RATES (%) IN QUEBEC, 1921–2001

Year	Union Density Rates (%)
1921	24.0
1931	21.6
1941	20.7
1951	26.5
1961	30.5
1966	35.7
1971	37.6
1976	34.8
1981	35.4
1985	38.2
1997	37.4 (41.9)
2001	36.6 (40.1)

Note: These data refer to union membership and the numbers are thus lower than those that one could get when looking at union coverage (e.g., the number of workers covered by a collective agreement). The data in parentheses refer to union coverage.
Source: Rouillard (1989, 124, 201, 289); Akyeampong (1997, 48; 2001, 49).

white-collar workers. CUPE leaders and local union officers were already deeply involved in the transformation of the FTQ and the representation vote at Hydro was perceived as a victory not only of CUPE, but of the FTQ. This experience demonstrated that the CSN's nationalist strategy could be offset by American and Canadian unions fully in touch with French-speaking Quebecers. It was also paramount that members of these unions enjoyed sufficient autonomy to determine their own policies and strategies in Quebec.

While acknowledging the importance of affiliation of locals to provincial federations, many Canadian trade unionists initially had difficulty in grasping the profound changes in Quebec. The greater degree of inter-union rivalry in Quebec and the CSN's successful raids against CLC locals in the early years of the Quiet Revolution pointed to the necessity of a stronger provincial federation to coordinate and defend the interests of American and Canadian unions. Even though affiliation to a provincial federation was not mandatory, locals supported a strong federation in Quebec in order to develop policies better suited to the context of the Quiet Revolution. Louis Laberge, an international business agent, was elected president of the FTQ in 1964 after a bitter struggle between the nationalist/progressive wing and a more conservative wing less sensitive to Quebec's conditions. Initially, the support for Laberge stemmed from the latter group, but the new president quickly realized that the federation and its affiliates had to drastically redefine their approach if American and Canadian unions were to remain a significant force in the province. After 1969, the FTQ took more nationalist positions which eventually led to their opposition to the provincial Liberals, and to their support of the Parti Québécois, the Bloc Québécois, and to the "Yes" coalition during the 1980 and 1995 sovereignty referendums.

LABOUR LEGISLATION

Labour legislation adopted in Quebec in 1944 followed the *Wagner Act* model and focused on the private sector. Amendments passed by the Liberals during the Quiet Revolution mostly concerned public service workers who had been under an interest-arbitration system and whose working conditions lagged the private sector substantially. Most significantly, public service workers received the right to strike during that period, including civil servants who had obtained the right to bargain under the *Public Service Act* in 1965.[2] The state initially granted these workers and their unions the same basic bargaining rights as their private sector colleagues (Cardin 1973). The Labour Code provisions were thus basically identical for both sectors, except for a provision for injunctions when a work stoppage threatened public health and safety. A series of major strikes in public services led to numerous injunctions and back-to-work legislation, and resulted in a more restrictive framework for public sector bargaining. If private sector bargaining followed a decentralized mode, collective bargaining in the public sector became increasingly centralized and bureaucratized, in addition to being inherently political.

The Labour Code

Despite its title, the Quebec Labour Code, unlike its federal counterpart, basically addresses collective rights. Other statutes cover individual employment rights. The pillars on which the Labour Code rests are identical to those defined in American and Canadian legislation: the right to organize and to certification, exclusive representation through majority rule, the duty to bargain, and the ability to enforce the collective agreement (Morin and Brière 1998; Dickman 1987). Quebec shares many features with other Canadian labour laws regarding the right of association, the certification process, unfair labour practices, strike prohibition and compulsory arbitration for police and firefighters, first contract arbitration, and the general prohibition to strike during the life of a contract. For many observers, the Quebec Labour Code is viewed as comparatively progressive legislation (Carter 1984). Quebec was among the first jurisdictions in Canada to provide for compulsory dues check-off when a union has been certified. It was also among the first jurisdictions to provide first contract arbitration. However, three distinct features of the Code stood out until the 1990s: the administrative machinery responsible for the implementation of this legislation, the anti-strikebreaking provisions, and the still existing but fragile decree system. Essential services have been a major issue.

Essential Services in Labour Disputes and Restriction to the Right to Strike

Essential services in labour disputes are those necessary for the protection of the public. The only essential-services measure in the Labour Code for the manufacturing and private services sectors stipulates that an employer cannot use replacement workers. The only distinction in the 1964 Labour Code for health care, education, and public services was the possibility of a court order, not to maintain essential services, but to suspend the right to strike for 90 days (Bernier and Lemieux 1994). However, the *Civil Service Act* adopted in 1965 contained essential services mechanisms for civil servants. The Labour Court could determine which essential services must be maintained in case of a work stoppage by civil servants, although this issue has never been a problem. The same cannot be said for other public sector and service groups.

During the 1960s and the 1970s, public sector unions struck frequently and obtained major gains in bargaining. Twenty-one work stoppages occurred in public transit in Montreal alone between 1975 and 1982 (Boivin and Déom 1995). The six most important bargaining agents in the public sector were involved in 48 bargaining situation between 1966 and 1989; for that period, nearly half (23) included a legal strike (ibid.). In half of these strikes the National Assembly resorted to special legislation.

In 1975, the Liberal government passed a law (Bill 253) requiring a binding decision on essential services prior to any work stoppages in health care. During the subsequent bargaining round, unions generally did not comply with this law. Pending charges against workers for violating this law were dropped shortly after the 1976 election of the PQ (Lemelin 1984). In 1978, the Parti Québécois government amended the Labour Code to create an essential services board for the health sector and agreement between the parties on essential services.[3] Though not permanent, this body was considered to be the forerunner of the present Conseil des services essentiels (Essential Services Council) created in 1982 by the PQ government.

The conseil deals in practice with two essential services regimes, one for public services and another for health care. Its mission is to make sure that a strike does not threaten public health and safety (Adell, Grant and Ponak 2001). The criterion for determining essentiality is thus narrow and does not take into account economic consideration or even any inconvenience that may result from strike action. However, in cases of illegal strikes, the conseil's mandate reaches beyond essentiality and includes the power for that board to end a strike, if it considers that the conflict is likely to be prejudicial to a service to which the public is entitled, including education.

In order for a strike to be legal, parties must first try to reach agreement on a list of essential services to be maintained, with the assistance of a mediator from the conseil (Lemieux 1996). In the absence of an agreement, the union submits a list of the essential services it is willing to provide. After representation from the parties, the conseil then decides which services will continue. If the conseil considers that a strike threatens public health and safety, it may, before reporting to the minister of labour, recommend changes to the list or the agreement. If the minister considers that services provided where a strike is apprehended or in progress are insufficient, he or she can suspend the strike. This has occurred six times since the creation of the conseil, but the possibility of such a suspension has encouraged parties to negotiate an acceptable level of essential services and enhances compliance with the conseil's decisions.

In November 1986, the Liberal government adopted Bill 160. Although the government did not have to use its provisions during the 1986 bargaining round, the purpose of this bill was to secure full compliance with essential services provisions in the health-care sector by penalizing non-compliance. Any worker, union officer or union can be fined for non-compliance with legal provisions regarding essential services. In addition, a union loses 12 weeks of dues check-off each day for an illegal strike. In addition to losing pay while on strike, each striker suffers an additional pay cut equal to the amount of time not worked during the illegal strike. Probably the harshest and most controversial provision concerns the loss of seniority; it stipulates that each complete or part of a day of illegal strike entails the loss of one year's seniority. Many illegal work stoppages occurred in the 1989 bargaining round, particularly from nurses refusing to work overtime or striking for a short period. As a result, a nurse not scheduled to work on a day of a strike would not be penalized, while one who was supposed to work but struck lost seniority. Employers themselves found this particular provision of Bill 160 extremely difficult to manage. Seniority of penalized employees was restored when the Liberal government put through Bill 157 in 1991. Furthermore, that same year, a judge from the Superior Court found that although Bill 160 was justified to assure the protection of the public, the provisions regarding the loss of seniority were disproportionate in regard to government objectives and that they generated injustice, thus nullifying the article concerning seniority. The Quebec Appeal Court, however, in a decision rendered on October 1998, found that Bill 160 provisions, including the loss of seniority, did not violate either the Canadian or the Quebec charters of rights.[4]

Consequently, a sharp contrast in the treatment of essential services exists between the health-care sector and those in other public services. At the outset, the high quotas, ranging from 55 to 90 percent, imposed on health-care unions do not allow the conseil much discretion in determining the appropriate level of essential services. In public services, however, the conseil was, for example, able to use its discretion to consider essential public transit in Montreal at peak hours during weekdays in order to avoid traffic jams that would obstruct circulation for firefighters, police patrol cars, and ambulance (Adell, Grant and Ponak 2001).

The Structure of Collective Bargaining: Centralization versus Decentralization

The role and presence of the state in the social and economic development of Quebec is probably the most important factor accounting for the "hypercentralized" (Hébert 1984) bargaining structure in the public sector.[5] This structure reflects the government's intent to fully control the bargaining agenda and strategy. This preoccupation with control stems from the importance of wage costs applied not only to its relations with unions but also with employers and their respective association in the education and health-care sectors. As shown in Table 6, collective bargaining in the private sector follows the Canadian decentralized pattern; 90 percent of bargaining units certified under the Quebec Labour Code are located in one workplace[6] covering 54 percent of workers under a contract, while the parapublic sector (education and health care) comprises less than 1 percent of bargaining units for almost 25 percent of workers covered by a collective agreement.

TABLE 6

DISTRIBUTION (%) OF COLLECTIVE AGREEMENTS AND WORKERS BY TYPE OF BARGAINING UNIT, 2002

Type of Bargaining Unit	% of Agreements	% of Workers
1 employer, 1 workplace, 1 union, 1 certification	90.30	53.90
1 employer, 1 workplace, 1 union, >1 certification	1.80	1.00
1 employer, 1 workplace, >1 union, >1 certification	0.16	0.18
1 employer, >1 workplace, 1 union, 1 certification	0.60	0.00
1 employer, >1 workplace, 1 union, >1 certification	0.60	0.60
1 employer>1 workplace, >1 union, >1 certification	0.00	0.10
>1 employer, 1 workplace, 1 union, >1 certification	0.00	0.10
>1 employer, >1 workplace, 1 union, >1 certification	1.00	12.50
>1 employer, >1 workplace, >1 union, >1 certification	0.00	24.00
Provincial bargaining unit (education)	0.57	6.30
Provincial bargaining unit (health and social services)	1.17	18.20

Source: Department of Labour, 2 June 2002.

When the right to strike was granted to education and health-care workers, collective bargaining took place at the local level. In 1966, Premier Jean Lesage proclaimed the end of the catch-up phase for public sector workers. Henceforth, conditions should follow the private sector pattern (Lemelin 1984). The government established norms in putting a cap on wage increases for school boards (ibid.). A series of strikes erupted at the end of 1966 and in early 1967, and led to the adoption of Bill 25.[7] The practical purpose of this bill was to end strikes, extend collective agreements through June 1968 and replace local bargaining by provincial bargaining for each category of school board (French Catholics, anglo-Catholics, and anglo-Protestants). Years after their inclusion under the Labour Code, public school teachers and hospital workers had thus shifted from a decentralized negotiation mode to a centralized one. This evolution was essentially linked to the political commitment that provincial expenditures would be controlled through limits on compensation, while the quality of services would be the same across the province.

The centralization process extended during the next bargaining rounds to other categories of personnel (e.g., office workers in school boards, CEGEP[8] personnel, and health-care and social services workers). Standing legislation defines the rules governing public sector bargaining structure and consolidating its centralized character for civil servants, office and blue-collar workers, and professionals.[9] It also addresses government agencies or Crown corporations labelled under "peripublic" — Hydro-Québec, Quebec Liquor Corporation, etc. Employers in this last sector must, before beginning negotiation, obtain government approval for the general guidelines regarding compensation and working conditions. The Act further stipulates that wage levels and schedules can only be negotiated for the first year; for the next two years, they are determined through regulation after consultation with unions and employers. In addition, the Institut de la statistique du Québec (ISQ) must issue annual public reports on wages and total compensation of public and parapublic workers to other Quebec workers. This bargaining procedure has never been followed, for each bargaining round since 1985 included three-year agreements on wages and wage schedules. However, the Institut de recherche et d'information sur la rémunération (IRIR) had been playing its role since its inception, before being replaced by the ISQ in 1999, by informing the general public and negotiating parties about the relative position of compensation for the public and parapublic sectors (Wavroch 1993); although not an actor directly present at the bargaining table, the

IRIR and then the ISQ established their credibility through a frame of reference for discussion of the merits of wage and other compensation issues.

Despite such a centralized framework, the number of bargaining units remains substantial and involves important coordination problems. For the 1988–90 bargaining round, 84 bargaining units existed in the health-care and social affairs sector and 27 units in the education sector (Hébert 1995).

MEANWHILE, IN THE PRIVATE SECTOR....

The Parti Québécois was elected in 1976 with strong support from unionized workers and also with an official and active endorsement from the FTQ. The PQ was committed to reform the Labour Code by introducing pro-union amendments, particularly provisions prohibiting replacement workers and granting the Rand formula. Later, the government focused on individual rights (Morin 1993): the *Charter of Human Rights and Freedoms*[10] (1975) and the *Charter of the French language*[11] (1977) included provisions protecting individual rights at the workplace. The National Assembly reformed the minimum wage system in 1979. That same year it radically transformed the legal and institutional framework regarding occupational health and safety. The global approach was based on prevention and granted the individual the right to refuse dangerous work assignments or conditions. Moreover, this legislation created an entire administrative structure based on the principle of joint worker-employer decision-making from the local and sectoral level to a provincial board.

A Three-Tier System and a New Labour Relations Board

Until the adoption of legislative amendments in 2001 creating a labour relations board similar to other Canadian jurisdictions, the administrative structure in Quebec consisted of a three-tier system: a certification agent, a labour commissioner supervised by a labour commissioner-general, and a labour court.[12] Upon receiving an application for certification, the labour commissioner-general designated a certification agent to verify that the group seeking certification was representative and had the right to certification. The certification agent determined the appropriate bargaining unit.

If the parties agreed on the bargaining unit, but disagreed on certain persons being covered by it, the certification agent issued a certificate. If there was an agreement on the bargaining unit, but the union represented between 35 and 50 percent of employees covered by the petition, the certification agent held a representation vote.

The labour commissioner was the second tier in the system and dealt with disputed applications, including allegations of unfair labour practices. A commissioner can order reinstatement and indemnity of workers disciplined because they had exercised a right protected by the *Labour Standards Act*.[13] Moreover, any employee with three years' seniority with a company could file a complaint against a dismissal not made for good cause. In such cases the labour commissioner acted as an arbitrator with the power to order reinstatement.

The third tier of the administration machinery was the Labour Court. On one level it acted in appeals of decisions of the labour commissioner, and at another level it has exclusive jurisdiction as the first instance in penal proceedings instituted for any offense under the Labour Code.

This three-tier system was complicated and extremely legalistic while generating important delays and narrowing the range of remedial responses. In 1987 the National Assembly amended the Labour Code and abolished the three-tier system and replaced it with a labour relations board similar to those existing elsewhere in Canada.[14] The National Assembly adopted the amendments, but the board was not created until the fall of 2002.

Employers were not enthusiastic about the creation of a labour relations board. One can expect that, during its first years, the new board mandate and power will be challenged as it renders its decisions. The judicial approach and mindset developed under the former three-tier system will remain.

Anti-Replacement Workers Provision

A major innovation in the Labour Code was the prohibition on the use of replacement workers during strikes. Moreover, there are more legal restrictions to the exercise of strikes where the public health and safety are an issue and where the lock-out is forbidden. The provisions go well beyond the prohibition of professional strikebreakers found in other jurisdictions. Duties performed by a bargaining unit employee cannot be carried out by the following replacement workers:[15]

- a member of the bargaining unit, unless that worker is providing services essential to public health and safety;
- anyone, worker or manager, hired after the beginning of negotiation;

- a person working for a contractor or for another employer;
- any manager working in another establishment, unless this establishment is part of the bargaining unit on strike or lock-out (e.g., food retailers);
- any employee working in another establishment;
- any other employee working in the establishment on strike or lock-out and who is not a member of the bargaining unit.

These provisions do not prevent an employer from transferring production to another establishment or to a contractor. Anti-strikebreaking provisions essentially aim at production in the one or many workplaces of the bargaining unit. The minister of labour, acting through an investigator, enforces this provision. The investigator system has produced compliance by seeking voluntary settlements (Fleury 1991). In roughly one-third of work stoppages that had occurred during the 1979–89 period, the union requested an investigation. A settlement was reached in 25 percent of cases, and the investigator found the employer in violation in slightly more than half the remaining cases; thus Boivin and Déom (1995) concluded that overall, strikebreakers were officially used in 13 percent of work stoppages.

Anti-strikebreaking provisions were introduced and adopted under the Lévesque government in 1977 after an intense debate; they were even strengthened by the same party during its second term in 1983. Employers opposed the inclusion of these measures because they would impair the ability to compete outside Quebec where such advantages for unions did not exist. They also feared that the number of strikes would increase if unions had too much bargaining power and managers became vulnerable to excessive demands. Data on work stoppages in Tables 3 and 8 show that the number of person-days peaked in 1976, more than a year before the enactment of these measures, and the occurrence and scope of labour strife afterwards followed a downward trend not dissimilar to other jurisdictions. These numbers strongly suggest that the decision to strike or lock-out is driven more by economic and commercial reasons than by the rules set in a labour code for replacement workers. The recession that hit the Quebec economy in the 1980s and again in the 1990s, the continuing globalization of commerce, and the general restructuring of economy, production, and labour markets with the development of a contingent workforce are much more significant in explaining the decline in labour strife. Anti-strikebreaking provisions have, however, contributed significantly to the reduction of violence during work stoppages. The most important employer association, the Conseil du patronat du Quebec, acknowledged this fact when it decided not to challenge these provisions in court because such action could damage the positive labour-management climate in Quebec.

The Decree System

This system is probably the most original feature of the Quebec legal framework. It was adopted during the Great Depression, when workers were suffering, and unions were too weak to negotiate significant improvements for their members. The clergy and the Catholic unions lobbied to import a European system, by which some collective agreement provisions were extended to workers in non-unionized shops (Beaulieu 1955). The system was designed to stimulate collective bargaining and labour-management cooperation by keeping wages out of competition (Bernier 1993). Decrees exist where a large number of employers with a relatively small number of personnel operate in a highly competitive environment.

The system still exists today, even though many employers are questioning its legitimacy and some decrees have disappeared, particularly in the garment industry. The system suffered different blows, for instance, when the construction industry was removed from decree jurisdiction or when joint committees lost control of vocational training in 1969. The system came under heavy attack in 1986 with the publication of a report that recommended its abolition.[16] Many non-union employers covered by decrees grew more resistant to the extension of the collective agreement, particularly in sectors such as ladies' garment manufacturing, where union density was falling. Despite pressures to eliminate decrees, the system remained in place as shown in Table 7, but the numbers keep getting smaller. The desire of employer and employee representatives to maintain the decree system is probably the main reason accounting for its survival (Hébert 1990).

Under the decree system, government may insist that a collective agreement shall bind employers and employees in a given industry, occupation or region. Both regional and provincewide decrees for an industry or occupation (e.g., garage employees in Montreal; men's wear for the whole province) exist. In the late 1990s, 29 decrees applied to 120,000 workers and 13,400 employers, including unionized and non-unionized workplaces.

Agreement provisions usually extend wages, classification of operations, hours of work, holidays, and vacations. The government may issue a decree extending a collective agreement with changes it considers appropriate if, among other reasons, the negotiated conditions of

TABLE 7

NUMBER OF DECREES, EMPLOYERS AND WORKERS, 1935–2001
(SELECTED YEARS)

Year	Decrees	Employers	Workers
1935	40	n/a	n/a
1948	100	18,000	200,000
1959	120	33,000	250,000
1970	75	18,000	140,000
1975	52	12,000	125,000
1985	42	17,250	144,662
1990	34	16,094	142,704
1991	33	16,246	140,347
1992	31	16,137	131,432
1994	29	15,441	126,178
1996	29	13,428	120,420
1998	27	11,508	112,101
2001	18	9,418	72,891

Source: Quebec. Ministry of Labour.

employment to be extended have acquired a "preponderant significance and importance." These conditions of employment must neither seriously hinder competitiveness nor impair job preservation and development. Joint committees supervise decrees (Déom and Boivin 2001).

Decrees are concentrated in low-wage sectors where small and medium-sized companies operate in highly competitive markets. This system has not hampered competition while it may improve conditions of work. Nor has it been a disincentive to unionization (Bernier 1993; Boivin and Déom 1995). Finally, the joint committee has provided an environment conducive to labour-management cooperation, particularly the development of industrial strategies and of training in the sector. The government has acknowledged that the elimination of decrees — in the garment industry, for instance — will lead to deterioration of working conditions. A greater gap between the union and non-union wage rates within an extremely competitive industry will create enormous pressure on the collective bargaining system.

THE 1970–1976 PERIOD: LABOUR MILITANCY
AND NATIONALISM

The 1970 provincial election, which led to the Liberal government of Premier Robert Bourassa, was also the first electoral test for René Lévesque and the Parti Québécois. Even though no formal link between the PQ and Quebec labour organizations has ever existed, a significant percentage of union officers were PQ activists. The adoption of the *War Measures Act* in October 1970 and the ensuing suspension of civil liberties brought major labour organizations, the Parti Québécois and other nationalist, progressive, and democratic forces in the province closer together. Union activists in the PQ helped to build its social-democratic agenda while promoting an increasingly sovereigntist agenda within their own organizations.

As union opposition to the Liberal government grew because of public sector wage controls, opportunities for joint action by the CSN, CEQ, and FTQ multiplied, including a common front of locals bargaining with the Quebec government. The socio-political and polarized climate generated confrontational tactics at the bargaining table, and person-days lost in work stoppages rose to an all-time high in 1976. Data in Table 8 eloquently contrast changes in the importance of labour strife in 1976, when the number of person-days lost exceeded six million before dropping to less than 500,000 for 1996.

The radicalization of labour action was accompanied by a radicalization of ideas. The general policies of the FTQ and CSN shared the following features: they strongly disputed capitalism; they sought a democratic and radical transformation of society, while existing governments were foes who delayed change and supported multinational corporations; in line with the heritage of the Quiet Revolution, they viewed the state as the engine for economic development (Tremblay 1972). Marxist rhetoric also inspired the CEQ in its analysis of the school system as an instrument of the business class (CSN-CEQ 1984).

These ideological pronouncements were made in era of confrontation. They were a tactical tool to mobilize membership and rally opponents of the Liberal regime and of employers, thus projecting labour-management conflict as a class struggle. The majority of trade unionists in Quebec were not Marxists. Union practices remained focused on collective bargaining and improvement of working conditions. The general conditions of labour militancy and growing nationalism added to the political tone of negotiation in the public and parapublic sectors. The

TABLE 8

NUMBER OF WORK STOPPAGES, WORKERS INVOLVED AND
PERSON-DAYS LOST, 1966–2001 (SELECTED YEARS)

Year	Number of Stoppages	Number of Workers Involved	Number of Person-Days Lost
1966	152	128,302	2,175,417
1967	148	153,273	1,653,670
1968	138	34,158	1,113,906
1970	134	85,431	1,490,690
1972	163	358,182	3,480,144
1974	412	197,370	2,690,483
1976	315	607,818	6,583,488
1977	299	61,466	1,433,421
1980	363	174,047	4,314,999
1983	253	156,760	2,384,822
1986	271	265,061	2,249,154
1989	244	297,672	1,609,763
1993	167	47,361	516,984
1997	103	22,502	324,020
1999	155	25,257	652,747
2001	113	52,666	499,451

Note: This table covers workers in Quebec under federal and provincial
jurisdiction, but does not allow us to discriminate between private and public
sectors.

Sources: Courchesne and Dompierre (1984, 56-57); Dompierre, Courchesne
and Martel (1987, 70-71); Morin (2002, 6).

discrepancy between the Marxist-inspired rhetoric used by top union leaders and the more practical values expressed at the grassroots and shop
levels eventually caused divisions between private and public sector unions.

Many workers in the private sector concluded that the CSN had
become too radical, too political and too focused on public sector issues.
The CSN experienced important divisions until the early 1980s, as Marxist-
Leninists infiltrated their ranks in public sector groups and strove to shape
union policies. Marxist-Leninists also existed in the FTQ, but the latter's
more decentralized structure and heavier membership concentration in
the private sector made it less influenced by ideologies.

A split occurred in the CSN in 1972, when 70,000 members, one-third of its membership, from the private and construction sectors founded the CSD (Centrale des syndicats démocratiques). Other groups such as those comprising the Alcan workers (Fédération des syndicats du secteur de l'aluminium), and civil servants (Syndicat des fonctionnaires provinciaux du Quebec) formed independent unions. The CSN share of union membership dropped in ten years from 30.5 percent to 19.2 percent, thus modifying significantly the trade union picture in Quebec (Rouillard 1989).

The CSN became predominantly a public sector organization, and its historical divisions helped increase the share of independent unions who represent almost an equal share of unionized workers in Quebec (Table 1). Moreover, with a majority of their membership in the public sector, the CSN, like the CEQ, developed policies that tended to view the state more as an employer than a relatively neutral third party who could balance both sides' interests.

The events that shook the CSN took place in 1972 while the president of the CSN was in jail for contempt of court along with the presidents of the FTQ and CEQ. The three labour organizations representing 210,000 members decided to coordinate their strategies through a "Common Front" to pressure government to change its wage policy. The government considered that the period of wage catch-up was over, so public sector wages should follow the private sector (Lemelin 1984). Unions challenged this policy and demanded wage levels based on the principle of a decent minimum wage. This demand mobilized public sector workers, because a significant percentage of CSN and FTQ members were low-wage earners. Conditions were thus ripe for a major confrontation which led to injunctions, contempt of court, and special legislation to end the strike. Another series of private sector strikes exploded, a majority affiliated to the FTQ, to protest the imprisonment of the three union presidents.

These strikes were probably the high point of politicization of a labour conflict in the history of Quebec. What happened? Once the crisis ended, government assigned new negotiators with new mandates to resume negotiation with the Common Front. The parties finally agreed on a $100 minimum weekly wage.

A second Common Front was organized for the 1975–76 bargaining round. Instead of using the same pressure tactics as in 1972, union strategists planned to give greater consideration to the influence of public opinion on the issues and the process of collective bargaining. Diversified pressure tactics in the workplace, sporadic rotational and one-day strikes proved efficient in bringing government to accept a contract that exceeded its own compensation limits. The scandal-ridden Liberals knew they were facing re-election problems, particularly from an increasingly powerful Parti Québécois, and they were ready to pay the price to get labour peace before the fall election.

TOWARD APPEASEMENT: ELECTION OF THE PARTI QUÉBÉCOIS

The labour scene facing the new PQ government in 1976 was very different from the one confronting the Liberals in 1960. Public sector workers were all unionized, and their conditions of work had improved greatly through collective bargaining. Public sector issues had dominated the industrial relations scene during the previous 15 years. The CSN not only suffered a severe financial crisis after losing one-third of its membership, but it also experienced an ideological and political crisis over the efforts of Marxist-Leninists to control the organization's agenda against the more moderate trade unionists. For many Marxists-Leninists, the PQ was a worse class enemy than the Liberals, because its social-democratic and petit bourgeois nationalistic program would distract the proletariat from its "revolutionary mission."

Meanwhile, the CLC affiliates in the FTQ had adapted to the Quebec environment more successfully. Paradoxically, FTQ locals from Canadian and American unions were the strongest supporters of the PQ. The importance of inter-union rivalry in Quebec compared to other provinces caused CLC to grant the federation control over many activities, so the FTQ had greater powers than other provincial federations. For example, the CLC permitted the Quebec caucus to choose one of the senior CLC vice-presidents. At the 1974 CLC convention, delegates supported the Quebec caucus against congress leaders when they transferred jurisdiction over regional councils and education, with the corresponding resources, from the CLC to FTQ. By 1993, the president of the FTQ claimed that his organization had achieved the status of "sovereignty-association" with the CLC (Fournier 1994).

During the 1970s, the political role of labour in Quebec changed fundamentally. Compared to the other labour organizations, which preferred to keep their distance publicly from political parties, the formal FTQ support for the Parti Québécois was in line with the tradition of the AFL-CIO support for the Democratic Party in the United States and the CLC's links with the federal New Democratic Party (NDP). The NDP never became a significant actor in Quebec because of its inability to integrate Quebec nationalism into its political and economic agenda. The path followed by progressive forces in Quebec blended social democracy with nationalism, thus continuing the course set at the beginning of the Quiet Revolution in the 1960s. In addition to sovereignty-association, the PQ's program included a wide array of social-democratic measures, including amendments to labour legislation. The presence of the Liberals as a common enemy was a unifying factor among the different unions and gained support for the PQ among union members. A significant number of members of the National Assembly elected in 1976 were former trade unionists, and Premier René Lévesque publicly acknowledged that his government was favourably disposed toward workers. During its first 1976–81 mandate the PQ government adopted amendments to the Labour Code sought by the labour movement but focused mostly on private sector issues (e.g., anti-strikebreaking provisions, first contract arbitration, Rand formula, etc.) and occupational health and safety.

Prior to the 1981 provincial election, the FTQ expressed its satisfaction with the PQ's first term in office and recommended its re-election. While the CSN had closer and more privileged contacts with the Liberals in the early 1960s, the FTQ had become the PQ's closest labour ally. Issues raised in the late 1970s and 1980s were less dominated by development of public administration and more by promoting economic development in the private sector. In contrast with the CSN and the CEQ, the FTQ, with a majority of its members in the private sector, was particularly sensitive to job protection and creation. The FTQ participated in large public summit meetings organized by government to bring consensus and cooperation between the principal socio-economic parties. The CSN and the CEQ expressed strong reservations about such exercises in tripartism or corporatism because they feared the labour movement risked co-optation. These two organizations had heavy concentrations of members in the public sector and were uncomfortable cooperating with a government who was also their employer and against whom they needed to mobilize members. However, they joined the socio-economic summit to avoid leaving the FTQ as labour's sole representative.

Despite a climate of cooperation, the volume of person-days lost remained high (see Tables 3 and 8). The first public sector bargaining round with the Parti Québécois was not accompanied by the same level of labour militancy and union solidarity as in the past. The PQ government, however, passed special legislation in 1979 to impose a 15 day cooling-off period. Serious divisions appeared within the third Common

Front when some health-care unions affiliated with the CSN resorted to one-day illegal strikes, while the FTQ and CEQ remained at work (Lemelin 1983; Rouillard 1981). Obviously many trade unionists had become less comfortable confronting the Parti Québécois in the context of the forthcoming 1980 referendum; public opinion did not view labour's demands as sympathetically as in the 1960s and early 1970s, particularly for a group that was seen as enjoying job security and that had made substantial gains through collective bargaining.

The Setback of the 1980s

Inflation declined in the 1980s. The purchasing power of negotiated wages for the 1985–89 period also fell. This trend to lower real wages affected both the private and public sector (Favreau 1989). Statistics on work stoppages reveal that, after more than a decade of labour militancy, the industrial relations climate became more peaceful, a situation that continued through the late 1990s; Figure 1 illustrates the decline in work stoppages after 1979.

FIGURE 1
PROPENSITY TO WORK STOPPAGES, QUEBEC JURISDICTION
1979–2001

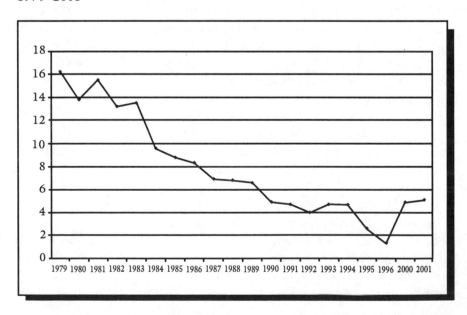

This is but one of the many indicators on how the recession of the early 1980s and the ongoing restructuring of world economy in the 1990s transformed not only the issues that unions and managers faced, but also the parties' strategies to settle their disputes. Practitioners faced problems different from those raised in traditional collective bargaining and contract administration. The term "industrial relations" was replaced by "human resources management" because of the development of programs geared more to the individual worker, such as training, career development and reorganization of work, and other questions traditionally outside the collective agreement

This first recession of the 1980s caused uncertainty regarding economic and commercial prospects and led managers to design more flexible and adaptable strategies. They found that Tayloristic and Fordist workplace arrangements did not fit into the new business environment. Unions in the private sector learned from their experience with massive layoffs that confrontational strategies were less and less suitable in this new context. Even public sector workers in 1983 experienced, under the PQ administration, wage cuts. In the following decade, major cuts in the number of jobs occurred as the provincial government fought for deficit reduction through restructuring, privatization, use of contingent workforce, rationalization, merger, and even closing of hospitals.

New values emerged and challenged trade unionists and managers. The welfare state, hierarchical order, and ideologies proposing global societal changes represented declining values while the local firm, small groups, pragmatism, individual achievement, and autonomy were replacing the former values (Larouche 1986). Managers seemed to be leading innovative practices while unions had to re-examine and redefine their approach; their responses generally vary according to the degree of exposure to competition and the threat of job losses. Unsurprisingly, private sector unions were thus the first to shift from confrontation to cooperation with management. This only widened the gap and emphasized the differences between private and public sector unionism. The creation of a wage solidarity fund in 1983 by the FTQ originated from a labour organization whose members were concentrated in industries experiencing huge layoffs. Twelve years later the CSN persuaded the government to create a fund offering similar fiscal benefits, not only with the purpose of creating jobs and stimulating the economy, but also of encouraging participative management in the workplace. This delay is probably due to the greater importance of public sector unions in the CSN, their proneness to ideological debate and preference to maintaining a distance from government; however, the structural characteristics of economic transformations and their permanency, the FTQ's success with its own fund, and the threat of job losses in the public convinced the CSN that innovative measures were necessary.

The 1990s: Lean Years in Public Sector and New Workplace Practices in the Private Sector

No real bargaining occurred in the public sector during the first half of the 1990s. PQ legislation controlled or froze wages, following the pattern of the federal government. Public sector unions resumed effective negotiations prior to the 1995 referendum, when they tried to improve conditions of work without compromising the chances for a "Yes" victory. Since the whole Quebec labour movement was part of the "Yes" coalition, public sector unions did not want to bear any onus for an eventual victory of their opponents.

Faced with a huge budgetary deficit, the Parti Québécois government imposed more drastic cuts. Mayors requesting special legislation used a huge compensation differential favouring municipal workers.[17] Municipalities claimed that they could not impose similar settlements on their unions as the provincial government. Consequently, the public sector contrasted with the private sector in terms of the labour climate and other conditions favouring a new social contract and the "social modernization" of the workplace (Bélanger, Grant and Lévesque 1994). Changes at the societal level fostered firm-level changes occurring at the three strate-

TABLE 9

NET INCREASES (%) IN NEGOTIATED WAGE SETTLEMENTS FOR 1986–1992 AND 1993–2001, QUEBEC

Category	1986–1992	1993–2001
Public sector	3.0	–1.7
Other unionized non-public sector	–1.3	2.4
Private sector	0.4	3.6
Municipalities	–4.4	0.1
Federal public sector	–7.6	1.1
All unionized workers	0.9	0.2

Source: Institut de la Statistique du Québec (2001, 162).

gic levels identified by Kochan, Katz and McKersie (1986): the long-term strategy and policy-making level, the collective bargaining and personnel level, and the workplace and shop floor level.

It was suggested earlier that, due to the specific historical and cultural conditions that developed since the Quiet Revolution, the provincial government was instrumental in bringing managers and unions together in cooperating and jointly committing themselves to both economic and job development. The strategic choice model proposed by Kochan, Katz and McKersie (1986) focuses at the firm level and not at the societal level. The Quebec experience suggests an addition to that model. Employee ownership corresponds to the strategic level. In addition to wage solidarity funds which allowed indirect participation of workers on boards of directors, the number of cooperatives increased to 175 in 1996 with 7,500 employees (Grant and Lévesque 1997). The increasing importance of employee and union involvement at the strategic level is one of the distinct features of the industrial relations system in Quebec. This situation developed with the support of labour and governmental institutions such as Société de développpment industriel. The FTQ solidarity fund finances worker economic and business training in order to help union representatives participate fully in policy-making and other long-term strategic issues. The presence of worker ownership can nurture a climate of mutual trust and union-management cooperation, but does not necessarily lead to innovative practices in the work process (Lebeau 1992). Between 1983 and 1993, firms associated with the FTQ solidarity fund experienced only four short work stoppages (Fournier, cited in Grant and Lévesque 1997).

A survey of over one hundred workplace case studies (ibid.) strongly suggests that most innovations occurred in the manufacturing sector, particularly in pulp and paper, metallurgy, and aluminum. The research also indicates that innovations in the organization of work were more frequent (86 cases) while changes in labour-management relations were second (76 cases). This study shows that innovations in work organization were often linked to transformations in labour-management relations.

This survey reflects changes at the collective bargaining and union-management relations' level where the terms of the social contract and major issues have been traditionally disputed and defined. Walton, Cutcher-Gershenfeld and McKersie (1994) refer to the present period as one of breaking with the existing paradigms that developed in an era where negotiations focused on incremental changes brought to collective agreements. The historical conditions in Quebec led to a fundamental shifting of the social contract from an "arm's length accommodation" relationship (ibid.) to greater union-management cooperation and employee commitment. One indication of this transformation is the growing number of collective agreements signed in the 1995–96 period that introduced joint labour-management committees (Baldino 1997).

Major changes in the social contract through long-term agreements appeared in the early 1990s. Although the Labour Code limited contract duration to three years, the union and employer at Sammi-Atlas in Sorel agreed to a six-year pact with union and employee participation programs. This accord also featured job guarantees. These changes were a prerequisite for a substantial government grant (Quebec 1993). The Sammi-Atlas case clearly spells out the active part played by the provincial government and its agencies in creating the conditions conducive to transformations in the workplace.

These contracts cannot be labelled "social" if they are not accompanied by significant changes in the basic values and approaches driving employer and union practices (Bourque and Vallée 1994). Collective bargaining may become continuous and the issues agreed upon may be outside the traditional language of a contract. Collective agreements may become "living" documents, open to frequent changes and adjustments based on verbal understanding and mutual trust (Harrison and Laplante 1994). This development does not suggest that all confrontation ends in union-management negotiations, but there is a significant trend in the private sector to move from traditional positional bargaining to more problem-solving and forms of mutual gains bargaining (Grant 1997; Grant and Lévesque 1997). For managers, collective agreements must become more flexible, not only in terms of compensation and the use of a contingent workforce, but also in the flexibility in the organization of work.

Lévesque *et al.* (1996) found that almost 60 percent of unions in a large sample were affected by different types of work reorganization. This third strategic level is probably the one where innovations occur the most frequently, according to Grant and Lévesque (1997). It is probably also the level where workers and their union can be the most influential. If union bargaining power once originated from the strike, present conditions indicate that workers and their unions are involved in overhauling Tayloristic and rigid work practices, which managers believe are essential, in order to improve productivity and profitability.

The principal forms of work flexibility appear to be reduction and merging of job descriptions, job enlargement, job enrichment, and training for multiskilling (Grant and Lévesque 1997). Because work reorganization not only involves technical activities, but also decentralization and reduction of hierarchical control, training programs must improve skills necessary for teamwork (Maschino 1995*a, b, c, d*). The significant presence of unions in sectors exposed to competition emphasizes the importance for employers encouraging and seeking union support in order to reorganize the work. Interestingly, the introduction of teamwork simultaneously has fostered union solidarity and workers' support for business objectives (Lévesque *et al.* 1996).

Private sector unions in Quebec have become increasingly committed to workplace transformation. Cautious at first, but more open by the end of the 1980s (FTQ 1987; Grant and Lebeau 1994), they became more proactive as the need to protect jobs grew more urgent for their survival and development (CSN 1991; FTQ 1993). The CSN, for instance, concluded that unions should even initiate and propose changes to employers because higher productivity cannot be achieved without improved deployment of human resources. Management and union representatives at the Conseil consultatif du travail et de la main d'oeuvre (CCTM)[18] reached an important consensus not only on the necessity to reorganize the workplace but also on the conditions to implement those changes (CCTM 1997). This significant agreement between the principal employer and union organizations provided more evidence of a new, more cooperative labour-management climate. Moreover, the active role of government in helping parties and providing them with a forum to reach such an accord illustrates again the government policy of consensus-building. Both union and management organizations acknowledge that, in order to achieve profitability, a firm must be able to adjust rapidly and use its personnel efficiently; job protection and training must become shared goals (ibid.). The document further states that work reorganization is no longer an exclusive management right, that unions have a legitimate voice in it. This position coincides with the recommendation of the professional association representing human resources and industrial relations practitioners. (Corporation professionnelle des conseillers en relations industrielles du Quebec 1992).

The major stakeholders seem to have learned that unilateral introduction of new forms of work and new technologies do not achieve expected results, based on a decade of experience (Harrison and Laplante 1995; Grant 1995). If employers are more often those who initiate workplace transformations, the policies and commitment of unions' parent organization influences the objectives and strategies of local unions on these issues (Lapointe and Paquet 1994).

Paradoxically, the government was instrumental in helping private sector parties create conditions favourable to innovation in production and labour relations. The pace of change on these issues is much slower and more difficult when government is itself the employer. Public sector unions, while experiencing a legislated two-year wage freeze, signed a letter of understanding in 1994 with the provincial government acknowledging budgetary constraints that required, in order to improve or even maintain services to the public, work organization to be deeply re-examined. Bill 102, adopted a year earlier, had extended the collective agreement for two years and frozen wages for the same period, but it also stipulated that compensation had to fall an additional 1 percent. The savings could be achieved through reorganizing work, and if not, through unpaid holidays similar to those experienced in Ontario under the NDP administration. Even though the letter of understanding raised hopes among union and employer representatives, both parties missed the opportunity to produce significant results. First, the continuing cuts in personnel and services prevented an environment conducive to mutual trust. Second, work reorganization is achieved more successfully in a context of decentralization, but the whole system of collective bargaining and the ensuing content of collective agreements is highly centralized and politicized. Centralization compounds the rigidity of provincially negotiated and implemented provisions. Additionally, the government and unions have a vested interest in maintaining a centralized bargaining structure that facilitates control for both sides. Centralized structures can hardly encourage adaptive responses to cutbacks. The changes of the 1990s were distinct in the public and private sectors.

CONCLUSION: A NEW SOCIAL CONTRACT FOR THE PRIVATE SECTOR ONLY?

Quebec's historical and cultural features have deeply affected industrial relations. The government's interventionist role magnified the importance of union pluralism. Indeed, the presence of government as an employer contributed to the development of two large, general categories of unionism: private sector and public sector. As collective bargaining experiences continued, an increasingly specific legal and institutional framework developed, not only within the whole sector of public services but also within some segments of the private sector (e.g., construction, decree system). Even in the latter sector, state interventionism influenced the pattern of collective bargaining. At the ideological level, nationalism provided the main ingredient in the shaping of strategies and objectives at the societal level.

Before the Quiet Revolution, nationalism took on a conservative form, as the Quebec ethos remained geared to religious, rural, and largely pre-industrial values. Economic modernization demanded a transformation of nationalism. As public institutions deemed necessary for social and economic development expanded, conditions for the emergence of a French-speaking business class were created. The modernization of Quebec and the relatively more prosperous early 1960s favoured a combination of nationalism with some basic social-democratic elements in order to favour the creation of a welfare state. The PQ inherited the Quiet Revolution and pushed it further, while leading a coalition of the largest groups of progressive forces in the province, including the labour unions. This created some degree of uneasiness in public sector unionism where government is viewed as an employer. Union support for sovereignty cannot alone explain the reduction in labour militancy. More generally, the transformation of commercial and economic conditions at the global level has been more influential in reshaping industrial relations in Quebec. The specific conditions which exist have, however, been crucial in determining the distinct institutional and strategic responses that the actors have generated in order to adjust to the new environment.

Industrial peace, such as the one experienced in Quebec in the 1990s (Boivin 2002), is a necessary condition to improve productivity and competitiveness and thus protect and generate jobs, but it is not itself a new social contract. The traditional approach to union-management relations in Quebec clearly is being overhauled. Employers had at first been able to gain some concessions from the unions. The benefits from these were usually short term. More fundamental and long-term changes required that both employers and unions express a genuine awareness of their mutual interests in their strategic choices, particularly regarding the link between business development and the capacity of employers to provide better job security and better conditions of work. Statistics on work stoppages clearly illustrate that unions and even managers no longer view strikes and lock-outs as the most appropriate and efficient tools in a context where issues regarding business and job survival matter more than those related to wages. Tactics suited to improvements in compensation in a context of economic prosperity and commercial expansion become questionable in the present environment, particularly in Quebec where unemployment rates are higher and where the economy is less diversified and more fragile than in Ontario. The future will show when and how public sector organizations and unions will reform their approach to union-management relations and to organization of the workplace.

The successes of the Action démocratique du Québec (ADQ) under the leadership of Mario Dumont in provincial by-elections in June 2002 could mean a challenge to the interventionist and welfare state approach expressed in the so-called Quebec model developed since the Quiet Revolution, but it is too soon to speculate on its impact on the evolution of industrial relations in the province.

NOTES

[1]Considering the period covered by this chapter, we will refer to this organization as the CEQ.

[2]S.Q. 1965, c. 14.

[3]These amendments were in line with recommendations from the Martin-Bouchard Report. This commission was created by the then new PQ government to study and recommend changes to the institutional and legal framework regarding collective bargaining in the public and parapublic sector. Yves Martin was a respected former deputy minister of education and Lucien Bouchard was already a prominent labour lawyer who later became premier.

[4]Procureur général du Québec c. Fédération des infirmières et infirmiers du Québec et al., C.A. 500-09-001449-911, 7 October1998.

[5]If we add to the public sector other public jurisdictions, like the federal sector, and other public services such as municipalities and Crown corporations, we find that, for 2001, over 47 percent of workers covered by a collective agreement in the province were in governmental services (Department of Labour).

[6]This percentage swells to over 95 percent when one includes collective bargaining with an employer with many workplaces or establishments (see Table 6).

[7]S.Q. 1966–1967, c. 63.

[8]Collège d'enseignement général et professionnel (CEGEP). These colleges provide professional and general training to prepare for following entry into the labour market or university.

[9]R.S.Q., c. R-8.2.

[10]R.S.Q., c. C-12.

[11]R.S.Q., c. C-11

[12]S.Q 2001, c. 31.

[13]R.S.Q., C. N-1.1, articles 124-131.

[14]S.Q. 1987, c. 85.

[15]The term "employee" here excludes managers and refers to workers who are unionized or who are legally unionizable.

[16]Groupe de travail sur la déréglementation, Réglementer moins et mieux, Québec, Les Publications du Québec, 1986.

[17]The annual report of the Institut de recherche et d'information sur la rémunération indicates that, for comparable jobs, municipal workers had in 1996

an average 27.9 percent lead over public sector workers in terms of total compensation (wages and fringe benefits) (IRIR 1997, 42). For 1998, this differential has climbed to 28.7 percent according to the last report from IRIR.

[18]This joint committee acts as an adviser to the minister of labour on any policy or legislative matter. As the most influential voice and representative of all employers in the province, the Conseil du patronat du Quebec sits with the representatives of the principal union organizations in the province.

REFERENCES

Adell, B., M. Grant and A. Ponak. 2001. *Strikes in Essential Services*. Kingston: IRC Press, Queen's University.

Akyeampong, E.B. 1997. "Statistical Portrait of the Trade Union Movement," *Perspectives on Labour and Income* 9 (3): 45-54.

—— 2001. "Fact–Sheet on Unionization," *Perspectives on Labour and Income* 13 (3):46-54.

Archibald, C. 1983. *Un Québec corporatiste?* Hull: Éditions Asticou.

Baldino, B.D. 1997. "Les conditions de travail modifiées en 1995-1996 lors du renouvellement des conventions collectives," *Le marché du travail* 18 (1-2):10, 106-11.

Beaulieu, M.-L. 1955. *Les conflits de droit dans les rapports collectifs du travail.* Quebec: Les Presses Universitaires Laval.

Bélanger, P.R., M. Grant and B. Lévesque. 1994. *La modernisation sociale des entreprises.* Montreal: Presses de l'Université de Montréal.

Bélanger, Y., R. Comeau and C. Métivier, eds. 2000. *La révolution tranquille, 40 ans plus tard: un bila.* Montreal: VLB éditeur.

Bernier, J. 1993. "Juridical Extension in Quebec: A New Challenge Unique in America," *Relations industrielles-Industrial Relations* 48 (4):745-61.

Bernier, J. and M. Lemieux. 1994. "La grève et les services essentiels au Québec," in *Grèves et services essentiels*, ed. J. Bernier. Sainte Foy: Les Presses de l'Université Laval and Conseil des services essentiels.

Bernier, L. 1995. "Adjusting to NAFTA: State Enterprises and Privatization in Quebec in Light of the Mexican and American Experiences," in *Quebec Under Free Trade,* ed. G. Lachapelle. Quebec: Presses de l'Université du Québec, pp. 191-209.

Boisvert, R. 1970. "La grève et le mouvement ouvrier," in *La grève de l'amiante*, ed. P.-E. Trudeau. Montreal: Éditions du Jour, pp. 345-78.

Boivin, J. 2002. "Comment se portent les relations du travail au Québec," *Effectif* 5 (2):10-18.

Boivin, J. and E. Déom. 1995. "Labour-Management Relations in Quebec," in *Union-Management Relations in Canada*, 3d ed., ed. M. Gunderson and A. Ponak. Don Mills: Addison-Wesley, pp. 455-93.

Boucher, J. 1994. "L'évolution du discours de la CSN sur les stratégies syndicales (1970-1990)," in *La modernisation sociale des entreprises*, ed. P.R. Bélanger, M. Grant and B. Lévesque. Montreal: Presses de l'Université de Montréal, pp. 259-78.

Bourque, R. and G. Vallée. 1994. "Ententes de partenariat ou ententes de longue durée? Inventaire et analyse juridique des contrats sociaux," *Info Ressources humaines* (February/March):16-20

Cardin, J.-R. 1973. "La philosophie du Code du travail," in *La politisation des relations du travail*, ed. G. Dion. XXVIIIème Congrès des relations industrielles de l'Université Laval. Quebec: Les Presses de l'Université Laval, pp. 79-97.

Carter, D.D. 1984. "The Labour Code of Quebec: Some Reflections and Comparisons," in *La loi et les rapports collectifs du travail. Quatorzième colloque des relations industrielles*, ed. M. Brossard. Montreal: École des relations industrielles, Université de Montréal, pp. 9-18.

Centre de Recherche et de Statistiques sur le Marché du Travail (CRSMT). 1994. *Conditions de travail contenues dans les conventions collectives 1992.* Quebec: Les Publications du Québec.

——— 1997. "La présence syndicale au Québec en 1996," *Le marché du travail* 18 (1-2):97.

Comité Interministériel sur les Décrets de Convention Collective. 1994. *Rapport du comité interministériel sur les décrets de convention collective.* Quebec: Les publications du Québec.

Commission Consultative sur le Travail et la Révision du Code du Travail. 1985. *Le travail: une responsabilité collective.* Quebec: Les publications du Québec.

Confédération des syndicats nationaux (CSN). 1991. *Prendre les devants dans l'organisation du travail.* Montreal: CSN.

CSN-CEQ. 1984. *Histoire du mouvement ouvrier au Québec*, 2d ed. Montreal: coédition CSN-CEQ.

Conseil consultatif du travail et de la main d'œuvre (CCTM). 1997. *Document de réflexion sur une nouvelle forme d'organisation du travail.* Quebec: Les publications du Québec.

Corporation Professionnelle des Conseillers en Relations Industrielles du Québec. 1992. *Relations du travail: Nouvelles pratiques.*

Courchesne, R. 1989. "Le processus de la négociation collective," *Le marché du travail: Les relations du travail en 1989* (décembre):24-32.

Courchesne, R. and A. Dompierre. 1984. "Grèves et Lock-out au Québec," *Le marché du travail* 5 (5):54-66.

Delorme, F., R. Fortin and L. Gosselin. 1994. "L'organisation du monde patronal au Québec," *Relations Indusrielles-Industrial Relations* 49 (1):9-40.

Denis, S. and R. Denis. 1995. "Trade Unionism and the State of Industrial Relations in Quebec," in *Quebec Under Free Trade,* ed. G. Lachapelle. Quebec: Presses de l'Université du Québec, pp. 213-37.

Déom, E. and J. Boivin. 2001. "Union-Management Relations in Quebec," in *Union-Management Relations in Canada*, 4th ed., ed. M. Gunderson, A. Ponak and D.G. Taras. Toronto: Addison-Wesley Longman, pp. 486-520.

Dickman, H. 1987. *Industrial Democracy in America: Ideological Origins of National Labor Relations Policy.* Peru, IL: Open Court.

Dompierre, A. 1997. "Grève et lock-out en 1996 – bilan," *Le marché du travail* 18 (5):6-10 and 79-88.

Dompierre, A., R. Courchesne and J.-M. Martel. 1987. "Grèves et lock-out en 1986," *Le marché du travail* 8 (5):69-81.

Drache, D. and M.S. Gertler. 1991. "The World Economy and the New Nation-State: The New International Order," in *The New Era of Global Competition*, ed. D. Drache and M.S. Gertler. Montreal and Kingston: McGill-Queen's University Press, pp. 2-25.

Dufour, G. 1980. "Les acteurs: l'organisation patronale," in *La gestion des relations du travail au Québec*, ed. N. Mallette. Montreal: McGraw Hill, pp. 365-87.

—— 2000. *Ghyslain Dufour témoigne de 30 ans du CPQ.* Montreal: Les Éditions Transcontinental.

Favreau, L. 1989. "Analyse de la rémunération et de la conjoncture," *Les relations du travail en 1989.* Quebec: Centre de Recherche et de Statistiques sur le Marché du Travail, pp. 65-76.

Fédération des travailleurs du Québec (FTQ). 1987. *Nouvelles stratégies patronales. Menace ou défi?* Montreal: FTQ.

—— 1993. *Face aux changements, De nouvelles solidarités.* Montreal: FTQ.

—— 1985. *Pour un progrès sans victime.* Montreal: FTQ.

Fleury, G. 1991. "Les dispositions anti-briseurs de grève: 1978-1989," *Le marché du travail* 12 (8):6-8 and 71-86.

Fournier, L. 1991. *Solidarité Inc. Un nouveau syndicalisme créateur d'emplois.* Montreal: Éditions Québec/Amérique.

—— 1994. *Histoire de la FTQ.* Montreal: Éditions Québec/Amérique.

Fournier, P. 1976. *The Quebec Establishment.* Montreal: Black Rose Books.

Fréchet, G. and J.-P. Simard. 1990. "Syndicats," in *La société québécoise en tendances 1960-1990,* cd. S. Langlois *et al.* Quebec: Institut québécois de recherche sur la culture, pp. 339-45.

Gagnon, M.-J. 1994. *Le syndicalisme: Québec: état des lieux et des enjeux.* Quebec: Institut québécois de recherche sur la culture.

—— 2001. "La FTQ comme acteur politique," in *La FTQ, ses syndicats et la société québécoise,* ed. Y. Bélanger, R. Comeau and C. Métivier. Montreal: Comeau & Nadeau, pp. 155-66.

Grant, M. 1990. "Vers la segmentation du syndicalisme au Québec," IN *Vingt-cinq ans de pratique en relations industrielles au Québec,* ED. R. Blouin. Cowansville: Éditions Yvon Blais, pp. 311-41.

—— 1995. "Les changements technologiques et les relations patronales-syndicales: vers de nouvelles stratégies," in *Changements technologiques et gestion des ressources humaines,* ed. R. Jaco and J. Ducharme. Montreal: Gaëtan Morin, pp. 245-77.

—— 1997. *Shifting from Traditional to Mutual Gains Bargaining: Implementing Change in Canada.* Kingston: IRC Press, Queen's University.

—— 2001. "La FTQ et la nouvelle organisation du travail: de la menace au défi," in *La FTQ, ses syndicats et la société québécoise,* ed. Y. Bélanger, R. Comeau and C. Métivier. Montreal: Comeau & Nadeau, pp. 67-82.

Grant, M. and B. Lévesque. 1997. "Aperçu des principales transformations des rapports du travail dans les entreprises: le cas québécois," in *Nouvelles formes d'organisation du travail,* ed. M. Grant, P.R. Bélanger and B. Lévesque. Montreal: Harmattan.

Grant, M. and F. Racine. 1992. "Les services essentiels et les stratégies de négociation dans les services publics," *Le marché du travail* 13 (4):68 and 73-78.

Grant, M. and J. Lebeau. 1994. "La FTQ et les nouvelles stratégies de gestion des ressources humaines," in *La modernisation sociale des entreprises*, ed. P.R. Bélanger, M. Grant and B. Lévesque. Montreal: Presses de l'Université de Montréal, pp. 270-79.

Harrisson, D. and N. Laplante. 1994. "Confiance, coopération et partenariat: un processus de transformation dans l'entreprise québécoise," *Relations industrielles-Industrial Relations* 49 (4):696-729.

Hébert, G. 1984. "Public Sector Bargaining in Quebec," in *Conflict or Compromise: The Future of Public Sector Industrial Relations*, ed. M. Thompson and G. Swimmer. Montreal: The Institute for Research on Public Policy, pp. 229-81.

——— 1990. "Le renouvellement du régime des décrets de convention collective," *Relations industrielles-Industrial Relations* 45 (2):404-13.

——— 1995. "Public Sector Bargaining in Quebec: The Rise and Fall of Centralization," in *Public Sector Bargaining in Canada: The End of the Beginning or the Beginning of the End?* ed. G. Swimmer and M. Thompson. Kingston: IRC Press, Queen's University, pp. 201-35.

Heron, C. 1996. *The Canadian Labour Movement*, 2d ed. Toronto: Lorimer.

Hudon, R. 1980. "Les groupes et l'État," in *L'État du Québec en devenir,* ed. G. Bergeron and R. Pelletier. Montreal: Les éditions du Boréal Express, pp. 263-84.

Institut de la Statistique du Québec. 2001. *Rémunération des salariés: État et évolution comparés 2001.* Quebec: Gouvernement du Québec.

Institut de Recherche et d'Information sur la Rémunération (IRIR). 1997. *Treizième rapport sur les constations de l'IRIR.*

Kochan, T.A., H.C. Katz and R.B. McKersie. 1986. *The Transformation of American Industrial Relations.* New York: Basic Books Inc.

Lapointe, P.-A. and R. Paquet. 1994. "Les syndicats et les nouvelles formes d'organisation du travail," *Relations industrielles-Industrial Relations* 49 (2):281-302.

Larouche, V. 1986. "La mobilisation des ressources humaines-orientations récentes," *La mobilisation des ressources humaines*, XLIème congrès des relations industrielles. Québec: Département des relations industrielles de l'Université Laval, pp. 31-51.

Lebeau, J. 1992. *Renouvellement des relations du travail chez Bestar Inc.* Mémoire de maîtrise en administration des affaires, Université du Québec à Montréal.

Lemelin, M. 1984. *Les négociations collectives dans les secteurs public et parapublic.* Montreal: Les Éditions Agence d'Arc Inc.

Lemieux, M. 1996. "La médiation et le règlement des conflits dans les services essentiels au Québec," *Relations industrielles-Industrial Relations* 51 (2):333-56.

Lévesque, C., G. Murray, S. Le Queux and N. Roby. 1996. *Syndicalisme, démocratie et réorganisation du travail: résultats d'une recherche effectués auprès des syndicats affiliés à la CSN.* Cahiers du Groupe de recherche sur les transformations et la régulation du travail, GRT, pp. 96-02.

Linteau, P.-A. 2000. "Un débat historiographique: l'entrée du Québec dans la modernité et la signification de la Révolution tranquille," in *La révolution tranquille,* ed. Bélanger, Comeau and Métivier, pp. 21-41.

Martin, Y. and L. Bouchard. 1978. *Rapport de la Commission d'étude et de consultation sur la révision du régime de négociation dans les secteurs public et parapublic.* Quebec: Éditeur officiel.

Maschino, D. 1995*a*. "Les nouvelles pratiques en milieu de travail au Québec," *Le marché du travail* 16 (9):6-8 and 87-94.

—— 1995*b*. "Les nouvelles pratiques en milieu de travail au Québec," *Le marché du travail* 16 (9):10 and 95-115.

—— 1995*c*. "Les nouvelles pratiques en milieu de travail au Québec," *Le marché du travail* 16 (10):9-10 and 81-99.

—— 1995*d*. "Les nouvelles pratiques en milieu de travail au Québec," *Le marché du travail* 16 (11):9-10 and 70-82.

Morin, D. 2002. "Les arrêts de travail au Québec: bilan de l'année 2001," *Travail-Actualités/Statistique-Travail,* pp. 1-17.

Morin, F. 1993. "La négociation collective selon le modèle de 1944 est-elle périmée?" in *La négociation collective du travail: adaptation ou disparition?* ed. C. Bernier *et al.* Sainte-Foy: Les Presses de l'Université Laval, pp. 13-14.

Morin. F. and J.Y. Brière. 1998. *Le droit de l'emploi au Québec.* Montreal: Wilson and Lafleur Itée.

Panitch, L. and D. Swartz. 1993. *The Assault on Trade Union Freedoms.* Toronto: Garamond Press.

Paquet, G. 1999. *Oublier la révolution tranquille.* Montreal: Liber.

Paquette, P. 1998. "Les stratégies de la CSN pour l'emploi," in *La CSN: 75 ans d'action syndicale et sociale,* ed. Y. Bélanger and R. Comeau. Sainte-Foy: Les Presses de l'Université du Québec, pp. 246-51.

Parent, A. and A. Dompierre. 1983. "Grèves et lock-out au Québec en 1982," *Le marché du travail* 4 (4):48-46.

Porter, M.E. 1990. *The Competitive Advantage of Nations.* New York: The Free Press.

Quebec. 1979. *Bâtir le Québec: énoncé de politique économique, Québec.* Quebec: Gouvernement du Québec.

—— 1982. *Le virage technologique: bâtir le Québec, phase 2.* Quebec: Gouvernement du Québec.

—— 1993. *Un modèle de partenariat: le contrat social d'entreprise,* rev. ed. Quebec: Gouvernement du Québec.

Rouillard, J. 1979. *Les syndicats nationaux au Québec de 1900 à 1930.* Quebec: Les Presses de l'Université Laval.

—— 1981. *Histoire de la CSN (1921-1981).* Montreal: Confédération des syndicats nationaux et Éditions du Boréal Express.

—— 1989. *Histoire du syndicalisme québécois.* Montreal: Les Éditions du Boréal.

Tremblay, L.-M. 1972. *Le syndicalisme québécois: Idéologies de la CSN et de la FTQ 1940-1970.* Montreal: Les Presses de l'Université de Montréal.

Trudeau, P.-E., ed. 1970. *La grève de l'amiante*. Montreal: Éditions du Jour.

Vadeboncoeur, P. 1961. "Projection du syndicalisme américain," *Écrits du Canada français* 9:149-259.

Walton, R.E., J.E. Cutcher-Gershenfeld and R.B. McKersie. 1994. *Strategic Negotiations*. Boston: Harvard Business School Press.

Wavroch, H. 1993. "Présentation de l'Irir," in *The Industrial Relations System- Le système de relations industrielles*, ed. T.S. Kutner. Proceedings of the XXIXth Conference of the Canadian Industrial Relations Association. *University of New Brunswick Law Journal* 2:671-80.

4 BRITISH COLUMBIA: THE PARTIES MATCH THE MOUNTAINS

Mark Thompson
Brian Bemmels

Résumé — La Colombie-Britannique est reconnue pour ses relations industrielles de nature combative, qui reflètent l'influence partisane de la politique provinciale. La réalité est en fait plus nuancée, mais la taille des parties en présence a toujours caractérisé les relations industrielles britanno-colombiennes. Les conflits de travail ont donc des répercussions importantes sur la vie de la province.

L'économie de la Colombie-Britannique repose sur les ressources naturelles. Le syndicalisme a surgi au cours du XIXᵉ siècle, et les employeurs étaient alors de grandes compagnies dont le siège social était situé à l'extérieur de la province. Les travailleurs ont établi une tradition de solidarité et pris une part active à la politique dès le début du XXᵉ siècle. En 1932, le mouvement syndical s'est d'abord associé à la Fédération du commonwealth coopératif (CCF), devenu le Nouveau Parti Démocratique (NPD). Craignant une victoire électorale du NPD, la droite a formé diverses coalitions afin de gouverner la province, mais le NPD est au pouvoir ou constitue l'opposition officielle depuis les années 1950. Les enjeux politiques ont souvent été liés aux relations industrielles.

Le style des gouvernements de droite a été brisé en 1972 par l'élection du NPD. Celui-ci n'a alors gouverné que trois ans, mais a adopté un code du travail novateur à la suite d'une vaste consultation des parties concernées, deux précédents en Colombie-Britannique. La structure juridique est restée en place après la défaite du NPD, mais le mouvement syndical a dû protester de façon vigoureuse contre les restrictions au droit de négociation dans le secteur public et la diminution du nombre de programmes sociaux en 1983. Plus tard dans la décennie, il a aussi résisté aux efforts déployés par les gouvernements pour apporter des modifications substantielles au code du travail.

La Colombie-Britannique est la province la plus fortement syndicalisée de l'Ouest canadien, bien que son taux de syndicalisation ait baissé depuis 1970. Les syndicats sont continuellement à la recherche d'accréditations, mais n'ont pu recouvrer le nombre de membres perdus à la suite de la diminution des emplois dans l'industrie primaire. La fédération provinciale des travailleurs est particulièrement influente du fait de l'éloignement physique et politique des bureaux centraux des syndicats. De nombreux syndicats locaux sont de compétence provinciale, ce qui fait qu'ils mènent des négociations à l'échelle de la province. Le mouvement syndical est aussi très actif sur le plan politique et entretient des liens étroits avec le NPD.

Les associations patronales sont plus fortes en Colombie-Britannique que dans la plupart des autres provinces. En plus des associations de négociation dans les secteurs de la construction, des soins de santé et des produits forestiers, il existe une association générale pour représenter le patronat : le *Business Council of British Columbia*. Ce conseil a été fondé pour défendre les intérêts des employeurs en matière de main-d'œuvre et d'emploi, mais s'est chargé d'autres responsabilités en plus au cours des années.

La Commission des relations de travail est l'organisme provincial le plus important au plan des relations industrielles. Elle a le mandat d'administrer la législation sur les relations de travail, de fournir des services de médiation et de statuer sur les litiges concernant les normes d'emploi. C'est le ministère du Travail qui applique la législation sur les normes d'emploi. La Commission des accidents du travail est, quant à elle, responsable de la santé et de la sécurité au travail. La Commission des relations de travail a longtemps favorisé des unités de négociation d'envergure, répondant ainsi au souhait des employeurs de s'unir face au militantisme syndical et d'éviter des structures de négociation fragmentées.

Grâce à l'adoption du premier code du travail par le NPD dans les années 1970, la province est devenue un chef de file en matière de droit du travail au Canada, sans pour autant modifier substantiellement ce droit. Le mouvement syndical a réussi à résister aux efforts déployés par les gouvernements conservateurs pour établir des cadres d'intervention courante de l'État lors des conflits de travail.

Les unités de négociation de grande envergure sont le sceau des relations industrielles de la Colombie-Britannique; les conflits sont donc parfois porteurs de perturbations sociales. En fait, les grèves ne sont pas plus nombreuses dans cette province que dans les autres, mais sont plus importantes de par leur ampleur. Entre 1971 et 2001, il y a eu vingt-huit grèves à l'échelle de la province, mais aucune au cours des huit dernières années du XXᵉ siècle. La fréquence des grèves a chuté dans les années 1990, comme ailleurs au pays. Un certain nombre de grèves de longue durée ont eu lieu dans des entreprises individuelles — qui avaient généralement des activités en dehors de la province — et concernaient un syndicat ou plus, ce qui confirme la tendance aux conflits de travail d'envergure.

Les salaires et conditions de travail en Colombie-Britannique sont légèrement supérieurs aux moyennes nationales. Le fossé entre les salaires versés dans cette province et ceux versés dans les autres provinces « riches », l'Alberta et l'Ontario, a été comblé dans les années 1980 et 1990.

Les relations industrielles britanno-colombiennes possèdent des caractéristiques distinctives — militantisme des syndicats, degré élevé d'organisation des travailleurs et des employeurs ainsi que liens étroits entre ces parties et les partis politiques représentant leurs intérêts. Le mouvement syndical est un acteur provincial de première importance, dont les employeurs et le gouvernement doivent tenir compte dans leurs prises de décision. Cependant, les partis de droite gouvernent habituellement la province, ce qui fait que les tensions sont toujours présentes.

Industrial relations in British Columbia has a reputation for high levels of conflict and developed organizations to represent both labour and management. The industrial relations climate was described as "explosive" by one knowledgeable participant. The province experienced a high incidence of strikes which came to resemble "wars of attrition" after stoppages began. The trade union movement was characterized as "just about the most powerful anywhere," seeking the transformation of society and the economic system. Employers responded by forming large organizations of their own to resist labour's demands (Weiler 1980).

Relations between labour and management are seen to mirror the adversarial nature of provincial politics, which are more divided and class-oriented than any other province in Canada (Blake 1985). The labour movement is an active and visible supporter of the New Democratic Party (NDP), while the employer community backed the Social Credit Party from the 1960s until its demise in the 1990s. When the provincial Liberal Party supplanted the Social Credit Party after the 1992 provincial election, business interests embraced it as the best hope of defeating the governing NDP.

Industrial relations is regarded as a significant aspect of the province's economic performance. In the 1970s and 1980s, wages in BC were routinely described as being among the highest in the world for particular occupations. Popular opinion attributed these wage levels to the militancy of the labour movement, and business interests believed that these conditions discouraged investment and job creation.

As with most perceptions, there are elements of fact and exaggeration in the popular view of industrial relations in the province. When the current state and history of industrial relations in British Columbia are examined carefully, one dominant theme is the size of the parties — large unions and employers, both of whom are well organized for dealing with each other, and disputes that reflect the capacities of the parties in terms of their absolute size and impact on the economy and society.

THE ECONOMIC ENVIRONMENT OF INDUSTRIAL RELATIONS

The BC economy traditionally has been driven by natural resources, beginning with mining in the late nineteenth and early twentieth century, followed by forest products and fishing in the mid- to late-twentieth century. Both national railway systems have had extensive operations, and several large natural ports on the Pacific Coast have made shipping and transportation major industries. In most countries, natural resources and longshoring are highly unionized industrial sectors, often characterized by labour militancy. British Columbia confirms this generalization.

The earliest labour activity on record in the province was in the coalfields on Vancouver Island in the 1850s. Miners protested poor working conditions there and hampered the development of the industry when they left the area in search of gold in other regions of the province. A gold rush in the 1860s sparked a boom in the province as thousands of people arrived seeking gold. Unionism was not a factor in the early days of gold mining, but mine owners continually attempted to thwart labour organization in coal mining. After the completion of the Canadian Pacific Railway in the 1880s, exploitation of silver, copper, and other minerals in the interior became feasible (Phillips 1988).

Early in the twentieth century, the forest products industry developed, first in the form of logging and basic saw milling, followed by pulp and paper and plywood. The two world wars stimulated this development, and the sector dominated the provincial economy by the 1970s, when approximately half of the gross provincial product originated in forest products.

Development of natural resources in a relatively isolated region such as British Columbia is a capital-intensive process, so that large corporations with headquarters outside the province were major actors in the economy. In the early twentieth century, absentee corporate owners were known for their hostility to unionism and contributed to the solidarity of the labour movement. These sentiments reinforced the general resentment in the province that major decisions too often were made elsewhere. While the sectors producing wealth changed over time, large companies have remained significant. As late as the 1980s, for instance, Canadian Pacific Limited was one of the largest employers in the province, through its ownership of a railroad, one of the nation's two air lines, controlling interest in the largest mining company in BC, and substantial holdings in the province's largest forest products company. Two major companies controlled a large number of mines in the province. Provincial government land-use policies favoured concentration of ownership in the forest products, to the benefit of a small number of companies controlled in British Columbia (Marchak 1988).

As Table 1 indicates, primary industries are not (and have not been) major direct employers in British Columbia. Agriculture is just under 2 percent of employment, and all other primary industries combined, while slightly above the national average, account for less than 2.5 percent of employment. However, their products generate much of the economic activity in other sectors, especially manufacturing. The manufacturing sector has never been large in British Columbia, but it has been dominated by the processing of forest products and minerals into lumber, pulp, paper, and mineral concentrates (Warburton and Coburn 1988). As a percentage of employment, manufacturing is substantially less than the national average, and well below Ontario and Quebec.

British Columbia experienced the relative decline of primary and secondary industries in the 1970s through the turn of the twenty-first century. This change reflected developments in Canada's economic structure, as employment growth occurred primarily in the service sector. The expansion of the welfare state in Canada fuelled job growth in health care and social services, but the largest areas of growth were in trade and business services. Consequently, the economic significance of small business increased.

TABLE 1
PERCENTAGE OF EMPLOYMENT BY INDUSTRY
BRITISH COLUMBIA AND CANADA, 2000

Industry	Canada	British Columbia
Agriculture	2.4	1.6
Forestry, fishing, mining, oil, gas	2.0	2.4
Utilities	0.7	0.6
Construction	5.6	6.0
Manufacturing	15.0	10.3
Trade	15.1	15.2
Transportation	5.1	5.7
Finance, technical services, management and administration	13.7	16.3
Education	6.3	6.6
Health care and social assistance	9.7	9.8
Accommodation, food services	6.5	8.3
Other services	4.5	4.9
Public administration	4.9	4.4
Unclassified	2.3	2.5

Source: Statistics Canada (2001).

These developments were a substantial shift in the economic structure of the province. Virtually since Confederation, large resource-exporting corporations controlled from outside the province had dominated the economy. The importance of these sectors stimulated the growth of a left-wing in provincial politics (Warburton 1988). During the 1990s, the most rapid job growth came from sectors such as tourism and high technology, where traditions of unionism were and are weak, and employees are more conservative than in resource industries.

THE POLITICAL ENVIRONMENT OF INDUSTRIAL RELATIONS

The dominant theme of modern British Columbia politics has been the continuing presence of a left-of-centre party, first the Cooperative Commonwealth Federation (CCF) and later the NDP, which in turn caused the "free enterprise," or non-socialist, parties to form coalitions to defeat the left-wing party of the day. (So strong is this tradition that an anti-socialist coalition was formed to run candidates in Vancouver civic elections in the 1950s.) In 1932, labour and socialist organizations from western Canada formed the CCF, an effort to unite the democratic left. The following year, the new party adopted an avowedly socialist political platform (the Regina Manifesto), including the "eradication of capitalism," nationalization of banks, and public ownership of major industries. The CCF quickly established itself in British Columbia. In the 1933 provincial election, it received almost 30 percent of the popular vote in a provincial election. This figure was only 10 percent less than that obtained by the Liberals, who formed the government, although the new party elected only seven members (Phillips 1967). Between the 1933 election and 2001, the CCF or the NDP gathered at least 30 percent of the popular vote. In a multi-party political system, this level of consistent support gives a party the reasonable hope of forming a government with a slight increase in its popularity. In the 1940s the Liberals formed an anti-CCF coalition with the Conservatives. The coalition, held together by the partners' shared fear of the CCF/NDP endured until 1952.

In 1951, a Conservative member of the legislature, W.A.C. Bennett, left his party and joined the Alberta-based Social Credit Party. While the Social Credit movement had supporters in several Canadian provinces as well as other nations, in British Columbia it was the vehicle of a new anti-CCF coalition under Bennett's leadership. He gathered members of the federal Liberal and Conservative parties and led the new party to victory in 1952.

Bennett's Social Credit Party governed British Columbia for 20 consecutive years. He is remembered as a builder. His government extended a provincially-owned railway to the northern region of the province in order to stimulate economic development there. He nationalized private electric utilities to form BC Hydro and promoted the construction of a network of dams and power plants on the province's major rivers. During his government, private interests constructed large smelters and mills. Throughout his career, Bennett portrayed himself as a "free enterprise" politician who would guard the provincial economy against the "socialist hordes" (Mitchell 1983).

Although the CCF experienced sporadic success federally, it remained the official opposition in British Columbia and also formed the government in Saskatchewan. During the 1950s, the principles of the Regina Manifesto, calling for the elimination of capitalism, were a barrier to recruitment in other provinces. However, ties between the BC Federation of Labour and the CCF remained strong in British Columbia, where the party won 35 percent of the popular vote in 1960. In an effort to broaden its electoral appeal elsewhere, the CCF and the Canadian Labour Congress (CLC) formed the NDP in 1961. The new party had close ties to organized labour, with a platform of promoting full employment, regulating big business and support for medicare. The transformation of the CCF had less impact in British Columbia than in other provinces. The NDP retained the support of CCF voters and ties between labour and the party remained close (Horowitz 1968).

Bennett's emphasis on economic development caused his government to be involved in labour disputes frequently, either in connection with its own projects or when major disputes threatened a business climate that the premier was anxious to protect. Bennett was a populist who could attack union leaders allied with the CCF or the NDP while appealing to members on the basis of his goals to stimulate the growth of the province. At the same time, Bennett had a tacit understanding with construction unions in particular that they would enjoy generous collective agreements, but would not interrupt major construction projects with labour stoppages. While Bennett's relations with large corporations were not close, the business community supported him as the only viable alternative to a labour-backed government. The importance of labour relations to Bennett's economic agenda caused frequent intervention into labour matters, either in the form of legislation or personal involvement in major labour disputes (Mitchell 1983). The alliances of the labour movement and the CCF/NDP and the links of the Social Credit Party to the business community inevitably raised the political profile of industrial relations issues.

Bennett's hold on provincial politics was broken in 1972, when the NDP elected its first government under the leadership of David Barrett. Ironically, the Barrett wing of the NDP had relatively few ties with the labour movement, but, in the tradition of NDP governments in the west, it was committed to labour law reform. The major contribution of Barrett to the development of labour relations was passage of the Labour Code. The Code was notable not only for its contents, but also the process by which it was drafted, both discussed below. While it redressed many of labour's objections to previous legislation, the Code was not a completely one-sided piece of legislation. Employers were strongly opposed to several provisions, while labour's criticisms were muted. Other provinces subsequently adopted several of its features.

The process leading to the adoption of the Code set a new pattern for labour law reform in British Columbia. Under the Bennett government, legislative change had been carried out in private, if not in secret, and little effort was made to accommodate varying interests of the parties. The Barrett government struck a neutral committee of experts to canvass the parties' wishes and reach its own conclusions about public policy. The committee's report was made public and widely debated. In the end, the government based its legislation on the committee's recommendations. In other jurisdictions, this process was not unusual. The federal government had followed a similar procedure in its revisions to the Canada Labour Code in the 1960s, for instance. But in the highly-charged political atmosphere of British Columbia, this degree of consultation was an innovation.

Labour policy was not the only accomplishment of the Barrett government. It expanded the scope of government in the economy by establishing a public monopoly over automobile insurance, increasing the royalties paid for oil and gas production, expanding postsecondary education, and protecting agricultural land.

Despite these efforts, the Barrett government's time in power was also cut short, partly because of labour relations. In 1975, three private sector strikes took place, one of which had an element of public safety and another had shut the pulp and paper industry down. The government passed special legislation to end all three stoppages. Later in the year, Barrett called an election and was defeated by Social Credit, by then led by W.A.C. Bennett's son, William. One of the causes of Barrett's defeat was the lack of organizational support from the labour movement, which was outraged by his interference in free collective bargaining.

Initially, the William Bennett government made few changes in the labour relations policy. Most of the initial concerns of the business community about the Labour Code had been allayed by their experience with it and the Labour Relations Board. Instead of returning to the previous pattern of intervention into labour matters, the new government made a number of small changes, generally favouring employers, and permitted the Labour Relations Board to function through its first two terms in office. However, public sector industrial relations became the major focus of tension between the government and the labour movement. In 1982, Bennett imposed wage controls over all elements of the public sector, following the lead of the federal government and leading six other provinces. Labour unsuccessfully resisted these measures in the courts and through administrative tribunals, and the broader public was generally indifferent to the complaints of public sector unions.

Labour relations became the focal point of provincial politics again in 1983. After winning re-election on a platform of government restraint that year, the Bennett government announced a package of legislative proposals to substantially change the conduct of public sector industrial relations. It eliminated or reduced a number of social welfare programs, including support for abused children, rent controls, and education (where severe budget cuts were imposed in the middle of the fiscal year). The major target of the proposed changes to the legal regulation of public sector industrial relations was the BC Government Employees' Union (BCGEU), the second largest public sector union in the province, which represented most employees of the provincial government. One bill would have limited the scope of negotiations for the BCGEU primarily to wages and economic issues. Another bill extended public sector wage restraints indefinitely, however, further limiting the scope of bargaining for the BCGEU and all other public sector employee groups. A third bill would have given public sector employers the right to dismiss employees virtually at will after the expiry of a collective agreement (Palmer 1987).

These proposals provoked a storm of protest, uniting public sector unions with community groups affected by the government's action. Protests escalated in the fall of 1983. A series of public sector strikes, both legal and illegal, began on 1 November 1983. The normal coordination role of the Federation of Labour was absent; as the movement was led by a handful of public sector union leaders and community activists. Private sector union leaders promised to join in a general strike if the government imposed back-to-work legislation on public sector unions. Whether private sector union members, who themselves had suffered severe layoffs in the recession of 1982–83, would have struck in support of job security for public sector workers will never be known. However, the threat of a mass confrontation brought the parties together. The president of the largest private sector union (then the International Woodworkers of America, IWA) met with Premier Bennett early in November 1983 and struck a deal to end the dispute. The government withdrew the bill that restricted bargaining for the BCGEU as part of a settlement of a new collective agreement. All public sector unions were given the right to negotiate layoff provisions (which most already had in their collective agreements) to gain exemption from the legislation giving employers broad rights to terminate workers (Thompson 1985). These measures placated public sector unions, but the government did not rescind its plans to cut social welfare programs. Many community activists were bitter at what they saw as a betrayal of their causes by organized labour (Palmer 1987). Tensions between private and public sector unions also remained.

The dramatic events of 1983 had repercussions elsewhere in Canada and were a turning point in the development of industrial relations in British Columbia. Until the Harris government in Ontario in the 1990s, no other Conservative government in Canada had attempted such massive changes to public sector industrial relations, and most avoided sudden reductions in social welfare programs (Thompson 1985). The BC Federation of Labour clearly disliked the divisive experience of confronting the government and it elected a moderate president from the private sector. Private sector employers maintained their distance from the public sector. However, the Social Credit political elite did not absorb the basic lesson of Operation Solidarity, the need to consult with the parties and at least attempt to gain consensus before changing labour legislation.

Premier William Bennett resigned in the summer of 1986 and William Vander Zalm was elected by the Social Credit Party to replace him as leader. Vander Zalm won election in his own right in October 1986. Shortly thereafter, before the new government was able to convene the legislature, a large strike erupted in the forest products industry. In general, 1986 was a year with a heavy bargaining agenda, so labour unrest was a prominent concern in the province. Under the existing law, the government could not end the forest products strike without passing special legislation. Ultimately, the strike was settled through mediation, but the premier resolved not to be left unable to act in similar circumstances.

He announced that revisions to the Labour Code would occur after an extensive process of public consultation (Leslie 1991).

In fact, the public consultation process was a sham. While the minister of labour was touring the province soliciting public suggestions for legislative change, a secret committee reporting directly to the premier drafted a substantial overhaul to the labour legislation and the law regulating collective bargaining by teachers. Public opinion favoured modest changes to the existing legislation, but the Vander Zalm government introduced wholesale amendments to the Labour Code. The changes favoured employers in virtually every respect. In addition, they gave the government extensive powers to end labour stoppages without any approval from the legislature (ibid.).

This legislation provoked another storm of protest by the labour movement. Labour did not rely on political help from other interest groups on this occasion, apart from the NDP caucus in the legislature. The legislation affected public and private sector unions alike. When the new law was passed, the BC Federation of Labour proclaimed a boycott of the law and set up the body to replace the Labour Relations Board to administer it. While exceptions to the boycott were granted, and a few independent unions did operate under the new legislation, labour's action was remarkably effective. The parties came to rely on private mediators and dispute-settlement systems instead of turning to government services. Labour refused to sit on any joint or tripartite committees established by the government and avoided cooperative mechanisms with leaders of the business community.

The boycott persisted until the election of an NDP government in 1992. Premier Vander Zalm was forced to resign as premier in the wake of a series of scandals involving him and members of his government. His labour legislation simply lost legitimacy. By 1990, even public sector employers were cooperating with labour by avoiding the use of the legislation, and the judiciary did not act against union members who violated it.

After the defeat of the Vander Zalm government in 1992, the new NDP premier, Mike Harcourt, appointed a subcommittee of special advisers composed of two highly-respected lawyers representing the parties and the province's leading mediator. After consulting widely, the committee issued a report recommending the repeal of most of the major changes in the existing statute (BC. Subcommittee of Special Advisers 1992). The report reflected consensus among the parties on all but three issues.

On the non-consensus issues, the government compromised: the new law banned replacement workers, but did not change the system of certification or expand the scope of picketing. The overall result was to return British Columbia to the mainstream of Canadian labour law.

After almost a decade of relative labour peace, British Columbia elected a new "Liberal" government headed by Gordon Campbell in 2001. The BC Liberal Party (not affiliated to the federal Liberal Party) was another version of the traditional "free enterprise" coalition united by a determination to defeat the NDP and consciously imitated right-wing governments in Alberta and Ontario. The Social Credit Party had collapsed in the wake of Vander Zalm's defeat. The Liberals were wildly successful, winning 77 of 79 seats, the biggest margin of victory in modern BC political history. Uncharacteristically, labour relations was not a significant issue in the 2001 election. The Liberals promised to replace the card check certification procedure with a mandatory vote. They also committed to maintaining the ban on strikebreakers, to respect public sector collective agreements and to make employment standards and workers' compensation legislation more "flexible," that is, to reduce worker entitlements.

During the first 30 months in office, the Campbell government honoured its commitment to impose mandatory representation votes and to retain the anti-replacement worker provision in the Labour Relations Code. However, it legislated major revisions to existing collective agreements in the health and education sectors and imposed (relatively generous) collective agreements covering nurses and teachers. Public sector unions were outraged by government actions.

Legislation covering health and social services workers was especially severe. Although the announced purpose of the legislation was cost reduction, the law did not affect wages directly. Rather, it removed collective agreement provisions covering workers' job security, including bumping rights and eliminated successor rights (i.e., the right of workers to retain union representation after contracting-out). Employers embarked on a major campaign of contracting-out non-medical work, and a number of small health-care facilities were de-certified. Arguably, this legislation was the most severe government intrusion into collective agreements in Canadian history — exceeding the public sector wage controls in the 1980s. As of early 2003, a challenge to the legislation under the *Canadian Charter of Rights and Freedoms* was underway.

Apart from labour legislation, health care, schools, and other social services were cut, especially in the rural areas of the province. The

NDP was left without even the status of an official party in the legislature, so public sector unions again became the focus of political opposition to the government. Private sector unions, weakened by high unemployment and employer initiatives, had little interest in opposing the government. The former woodworkers union (which retained the initials "IWA") needed the government's cooperation in resisting a lumber tariff imposed by the United States. By early 2003, the Campbell government had avoided any legislation that threatened the interests of the major private sector unions in the province. Late in 2002, it struck a low-profile committee to review the Labour Relations Code.

UNION DENSITY AND ORGANIZATION

British Columbia is the most heavily-unionized province in western Canada. Union membership rose during most of the post-World War II years, but union density declined slowly, in keeping with national trends. Union density in British Columbia peaked at 55.4 percent in 1958, and with only a few exceptions has been in a long-term decline ever since. However, as Table 2 indicates, union membership has increased almost every year since 1960, but the rate of increase has not kept pace with the growth in employment, thus leading to the decline in union density. Once the most heavily unionized province in Canada (with the occasional exception of Newfoundland), by 2002, British Columbia was slightly below the national average for the rate of unionization. This trend has also been reflected in the proportion of all union members in Canada that are in the province. Traditionally, BC accounted for approximately 15 percent of all Canadian union members. Since 1970, that proportion has fallen slowly, from about 14 to 13 percent at the turn of the twenty-first century.

The growth of the labour movement in British Columbia generally reflected national patterns. In the early years of the province, most union members were in mining, railways, and construction. Later, membership rose in lumber, pulp and paper, and transportation. Although public sector unionism first appeared during the period of World War II, it rose sharply in the 1960s and 1970s. By 2002, the three largest unions in the province were in the public sector. After 1990, a number of union mergers occurred, especially involving the Canadian Auto Workers, which became the ninth biggest union in the province, with virtually no members in British Columbia in its core jurisdiction of the assembly of autos or tractors and manufacture of parts.

TABLE 2
UNION MEMBERSHIP AND DENSITY, BRITISH COLUMBIA
(SELECTED YEARS)

Year	Membership	Density* (%)
1960	215,437	41.8
1965	237,864	37.2
1970	310,222	38.3
1975	401,608	39.1
1980	480,680	38.1
1985	466,864	36.6
1990	502,036	32.3
1995	545,219	30.4
2000	590,380	30.3
2001	594,070	30.4

Note: *After 1991, union density is based on "total employment." Previously, density was calculated on "paid employment."
Source: British Columbia. Ministry of Skills Development and Labour (2001).

In the 1990s, the labour movement made a special effort to organize private sector service employers. It found the path to success difficult, but more successful after the NDP government made numerous revisions to the Labour Relations Code in 1993. One of the key changes to the Code in 1993 was the re-introduction of automatic certification without an election for applications where the union had at least 55 percent of the employees signed up at the time the application is made. The number of certifications granted almost doubled after 1993 relative to several years before the revisions to the Code.

Between 1993 and 2001, the era of certification by card checks, about 25 percent of all certifications were in health and social services. Another 20 percent were in construction, where organizing is continuous. Labour's most numerous organizing victories were in health and social services as the provincial government relied more heavily on private or non-profit establishments for the delivery of health and social services. A few high-profile successes for labour occurred in the fast food industry (such as Kentucky Fried Chicken, Starbucks, and 7-11), but most of the private sector service sector remained non-union. The Federation of Labour established a special unit to support affiliates' organizing efforts.

During the same period, the labour movement was able to organize approximately 10,000 new members a year through certification, out of an average of slightly more than 1.5 million paid workers in British Columbia, (about 0.7 percent annually). This lack of resounding success at union organizing following the 1993 revisions to the law led to additional attempts by the NDP government to revise the Code. The labour movement wanted the introduction of "sectoral bargaining" for service industries, which would guarantee an immediate standard sectoral agreement for any newly certified units, but strong resistance from the business community resulted in only minor revisions to the Code in 1998, which did not include a sectoral bargaining scheme.

Several distinctive features of the British Columbia labour movement are rooted in its history. In its formative years, workers in resource industries dominated the labour movement in the province. The climate of labour relations in the province reflected many of the features of employment relations in such settings: employers were usually large firms controlled from outside the province; workforces were concentrated in isolated communities; and product markets (and hence employment opportunities) were driven by international markets. This combination of circumstances produced a greater sense of class among British Columbia workers than their counterparts in other regions. Later, construction unions became entrenched as the province built its infrastructure. Unlike their counterparts elsewhere in North America, these unions took positions similar to the resource workers. This class sentiment had several consequences for the development of labour relations in the province.

The labour movement in British Columbia has been heavily involved in provincial politics since its earliest years. Their sense of working-class solidarity caused workers in the province to embrace political action when unionists elsewhere were influenced by the apolitical traditions of craft unionism. In a thinly-populated province, the lack of other organized interest groups gave labour an advantage politically. Factors such as family traditions, ethnicity, and religion, which influence voter behaviour in other provinces, have been relatively unimportant in BC (Blake 1985). Union members first tried to form an independent labour party in BC in 1899. In 1905, labour-backed members of the legislative assembly held the balance of power, which they used to secure legislation regulating hours of work. Later, workers voted heavily for a socialist party. When the CCF was founded in 1932, its doctrines were well received in the province, and the NDP has continued that tradition through the 1990s (Phillips 1967). Since the CCF and NDP appeared, unionists have been prominent in both parties; either in opposition or in government, the NDP caucus has always included several people who have launched their political careers as union officials. Prominent union leaders, including officers of the BC Federation of Labour, also occupy leadership positions in the NDP. During the 1992–95 period, for instance, the president of the provincial NDP was a senior staff official of the BC Government Employees' Union. Subsequently, the provincial secretary of the party was a former president of a college teachers' union. Labour-backed Vancouver civic parties have elected city councilors in Vancouver and other municipalities in the Lower Mainland. In 2002, a labour-backed Vancouver civic party swept the election, although not based on issues linked to provincial politics.

Within the BC labour movement, the provincial Federation of Labour plays an especially prominent role. Distance from headquarters in Central Canada or the United States and a distinctive political culture (including a strong left-wing orientation in many unions) has traditionally diminished the influence of national or international union leaders. The federation has filled the leadership position that national or international union officials occupy in other regions. The president of the federation is a major political figure in the province, even when right-wing governments have been in power, and especially when the NDP governs. Presidents have intervened privately to resolve both labour-management and intra-union disputes. They consult with business leaders about labour relations and broader economic issues. For example, the federation and its affiliates have supported the organization of a labour-sponsored investment fund under federal legislation and a development company for the city of Vancouver. The president of the Federation of Labour has represented labour on boards of both organizations. Labour organizations take an active part in many community activities. When the NDP has governed, labour officials receive appointments to many boards, where they sit with representatives of business and other interests.

British Columbia unions also have a capacity for organizing large strikes and demonstrations. Relying on strong membership support and political experience, labour leaders have mounted massive demonstrations of support. The earliest of these events occurred during World War I. Later, there were demonstrations in the 1930s to protest high levels of unemployment. In 1976, the labour movement took an active part in a national "Day of Protest" against the federal government's Anti-Inflation Program, and in 1983 the province was on the verge of a general strike.

One consequence of the class sentiments and early history of labour in British Columbia was the continuing influence of the left. As late as 1983, for instance, the "Communist Party [had] significant influence in the trade unions" (Palmer 1987, 29). While the number of active members of left-wing political parties was not large, their leadership roles in several unions and the Vancouver and District Labour Council were sources of energy and militancy for the labour movement in general.

The political activism of British Columbia unions highlights another feature of the labour movement — the lack of influence of outside labour organizations. While unions in BC were organizing politically, the official doctrine of the major national labour central and many of its affiliates was to discourage ties to political parties. Until the 1990s, prominent unions in British Columbia often were dissident groups which had broken away from the mainstream of the labour movement. This tradition was especially strong in mining and smelting, but also has been present in the pulp and paper industry. Conversely, when construction unions separated from the CLC in the 1980s, their affiliates continued to participate actively in the BC Federation of Labour chartered by the CLC. Some of these divisions were based on ideology. The influence of the left was traditionally stronger in British Columbia than in other provinces. In other cases, the divisions within the labour movement apparently reflected the broader BC sense of alienation from Central Canada or the United States.

A significant structural feature of the labour movement in the province is the centralized structures of many local unions in the private sector. The IWA, Food and Commercial Workers, and several construction unions have locals with a jurisdiction covering all or most of the province. In part, this structure recognizes the dominance of the Vancouver region to the economy of the province. Union structure is both a cause and effect of centralized bargaining structures discussed below. Unions with central leadership found it easy to adapt to centralized bargaining, and their structures led many employers to form comparable organizations to avoid being whipsawed by labour. The existence of such organizations was a factor in government or labour board decisions to promote or impose centralized bargaining, discussed below.

EMPLOYER ORGANIZATIONS

Employers in British Columbia are highly organized by Canadian standards. This factor confirms experience elsewhere that strong employer organizations typically are a response to strong unionization and especially central trade-union leadership. In addition, public policy in British Columbia traditionally favoured centralized bargaining units, which virtually forced employers to organize on industry lines for collective bargaining.

In BC there is a single organization (the Business Council of British Columbia, BCBC) that represents large employers in lobbying and the exchange of information in labour relations matters. The BCBC (then known as the Employers' Council) was formed in 1966 in response to the ability of the BC Federation of Labour to exchange information and encourage cooperation among its affiliates. Policies are approved by a board of governors consisting of the presidents of most of the province's major employers. While it initially concentrated on industrial relations matters, the council has expanded its scope. It deals with workers' compensation policies, environmental issues, public human resource development policies, provincial economic developments, and general relations between its constituents and the provincial government. As the organization evolved, some non-union firms became affiliated, and their representatives began to assume leadership roles. However, the council does not participate in labour-management negotiations (Sovka and Loseth 1993).

The council takes an active part in public policy debates in the province, especially in the areas of employment, the environment, and the economy. Senior officials have ready access to the government of the day, including the NDP, and they consult privately with their counterparts in the labour movement frequently. Although British Columbia lacks formal mechanisms for labour-management consultation, at the level of peak associations, these discussions have taken place since the 1980s. The Business Council actively participates in consultation on labour policy issues, including nominating individuals to conduct reviews and presenting briefs when public processes occur.

In 1993, the Coalition of BC Business was formed to organize opposition from small employers to impending amendments to the provincial labour code. After the legislation was enacted, the coalition, comprised of industry associations rather than individual employers, continued to act as a spokesperson for small employers on legislative matters, concentrating on employment issues. From its inception until 2003, the president of the coalition was the regional vice-president of the Canadian Federation of Independent Business. The coalition has taken a more hostile stance toward collective bargaining and the institutions of industrial relations than did the Business Council. A prominent member association is composed of predominantly non-union construction companies, for instance, and their senior official became president of the coalition in 2003.

Industry associations have a long history in the province. One of the oldest and most important organizations, Forest Industrial Relations (FIR), arose out of a research agency employers founded during World War II, when the IWA was organizing logging and wood products operations. FIR appeared in 1946 and in the following decade similar associations were formed in the interior of the province. The FIR model appealed to other employers facing militant unions. Pulp and paper producers formed their own association in 1946 (Saunders 1979). In 1969, the Construction Labour Relations Association (CLRA) was formed with the support of the Employers' Council to offset the whipsawing tactics of construction unions. When the construction unions resisted the employers' organization front in the 1970s, the Employers' Council, with many members who purchased construction, encouraged a united front with construction employers in bargaining (Rose 1980).

During the 1970s, the employer association model was adopted widely. Companies in such varied industries as trucking, hospitals, municipal government, supermarkets, hotels, brewers and automobile dealers formed organizations to represent them in labour relations. A crucial element in this process was the inclusion of a provision for "accreditation" of employer associations in the provincial labour code, discussed below. By 1979, 25 employer associations existed to bargain with labour (Saunders 1979). As union militancy waned in the 1980s, however, a number of private sector associations disbanded, leaving employers to negotiate individually. However, the construction, fishing, and forest products industries retained the association bargaining system. In addition, the provincial government mandated employer associations for the health sector, public education, and colleges in 1996 as part of a general effort to centralize its controls over negotiations.

GOVERNMENT AGENCIES

The focus of government action in BC industrial relations is the Labour Relations Board (LRB). The LRB is responsible for administering the Labour Relations Code, the major piece of industrial relations legislation in the province. In 2002, the government added responsibility for employment standards appeals to the board's responsibilities. The Ministry of Labour (which has functioned under several titles) obviously influences policy and occasionally intervenes in major disputes. Within the Ministry of Labour, the Employment Standards Branch enforces the *Employment Standards Act* and supplies investigative staff to the LRB. In addition, it administers apprenticeship programs and other government policies covering working people. A system of expedited grievance arbitration exists, and the ministry appoints arbitrators when the parties are unable to agree from a list compiled with the advice of the parties. Occupational health and safety are regulated by the Workers' Compensation Board (WCB), which administers a separate system for resolving disputes. The WCB has a history of controversy and has been the subject of disputes between labour and management over the administration of its insurance function.

Despite several efforts to establish permanent consultative bodies on labour relations and economic issues in the province, no formal organization exists. Informal consultation, often involving the president of the Business Council and officers of the Federation of Labour, is frequent, and these contacts may explain the parties' lack of enthusiasm for a formal structure. The scope of the responsibilities of the LRB is wider than any other province. Unlike other provinces, BC has avoided the creation of multiple tribunals to rule on issues of labour relations law and policy. In addition to the enforcement of labour relations legislation, that is, receiving petitions for certification, determining (or varying) appropriate bargaining units, ruling on allegations of unfair labour practices, issuing orders with regard to unlawful strikes or the regulation of picketing and the like, it has other responsibilities. It provides mediation services for both the public and private sectors. The board regulates labour relations in the public sector, including police and fire personnel and the provincial public service. Appeals from grievance arbitration awards must go to the LRB, whose authority is sheltered extensively by legislation from judicial review. The board's authority to regulate picketing is extensive. The comprehensive jurisdiction of the LRB ensures that it will be seen in the labour relations community as a protector of the interests of both unions and management and adds to its moral authority and the acceptability of its policies (Adams 1997).

The basic structure of the board is not unusual. It consists of a chair, several vice-chairs and a number of members. The chair and vice-chairs are full-time positions. Members are part-time positions drawn from employer and union circles. Beyond their capacity as representatives of labour or management, the members are chosen for their backgrounds in the major industrial sectors of the province. Panels of three persons normally decide cases. For more significant issues, the chair and several vice-chairs may constitute a panel.

The LRB really dates from the passage of the Labour Code in 1973. The Code deliberately expanded the jurisdiction of the board and established structures to make it a professional and respected administrative tribunal. Except for the period between 1987 and 1992, appointments to the chair position and most vice-chairs have been non-political. Chairs have been drawn from the labour relations bar of British Columbia, generally after serving as a vice-chair. None has served beyond the initial five-year appointment provided in the statute.

The LRB's responsibility for mediation in interest disputes is also unusual among Canadian jurisdictions. This innovation occurred in 1987, when the Social Credit government of the day made sweeping revisions to labour legislation. Previously, mediation services had been provided by the Ministry of Labour. Most of the 1987 changes were repealed in the 1992 reform, but mediation remained a function of the board. In practice, there is a vice-chair for mediation who administers the function more or less independently of the adjudication functions of the board, which are directed by a separate vice-chair.

Policy decisions of the LRB have both reflected the industrial relations reality of the province and have shaped the course of relations between the parties. A notable example has been the promotion of large bargaining units. Faced with large local unions and well-organized employers, the LRB consistently favoured industrywide or at least regional bargaining units. The origins of these policies, which contrasted with the Canadian pattern of craft or enterprise bargaining units, pre-dated the Labour Code in 1974. However, the Code passed during the Barrett government made explicit provision for the accreditation of employer associations, the only province in Canada to have such a provision outside construction. Accreditation in the BC context is the mirror image of union certification, that is, an employers' association gains exclusive bargaining rights on behalf of member companies.

Under this policy regime, the LRB first favoured all-employee single units for individual employers. Secondly, the board accredited employer associations in a number of industries outside construction in both the public and private sectors, including trucking, breweries, hospitals, hotels, local government, and forest products (Weiler 1980). The accreditation of employer groups strengthened their position vis-à-vis strong unions and confirmed the existing practice of employer organization. Board policies virtually barred individual employers from withdrawing from an association if they were dissatisfied with majority decisions in collective bargaining. The Code also gave the board the authority to certify councils of unions, another unusual feature in Canadian labour law. When multiple unions did exist due to craft certifications, the board was able to certify a council to represent all unions. When necessary, the board virtually dictated the rules by which council members would make decisions on collective agreements (ibid.).

These decisions reinforced the traditional structure of collective bargaining in British Columbia. They were designed to reduce opportunities for labour disputes, a common theme in labour policy across the country in the 1970s. However, they also guaranteed that when labour disputes did occur or were even threatened, they attained a high profile in the province and among customers and investors elsewhere.

During the 1990s, the LRB and labour legislation responded to other changes in the industrial relations climate, and it facilitated the decentralization of bargaining structures. Industry associations in a number of sectors either were de-accredited or ceased to function as bargaining agents. In particular, industrywide bargaining in the pulp and paper industry ended, to be replaced by a system of pattern bargaining that produced several long disputes at a single company.

LABOUR LEGISLATION

During the era of W.A.C. Bennett, labour legislation in British Columbia was haphazard and controversial. After World War II, the government passed legislation incorporating the basic principles of the wartime regulations. Subsequent amendments encouraged intervention by the courts in labour disputes and picketing was more restricted than in any other jurisdiction in North America (Matkin 1975). Unsurprisingly, legislation also restricted the use of union dues for political purposes. Employers and the government frequently obtained injunctions from the courts to end strikes.

The most far-reaching and controversial piece of labour legislation in the W.A.C. Bennett government was the *Mediation Commission Act* (MCA). This law was enacted after a prominent jurist was asked to visit Sweden to examine that country's labour relations system. The report recommended the establishment of a permanent commission to settle labour disputes, without the power to decide collective bargaining disputes through arbitration. Instead, the government enacted the MCA, which provided for a system of compulsory arbitration of disputes which the government saw as injuring the well-being of the province. The commissioners did not mediate. Instead, they had comparable status to judges.

The concept of compulsory arbitration outraged the labour movement. The BC Federation of Labour boycotted the commission and threatened a general strike if any union officials were punished for observing the boycott. A few non-affiliated unions did participate in arbitration. The decisions of the commission were so out of touch with the realities of industrial relations that virtually all unions came to boycott its proceedings. Ultimately, the government was forced to resort to other forms of intervention in order to deal with major labour disputes; despite the legal authority it possessed to invoke the commission (ibid.).

When the NDP was elected in 1972, the first law that was passed repealed the MCA. The government then initiated the consultative process that led to the Labour Code. The labour minister (a former union official) was under intense pressure from the labour movement to follow the previous pattern of labour law reform and to pass legislation reflecting labour's priorities only. He resisted these pressures and appointed a Commission of Inquiry composed of two lawyers, one each associated with management and labour, and a neutral chair who was a professor from the University of British Columbia. The commission solicited the parties' views and prepared recommendations for change that commanded broad support. The commission's report was debated extensively and legislation was enacted following most of the recommendations. Employers resisted many aspects of the law, and labour objected strenuously to a few provisions (Weiler 1984). Within the legislature, however, the new law was seen as relatively balanced.

The Labour Code contained many innovations for British Columbia, although almost all of its provisions existed in at least one other jurisdiction. The new law contained a strong commitment to collective bargaining, balanced by equally strong support for stability in labour relations (ibid.). The chosen vehicle for reconciling these two objectives was a powerful Labour Relations Board and the virtual exclusion of the courts from labour relations matters, and replacing them with enhanced powers for the Labour Relations Board. The board received the power to regulate picketing and strikes, broad authority to interpret and administer the statute, the right to offset the effects of employer unfair labour practices and the function of mediating grievances. The board was formally tripartite for the first time. Protections of the Code were extended to police forces and fire departments. Striking unions were given the right to picket other employer operations not involved in a dispute. Unions whose members provided essential services received the option of choosing interest arbitration instead of exercising their right to strike. The rights of individual union members were expanded and employer associations in all industries could apply for accreditation (Arthurs 1974).

Despite some doubts about the constitutional authority of the province to exclude the courts from labour relations matters, the Code was highly successful. The first chair, a former Ontario law professor, Paul Weiler, skillfully crafted a series of early decisions that implemented the principles in the legislation. No serious constitutional challenges to the board's authority were launched. Amendments in 1975 expanded coverage to include professionals and set out a comprehensive legal framework for grievance arbitration. Other changes in 1977 gave unions automatic access to the Rand formula for union security (Kelliher 1984).

Given the history of labour legislation in the province, perhaps the most remarkable commentary on the Code was that it survived the change in government in 1975. In fact, the president of the Employers' Council (as it was then named) publicly called on the new Social Credit government not to tamper with the Labour Code. All neutral and partisan members of the board were offered re-appointment, and Weiler remained as chair until he resigned to accept an academic appointment. After the change of government, Weiler advised the incoming minister of labour to retain the balanced approach of the Code and the Labour Relations Board (Weiler 1984).

The exception to the theme of continuity in labour legislation was an ill-fated attempt by the Social Credit government to enact essential services legislation. The original Code expanded the right to strike of workers likely to render essential services, but relied on preventative measures to avoid stoppages that might be seen as damaging to the public interest. The 1975 amendments gave the board the authority to designate services essential to prevent "immediate and serious danger to health, life or safety." In the wake of disputes in BC Rail and the ferry system, which had serious economic effects without endangering health, life or safety, the Bennett government imposed legislation covering essential services in 1977. The scope of the legislation exceeded the amended Code, and a commission was established to deal with such strikes. The commission had a range of powers to end disputes, in addition to the designation of essential services. The interventionist nature of the statute, the lack of general consultation or any effort to balance conflicting interests aroused labour's opposition to the new law. The Federation of Labour called a boycott of the commission, and it never really functioned (Kelliher 1984).

The fate of the Essential Services Disputes Commission was a forerunner of the fate of the next major change in BC labour legislation, the 1987 *Industrial Relations Act*, enacted by the Vander Zalm government. The lack of true consultation and one-sided nature of the law aroused labour's opposition. For instance, a ballot was required for union certification, breaking with the mainstream of Canadian labour law, which provided for certification based on union membership (Weiler 1980). Decertification was made easier. Picketing and economic boycotts were restricted. The chair of the commission was given wide authority to intervene in labour disputes, and other mechanisms were established to limit the impact of labour disputes. The BC Federation of Labour again called a boycott of labour law. While the boycott had a number of important exceptions, it served the purpose of bringing the legislation and the Industrial Relations Commission, which replaced the Labour Relations Board, into disrepute. The Harcourt government followed the procedures used by Barrett 20 years earlier in reviewing labour legislation. It appointed an advisory committee and accepted the committee's consensus recommendations. Government made political choices for the three issues in contention. It acceded to labour's demands for a ban on replacement workers, but retained most of the *Industrial Relations Act* restrictions on picketing and declined to provide for broad-based certifications in traditionally non-union sectors (BC Subcommittee of Special Advisers 1992). When the legislation (the Labour Relations Code) was enacted in 1993, British Columbia was very much in the mainstream of Canadian labour law, except for the ban on replacement workers. At that time, both Quebec and Ontario had such restrictions, and similar provisions were under consideration for the federal jurisdiction. (Subsequently, the Harris government in Ontario repealed the ban on replacement workers, and the federal Parliament enacted a more limited provision.)

The 1992–93 experience again demonstrated the need for broad and honest consultation before the enactment of changes to the labour law in British Columbia. In the subsequent provincial election, the opposition attempted to make labour law a political issue, but ultimately committed itself to the elimination of the ban on replacement workers, mandatory representation votes for certifications and a small number of less significant changes. After the NDP was re-elected, the government appointed yet another committee to review labour legislation composed of three experienced labour lawyers. The committee recommended no significant changes to the Code, and the government added only a provision covering the construction industry in 1998. Even these rather modest changes provoked controversy, a massive public relations campaign from the non-union construction industry and an extended debate by the opposition in the legislature.

LABOUR DISPUTES

BC labour relations have long had a reputation for high levels of strike activity. Some of this reputation is based on fact, but the pattern of labour disputes in the province is more varied than a simple count of the number of strikes. Measurement of strike activity is itself a complex process, but our analysis of stoppages in BC will focus on four areas: person-days lost due to strikes, the number of strikes, the average size and the duration of strikes, and the impact of large strikes.

Overall, British Columbia has followed national patterns of declining strike activity over the last decade. As shown in Table 3, person-days lost due to strike activity in BC was high in the late 1970s and early 1980s, but declined to low levels in the 1990s. British Columbia, Newfoundland and Labrador, and Quebec stand out with very high levels of lost time due to strike activity in the late 1970s, but like British Columbia, Quebec and Newfoundland and Labrador have declined to join the other provinces at low levels in the 1990s. Since 1970, British Columbia has accounted for approximately 12 percent of all strikes, a level that has not changed greatly over time.

The reason why person-days lost per 1,000 employees in British Columbia is almost double the Canadian average is the large size of strikes in BC. The average number of workers per strike in British Columbia is more than double the Canadian average, and is also more than double the average size of strikes in every other province except Quebec, where average strike size is about two-thirds the size of strikes in British Columbia. Average strike duration in British Columbia is below the Canadian average and below the average for all of the other provinces except Saskatchewan and Quebec. Average strike duration in BC has declined slightly over the 1970–2001 period, but this trend is not statistically significant. The average strike size in BC has remained stable over the period.

In sum, the strike statistics reveal that British Columbia had very high levels of person-days lost due to strikes in the 1970s and early 1980s, but this has declined to low levels matching the other provinces in the 1990s. This decline is due to a very significant reduction in the number

TABLE 3
WORK STOPPAGE SUMMARY STATISTICS, BY PROVINCE, MEANS FOR 1970–2000

	Total	BC	AB	SA	MA	ON	PQ	NS	NB	NF
Number of strikes	629.5	74.9	20.3	19.8	15.8	203.1	224.5	23.2	21.7	23.6
Number of strikes/ employment	66.4	62.3	20.1	48.7	34.2	48.3	81.8	74.0	87.4	140.9
Person-days lost/ employment*	393.3	724.9	144.1	217.7	160.1	366.9	574.3	254.7	314.4	782.4
Average strike duration	21.8	16.6	30.0	15.5	26.3	19.7	16.3	13.1	32.9	19.0
Average number of strikers	405.6	1287.4	358.1	325.3	511.6	435.5	531.7	112.6	271.0	196.4
Person-days lost per strike	6,286.5	8,327.3	7,686.0	4,486.9	5,767.6	7,538.3	6,203.3	3,865.8	4,595.7	5,451.2

Note: *Per 1,000 employees in the province.
Source: Human Resources Development Canada, unpublished data.

of strikes. The average strike duration is below the Canadian average and has declined only slightly. The most distinguishing feature of strikes in British Columbia is their large size relative to strikes in the other provinces.

In general terms, industrial relations in British Columbia has been dominated by large provincewide disputes, involving thousands of workers. This pattern is consistent with the presence of large bargaining units and the insulation from market pressures that bargaining through employers' associations can provide. During these stoppages, BC employers engaged in a dispute were protected from competition within the province, although obviously alternate sources of supply may have existed elsewhere.

Between 1970 and 2001, a total of 28 provincewide strikes occurred in British Columbia, which caused the loss of at least 50,000 person-days. While the number is large, the incidence of these disputes was concentrated in a handful of bargaining relationships. Eleven disputes occurred in the forest products industry (pulp and paper and lumber/logging), four in construction and two in fishing. Each of these disputes involved many employers in the industry. Between 1973 and 1982, the period of highest strike activity, 75 percent of person-days lost in labour disputes were accounted for by the construction, lumber, and pulp and paper industries (Allen 1986). In addition, other strikes involved single employers with multiple locations: BC Hydro, BC Telephone, Safeway, the Insurance Corporation of BC, the provincial government, and the health and education sectors. In addition, large strikes involving multiple employers in one region of the province occurred on eight other occasions, including local government, trucking, longshoring, supermarkets, and breweries.

Arguably, these high-profile disputes were instrumental in giving British Columbia its reputation for labour unrest. In a relatively isolated jurisdiction, these were major events. Two strikes in the forest products sector were factors in changes of government, for instance. The effects of extended walkouts in isolated communities heavily dependent on a single industry were profound.

In terms of the total impact on the economy, however, smaller and longer strikes were also important. Taking 50,000 person-days lost as the definition of a major dispute, the mining industry, which was always bargaining separately for each site, had a total of 11 such stoppages, more than all other sectors combined. Other large strikes did not follow such a strong pattern, as they occurred in manufacturing, publishing, restaurants, local transit, and airlines. After the de-accreditation of the employers' association in the pulp and paper sector, the unions chose one employer as the pattern setter, and it experienced two long strikes at several locations.

TERMS AND CONDITIONS OF EMPLOYMENT

Compensation in British Columbia traditionally has been higher than in other provinces, although the margin has been small. Relatively high union density and labour militancy may have contributed to these circumstances. From the 1940s through the mid-1980s, BC wages were approximately 5 percent higher than Ontario's. A high point of about a 13 percent advantage was reached in the early 1980s, shortly before the William Bennett government launched its campaign to weaken unions. For whatever reasons, the gap between British Columbia and Ontario narrowed later in the decade to approximately its normal level of 5 percent. The most significant advantages for BC workers have been in forest products and construction. In forest products, workers have been able to capture economic rents from public ownership of timber reserves, and construction workers were able to capitalize on their monopoly position during the era of large projects in the period of W.A.C. Bennett's government and the boom in the early 1980s before the world's fair in Vancouver. Conversely, wages in commercial services, finance, and personal services are lower than in Ontario (Allen 1986). Since the early 1980s, perhaps coinciding with Bennett's anti-union campaign, wages in British Columbia have declined relative to the rest of Canada, as the province's economic growth lagged behind other jurisdictions: Alberta, Ontario, and Newfoundland and Labrador in particular.

CONCLUSIONS

This review demonstrates the reality of regional differences within a national system. While industrial relations in BC shares most of the structural features of other provinces, it has distinctive features, especially the high degrees of organization by both parties, the close links between labour policy and partisan politics and a level of class solidarity by labour and management that is unusual in the twenty-first century.

The development of industrial relations in the province demonstrated the importance of economic factors in the formation of social attitudes. A resource-based economy dominated by large corporations in turn bred a militant labour movement committed to political action. These factors helped produce a political culture that fed on class differences, lacking some of the pragmatism found in other provinces and in the federal government.

As the economic and social importance of resource industries and large corporations diminishes in British Columbia, an obvious question arises about industrial relations. Will the parties' traditional attitudes and practices continue to be relevant in an economy increasingly dominated by services and small business? Despite a legislative regime and a government favourable to labour's interests, union density fell during the NDP's time in office in the 1990s. Of the largest unions in the province, three predominantly private sector unions (the CAW, the Wood Workers, and the Hotel and Restaurant Workers) reported an absolute increase in membership between 1992 and 2001, and the CAW expansion was largely due to mergers with existing unions.

Apart from legislation enacted in the 1970s, BC industrial relations has not been especially innovative. Rather, the parties have performed traditional functions more skillfully than most of their counterparts elsewhere in Canada. The labour movement in particular has maintained the organizational resources necessary to defend its interests, even in the face of government and employer hostility. Moreover, many of its leaders appreciate the need to expand their membership in the service sector. They have increased resources devoted to organizing and have pressed the government to enact legislation that would facilitate collective bargaining in traditionally non-union sectors. Employers in traditionally unionized sectors have learned to deal comfortably with labour, and attitudes of mutual respect prevail, especially at the senior levels of employer organizations. The small business sector, however, is dedicated to the prevention of unionism while being respectful of the general culture of the province.

REFERENCES

Adams, G.W. 1997. *Canadian Labour Law*. Toronto: Canada Law Book.
Allen, R.C. 1986. "Trade Unions and the BC Economy," in *Restraining the Economy: Social Credit Economic Policies for BC in the Eighties*, ed. R.C. Allen and G. Rosenbluth. Vancouver: New Star Books, pp. 225-53.
Arthurs, H. 1974. "The 'Dullest Bill': Reflections on the Labour Code of British Columbia," *University of British Columbia Law Review* 9:280-302.
Blake, D.E. 1985. *Two Political Worlds: Parties and Voting in British Columbia*. Vancouver: University of British Columbia Press.
British Columbia. Ministry of Skills Development and Labour. 2001. *BC Labour Directory*. Victoria: Ministry of Skills Development and Labour.

—— Subcommittee of Special Advisers. 1992. *Recommendations for Labour Law Reform: A Report to the Honourable Moe Sihota Minister of Labour.* Victoria: Ministry of Labour and Consumer Services.

Horowitz, G. 1968. *Canadian Labour in Politics.* Toronto: University of Toronto Press.

Jamieson, S. 1962. "Regional Factors in Industrial Conflict: The Case of British Columbia," *Canadian Journal of Economics and Political Science* 28 (3):405-16.

Kelleher, S. 1984. "Ten Years with the 'Dullest Bill': The Evolution of Policy and Practice under the Labour Code," in *The Labour Code of British Columbia in the 1980's,* ed. J.M. Weiler and P.A. Gall. Vancouver: Carswell Legal Publications, pp. 5-24.

Leslie, G. 1991. *Breach of Promise: Socred Ethics Under Vander Zalm.* Vancouver: Harbour Publishing.

Marchak, M.P. 1988. "Public Policy, Capital and Labour in the Forest Industry," in *Workers, Capital and the State in British Columbia,* ed. Warburton and Coburn, pp. 177-200.

Matkin, J. 1975. "Government Interventions in Labour Disputes in British Columbia," in *Collective Bargaining in the Essential and Public Service Sectors,* ed. M. Gunderson. Toronto: University of Toronto Press, pp. 79-100.

Mitchell, D.J. 1983. *W.A.C. Bennett and the Rise of British Columbia.* Vancouver: Douglas & McIntyre.

Palmer, B.D. 1987. *Solidarity: The Rise and Fall of an Opposition in British Columbia.* Vancouver: New Star Books.

Phillips, P. 1967. *No Power Greater.* Vancouver: British Columbia Federation of Labour.

—— 1988. "The Underground Economy: The Mining Frontier to 1920," in *Workers, Capital and the State in British Columbia,* ed. Warburton and Coburn, pp. 35-54.

Rose, J.B. 1980. *Public Policy, Bargaining Structure and the Construction Industry.* Toronto: Butterworths.

Saunders, D. 1979. "Group Bargaining," *UBC Business Review* 14:39-44.

Sovka, R. and M. Loseth. 1993. "The Business Council of British Columbia." Unpublished paper, University of British Columbia, Vancouver, BC.

Thompson, M. 1985. "Restraint and Labour Relations: The Case of British Columbia," *Canadian Public Policy/Analyse de Politiques* 11(2):171-79.

Warburton, R. 1988. "Conclusion: Capitalist Social Relations in British Columbia," in *Workers, Capital and the State in British Columbia,* ed. Warburton and Coburn, pp. 263-88.

Warburton, R. and D. Coburn, eds. 1988. *Workers, Capital and the State in British Columbia.* Vancouver: University of British Columbia Press.

Weiler, P. 1980. *Reconcilable Differences: New Directions in Canadian Labour Law.* Toronto: Carswell.

—— 1984. "The Process of Reforming Labour Law in British Columbia," in *The Labour Code of British Columbia in the 1980s,* ed. J.M. Weiler and P.A. Gall. Vancouver: Carswell Legal Publications, pp. 25-34.

5 MANITOBA: BEYOND THE CLASS DIVIDE?

John Godard

Résumé — Ce chapitre traite du caractère unique des relations industrielles au Manitoba. Ces relations ont été particulièrement marquées, d'une part, par la division des classes toujours présente au cours de l'histoire de cette province et cause profonde de la Grève générale de Winnipeg et, d'autre part, par les conditions précaires auxquelles l'économie manitobaine a été confrontée, économie qui a décliné depuis 1910 par rapport à celle d'autres grandes villes canadiennes. La prise de conscience de la part du patronat et des syndicats de la nécessité de maintenir la paix dans les industries en dépit des antagonismes de classe profondément ancrés a entraîné des relations industrielles instables, caractérisées par relativement peu de grèves dans l'ensemble des industries, quoique des mouvements de grève et du radicalisme syndical se soient manifestés périodiquement.

Les relations industrielles manitobaines ont aussi subi les changements de cap importants de l'orientation de la politique tantôt de droite tantôt de gauche, selon que le Parti progressiste conservateur ou le Nouveau Parti Démocratique détenait le pouvoir. Ce fut particulièrement le cas lorsqu'un gouvernement conservateur a pris le pouvoir à la fin des années 1980. Ce gouvernement a constamment orienté la province vers la droite, s'engageant dans une voie néoconservative qui a mené, entre autres, à l'affaiblissement des protections offertes aux travailleurs par le droit du travail. Cette façon de faire a accentué considérablement la division des classes et conduit, en 1996, au second mouvement de grève, en importance, depuis la Grève générale de Winnipeg. Il semble aussi qu'elle ait procuré quelques grands avantages aux Manitobains, au lieu de conduire la province à une économie de bas salaires. On peut affirmer que le gouvernement avait peu de choix, compte tenu des conditions économiques de l'époque et que ses succès mitigés reflètent les difficultés particulièrement grandes avec lesquelles la province était aux prises. Pourtant, il est clair *a posteriori* que la solution néoconservative ne convenait pas au Manitoba, tant du point de vue économique que politique.

En haussant les niveaux d'éducation et de compétence tout en veillant à ce que la main-d'œuvre manitobaine continue de représenter une sorte de « marché » pour cette formation améliorée, le Manitoba devrait être capable de se constituer une niche distinctive au sein de l'économie nord-américaine. Mais il faudra des politiques qui tiennent compte davantage du rôle des travailleurs et de leurs représentants syndicaux, non seulement dans le milieu de travail mais aussi dans la conception des politiques économiques et sociales. Autrement dit, il faudra adopter des politiques permettant au Manitoba de dépasser la division des classes et les faux-fuyants politiques qui lui sont associés.

Cette orientation stratégique n'est pas encore perceptible au début des années 2000. Bien que l'élection d'un gouvernement NPD en 1999 ait provoqué un mouvement d'abandon du néoconservatisme et un léger renforcement du droit du travail, ce gouvernement semble se satisfaire de suivre une voie plus proche de celle du gouvernement progressiste conservateur de Duff Roblin des années 1960 que de celle d'un parti social démocrate moderne préoccupé de conclure une entente durable avec les syndicats et le patronat. Ses politiques semblent plutôt indiquer la fin de la tradition sociale démocrate du NPD manitobain et, donc, un changement fondamental de la vie politique dans cette province. Cependant, la division des classes demeure, sinon intacte, du moins présente dans les relations industrielles.

INTRODUCTION

In his classic comparison of the United States and Canada, Lipset argued that, while the US was born of individualistic, frontier expansion, Canada was born of a more organizationally driven one. The result, according to Lipset, has been that Canadians are more supportive of state initiatives and more sympathetic to collective action than are Americans. This has affected both politics and labour relations, as reflected in more social democratic state policies and a more socially oriented labour movement (Lipset 1964, 1990).[1]

To the extent that the Lipset theory can serve as a starting point for understanding labour relations in any Canadian region or province, Manitoba comes the closest. The province's early growth was fuelled by the fur-trading companies, followed by the grain trade and the westward expansion of the railways. Yet, by the early 1900s, Manitoba also experienced a rapid influx of Eastern European immigrants sympathetic to socialist doctrines, thereby laying the foundations for stronger class divisions than assumed under the Lipset thesis. Complicating matters has been the province's economic experience since this influx. Once the metropolis of the west, Manitoba has faced decline relative to most other provinces since the second decade of the twentieth century, with an increasingly fragile economy and an often insecure business community.

This unique context has given rise to a labour relations environment that is distinct from that of other Canadian provinces. Early class divisions created the preconditions for labour unrest and radicalism. Yet this unrest and radicalism have been dampened by the fragile economy and the awareness of both the labour and management communities of the need to maintain industrial peace. Thus, while labour-management relations in all market economies reflect a dynamic tension between underlying sources of conflict and overarching sources of cooperation, this tension has been especially strong in Manitoba. As a consequence, industrial relations in Manitoba has been volatile in nature, with relatively low levels of industrial strife overall, yet sporadic outbursts of strike activity and labour radicalism.

By far the greatest outburst of this radicalism was the famed Winnipeg General Strike of 1919, which was to have a formative impact on industrial (and class) relations in Manitoba throughout the remainder of the twentieth century. Accordingly, this strike is taken as the point of departure for this chapter. This chapter then reviews Manitoba's development since the strike, focusing on economic, political, and legal events, and their implications for industrial relations. Finally, the current context of industrial relations in Manitoba is addressed, placing particular emphasis on developments throughout the 1990s and their implications for the future.

A DEFINING MOMENT: THE WINNIPEG GENERAL STRIKE OF 1919

The Winnipeg General Strike is probably the closest to a true class conflict that Canada has witnessed.[2] On 2 May 1919, 27,000 union and non-union workers walked off the job, virtually shutting down the Winnipeg economy for six weeks, and spawning a wave of sympathy strikes across the country. Support was so strong that even the local police refused to take the side of employers (and government), a stand for which they were dismissed *en masse* by the municipal government, to be replaced by a volunteer militia. Concerned that the strike was the beginning of a general insurrection throughout the west, the federal government called in the Royal Northwest Mounted Police to maintain order. The strike ended when the police shot into a crowd of strikers, killing one and wounding another 30 (one of whom later died). The city was subsequently placed under martial law, and, with the strikers too demoralized to continue, the strike ended in defeat two days later. Thousands of workers were subsequently fired, blacklisted, or harassed by the police, and many of their leaders were jailed or deported.

The Winnipeg General Strike had lasting effects on Manitoba industrial relations, for it cemented emerging class divisions, divisions that have remained in varying degrees ever since. This strike can be explained at two levels. The first entails the immediate causes of the strike, of which three may be identified. First, there had been widespread discontent over declining incomes and deteriorating working conditions, attributable in considerable measure to inflationary government policies and high unemployment after World War I. Second, radicalism had been growing within the labour movement, particularly as reflected in the decision, at a convention in Calgary in March of 1919, to found the One Big Union (OBU) as a class-wide alternative to the perceived narrowness and conservatism of the dominant Canadian labour federation of the time, the Trades and Labour Congress (see Smith 1984). The third cause, which ignited the strike, was the refusal of Winnipeg employers in the metal and building trades to accommodate worker demands for improved wages and working conditions or to even meet with their union representatives in the days leading up to the strike.

This first level explanation provides a reasonable understanding of the rationale and immediate causes of the strike. But it really does not address, specifically, why this strike occurred in Winnipeg.[3] Workers across the country held many of the same grievances as their counterparts in Winnipeg in the years immediately preceding, during, and after World War I. The second level explanation addresses this question, identifying underlying preconditions for the strike which were unique to Winnipeg. These preconditions reflect Winnipeg's early development.

Winnipeg was, by the first decade of the twentieth century, the metropolis of the west. Not only had it become the funnel through which western grain would be shipped to points throughout the world, it had also become the major point of supply for the western prairies, and hence a major centre for manufacturing, wholesale trading, and immigration. Between 1900 and 1910, its industrial output quadrupled, and its labour force more than tripled in size (Morton 1967). In the words of a special correspondent to the *Chicago Record Herald* who visited the city in 1911:

> No city, in America at least, has such absolute and complete command over the wholesale trade of so vast an area. It is destined to become one of the greatest distributing centres of the continent as well as a manu-

facturing community of great importance (William E. Curtis, as cited in Newman 1998, 406).

An important component of Winnipeg's growth was the rapid influx of British and Eastern European immigrants, creating a "new" working class that was strongly influenced by European class traditions and much more sympathetic overall than its central Canadian counterpart to socialist reform and to industrial unionism. Both political activism and labour militancy thus became widespread prior to World War I (see Smith 1984; Bercuson 1974), and Winnipeg became largely divided between the poor "north end," with its immigrant working class, and the affluent "south end" from which the voluntary militia was subsequently drawn during the strike. By the outbreak of the war, there were 82 local unions in Winnipeg, representing 10,000 members, and Winnipeg had become the third largest centre of union activity in the country (Smith 1984), with a number of active working-class political organizations. In short, Winnipeg had become a fertile ground for the kind of class conflict that was to emerge in 1919.

Winnipeg's position as the metropolis of the west had also begun to gradually collapse in the years preceding the war. Though partly a reflection of worldwide economic recession, Winnipeg's position appears to have been threatened by three factors. First, the opening of the Panama Canal in 1914 provided an alternative route for grain shipment, thereby threatening Winnipeg's dominance in the grain trade (Phillips 1990). Second, changes in the railway regulatory structure after 1907 substantially weakened Winnipeg's competitive position as a transportation hub (ibid.). Third, there had been a growth throughout the west of large retail stores that had no need of Winnipeg's wholesalers, gradually undermining Winnipeg's dominance as a commercial centre (Bellan 1978). This combination of factors meant not only that Winnipeg employers found themselves in more dire economic straits than otherwise, it also likely resulted in a growing insecurity among business owners and government officials, creating a climate of employer and government intransigence and hence unwillingness to make even minor concessions to workers and the labour movement. In short, the unique composition of the Winnipeg working class coupled with economic insecurity appear to have laid the foundations for the Winnipeg General Strike.

In addition to their importance for explaining the strike, these two factors continued to have important implications for Manitoban labour relations throughout the twentieth century. The Winnipeg working class retained a strong ethnic heritage, and though the north end/south end division may not have been quite as deep by the end of the century, it continued to be reflected in voting patterns and to serve as an important metaphor for broader class divisions (Bercuson 1974). In part because of this division, the political left continued to be a major force in provincial politics. Equally important, the decline of Winnipeg's position proved not to be a temporary development, but rather the beginning of a long-term and seemingly irreversible decline relative to most other major cities (Gonick 1990). Winnipeg has continuously aspired to regain its former economic stature, but has never quite succeeded. Thus, these two factors, coupled with the General Strike itself, are important to understanding both the economic and the political context of industrial relations in Manitoba as they have developed to this day. Below, each of these contexts is discussed in greater detail, before turning to the contemporary structure and complexion of Manitoba industrial relations.

THE MANITOBA ECONOMY: FIGHTING DECLINE

Since 1919, Manitoba has experienced a gradual erosion of its traditional economic base. Once large and prosperous rail yards and meat-packing abattoirs have now all but disappeared from Winnipeg, taking with them a preponderance of "good jobs" generated during the post-World War II era and before. Winnipeg is no longer the major centre for grain shipments that it once was, and garment manufacturing, once an important industry, now accounts for under 1 percent of all jobs. Helping to offset these declines has been expansion in motor vehicle and parts manufacturing and in furniture manufacturing, with the former now representing the province's largest export category. The aerospace industry has also grown substantially. The province has thus managed to maintain a relatively healthy and diverse manufacturing sector despite the decline of its traditional economic core. As of 2001, manufacturing accounted for 12.7 percent of employment, compared to 15 percent for Canada as a whole (Statistics Canada 2002b).

The grain industry has also maintained a strong presence, even though Winnipeg is no longer a major centre for grain shipping. The head offices of the Canadian Wheat Board, the Canadian Grain Commission, and most major grain-handling companies are located in Winnipeg, along with the Winnipeg Commodities Exchange, on which some grains are traded. Equally important, the province as a whole continues to have a relatively strong agricultural base, despite a long-term decline in agricultural employment (to 5.3 percent as of 2001), and a concomitant rural migration into Winnipeg. The decline in agriculture has also been offset somewhat by northern development, though this development has generated only a limited amount of employment.

Manitoba's economy is bolstered by a relatively large public sector, with the municipal, provincial, and federal governments serving as Winnipeg's three largest employers (Nairne 1998), and by a relatively strong financial and insurance sector, led by James A. Richardson and Sons, Investor's Group, and Great-West Life Assurance, all of which have their head offices in Winnipeg. The dominance of the public sector in many respects reflects both the social democratic heritage of the province and particular economic features that mandate a larger number of public sector employees per capita. The financial industry can, historically, be attributed in considerable measure to the grain trade.

It may thus be argued that Manitoba has done reasonably well given the difficulties that it has faced. Yet it has still fallen behind relative to the rest of Canada. Winnipeg, which now accounts for 80 percent of the provincial output outside the agriculture and mining industries, has dropped from the fourth to being the eighth largest Canadian city over the past century. As of 2001, Manitoba had experienced a negative net population migration every year except one (1999) over the preceding 15 years (Manitoba. Bureau of Statistics 1999, 2002). Although this was more than offset by natural population increases, the provincial population still grew by only 12 percent in the quarter-century from 1976 to 2001, which was only one-third of the growth rate for Canada as a whole (Statistics Canada 2002a). As revealed in Table 1, a potential bright spot has been Manitoba's relatively low unemployment rate compared to the Canadian average and to that of its provincial neighbours (especially Ontario). Yet even this may in considerable measure reflect the province's low population growth rates. Throughout the 1990s, for example, Manitoba had one of the lowest rates of job creation of all provinces, registering an employment growth of only 5.7 percent, compared to a national average of 11.7 percent (Nairne 2000).

It follows that, even if Manitoba has managed to maintain a relatively healthy economy, its position has remained precarious. This position has arguably meant a continuing sense of insecurity within its business class, and a labour movement that has had to remain mindful of the fragile constitution of the Manitoba economy despite the class divide emergent in the early twentieth century. Moreover, although the province appears

TABLE 1
AVERAGE UNEMPLOYMENT RATES, 1976–1995

	Manitoba	Canada	Ontario	Saskatchewan
1976–95	7.9	9.4	8.2	6.8
1996	7.5	9.7	9.1	6.6
1997	6.6	8.5	8.5	6.0
1998	5.7	7.2	7.2	5.9
1999	5.5	6.4	6.4	6.1
2000	4.9	6.8	5.7	5.2
2001	5.0	7.2	6.3	5.8

Source: Statistics Canada (2002*b*).

to date to have done reasonably well under the Free Trade Agreement and the North American Free Trade Agreement, these agreements would also appear to have increased the perceived (if not actual) level of precariousness by further weakening the province's position as an east-west lynchpin and rendering it more susceptible to employer threats of relocation. This has become especially evident in recent political patterns and labour policies (see below).

POLITICAL PATTERNS AND LABOUR POLICIES

Although the precariousness of the Manitoba economy may have limited the level of conflict in industrial relations, the class divide has been evident in political patterns ever since the Winnipeg General Strike. In particular, the province has had a strong social democratic movement (often badly split internally), primarily represented since the 1930s by the Cooperative Commonwealth Federation (CCF) and its successor, the New Democratic Party (NDP). It has also had a strong right-wing conservative element, comprised largely of rural communities in the southern half of the province and small-business owners. The latter has been partly balanced off by a somewhat more moderate conservative element consisting of managerial and professional voters and dominated by members of the traditional business establishment. Because of its economic power, this element has historically had an important behind-the-scenes influence.

But it has tended to be small in numbers, so on the surface, provincial politics has tended to be defined by a strong "right-wing," a strong "left-wing," and a relatively weak "centre." Coupled with Manitoba's precarious economic position, this has made for a more fractious political environment than has characterized most provinces. Because this has had consequences for the complexion of labour relations, it deserves a brief recounting.

As in other Canadian provinces, both provincial and civic governments remained hostile to labour prior to World War II, often playing a key role in defeating strikes (Phillips 1990). All the same, Manitoba had a vibrant (though divided) "left" during this period. Labour and socialist parties elected 11 representatives in the 1920 provincial election, and maintained between 10 and 20 percent of the popular vote throughout the 1930s (Black 1990). In federal elections throughout this period, the percentage of Manitobans voting for parties of the left remained far above that of the rest of Canada (see Table 2), with the leftist vote consistently exceeding 40 percent in municipal elections in Winnipeg (Black 1990), and for a brief period in the mid-1930s labour and a lone Communist came to control Winnipeg City Council. But the left was racked with extensive divisions between reformist and revolutionary currents, and so its accomplishments were minimal (ibid.).

Support for the left continued to grow during World War II, and a long-standing split between social democratic and revolutionary elements largely disappeared by the end of the war, with the former coming to dominate. Reflecting the tenor of the times, the provincial government

TABLE 2
PROPORTION OF VOTES FOR LEFT PARTIES IN FEDERAL ELECTIONS, MANITOBA AND CANADA, 1926–1945

Election	Manitoba	Canada
1926	8.7	1.5
1930	10.2	1.3
1935	22.7	9.6
1940	19.4	8.5
1945	36.5	17.8

Source: Black (1990), based on Statistics Canada data.

passed the *Labour Relations Act* in 1948. This Act resembled other legislation adopted across Canada, granting workers the right to organize
unions free from employer interference and to bargain collectively with
their employer once organized.

Following the immediate postwar years, there have been widespread swings in government, reflecting the ideological divisions noted
above. In 1949, Manitobans elected a Liberal-Progressive government,
based largely on rural support. At the time, the ideology of the Liberal-
Progressive Party was as close to *laissez-faire* conservativism as could be
found anywhere (Snidal 1967), and this was reflected in the new government's policies. Intent on reducing the debt from the Great Depression,
the government embarked on a fiscal austerity program that delayed badly
needed expenditures on infrastructure and public services (Gonick 1990)
and appears to have been partly to blame for a slower rate of economic
growth than was characteristic of other provinces throughout the 1950s
(63 percent compared to 79 percent) (ibid.).

Then, in 1959, a strongly pro-development Conservative government led by Duff Roblin was elected. The Roblin government has
been characterized as "non-ideological" (Wiseman 1983), and was probably the only government to directly represent the traditional Manitoba
business establishment since World War II. It was by no means a friend of
labour. But, partially in response to a bitter six-month strike at the Brandon
Packers' plant in 1960 in which the employer attempted to use replacement workers to break the union, and the labour movement's bitterness
over pro-employer legislation subsequent to this strike, the government
decided to seek a more cooperative relationship with labour. To this end,
it established the Labour Legislation Review Committee, comprised of
both labour and management representatives, with the mandate of undertaking a continuing and comprehensive review of labour legislation
and labour-management relations in the province. Since renamed the
Labour-Management Review Committee, this body was to play a significant role in most subsequent changes to labour and employment
legislation.

In keeping with its more activist, pro-development policy, the
Roblin government also established massive incentives designed to foster
northern forestry, mining, and hydro-electric projects. But this strategy
met with limited success. After considerable internal turmoil, and ultimately Roblin's replacement by a new, right-wing leader (Walter Weir) in
1967, it was defeated in the election of 1969, to be replaced by the province's first NDP government, led by Ed Schreyer.

The Schreyer government turned the province's direction back to the left. It implemented the most progressive package of tax and social reforms in the country, and while it generally avoided direct conflict with the business community (Gonick 1990), it introduced public automobile insurance and, more importantly for this chapter, pro-labour reforms to the *Labour Relations Act*. The main features of these reforms included expanded coverage of the labour force, extended and strengthened unfair labour practice provisions, measures to facilitate union organization, provisions intended to expedite the bargaining process and to encourage the parties to bargain responsibly, compulsory check-off of union dues, and provision for bargaining over the effects of technological change during the term of an agreement (Manitoba. Department of Labour 1973). These changes were largely consistent with the wishes of the Manitoba Federation of Labour (MFL), with one exception. They did not ban the use of strike-breakers, which had been a major priority of the labour movement since the Brandon Packers strike.

Although the first "pro-labour" government elected by Manitobans, the Schreyer government's cautiousness alienated many of its key supporters, including labour (Gonick 1990). Particularly damaging was its handling of a 1976–77 strike at a steel fabrication plant (Griffin Steel) in which the employer hired permanent strike-breakers, and a settlement was never reached. This led to major splits within the NDP (Wiseman 1983). In part as a result, the Schreyer government was defeated in 1977, replaced by a Conservative government committed to moving the province sharply back to the right. It slashed public spending and cut taxes by 6 percent, just as the world economy was plunging into recession. Not only did Manitoba experience the worst economic performance in Canada in terms of gross domestic product (GDP) growth, job growth, investment, and housing starts (Gonick 1990), there was also a wave of labour and social unrest, partly due to the actions of private sector employers inspired by the government's austerity program, but also in reaction to massive cuts to social programs. Strike activity was higher in 1978 than in any other year since the 1919 General Strike.

The NDP was returned to office with a strong majority in November 1981, under Howard Pawley. Though the Pawley government only partly delivered on its pre-election promises to the labour movement, it did enact legislation favourable to labour. These included first contract arbitration, a ban on permanent striker replacements, provision for expedited arbitration of grievances, and provision for grievance mediation. Perhaps most notable was the enactment of final offer selection (FOS) legislation in 1987. This legislation was largely in response to a demand by labour for a ban on the use of replacement workers during a strike. But rather than implement such a ban and risk upsetting the business community, FOS was designed to effectively undermine the use of these workers as a union-breaking strategy, by enabling unions (after a favourable membership vote)[4] to have the final offers of each party submitted to a "selector," who would then choose the most "reasonable" offer. Not only would this end the strike, it would also reward the most reasonable party, in theory serving as a disincentive against intransigence in negotiations.

Given the economic climate and the belief that other jurisdictions were becoming more hostile to labour, these reforms were sufficient to maintain the labour movement's support (see Black 1990). Yet the Pawley government was strongly committed to social programs and public investment, so instead of cutting spending during the recessionary period of the early 1980s, it relied extensively on government spending to counteract the recession. This strategy produced a substantial deficit, and to combat this deficit the government introduced massive, and highly unpopular, tax increases in 1986. These increases, coupled with other difficulties, led to its defeat two years later.

The Pawley government was replaced by a minority Conservative government, and then, in 1990, a majority Conservative government that governed until 1999. Led by Gary Filmon, this government was elected on a campaign of moderate change, but over the course of its mandate, its agenda shifted further and further to the right, favouring rural and small business interests. In the government's first full term, it repealed the final offer selection legislation of its predecessor and introduced several, though typically minor, anti-labour reforms. For example, the government expanded employer "free speech" rights, that is, rights to communicate with employees during an organizing campaign. It also raised the level of support necessary for automatic or "card" certification from 55 to 65 percent. These reforms angered the labour movement, which mounted a campaign against the government in the April 1995 election. Despite this campaign, the Filmon government succeeded in winning another term.

After its re-election, the Filmon government stepped up its attack on labour. First, under the guise of improving the rights of individual union members, it enacted a number of anti-labour amendments to the *Labour Relations Act*. These included:

1.   elimination of the union card system for automatic certification altogether, replacing it with a mandatory certification vote, nor-

mally to be held within seven working days of union application for certification,

2.   cumbersome financial reporting requirements for unions, which could be initiated at the request of any single union member,

3.   the right for the minister of labour to order a ratification vote on the employer's last offer during a strike, if requested by the employer,

4.   a requirement that unions establish a process to enable individual members to opt out of political contributions through their dues,

5.   restrictions on expedited grievance mediation/arbitration procedures to cases involving an employee's dismissal or a suspension of more than 30 days, and

6.   a provision permitting employers to fire striking workers "for a cause for which the employee might have been discharged outside the context of a strike or lockout."

Of these reforms, the provision allowing for employees to be fired for strike behaviour seemed especially punitive, because it rendered striking employees subject to discipline for behaviours that are commonplace during a strike (for example, speaking against their employer in public). But the elimination of automatic card certification was perhaps the most harmful. There is strong evidence that automatic certification has important implications for union organizing success, even where there are procedures in place to expedite the voting process (Godard 2003). Perhaps as a result, the "win rate," or percentage of organizing attempts in which the union won certification, dropped from an average of 75 percent in the three years prior to this legislation to 64 percent in the three years after, returning to its former level only after the Filmon government was voted out of office in 1999 and its reforms were partly reversed.

Second, the government followed an agenda of public sector cuts and privatization, including the sale of the Manitoba Telephone System (Phillips and Stecher 2001). In response to a strike by home-care workers (see below), it also introduced legislation enabling the government to unilaterally, and at any time during, before, or after a public sector strike, designate essential services, subject only to appeal to the labour board by the union affected. The government also introduced changes to bargaining in the public school system. The minister of education was given the authority to unilaterally determine bargaining structure and representation, and the system of compulsory arbitration in the school system was modified to eliminate the right of teachers to arbitration over class sizes and to require arbitrators to place higher priority on a school board's budget and hence ability to pay when deciding awards.

The effects of the government's cut-backs to the civil service were muted by a long tradition of non-militancy among the majority of members in the Manitoba Government Employees Union (MGEU). Although government actions created substantial tensions between the union and management, and a politicization of many elements of the union membership, the working arrangement between the MGEU and the Civil Service Commission was not seriously injured (ibid.). Yet the government's aggressive position did contribute to a series of bitter quasi-public sector strikes in late 1995 and in 1996, including a 23-day strike at the University of Manitoba over academic freedom. In response to government pressures, management demanded the elimination of layoff provisions that faculty believed prevented them from being singled out for their academic and political beliefs (Godard 1998). Other strikes included a five-week provincewide home-care worker strike over contracting-out, a two-month strike by personal-care home workers over proposed cuts to wages and seniority provisions, and a four-month strike by casino workers over pay and benefit levels, in which replacement workers were used. The government also appeared to side with the employer in a number of private sector strikes (Stecher 1997).

Overall, the second highest number of days lost to strike activity since 1919 occurred in 1996, behind only the strike wave of 1978. While this was not entirely due to government actions, the government helped to create a climate that made the labour movement increasingly insecure and employers increasingly emboldened. Government actions appear to have been motivated in part by deficit problems (as in other jurisdictions, the deficit ballooned out of control during the 1992–93 recession) and by a desire to create a more positive climate for investment. But it also appears that they were motivated by pressures from rural members to adopt a more conservative agenda, and, perhaps, were intended as retribution for the labour movement's active anti-government position in the preceding election.

As happened after the widespread labour unrest of 1978, the ruling Conservative government was replaced in 1999 by a majority NDP government. The Filmon government's demise was not entirely due to its labour policies. After 11 years in office, a certain "fatigue factor" had set in, and like other provincial governments, the Filmon government was attacked for its health sector cutbacks. It had also been embarrassed by its connection to a vote-rigging attempt in the 1995 election. Finally, the government's election strategy was disastrous. The Manitoba Conservatives relied on strategists from the Progressive Conservative Party of Ontario, who convinced their Manitoba counterparts to promise policies from that province, most notably massive tax cuts. Although the Conservatives promised to balance this policy with eventual spending increases made possible through economic growth, Manitoba voters rejected it, believing that it would likely bankrupt the province and ultimately undermine social programs.

Perhaps more fundamentally, the Filmon government had been able to justify its cutbacks on the basis of the need for a balanced budget. After this was achieved in 1997, the government's mandate for further reform was exhausted. Manitobans also just did not trust the government's apparent intention to move the province even further to the right. The special features of the Manitoba context, including the strength of the labour community, appear to have rendered the government's economic and fiscal policy politically infeasible once the budget was under control.

The Filmon years have been characterized as a neo-conservative economic "experiment" (Black and Silver 1999). This experiment was of course not unique to Manitoba. But some of the conditions that gave rise to it may have been. As noted earlier, the advent of free trade accelerated the Canadian economy's shift toward a north-south alignment, further eroding Manitoba's role as the lynchpin in an east-west economy. A new economic strategy was thus needed (Black and Silver 1999). Yet the economic success of the Filmon government's policies was at best uncertain, at least as of the end of the Filmon government's mandate (ibid.; also see below). Socially and politically, they only exacerbated the class divide. Although the Filmon government may have been able to move the province substantially to the right, neo-conservative policies that may be politically feasible in other provinces simply did not fit with the Manitoba reality and, judging by the fates of earlier right-wing governments, never have.

The election of the NDP brought with it some initial expectation of a substantial shift in labour policy. Not only was the new premier, Gary Doer, a former president of the MGEU, the new government's orientation was also thought to be similar to the "third way" of the Blair (Labour) government in Britain, which had at the time begun to implement a number of workplace consultation rights and mildly progressive legal reforms (Metcalfe 1999; Wood and Godard 1999). Yet no such shift took place (to the date of this writing). In 2000, the Doer government enacted a number of labour law reforms, but these tended to be mild for an

NDP government, only partially reversing the legislation passed by the Filmon government. The main changes were:

1. Restoration of the provision for card certification, but with a 65 percent sign-up requirement.
2. Introduction of a provision under which the Labour Relations Board can order arbitration once a strike had lasted 60 days or more, if so requested by either the union or the employer, and provided that the board is satisfied that a settlement is unlikely in the next 30 days and that the party requesting arbitration has been bargaining "sufficiently and seriously."
3. Elimination of the provision broadening the right of employers to fire employees for their behaviour during a strike or lockout.
4. Elimination of the union financial reporting requirements enacted by the Filmon government.

Despite their mildness, these reforms met with a massive attack from elements in the business community. Partly as a result, the Doer government subsequently showed little appetite for further reforms (at least as of this writing). With the exception of some strengthening of health and safety laws and a reversal of Filmon government reforms to public school arbitration criteria, it made few changes that might distinguish it as a social democratic government, largely, it seems, for fear of alienating the business community.

The Doer government's timidity became especially apparent in early 2002, when a local bus manufacturer (MCI) controlled by a New York-based private equity firm threatened to move its operations to the southern United States unless its approximately 1,000 union workers voted in favour of contract amendments that would undermine job security, freeze pay levels, and extend the collective agreement to 2010. The employer refused to negotiate over these changes or to offer any effective *quid pro quo* (e.g., profit-sharing) and, after a vote in which the edict was rejected, announced that it would leave the province in the fall of 2003. Perhaps not coincidentally, this was the expected time of the next provincial election. The employer also claimed, however, that it would reverse this decision if another vote was held and workers voted in favour, provided that union leaders did not advise their members in advance and the vote was supervised by the Labour Board. Premier Doer not only failed to voice concerns over the employer's tactics, he placed considerable pressure on union leaders to hold a second vote and publicly recommended that workers vote in favour. Another vote was held, and the workers did vote in favour. But any benefits to be derived from the premier's inter-vention remained elusive as of June 2003.[5]

The government's weak labour law reforms, coupled with the MCI debacle and with public statements by the premier, suggest an end to any social democratic tradition within the Manitoba NDP, if not in general, then at least in the area of labour relations policy. Although labour lead-ers have been muted in their public criticisms of the Doer government, they have been clearly disappointed by its policies. Considered in con-junction with the business community's reaction to those labour law re-forms that have been implemented, it seems that the class divide remains alive and well in Manitoba.

Current Structure of Industrial Relations

In spite of the Filmon government's labour policies and the Doer government's subsequent timidity, the Manitoba labour movement ap-pears to have remained relatively healthy. As of 2001, union density was estimated to be 35 percent, behind only Newfoundland and Quebec, and substantially higher than the national average of 30 percent.[6] Otherwise, the structure of labour relations in Manitoba has remained in most re-spects unremarkable. As of the early 1990s (the last date for which infor-mation is available), roughly four in ten union members were in unions affiliated only with the Canadian Labour Congress (CLC), and another three in ten with both the American Federation of Labor-Congress of Industrial Organizations (AFL-CIO) and the CLC (Manitoba Depart-ment of Labour 1992). This closely mirrored the figures for Canada as-a-whole, especially if the Canadian-wide figures are adjusted to allow for Quebec, where there are a number of additional federations. Finally, there is a single provincial labour federation, the Manitoba Federation of Labour.

There are no employer organizations distinctive to the province. Virtually all collective bargaining is at the employer or establishment level, so there are only a few industry associations (in construction and garment manufacturing) established specifically for the intention of collective bar-gaining. However, the Manitoba chapter of the Canadian Federation of Independent Business took an especially high profile on industrial relations issues in the late 1990s, with its president, rather than a government official, serving as the main spokesperson for the 1997 changes to the *Labour Relations Act* by the Filmon government.

In addition, Manitoba has a unique joint labour-management body, the Manitoba Labour-Management Review Committee, consisting of a chairperson, a vice-chairperson, a government representative, a secretary, and equal numbers of labour and management representatives. As discussed earlier, this committee was first established by the Roblin government in 1964, although it was referred to at the time as the Labour Legislation Review Committee, and has frequently been referred to as the "Woods Committee," after its first chairperson, McGill University professor, H.D. Woods. It has historically played an active advisory role in helping to formulate policy, and has been involved in almost all legislation. Its role was diminished under the Filmon government, which largely ignored its recommendation that the government make only small changes to labour law when it enacted its 1996–97 amendments. However, it was revived by the Doer government in early 2000 and restructured to include fewer labour and management representatives (from 12 to 5 of each), in order to make it less unwieldy.

Current Labour Law and Policy

Labour laws in Manitoba are also similar to those of other Canadian jurisdictions. In general, workers have a legally protected right to organize unions and engage in collective bargaining free from intimidation. With the exception of teachers, police, and fire-fighters, who have a right to compulsory arbitration should a settlement not be achieved, workers enjoy the right to strike provided that a good-faith attempt has been made to reach agreement and certain timeliness restrictions have been met. Employers continue to have a right to employ replacement workers during a strike, but strikers have a right to displace any such workers once a strike is over.

Despite these broad similarities, Manitoba also has a number of provisions that differ from those of other provinces. Perhaps in reflection of Manitoba's unique industrial relations context, these are directed primarily at conflict resolution. The one with perhaps the most commonality to other provinces is first contract arbitration, although this is not available in a number of other provinces. However, the provision in the August 2000 reforms allowing the minister of labour to order arbitration after a strike has lasted 60 days is unique. This provision provides workers with some assurance that the strike will be settled within a reasonable period of time if they make a reasonable effort to reach a settlement, and employers with less incentive to try to undermine the union. In particular, it discourages employer attempts to break unions by either shutting down until striking workers give up or by hiring replacement workers with the intention of extending a strike indefinitely. It would thus appear to be a substitute for the system of final offer selection enacted by the Pawley government — one that is much simpler and potentially more effective.[7]

Another distinguishing feature is an expedited arbitration procedure (mentioned above), under which either the union or the employee can apply to the labour board to have a grievance expedited if that grievance involves unjust dismissal or suspension of more than 30 days, or if the board considers the matter to be "of an exceptional nature." There are also provisions under the law for grievance mediation, under which the parties can request a mediator to help them resolve a grievance, and for the minister of labour to order mediation in the event of an impasse in collective bargaining. Under the latter provision, the mediator is required to issue a report to the minister and the parties if a settlement is not reached, and this may be released to the public, thereby placing pressure on the parties to reach a settlement lest a report critical of their position is issued. A further difference, one that is not related to conflict resolution per se and is used infrequently, is a provision that allows the Labour Relations Board to award punitive damages of up to $2,000 in the event that an unfair labour practice has been held to occur, but the aggrieved party has not lost income as a result and hence is not eligible for a compensatory award. Finally, Manitoba is the only province that does not permit strikes by teachers.

Dispute Patterns

As discussed earlier and illustrated in Figure 1, Manitoba has historically experienced considerable volatility in labour disputes. On a year-by-year basis, strike activity has tended to be relatively low. Yet there have been a number of years in which it has markedly increased. Because the population of the province is relatively small, and the number of annual strikes is also small, such increases have in some years reflected either random fluctuations or a "contagion" effect, under which particular employers or unions have decided to adopt more aggressive bargaining policies, and a few others have followed. But in other years, they have tended to reflect more broadly-based conflicts. This is explained by the Manitoba industrial relations context. As discussed earlier, the fragile nature of the economy has led union leaders and their members to be more reticent about striking (and, perhaps, employers more likely to stand firm if a strike occurs), yet the class divisions which have characterized the province have

FIGURE 1
STRIKE ACTIVITY IN MANITOBA, 1910–2001

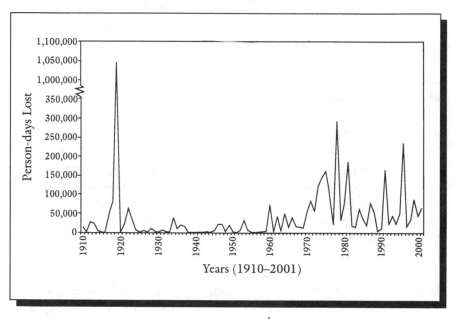

Source: The Labour Gazette, Strikes and Lockouts in Canada, as obtained from the Manitoba Department of Labour.

also led to a somewhat stronger impulse to conflict, an impulse that is suppressed only as long as workers do not perceive themselves as under direct attack. Thus, the two sets of opposing forces that define industrial relations, one for conflict and one for cooperation (see Godard 2000), have been stronger in Manitoba than in most other provinces. While labour and management may have an even greater interest than their counterparts in other provinces in maintaining some semblance of a truce, this truce has tended to be a fragile one.

It is also notable that this truce tends to break down when Conservative governments are in power. Since the first NDP was elected in 1969, the four worst years for strike activity have all been under the Conservatives (1978, 1981, 1991, and 1996), even though these two parties have been in office for equal periods of time. Moreover, while there have also been years with relatively high strike activity under NDP governments, most notably from 1973 to 1975, record high levels of strike activity occurred throughout the country in those years. Thus, while these years may have also reflected more broadly-based conflicts, these conflicts were not unique to Manitoba.

Why has the election of Conservative governments brought increased conflict to Manitoba? One answer is that it both emboldens anti-union elements in the business community and gives rise to a more insecure and hence combative labour movement, especially if this election is accompanied by the introduction of pro-employer labour legislation, as in 1978, 1991, and 1996–97.[8] Yet it appears that a more general, class-based explanation may also apply, particularly in Manitoba. Specifically, strike levels also rise because social programs and the public sector are perceived to be under threat, thereby bringing broader class divisions to the surface. This was the case in Manitoba's two worst years since the Winnipeg General Strike, 1978 and 1996. In both years, broader social coalitions emerged to fight initiatives of right-wing governments, and these coalitions encouraged and supported industrial unrest. Again, this is consistent with the special context of industrial relations in Manitoba, with its underlying class divisions and the political shifts this has engendered. Also consistent with this tradition has been a tendency for governments to either modify their approach to labour (as did the Roblin government in the 1960s) or to be defeated in the subsequent election (as did the Weir, Lyon, and Filmon governments in 1969, 1981, and 1999, respectively).

CURRENT INDUSTRIAL RELATIONS INITIATIVES AND CLIMATE

Few noteworthy or unique innovations in collective bargaining or contract provisions have occurred in Manitoba. However, as with employers in other provinces, there has been considerable experimentation with the adoption of progressive human resource management practices and new forms of work organization. The extent to which this experimentation has given rise to "transformed" labour-management relations, characterized by radically redesigned work processes and high levels of trust and commitment, is not clear. There *have* been a few noteworthy cases. One has been Winnipeg's third largest private sector employer, Palliser Furniture (Nairne 1998), which has established a training and educational program which it refers to as "Palliser University." Another is Bristol Aerospace, which has implemented a system of autonomous work teams which are allowed substantial control over the work process. Still another is Friesen's Corporation, which is known for its progressive management practices and employee stock ownership scheme.

Despite these noteworthy cases, a 1996 survey of 204 large and medium-sized (over 50 employees) Winnipeg employers indicated that truly transformed workplaces were relatively rare (see Winnipeg 2000 1997). As indicated in Table 3, a large minority of these employers reported internal progression policies and merit-based promotion. But many employers have used these practices for decades. More relevant is the extent to which these employers have adopted more participative practices and, in particular, how far they have moved from traditional methods of designing work and instead adopted a system of autonomous work teams. As indicated in the table, 35 percent did report some form of participation program, but only 15 percent had implemented alternative job designs. In addition, this survey did not address how seriously these reforms had been implemented, so it is impossible to determine if they had been adopted superficially, in response to contemporary management fads, or whether sincere attempts to transform the workplace had occurred.

Evidence on the effects of new forms of work organization is somewhat mixed (see Godard 2001, 2004). Perhaps more important is whether employers invest extensively in vocational training for employees, as such training is typically viewed as essential if employers are serious about "empowering" workers. In effect, such training suggests that an employer is following the kind of "high-skill," "high-performance" strategy often assumed by proponents of new work practices. Yet Table 3 indicates that vocational training remained relatively rare as of the mid-1990s, with only 13 percent of respondents reporting that they had such a program involving at least half of their employees. Again, the study did not indicate just how intensive these programs were, so even this figure may over-estimate the extent to which "high-skill" strategies had been adopted.

The study of work practices also included Calgary and Kansas City. Generally, it found that Winnipeg employers were neither less nor more likely to adopt progressive human resource management practices than were their counterparts in these other two cities, although Calgary respondents did report a significantly higher propensity to adopt formal participation programs — a finding that may reflect lower union density in that city and possibly a use of these programs to prevent workers from organizing unions.

More important, however, was the relative pessimism of Winnipeg respondents. They were on average less optimistic about their companies' prospects for growth, in both jobs and output, and less positive about their city than employers in the other two cities. This may reflect concrete problems confronted by employers, or it may reflect a

TABLE 3

MANAGEMENT AND HUMAN RESOURCE PRACTICES OF
WINNIPEG EMPLOYERS, 1996

Practice	Percent Reporting Practice (%)
A system that encourages filling employment vacancies by promotion rather than hiring externally.	71
A merit-based promotion process.	70
A flexible or alternative work scheduling program for some of your employees.	56
Wages and benefits that are considered to be above the industry average.	45
A variable pay program for non-management employees, based on incentives or performance.	36
A formal employee-participation program that encourages your employees to contribute input into the operation and organization of the work area.	35
A company-sponsored, non-vocational training program for non-management employees.	19
A formal human resource strategic plan, integrated with the overall organizational business plan and strategy.	18
Personal or family care programs beyond those required by law.	18
Formally implemented job designs for non-management employees based on job rotation, enlargement, or self-directed work teams.	15
A company-sponsored, vocational training program involving at least half of your employees each year.	13

Source: Based on a 1996 survey mailed to the CEO or human resources manager of the larger corporations in Winnipeg (most had a minimum of 50 full-time employees) conducted by Prairie Research Associates on behalf of Winnipeg 2000. Of an initial sample of 410 firms, 204 participated.

particular psyche.[9] Either explanation is consistent with a basic theme of this chapter: that Winnipeg has historically had to fight relative decline, resulting in a somewhat less confident and secure management community. Moreover, although a parallel survey of workers in each of the three communities revealed few differences in worker attitudes, the employer survey indicated that Winnipeg employers rated the quality of labour-management relations in their city less favourably than their counterparts in the other two cities (Winnipeg 2000 1997). Whether this reflects poorer relations in their own firms is not clear. It more likely reflects the high level of labour unrest in Winnipeg in 1996, as earlier discussed. But it is also consistent with another argument here: that class antagonisms have remained more widespread in Winnipeg than elsewhere, even if these antagonisms tend to be muted by the precariousness of the economy.

PROSPECTS FOR THE FUTURE: BEYOND THE DIVIDE?

It has been argued that Manitoba's growth during the Filmon era entailed a "low pay–low cost" government strategy, reflected in attacks on the labour movement and the cutting of social services and post-secondary education funding in an attempt to establish a low-tax, low-cost business environment (e.g., Black and Silver 1999). Critics have focused in particular on low-paying call centre and hog-processing jobs attracted by the government, especially a massive hog-processing operation in Brandon, where the employer has since been forced to import labour from Mexico because the wages paid are too low to attract and retain Canadian workers (see Smith 2002).

The statistical evidence suggests some support for this argument. By the end of the Filmon government's tenure, the average wage for hourly paid workers was generally unchanged relative to the national average, at 90.9 percent. But average weekly earnings had dropped, from 91.7 percent of the national average as of 1988, when the Filmon government took office, to 89.1 percent by 1999, when it left office (Statistics Canada 2001), leaving Manitoba earnings among the lowest in Canada. Meanwhile, the cost of living had increased by five percentage points more than for Canada as a whole (34.6 versus 29.5 percent, respectively), suggesting an even greater decline in the relative standard of living. Moreover, and perhaps reflective of a growth in low-wage, low-skill jobs, Manitoba's productivity growth per hour worked averaged 1 percent per year from 1989 to 1998, compared to an average of 1.29 percent for Canada as a whole. It was ahead of only Nova Scotia's, PEI's, and New Brunswick's (Centre for the Study of Living Standards 2002). Finally, capital investment in Manitoba, per capita, remained at only three-quarters of the national average throughout the 1990s (Manitoba. Bureau of Statistics 2002, Table 34; Statistics Canada 2002a).

Regardless of how strong the evidence of a low-pay economy may or may not be, and regardless of what the Filmon government's intentions may have been, there can be little doubt that Manitobans could benefit from a strategy focused more on the creation of "high-pay" jobs, not just because such a strategy means improved living standards and government revenues if successful, but also because it could help to reverse Manitoba's negative migration trends. To this end, Manitoba enjoys a number of advantages presently, including the lowest electricity rates on the continent, a low cost of living, and a relatively high quality yet inexpensive labour force.[10] By enhancing skill and education levels while ensuring that, for these levels, Manitoba's labour force continues to represent something of a "bargain," the province could develop a distinctive niche in the North American economy, one that could render it a more attractive place to work and live.

The province's ability to develop such a niche will be substantially improved if it can also foster a less adversarial labour relations environment. In view of the Manitoba context, this will require the adoption of policies that ensure a more inclusive role for workers and their representatives, not only in the workplace (see Godard 2002), but also in government policy. In North America, such a possibility often seems a pipedream. But the experience of a number of nations suggests that it need not be if it is cautiously designed and enacted to fit the Manitoba context (Baccaro 2002). The history of antagonism between the labour and business communities may no doubt be viewed as a serious impediment to doing so. Yet the precariousness of the Manitoba economy may also render it especially suited to such an arrangement, and Manitoba's history and traditions suggest that the chances for any strategy to succeed may be substantially greater if labour is explicitly included.

In their first budget, proclaimed in May 2000, the NDP took a step in the direction of a higher skills strategy, making provision to double enrolment in the community college system within five years and to cut university tuition by 10 percent. It has also subsequently revealed a strong interest in the development of science-based sectors (e.g., biotechnology) and of hydroelectric power. But although the NDP seems to have built a generally positive relationship with the business community, it appears to have done so in large part by distancing itself from the labour community. The Doer government has made some attempt to overcome the class divide, but it does not, as of this writing, appear prepared to adopt the kinds of policies that are really needed to do so. Instead, every indication has been that it is content to follow a course more consistent with that of the 1960s' Progressive Conservative government of Duff Roblin than with that of a modern social democratic party concerned with achieving a lasting, balanced accord between labour and management or fostering more democratic workplaces (e.g., consultation or co-decision rights).[11] This may reflect a belief that the labour and business communities are not ready to work more closely with one another, but it would also seem to reflect an unwillingness to take the risks needed to move forward. Either way, it means not only that the NDP's economic strategy will likely meet with limited success, but also that the province will miss the opportunity to achieve the kind of egalitarian workplace relations and labour-management partnership arrangements characteristic of, and hence needed to catch up to, more advanced democratic societies such as those in northern Europe.

CONCLUSIONS

This chapter has emphasized the unique nature of industrial relations in Manitoba, particularly the tensions between the influence of historical class divisions and precarious economic conditions. It has also emphasized the neo-conservative "experiment" of the Progressive Conservative government throughout the 1990s. Not only did this experiment appear to aggravate the class divide substantially, it seems to have provided few major benefits to Manitobans, despite the costs involved. A case can be made that the government had little choice in view of the economic conditions of the time and that its limited success reflects the especially difficult conditions faced by the province. Yet as also illustrated by experiences of the Filmon government's Conservative predecessors throughout the postwar era, the neo-conservative alternative would seem to be especially ill-suited to Manitoba, both economically *and* politically. Rather than further aggravate the class divide, as right-wing policies have always done, Manitoba needs policies that will move it beyond this divide. Although the policies and practices of the NDP government elected in 1999 have embodied a shift away from neo-conservativism, they have also fallen far short of establishing a truly new direction, especially in industrial relations. It is thus unlikely that Manitoba will be able to move beyond its class divide, at least in the immediate future.

NOTES

I thank Gerry Friesen, Julie Guard, Terry Hercus, Paul Phillips, Joe Rose, and Mark Thompson for their comments on earlier versions of this paper. I also thank Glenda Segal of the Manitoba Department of Labour and Janet Duff of the Manitoba Labour Board for their assistance.

[1]The evidence in support of this thesis is mixed. A 1996 Angus Reid survey of 1,495 Canadians and 1,750 Americans found that Canadians were more supportive of state intervention in the economy, but that there was little difference in US and Canadian views toward unions. In the US, 70 percent stated support for unions, compared to 67 percent in Canada (Lipset and Meltz 1997).

[2]For a more extensive discussion of this strike and the events surrounding it, see Smith (1984, 35-54) and Bercuson (1974).

[3]There was also widespread strike activity in BC (Phillips 1967, 73), and the previous year witnessed a general strike in Seattle. Yet the Winnipeg General Strike is perhaps the most famous event in Canadian labour history, and seems to have had a defining effect on Manitoba that remains to this day. In 1994, there were a number of activities to commemorate the 75th anniversary of the strike, and favourable mention of the strike still offended some members of "old" Winnipeg families.

[4]Such a vote could be held either 60 to 30 days before contract expiry or 60 to 70 days after expiry. It could also be called by employers, although of the 86 applications made while FOS was in place, no employer application was supported by the employees. See Kelly (1991).

[5]After the workers voted in favour, the employer announced that it would still be moving unless the three levels of government provided an acceptable incentive package. In January 2003, a $20 million government support package was announced, based on promised job increases. But as of May 2003, MCI announced that, due to poor markets, it would be embarking on substantial lay-offs. They also announced that they would extend the summer shut-down period (normally four weeks) to eight weeks unless workers agreed to a reduced workweek. The workers voted against doing so.

[6]This is largely because (as of 2001) the Manitoba public sector accounts for 35 percent of all employees and has a density of 75 percent, compared to 30 percent and 70 percent, respectively, for Canada as a whole. Private sector density is 19 percent, compared to 18.3 percent for Canada as a whole (Godard 2003).

[7]The effectiveness of the FOS system has been a matter of some debate (e.g., Kelly 1991; Black and Silver 1990; Grant 1990). A major criticism is that it favoured unions because employer requests for FOS had to be approved by a vote of employees.

[8]Note that the 1991 reforms were not passed until the following year, which is why the 1991 figure at first appears inconsistent with the date of enactment.

[9]This latter possibility tends to be borne out by the tendency for respondents in Winnipeg to rate the availability of low-cost utilities less favourably than their counterparts in the other two cities, even though Winnipeg has less costly hydro rates (Winnipeg 2000 1997, 38).

[10]As of 2001, Winnipeg was tied with Regina for the lowest cost of living of all Canadian capital cities (see Manitoba. Department of Finance 2001). Consumer Price Index data indicate that the cost of living in Winnipeg was 92 percent of the average for cities with over 500,000 occupants.

[11]For example, the Doer government's interest in hydro-electric development parallels that of the Roblin government.

REFERENCES

Baccaro, L. 2002. "What is Dead and What is Alive in the Theory of Corporatism?" Paper presented at the *British Journal of Industrial Relations* Conference on Politics and Industrial Relations, Windsor Great Park, Windsor, England, 16-17 September.

Bercuson, D. 1974. *Confrontation at Winnipeg: Labour, Industrial Relations, and the General Strike*. Montreal: McGill-Queen's University Press.

Bellan, R. 1978. *Winnipeg's First Century*. Winnipeg: Queenston House.

Black, E. 1990. "Labour in Manitoba: A Refuge in Social Democracy," in *The Political Economy of Manitoba*, ed. J. Silver and J. Hull. Regina: Canadian Plains Institute, University of Regina, pp. 92-127.

Black, E. and J. Silver. 1990. "Contradictions and Limitations of Final Offer Selection: The Manitoba Experience," *Relations industrielles-Industrial Relations* 45 (1):146-65.

—— 1999. *A Flawed Economic Experiment: The New Political Economy of Manitoba*. Winnipeg: Canadian Centre for Policy Alternatives.

Centre for the Study of Living Standards. 2002. "Productivity Tables." At <http://www.csls.ca/ptabl.html>.

Godard, J. 1998. "Strikes and the Law: A Critical Analysis," *Relations industrielles-Industrial Relations* 53(2):258-77.

—— 2000. *Industrial Relations, the Economy, and Society*, 2d ed. Toronto: Captus Press.

—— 2001. "High Performance *and* the Transformation of Work? The Implications of Alternative Work Practices for the Nature and Experience of Work," *Industrial and Labor Relations Review* 54 (4):776-805.

—— 2002. "Labour Unions, Workplace Rights, and Canadian Public Policy." Paper presented at the Annual Meeting of the Canadian Industrial Relations Association, Toronto, 22-24 June.

—— 2003. "Do Labor Laws Matter? The Density Decline and Convergence Thesis Revisited," *Industrial Relations*, forthcoming.

—— 2004. "A Critical Assessment of the High Performance Paradigm as Best Practice in Liberal Market Economies," *British Journal of Industrial Relations*, forthcoming.

Gonick, C. 1990. "The Manitoba Economy Since World War II," in *The Political Economy of Manitoba*, ed. J. Silver and J. Hull. Regina: Canadian Plains Institute, University of Regina, pp. 25-48.

Grant, H. 1990. "Contradictions and Limitations of Final Offer Selection: The Manitoba Experience. A Comment," *Relations industrielles-Industrial Relations* 45 (1):166-68.

Kelly, L. 1991. "Manitoba's Experience with Final Offer Arbitration," *Labour Law Journal* (June):381-84.

Lipset, S.M. 1964, "Canada and the US: A Comparative View," *Canadian Journal of Sociology and Anthropology* 1:173-85.

—— 1990. *Continental Divide: The Values and Institutions of the United States and Canada*. Boston: Routledge.

Lipset, S.M. and N. Meltz. 1998. "Canadian and American Attitudes Toward Work and Institutions," *Perspectives on Work* 1 (3):14-19.

Manitoba. Bureau of Statistics. 1999. *Manitoba Statistical Review*, April.

—— 2002. *Manitoba Statistical Review*, April.

Manitoba. Department of Finance. 2001. "The Manitoba Advantage." Appendage to the 2001 budget speech.

Manitoba. Department of Labour. 1973. *Annual Report, 1973.* Winnipeg: Government of Manitoba.

Metcalf, D. 1999. "Prime Minister Blair's New Industrial Relations Program," *Perspectives on Work* 3 (1):12-17.

Morton, W.L. 1967. *Manitoba: A History.* Toronto: University of Toronto Press.

Nairne, D. 1998. "Prosperity, But at What Cost?" *Winnipeg Free Press*, 7 October, p. A8.

—— 2000. "Mistake Erases Job Growth," *Winnipeg Free Press*, 14 February, pp. A1-A2.

Newman, P.C. 1998. *Canadian Establishment*, Vol. 3, *Titans: How the New Canadian Establishment Seized Power.* Toronto: Viking.

Phillips, P. 1967. *No Power Greater: A Century of Labour in British Columbia.* Vancouver: BC Federation of Labour Boag Foundation.

—— 1990. "Manitoba in the Agrarian Period: 1870-1940," in *The Political Economy of Manitoba*, ed. J. Silver and J. Hull. Regina: Canadian Plains Institute, University of Regina, pp. 3-24.

Phillips, P. and C. Stecher. 2001. "Fiscal Restraint, Legislated Concessions and Labour Relations in the Manitoba Civil Service 1988-1997," in *Public Sector Labour Relations in an Era of Restraint and Restructuring*, ed. G. Swimmer. Oxford: Oxford University Press, pp. 96-126.

Smith, D. 1984. *Let Us Rise: An Illustrated History of the Manitoba Labour Movement.* Vancouver: New Star.

—— 2002. "Slaughterhouse Lies," *Manitoba Alternatives* (CCPA) 2 (2/3):12-14.

Snidal, D.J. 1967, "A Financial History of Manitoba from 1950 to 1965." Master's thesis, University of Manitoba.

Statistics Canada. 2001. *Annual Estimates of Employment, Earnings, and Hours.* Ottawa: Communications Canada.

—— 2002*a*. *Canada at a Glance.* Ottawa: Statistics Canada.

—— 2002*b*. *Labour Force Survey Estimates* CANSIM II, Table 282-0008. Ottawa: Statistics Canada.

Stecher, C. 1997. "1996: A Year of Turmoil in Labour-Management Relations," *The Newsletter.* Winnipeg: Labour and Workplace Studies, University of Manitoba, Spring.

Winnipeg 2000. 1997. *Winnipeg's Workplace: Report on the Survey of Managers and Employees*. Winnipeg: Prairie Research Associates Inc.

Wiseman, N. 1983. *Social Democracy in Manitoba: A History of the CCF-NDP*. Winnipeg: University of Manitoba Press.

Wood, S. and J. Godard. 1998. "The Statutory Union Recognition Procedure in the Employment Relations Bill: A Comparative Analysis," *British Journal of Industrial Relations* 37 (2):203-45.

6 SASKATCHEWAN: SOCIAL EXPERIMENTATION, ECONOMIC DEVELOPMENT AND THE TEST OF TIME

Larry Haiven

Résumé — La Saskatchewan a toujours été une des provinces canadiennes les moins industrialisées et les moins densément peuplées. Par contre, elle a été une des plus dynamiques et progressives en matière de participation et d'initiative des citoyens, de droit du travail et d'aide sociale. Elle a été le foyer d'un des mouvements coopératifs les plus visionnaires et dynamiques du pays, la première province à accorder le droit de vote aux femmes, la première à élire un gouvernement s'affichant ouvertement social démocrate et la première à mettre en vigueur le droit moderne du travail. Elle a été l'initiatrice de l'assurance-maladie et de la législation en matière d'hygiène et de sécurité du travail, ainsi que la première province à nationaliser une grande industrie primaire. Bref, elle a été un creuset d'expérimentation économique et sociale. Cette audace prend sa source dans une population d'agriculteurs et de manœuvres, dispersés dans un vaste territoire, rudes et indépendants, mais ayant un penchant pour les solutions collectives.

Chercher à tirer plus de revenus des abondantes richesses naturelles a été à la base de l'économie politique de la Saskatchewan. Cette quête a entraîné une double désaffection : la désaffection envers la « grande entreprise et le monde de la finance » qui, après avoir méconnu cette province, en ont exploité la vulnérabilité; la désaffection à l'égard du gouvernement fédéral perçu comme le représentant politique des élites distantes. Cette double désaffection s'est accentuée quand cette province agricole a découvert et entrepris d'exploiter d'abondants gisements de pétrole, de potasse et d'uranium.

Cette double désaffection a provoqué en retour deux tendances opposées. Principalement, une forte propension au populisme, de droite ou de gauche à divers degrés, qui prônait la méfiance envers le pouvoir et la participation du citoyen, faisait valoir la « sagesse » des gens ordinaires et, paradoxalement, encourageait le culte envers le leader charismatique et visionnaire. À l'opposé, une technocratie composée d'experts, de fonctionnaires et de professionnels qui préconisaient le développement de la province, le modernisme, l'efficacité et l'expertise. Le populisme et la technocratie ont eu tous deux des versions de droite et de gauche.

L'existence de variantes de droite et de gauche de ces tendances illustre un autre trait marquant du terrain politique de la Saskatchewan : la bipolarité de la politique. On pourrait vraiment dire que la politique a été plus polarisée en Saskatchewan que dans les autres provinces.

La bipolarité s'est reflétée sur les relations industrielles dont le parcours est particulièrement à l'image de montagnes russes. Lorsque des partis sociodémocrates (la CCF ou le NPD par la suite) étaient au pouvoir, les syndicats pouvaient s'attendre aux lois, règlements et politiques les plus favorables aux travailleurs en Amérique du Nord, et ces attentes n'ont pas été déçues, jusqu'à l'arrivée du dernier gouvernement NPD. Par contre, lorsque des partis plus axés sur le marché étaient à la tête du gouvernement, les travailleurs perdaient une bonne partie de ce qu'ils avaient gagné précédemment, parfois même la totalité. Toutefois, les sociodémocrates ont pu se vanter d'avoir été au pouvoir pendant 44 ans sur 61 durant la dernière partie du XXᵉ siècle. Au cours de la dernière décennie, leur zèle traditionnel à l'égard de la réalisation de réformes s'est peu manifesté. Ni les syndicats ni le patronat ne s'en sont réjouis, mais ce peut bien être la clé d'une résistance de l'électorat presque unique au Canada.

INTRODUCTION

Saskatchewan has always been one of the least industrialized provinces in Canada and one of the smallest in population. Yet in citizen activism and self-help, in labour law and in social welfare provision, it has been one of the most innovative and progressive. It was home to energetic cooperative movements, the first province in which women voted, first to elect an avowedly social-democratic government and first to enact modern labour law. It was the originator of medicare and groundbreaking occupational health and safety legislation, and first to nationalize a major resource industry. In short, it has been a crucible of economic and social experimentation. The origins of this adventurousness lay in a population of farmers and labourers, widely dispersed, rugged and independent, but with a penchant for collective solutions.

Like Manitoba and Alberta, Saskatchewan became part of Canada with the transfer of "Rupert's Land" from the Hudson's Bay Company to the new Dominion in 1868. This treasure of fertile land and natural resources drew the business-state consortium in central Canada to colonize the west as an economic hinterland. The plan was simple: to establish a breadbasket by populating the region with farmers who would also be a market for central Canadian manufacturing. Eventually, the need for infrastructure to support the population and industries outstripped the meager revenues of the provinces (even with the federal government stipend in lieu of land and resource sovereignty). This led to demands for more control of their politics and economics, and the next one hundred years were spent seeking equality in the Canadian political economy.

Thus, the major themes in the history of Saskatchewan's political economy were formed. Most important was the search to capture more of the revenues from the abundant natural wealth. This quest produced twin alienations — alienation from "big business and finance" that at first ignored then exploited the development of the vulnerable province, and alienation from the central government, which was seen as representing the remote elites.

UNDERLYING TRENDS

These alienations in turn fuelled two divergent trends. Foremost was populism — of both the left-wing and right-wing varieties, so much that "it is clear that Saskatchewan political life has been affected by popularly-based critiques of elite economic and political power more than any other Canadian province" (Dunn and Laycock 1992, 221). Populism has stressed distrust of authority, citizen participation, the "wisdom" of the ordinary folk, and the cult of the charismatic and visionary leader. A contrary trend involved local citizens assuming control of their political and economic future. A technocracy of experts and bureaucrats emerged, stressing province-building, efficiency, and expertise. Both populism and technocracy divided into left-wing and right-wing versions.

The existence of left- and right-wing variants in the foregoing trends illustrates another important feature of the Saskatchewan political terrain: bipolarity of politics. A Liberal government, which took pains to distance itself from the federal Liberals, led the province from its inception in 1870 to 1929 with a platform of populism and championing farmers' interests. Also, Premier Walter Scott, a former Regina newspaper publisher, considered himself a friend of labour. He recognized a typographical union in his shop and supported labour's broad aims in his publications. But through its first quarter-century, opposition was building and the Liberals were finally defeated in 1929 by an unusual coalition: Conservatives desiring an end to non-Anglo-Saxon immigration and to French in schools; Progressives, an agrarian party born of the disastrous farm economy in the years surrounding World War II, and socialistic elements of the farmer and workers' movements (who had elected a few independents but did not unite as a party until 1932). While the Liberals did come back in 1934 for another ten years, the Farmer-Labour Group, later called the Cooperative Commonwealth Federation (CCF), consolidated its support among a population ravaged by droughts and economic downturns beginning before World War I. After World War II, the CCF became the first social democratic government in North America. Over the next 50 years, Saskatchewan politics seesawed back and forth between the CCF-New Democratic Party (NDP) and a single party of the right.

For half a century, the parties on each side of this political duality followed a predictable electoral cycle: one took power exploiting a populist sentiment in a population tired of the complacency and bureaucracy of the incumbents. It then offered its own technocratic response to the development problems of the day (mild socialism for the CCF-NDP, free-market for the rightist party). But the structural economic problems of a hinterland economy limited government. A frustrated electorate later returned the other party, responding to its populist appeal.

For the labour movement, the political bipolarity was a mixed blessing, a political roller-coaster ride. With the CCF-NDP in power, labour could expect and did receive (until the NDP regime in the 1990s) some of the most pro-labour legislation, regulation, and policy in North America. With the more market-oriented parties in power, labour's gains were eroded and sometimes reversed.

Behind the changeable relationship between labour and government in Saskatchewan's political economy stood a more volatile relationship — between farmers and workers. At times the interests of the two groups of producers coincided, especially when it came to opposing domination by big finance and the central government and when economic recession made both desperate. Both were building collective institutions: unions and agricultural/consumer cooperatives. But there were opposing interests as well. While workers are always employees, subject to the vagaries of a boss, farmers are in essence independent small business people, a *petit bourgeoisie*. Indeed, farmers are often employers, both of farm labour and as collective owners of cooperatives and, later, as owners of agribusinesses. It is ironic that some of the bitterest labour disputes in Saskatchewan have been at producer and consumer cooperatives. Even as the first CCF-NDP regime (1944–64) introduced unprecedented improvements in labour law, it exempted farm labour and hesitated for many years to lower the maximum hours that employees could work in a week. Farmers and workers have also found themselves at odds whenever it came to the movement of crops to market, especially when there is a labour dispute on the railways or in the ports. While Saskatchewan's history includes many instances of collaboration between workers and farmers, it also abounds with strife between them. But more importantly, the political complexion of the province has emerged from the changing electoral alliances that politically influential farmers have made, sometimes with workers and the urban middle class, sometimes with merchants and small capitalists.

The Radical Tradition and the Trade Union Movement

Though small in comparison to the other western provinces, Saskatchewan's labour movement shares the radical tradition that sharply divided eastern Canada from western Canada. One of the first formative influences was the National Policy itself.

> For western Labour ... the major villain was the National Policy. Tariff protection, while of undoubted benefit to both labour and management in central Canada, was a disaster for the West. Not only did it raise prices, but western employers, desperate to undercut Ontario competition in order to survive, were forced to pay their workers lower wages (Abella 1975, 6).

Stuck in the downside of a two-sided economic policy, western workers developed a fierce strain of independence from their fellow trade unionists to the east. While the latter endorsed the conservative and non-ideological craft unions, the westerners were quick to take to a more industrial, class-conscious, and political unionism. Western employers, already indisposed to unions of any sort, fought doubly hard to crush the radical upstarts.

When the federal government, under national emergency powers, seized authority over wages, hours, working conditions, and union-management relations, the Trades and Labour Congress's (TLC) Ottawa headquarters took control of dealings with government away from local

unions, councils, and federations. This worsened the enmity between unionists in the metropolis and the hinterland. Tensions rose when the federal government made strikes in war-related industries illegal in 1918 and
prescribed instant conscription and military law for draft-age violators.
Along with fellow unionists in Calgary and Winnipeg, Regina's labour
council called for a general strike (Cotterill and Davies n.d., III-12[1]). A
ten-day general strike of Winnipeg civic workers in 1918 ended in a labour victory, setting the stage for an unprecedented round of unrest a
year later.

The end of the war brought no reprieve from the war's hardships,
but the gap between hope and reality, especially for the thousands of west-
ern-Canadian veterans returning to unemployment, lit the powder keg.
After being overwhelmed at the 1918 TLC convention, western delegates
vowed to hold their own convention in Calgary the following year. The
delegates vented their bitterness and a majority called for a new Canadian
union movement based on industrial unionism and political action of a
new type. Emboldened by the Russian Revolution, a majority resolved
that: "the system of industrial soviet control by selection of representatives from industries is more efficient and of greater political value than
the present system of government by election from [geographical]
districts." The delegates adopted "proletarian dictatorship" as the way to
achieve socialism, and sent greetings to the new Bolshevik regime in Rus-
sia and called for a referendum among labour to establish the "One Big
Union" (OBU).

The frustrations boiled over later that year in a wave of strikes
across the west. The culmination was the Winnipeg General Strike, re-
counted in Chapter 5 on Manitoba in this volume. In support of the
Winnipeg strikers, trade unionists in cities across Saskatchewan struck.
Railway workers in various centres walked out. In Saskatoon and Prince
Albert, unionists held general strikes lasting several days. But these dissipated from internal dissension and the federal labour minister's warnings
that the Winnipeg event had been plotted by Bolshevik agitators (ibid.,
III-29).

The One Big Union, which had a meteoric rise and fall in the
months after the Winnipeg General Strike, agitated the labour scene in
Saskatchewan. One target of its organizing attempts was the soft coal and
lignite fields on the province's southeastern border, where typically feudal
"company town" conditions existed (use of company housing and company stores as a condition of employment). Though many of the miners
were already represented by the United Mine Workers Union of America,

the owners used the wartime emergency and the provincial police to break a strike and to fire strike leaders in 1917. In 1920, dissatisfied workers joined the OBU. When workers struck again, the employers struck back. Employer agents and the police kidnapped the OBU organizer, drove him across the US border and threatened him with tarring and feathering if he ever returned. Other OBU organizers in the province were expelled from towns and cities by the police, and members were harassed (ibid., III-31).

While the labour radicalism that erupted in 1919 submerged in the face of repression, fatigue and the high economic spirits of the 1920s, the seeds of a new political movement had been planted. With the onset of the Great Depression in 1929, the seeds took root.

The Rise of the CCF

The Depression hit Saskatchewan harder than most provinces. The net value of farm production was negative between 1931 and 1934 and again in 1937 through a combination of lack of demand and "dust bowl" conditions. Joblessness was worse than the 15 percent national average, with 20 percent of wage earners out of work (not counting the many young people on the road and rails) and wages for those still working collapsed.

With the establishment of unemployed relief camps (most federal, some Saskatchewan initiatives), the movement to organize residents was especially strong in the province. Attempts to move activists from Saskatoon's provincial camp in 1933 resulted in the death of an RCMP constable. The federal camp at Dundurn, Saskatchewan, was the largest in the country, with 2,000 residents. When frustrated camp workers across the country organized the "On to Ottawa Trek" in 1935, the federal government chose Regina, a known hotbed of dissent to stop the march. This culminated in the "Regina Riot," the death of a police officer, the injury of hundreds of other people and the arrest of scores of strikers.

A more lasting movement emerged on the moderate left. In 1930, the new United Farmers of Canada (Saskatchewan Branch) and an equally new provincewide Labour Party united in Saskatoon under M.J. Coldwell. The next year, similar elements across the country met in Calgary to form the CCF. The program of the new party was adopted in Regina two years later as the "Regina Manifesto" and, while committing to the path of parliamentary reform, called for socialization of the commanding heights of the economy and state economic planning. In the1934 provincial election, the Farmer-Labour Party (as it was called provincially until 1935) became the Official Opposition in the Saskatchewan legislature. In 1935, two CCFers, Coldwell and T.C. Douglas were elected to the federal Parliament and in the 1938 provincial election the CCF retained its Official Opposition status despite a challenge from the right-wing populist Social Credit.

During the Second World War, Saskatchewan changed from a province of rural farmers to one of urban workers. The proportion of small independent farmers was dwindling as young people left the farms for jobs in the cities and the armed forces. Technology and the trend to larger farms rendered many of them less necessary anyway. Even those still on the land started to move to larger communities.

Events in the United States helped push change as well. The *Wagner Act,* passed in 1935, spurred demands for recognition and protection of trade unions and collective bargaining. The idea of industrial unionism, no stranger to the western labour movement, attained greater legitimacy with the growth of the Congress of Industrial Organizations (CIO) and of its Canadian emulator, the Canadian Congress of Labour (CCL).

UNIONISM COMES OF AGE

In 1938, the Saskatchewan Liberal government took a first step toward modern labour law, passing legislation protecting unionism and collective bargaining, though not compelling employers to bargain and exempting civil servants from coverage. The federal order in council PC 1003, passed in 1944, finally brought comprehensive labour legislation to Canada. Its features are well known. But in several aspects it differed greatly from the Saskatchewan CCF government's labour legislation, which followed it by several months. One of the most important differences was when strikes could legally occur. As Cotterill and Davies so aptly put it, in PC 1003 "strikes were delayed as long as possible for as many reasons as possible" (Cotterill and Davies n.d., V-23). The new federal law forbade work stoppages during the life of the collective agreement. Disagreements between union and management over the application, interpretation or alleged violation of a collective agreement during its term had to be submitted to binding arbitration. And upon expiry of the agreement, the parties had to exhaust attempts at conciliation by government officers. Moreover, even legally sanctioned work stoppages considered harmful to the war effort could be ended unilaterally by the government and submitted to arbitration. Finally, the new law applied only to workers in private industry. Government employees were not covered.

Nevertheless, the passage of PC 1003 in 1944 provoked a huge surge in union organizing, not least in Saskatchewan, where workers in workplaces such as packing houses, metal fabricating plants, dairies, hospitals, and retail establishments were eager to have collective representation. The CCL industrial unions gained more legitimacy and organized vigorously. Many of the TLC craft unions also actively signed up new members, but these activities received less support from their headquarters. Especially frustrating was the insistence by the TLC that craft unions confine themselves to their craft jurisdiction, even if it resulted in workers being unrepresented. The CCL unions also were much more willing than their TLC counterparts to engage in politics and, encouraged by the CCF's promise to adopt a Wagner-type labour legislation if elected, endorsed the party as "labour's political voice."

Labour Reform and the First CCF-NDP Regime

In June 1944, under the leadership of T.C. "Tommy" Douglas, the CCF swept to power, capturing 89 percent of the seats. So strong was the popular groundswell behind the victory that the CCF-NDP held power for the next 22 years. While there were strong economic, political, and social reasons why the CCF won the election, one cannot ignore Douglas's personal magnetism. He was a powerful speaker, a visionary who combined political pragmatism with a strong policy agenda.

From its origins the CCF combined the tendencies of Fabianism and populism. Fabianism embodied the belief that through planning by well-intentioned experts and judicious use of the public sector, government could tame the more disorderly features of capitalism. Populism responded to charismatic leaders with vision who spoke directly to "the common people." Douglas personified both tendencies and managed to keep them from conflicting. With the added feeling of optimism that swept the whole country after World War II, Saskatchewan was ripe for the social policy innovation. However, the new government owed more of its success to the farm population than to the trade unionists. Douglas's road to power emerged from a rural, not urban, base.

> [H]is clerical indignation about poverty, his prophetic condemnation of those who dared put interest payments before human need, and his witty advocacy of cooperative principles had been just what Depression farmers and their small town suppliers had wanted to hear (Cotterill and Davies n.d., VI-10).

The relative scarcity of labour votes reflected the provincial population. While the labour movement strongly supported the new government, the working class was quite small compared to the more industrialized provinces. Farming organizations exerted more influence than the unions over the government. Labour's relative weakness set the Saskatchewan CCF-NDP apart from its counterparts in the rest of the country for years to come. Despite this situation, Douglas strongly supported union rights, often citing his youthful experiences amid lead and arsenic poisoning in a Winnipeg print shop. His personal charisma protected the innovative approach to labour legislation from more conservative elements of the party. Since most employment matters were still under wartime federal jurisdiction, Douglas had time to develop his own approach to labour-management relations. Two prominent Ontario labour lawyers who were CCF supporters and a Saskatchewan civil servant wrote new industrial relations legislation.

Lipset branded the resulting *Trade Union Act* (1944) "the most pro-union legislation in the democratic capitalist world" (1968, 279), right-wing opponents called it "the most far-reaching and drastic labour legislation in Canada" and "discriminatory, class legislation of a coercive and punitive nature."[2] Yet opposition to it was weak. Large and medium-size employers were few, with a small voice. Most citizens were farmers, and the Act did not cover farm laborers.

While broadly similar to the Wagner/PC 1003 model, the new law broke new ground in several ways. It was at least 25 years ahead of its time in granting the public sector the right to unionize and bargain collectively. Moreover, the new law allowed strikes in the public sector, which many Canadian governments still refused to do in 2003. Of course, this meant that the government and public employers could also lock their employees out. While it may have been a bold move, some in the CCF-NDP would regret it in the future, when public sector workers started taking their new power seriously. Another innovation was union security. Saskatchewan was the first province to require new employees to join a certified union and obliged employers to check off the dues of everyone in the bargaining unit.

The third innovation, and arguably the most important, allowed work stoppages at any time — both during and after the term of the collective agreement. Fifty years later, after all jurisdictions in Canada have succumbed to the mid-contract strike ban, it is easy to overlook the significance of this issue. Indeed, the fact that it *is* overlooked by labour, by academics and by public policymakers today speaks volumes about what has happened to industrial relations in this country.

From 1944 to 1983, Saskatchewan was the sole regime in Canada where strikes mid-contract were allowed. Moreover, the original *Trade Union Act* included (and continued to include) mid-contract bargaining as part of the duty to bargain in good faith. Cotterill and Davies are among the few Canadian commentators to understand how the ban on work stoppages put a permanent chill on labour relations.

> All this anti-strike legal insulation [outside of Saskatchewan] provided no encouragement to those who might be willing to work out compromises. Instead, it encouraged the stubborn posturers on both sides to come to the fore....
>
> when it came to grievances ... the fact that both sides were again insulated from economic risk discouraged compromise until the mandatory, time-consuming and expensive arbitration process was finished.... With all of the employee frustrations piling up as a result of long delayed grievance settlements and long drawn out contract bargaining, employees had an understandable propensity to explode in abnormal fury at that one moment when they could, at long last, legally stop work and legally apply some economic heat on their well protected employers. It was therefore not surprising that, despite its plethora of penalties against work stoppages, Canada would eventually acquire world-wide notoriety for the frequency, duration and bitterness of its strikes (Cotterill and Davies n.d., VI-15).

Indeed, in retrospect, it can be seen that Douglas's CCF regime was concerned not only or even primarily with pleasing the trade union movement. Just as Mackenzie-King's PC 1003 responded nationally to a postwar surge of labour militancy, the goal of Saskatchewan's *Trade Union Act* provincially was to regularize, institutionalize, in essence, to create an orderly labour relations system so that it could pursue long-range financial planning without experiencing costly labour disputes (Makahonuk 1997, 17). The difference was that Saskatchewan was more decidedly pluralist than its federal counterpart. It could see more clearly that, like a vaccination, a little bit of industrial conflict could be injected to protect the polity against a lot of industrial conflict. To be sure, Saskatchewan faced a much smaller threat from labour than did Ottawa in 1944.

If the CCF-NDP is not recognized for its early workplace reforms, it is well known for changes to the "social wage," that is, state regulations and benefits to protect the population from the market. The Douglas government was influenced by the hardships of the Great Depression. Later, the Blakney regime attempted to garner the profits from resource exploitation, and the Romanow government of the late twentieth century cautiously retreated from social policy innovation.

The most famous of the "social wage" programs was medicare, the result of a Douglas election promise. It covered hospital services in 1947 and extended to physicians' services after a bitter strike in 1962. But the CCF introduced other innovations as well — public crop insurance and government-owned automobile insurance. Crown corporations bought private telephone and electric utilities and extended service to the rural population.

SOCIAL POLICY AND ECONOMIC POLICY: THE DILEMMA

The CCF-NDP in Saskatchewan has always had difficulty in reconciling its social and economic policies. Social policy has always been tempered and constrained by the problem of revenue-generation, which has, except for some notable exceptions, been left to the private sector. The NDP's labour policy has been caught between social policy and economic policy, partly affected by the desire to extend at least some of the welfare state to the workplace and partly affected by the need to promote capital accumulation.

Almost coincident with the CCF victory, Saskatchewan economic development changed forever with the discovery of a prodigious supply of oil and gas, potash, and uranium. The challenge was whether a previously poor agricultural province could develop this bounty under public control. The CCF's founding document, the Regina Manifesto, called for public ownership and development of natural resources. After considerable debate, the government offered development of these resources to the private sector and attempted to recover as much of the rent as possible through royalties.

The price was steep. Private resource companies knew their greatest leverage occurs right at the beginning, when local administrative and technical expertise is low. In negotiations with the government, they would try to set the royalty rate as low as possible and lock the rate in as long as possible. Potash provides an excellent example.

A low royalty structure was established for 21 years. The presence of Cold War anti-socialist sentiment and the federal government's refusal to partner with the province in resource development also appears to have contributed to the decision. The essentially passive approach to resource development marked by this decision had profound implications for the province's future and for the political complexion of the Saskatchewan CCF-NDP (and to the party across the country) in the years to come, especially when the government subsequently tried to take a more activist role in resource development.

First, in the case of potash, failure to take ownership in the development of these resources put the government at a disadvantage in assessing, monitoring, and controlling the pace of investment and the exploitive capacity of those resources. This position cost the people of Saskatchewan literally billions of dollars in dissipated rents. Second, it entrenched the Saskatchewan government as a junior, rather than a senior partner in the province's economic development, driven more by the vagaries of capital and commodity markets than by its own policy. Third, future non-NDP governments found it much easier to collaborate with resource companies or to undo any short-term economic policy that the NDP had put in place. Fourth, the CCF-NDP focused on social policy while allowing private enterprise to expand its influence. Eventually government efforts to raise revenues had to appease the private owners of its resources, even if it meant entering the vicious circle of lowering royalties and accelerating depletion of the non-renewable resource. Fifth, the unions and workers in these industries identified more with the needs and problems of their employers than with those of fellow trade unionists, or the province as a whole. Later, NDP governments attempted to buy some of these industries back. But with the original decision to defer to capital already taken, it was an uphill battle (Richards and Pratt 1979).

A Changing Province

On the other hand, the government's foray into social services, Crown corporations, and commercial ventures changed the provincial labour market, industrial relations, and politics in two significant ways. The province produced a corps of highly trained public managers and a new upper middle class. And, together with the burgeoning private resource industries, it led to an impressive expansion of the unionized working class of the province. Spurred also by the new labour law, the number of trade union members increased more than threefold by the time the NDP was defeated in 1966.

By 1966, the demographic and political makeup of the province had changed dramatically. The previous peak in population had been in

1936 with 931,000 people, with three out of five engaged in farming. The Depression and its aftermath reduced the population by 100,000 in ten years. By the time the population returned to the 1936 level in 1961, the proportion engaged in farming was down to one in three, with the number of operating farms cut by 30 percent! Yet the average farm size increased by 70 percent and wheat production climbed by almost a third.

> Farmers were doing to themselves what they had prevented external in-stitutions from doing — forcing one another off the land as the big bought out the small, creating class divisions between large, well-capitalized farmers often using hired labour and small, undercapitalized farmers increasingly reduced to tenant status (Richards and Pratt 1979, 107-08).

Several factors contributed to the NDP defeat in 1964. Changes in the farm population, the growth of a much larger working class and the development of a sizeable professional, entrepreneurial, and managerial middle class combined to alter and polarize the Saskatchewan electorate from 1944. A sizeable group of rural and farm supporters left the party as the urbanites and trade unionists gained more prominence up to the found-ing of the NDP in 1961. One of these was the Liberal leader Ross Thatcher, who left in 1955 and soon began articulate attacks against the socialist evils of his former colleagues. Neighbouring Alberta was booming from an oil bonanza and with the Saskatchewan potash boom finally begin-ning, many in the province felt that this product would do the same for them. Thatcher's free market rhetoric seemed to match the upbeat mood better than the NDP's collectivist status quo. The electorate was also weary after the acrimonious doctors' strike over the introduction of medicare in 1962. Not to be overlooked were a series of public sector and Crown corporation labour disputes, which contributed to the (mostly incorrect) impression that the public sector and its workers were overpaid.

Despite Thatcher's small electoral majority over the NDP (and an even slimmer lead in the popular vote), he took a hatchet to the pro-gressive labour policy of the former government. In the Liberal's *Trade Union Act* "conscientious objectors" opposed to unions on religious grounds could assign the equivalent of their union dues to an outside charity (but would be covered by the collective agreement). Employees belonging to a professional association could exempt themselves from unionization. Employers were given greater freedom to campaign against union organizing drives. The onus in cases of dismissal for union activity shifted to the union. Decertification, previously available only at contract's end, was available during a contract. The minimum union support to hold a certification vote increased to 40 percent, then 60 percent. Minimum fines for transgressing the Act were lowered from $200 to $25. Employers could change terms and conditions of employment during a certification attempt if they could prove they were unaware the union had majority support.

Strangely enough, the Liberal government did not remove the right to strike in mid-term, although this was unique to Saskatchewan. It could be that the government and its business supporters relished the prospect of "taking on" the unions at any time.

But when Saskatchewan Power Corporation employees went on strike in 1966, the government clearly preferred the legislative route to put an end to conflict. Thatcher brought in the *Essential Services Emergency Act*, giving Cabinet the power to end any strike involving the delivery of water, heat, electricity, gas, and health services and to impose binding arbitration. Unions who flouted the obligation to do everything reasonably possible to end such a strike could be decertified; members who resisted could be fired.

With record-setting wheat crops and a buoyant economy, Thatcher called an election after three years. While the Liberals increased their majority by a small amount, both they and the NDP gained at the expense of the Conservatives. The province was still divided, but a new pattern was emerging with the NDP taking a majority of urban seats and the Liberals, rural seats.

Having cut back the public service in his first term, Thatcher continued his attacks. Further amendments to the *Trade Union Act* included giving employers the right to alter unilaterally terms and conditions of employment during negotiations. Votes on contract offers could be imposed 30 days after a strike began. "Hot cargo" clauses in collective agreements became illegal. Yet despite the increase in government coercion in labour relations, the average annual person-days lost due to work stoppages was three times higher during the Thatcher years than in the 20 years of the CCF.

While making some modest increases in the "social wage," Thatcher's government fell behind most of the other provinces. By the end of its term, the minimum wage was about 20 percent lower than Ontario, British Columbia, Alberta, and the federal jurisdiction. The maximum hours of work without overtime were the same (44 hours per week) as those set by the CCF in 1944 while most other provinces had long since moved to 40 hours. Thatcher imposed a "utilization fee" (later dubbed a "deterrent fee") for hospital and doctor visits, which succeeded in deterring only the poor and angering everyone. As a result, the NDP swept back into power with its highest popular vote since 1944.

LABOUR POLICY AND ECONOMIC POLICY: THE BLAKENEY CONUNDRUM

Spurred on by the left-wing nationalist "Waffle" group whose candidate had run a surprisingly strong leadership challenge to the moderate Alan Blakeney, the party's election platform "A New Deal for People" was the most progressive since 1944. Not only did it propose strong social policy, it also called for changes in economic policy — a type of public ownership of land, reluctance to increase the foreign ownership of Saskatchewan's economy and, indeed, the feasibility of nationalizing the potash industry. Yet the Waffle's influence was mercurial. In 1969 its members controlled the provincial NDP executive and had more than nodding support from the leader Woodrow Lloyd, but more moderate party leaders staged a coup and ousted Lloyd as leader.

Alan Blakeney's new government was considerably different in composition than the previous CCF. "The old left agrarian-labour alliance dating back to the latter days of the CCF was increasingly replaced by a leadership corps of party apparatchiks, lawyers, co-op bureaucrats, and of other professionals and middle level managers" (Brown 1995, 8). So the new government was torn between two inclinations.

> Blakeney found himself between a program considerably to the left of his basic inclinations and a party leadership and caucus the majority of which was to his right. He opted for caution. Unlike the first CCF government when Douglas' cabinet contained members enthusiastic to implement the party's economic program, Blakeney's initial choices for portfolios bearing on economic policy were — the Agriculture minister excepted — basically hostile or indifferent to the thrust of the party's economic policy (Richards and Pratt 1979, 255).

But the new government was less timid in its social policy. It had more trade unionists in caucus than ever, one of whom, railway man Gordon Snyder, was named minister of labour. The government received strong support from and owed a debt to the trade union movement, a force in the province, so labour law reform was among its first priorities. Immediately, the government repealed the *Essential Services Emergency Act*. It also introduced a new *Trade Union Act* (TUA).

The new TUA expanded the scope of employees to whom collective bargaining applied, including professionals. The Labour Relations Board was strengthened and restricted to representatives from government, business, and labour. Minimum membership support for representation votes was reduced to 25 percent and, for the first time, automatic certification (without a vote) was available to unions with evidence of majority support from the bargaining unit. Employers were forbidden to express their views to employees during a certification drive. The Liberal provision for a vote on the employer's last offer after 30 days on strike was repealed as was the prohibition against "hot cargo" clauses. Penalties for violations were also increased. A new technological change clause obliged the employer to provide 90 days' notice of the nature and impact of the change on employees. Failing such notice, the union could delay the change and any layoffs by 90 days. Few other provinces would introduce such a provision. On the other hand, several of the old Liberal provisions were allowed to remain, for instance, exclusion from the bargaining unit on religious grounds.

The government passed a *Construction Labour Relations Act*, which compelled unionized contractors to engage in industrywide bargaining. It also prevented unionized contractors and firms from establishing subsidiaries for the purpose of evading unions (see Rose and Wetzel 1986; and Wetzel 1984).

A revised *Labour Standards Act* established the 40-hour week with time and a half overtime, a national pace-setting basic three weeks vacation for all (with four weeks after 20 years' service), equal pay for similar work and 18 weeks unpaid maternity leave. The minimum wage was the highest in Canada during much of the Blakeney regime.

A new *Occupational Health and Safety Act* broke ground in North America, establishing the "three employee rights": the right to participate (with health and safety committees in workplaces of ten or more employees); the right to be informed of workplace hazards; and the right to refuse unsafe work.

Other social policy innovations included a provincewide dental plan and prescription drug plan, free aids to disabled people and a senior citizen's benefits program. All of the above were accomplished without the government incurring a deficit. Indeed, the government was able to claim it had accumulated $1 billion in a Heritage Fund by the end of 1981 (Sass 1994).

The Blakeney administration has been celebrated as a laudable social democratic regime, a kind of golden age (especially). Yet some scholars evaluating this period see it in a more critical light. While Blakeney's reforms clearly eclipsed the old Thatcher legacy, the 1970s were a time of social reform throughout the country. The Blakeney regime comprised two periods:

> The first period (1971–76) represents a phase of modest growth in social policy developments and in expenditures on social assistance. During the second period (1976–1982), social spending tended to decline as the policy priorities of the NDP shifted from manifest social concerns to economic priorities, particularly in the area of government control of natural and mineral resources (Ternowetsky 1994, 149).

Despite the unparalleled growth of the provincial economy during the Blakeney years and the various social programs it initiated, income inequality was only moderately affected. In other words, "higher income groups were the main beneficiaries" of the windfall (ibid.). Behind the scenes nationally and internationally, darker economic forces were at work polarizing the labour market, shrinking the middle class, and further impoverishing the poor. And when national inflation figures went into double digits in the mid-1970s, the Blakeney government joined the wage-restraint bandwagon and stopped social innovation.

But even economic development had problems. Having foregone the opportunity to develop its resources in the first CCF regime, the government faced resistance from private firms in the resource sector. The biggest problem was potash. Caught in a three-way fight with the companies and the federal government over the division of revenue from this resource, Saskatchewan risked losing substantial revenues from a bonanza — a product in which the province had an almost global monopoly. Immediately after the 1975 election, the government nationalized a large proportion of the potash industry (Laux and Molot 1981).

The province also entered the oil and gas industry by setting up the Saskatchewan Oil and Gas Corporation (Sask Oil) in 1973. Although it gave the government a needed "window" on the industry, the enterprise was never a major player. With the discovery of a major uranium deposit and expansion of the nuclear power industry, the uranium looked like a great potential money-maker. The Blakeney government wanted to maximize the benefits of the resource, including a refinery. It forced the uranium companies to give equity in the new uranium properties to a Crown corporation. Unlike potash, the industry was not hostile to government involvement. A provincial government partner could help the industry weather political and environmental storms (Gruending 1990).

With a large proportion of the provincial workforce employed by government and Crown corporations, the government had an opportunity to experiment with new forms of work organization and democratization of the workplace. But only a few, half-hearted attempts were undertaken and these came to little. As Laux and Molot said of potash:

> The Potash Corporation of Saskatchewan chose to retain private-sector mine managers to ensure a smooth transition to state ownership, and [was not] concerned with experimentation despite individual expressions of embarrassment over the lack of meaningful changes from senior government and PCS officials (Laux and Molot 1981, 212).

For the most part, the government relied on private sector managers for its Crown enterprises. Indeed, one of the potash mines taken over was not unionized and managers made no initial attempts to recognize a union. While some trade unionists sat on the boards of some Crown corporations, "the government believed that workers should not be from the bargaining unit within the particular crown corporation" (Sass 1994). The government finally set up a Work Environment Board within the Potash Corporation in 1982 to create some worker participation. But when the unions involved encroached upon traditional managerial rights, corporation managers balked, preferring milder "quality of work life" programs (Sass 1994). The government did not pursue the project any further. The unions involved were cautious.

> The unions, in particular the Steelworkers [were] more skeptical than enthusiastic about direct participation in decision making, preferring a limited adversary relationship via collective bargaining.... The miners [were] concerned with job security rather than solidarity across the industry. Political consciousness and knowledge about forms of industrial democracy that do not inevitably lead to co-optation are lacking. This lack is in turn due to the absence of any traditional commitment to democracy in the work place by the N.D.P. Without political pressure for change ... state managers [are not expected] to abandon the priority to pragmatism — business as usual (Laux and Molot 1981, 212-13).

Public sector strikes divided the Blakeney government and the labour movement. Such disputes are always difficult for governments, especially when they involve "essential services" and the government's professed support for the right of those workers to strike. The government emerged from a 1979 strike by its civil servants with a strained relationship. But when hospital workers represented by the Canadian Union of Public Employees walked out just before the 1982 election campaign, the government was especially embarrassed and angry. It recalled the legislature and passed emergency legislation ordering the strikers back to work and banning any strikes during an election campaign in perpetuity. To many in the government, the strike was a betrayal by the union movement; to many trade unionists, the government actions were worse. While many factors caused the NDP defeat in 1982, labour's disenchantment with the party was surely one.

THE TIDE TURNS: THE DEVINE REGIME

The election results followed the familiar trend to bipolarity in Saskatchewan politics. The left populist NDP had defeated the increasingly "out of touch" Liberals. Now the right populist Conservatives under Grant Devine had defeated the increasingly "out of touch" NDP, capturing 54 percent of the popular vote and 55 of 64 seats. Given that the NDP boom years had not translated into income gains by ordinary people, it is not surprising that Blakeney himself attributed the loss to "a perception that our government was well off, but the people were not" (Gruending 1990). Devine promised to address these concerns. Economic development had brought prosperity. But if cautious engagement with the private sector had marked the NDP regime, Devine promised that greater intimacy with business would bring prosperity. In the age of Reaganism and (Margaret) Thatcherism, institutions that interfered with the free market damaged prosperity. Targets included social programs and especially trade unions.

The new labour minister had been a manager of a firm found guilty of several violations of labour laws. His overhaul of the *Trade Union Act* brought back many of the provisions of the Thatcher Liberals, except that this time a more powerful employer lobby had more direct input (Pitsula and Rasmussen 1990). Exemptions to inclusion of employees in the bargaining unit were expanded. Employers could delay certification by arguing that they were building up their workforce. Unions could be sued or sue under their own name. The old provision allowing employers to urge captive employee audiences against joining a union was returned and strengthened. As before, employers could invoke a vote on their final offer after 30 days of a strike. Moreover, all employees, even strikebreakers, could vote on the offer.

The Devine government also broke the 40-year convention of allowing strikes during the term of collective agreements, joining all other

Canadian jurisdictions in prohibiting such work stoppages. This move appeared to be pure spite. Despite the historical absence of a ban on mid-term strikes, there was no evidence that Saskatchewan unions had abused the right. Indeed Saskatchewan unions were *less* inclined to strike during collective agreements than their counterparts in other provinces. We also observe this when we compare strike activity in Canada as a whole to that in other countries where the mid-term ban does not exist. This strongly suggests that the possibility of strikes at any time during the collective agreement may actually diminish a conflict.

Other industrial relations changes were reflected in rulings of the Labour Relations Board, which undercut several venerable union rights. Perhaps the most significant ruling concerned union protections during collective bargaining. It reinterpreted the proscription on employers changing terms and conditions of employment during negotiations. Rather than following the tradition of barring such changes unless the union agreed, it allowed employers to discharge the onus merely by giving the union notice and "bargaining," that is, engaging in the form, if not the content, of negotiations.

The building-trades unions were especially hard-hit. The provincial unemployment rate doubled with two-thirds of plumbers, pipe fitters, and labourers jobless. Employers took the opportunity to lobby the government to allow them to evade unions. The government responded in 1984 by repealing the *Construction Labour Relations Act*. Very soon, almost all contractors had established non-union "spin-off" subsidiaries. Moreover, the employers' Construction Labour Relations Council terminated all collective agreements. The Labour Relations Board ruled that some spin-off firms were still bound by the union certificates of their sister or parent companies, but were no longer bound by the collective agreements. To hold onto their dwindling memberships, the unions agreed to major concessions. But even 25 percent cuts in pay were often not enough for employers. Soon, union membership plunged to less than a half and few of those members were working.

Not surprisingly, for the first time since 1944 Saskatchewan's union density dropped, from 32.9 percent to 29.2 percent with the number of certification applications falling from 183 in 1982–83 to a mere 78 by 1987–88 (McQuaig, Sass and Stobbe 1990).

The Devine government soon confronted the public sector. In 1985, faced with employer proposals to undermine job security, work hours, and the scope of its bargaining unit, the Saskatchewan Government Employees Union conducted rotating strikes. The government responded by legislating the strikers back to work and became the first government in the country to invoke the "notwithstanding clause" to avoid any application of the *Charter of Rights and Freedoms*. The government used the notwithstanding clause again by forcing decertification of public employees when restructuring public institutions. In the case of the province's postsecondary technical institute, the decertified union was forced to reorganize its old members.

The capricious nature of the government's industrial relations policy was epitomized in a 1988 strike by University of Saskatchewan professors just before final examinations. Not only did the government legislate the strikers back to work, it also refused to impose interest arbitration or a settlement. It merely postponed the strike by a few weeks until after all the students had written their exams and left for the summer, thereby removing the union's leverage.

The Conservatives also placed their stamp on labour standards. The minimum wage fell by 28 percent in purchasing power by decade's end. Though complaints against employers rose by 37 percent, there was a drop of 87 percent in the number of prosecutions (ibid.). In 1986, the branch stopped routine inspections altogether, eliminating the element of surprise.

Previously a national leader in occupational health and safety provision, Saskatchewan retreated under Devine. The government allowed workplace inspection and support for workplace committees to deteriorate. It also loosened a number of regulations. A deputy minister of labour typified the government's attitude, saying, "We're open for business and that means that we're not going to put employers out of business by pursuing academic occupational health and safety rules" (ibid., 168). The Workers' Compensation Board toughened up its scrutiny of worker claims and forced many disabled claimants off benefits to take lower paying jobs.

In 1989, the government offered the Potash Corporation of Saskatchewan for sale and began to privatize SaskEnergy. The NDP opposed the sale. Although the government eventually reversed the decision to sell SaskEnergy, it tried to privatize public auto insurance, another popular program, and its fate was sealed.

THE INDUSTRIAL RELATIONS SYSTEM AND
THE PARTIES IN THE 1990s

Early in the twenty-first century, the major features of Saskatchewan industrial relations can be identified. Saskatchewan has largely moved away from its origins as an agricultural province. Since 1951, farming income has dropped from 50 percent of the total to virtually zero, while employment income has risen from 30 percent to almost 60 percent. The fate of agriculture as an income generator was vividly demonstrated in the late 1990s as farm incomes fell to levels as low as in the Great Depression.

Employment in agriculture has dropped, but more gradually than income derived from it. By 2001, agricultural employment was about one-fifth of the provincial total. Non-farm employment has risen steadily, with services adding the lion's share, and manufacturing and extractive industries growing moderately. Employment in public administration rose to a peak in the mid-1980s and has declined in absolute and proportional terms since then. Despite the drop in agricultural employment, the farm still casts a long shadow on the province's labour scene. There is much employment in the production of food products and various consumer cooperatives and credit unions. Several major manufacturing firms produce agricultural equipment (although some of these firms were wiped out in the late-1990s slump in agriculture). And while not a large employer at the moment, the agricultural biotech industry is growing by leaps and bounds. Thus, age-old farmer-worker relationships, both affable and adversarial, persist.

Unemployment in Saskatchewan is consistently below the national average, while generally following the fluctuations of the national economy, Saskatchewan has seldom had more than 8 percent unemployment. A major reason for the Saskatchewan experience is that many people who would otherwise be unemployed return to the farm in economic downturns. Low employment in manufacturing and extraction also contributes to the muting of unemployment.

Overall union density in Saskatchewan in the latter part of the twentieth century remained close to the national average figure of about 30 percent. Patterns of unionization did differ somewhat from the national figures. While Saskatchewan did not achieve the national density levels in manufacturing and public administration, it has exceeded the national levels in the public sector, health care and social assistance, and in extractive industries and agriculture. The latter three, however, do not make up a large part of employment in the province (and consequently not a large proportion of unionized employees).

The vast majority of union members (over 75 percent of the total) are employed in the broad public sector. Indeed, for the last two decades of the twentieth century, public sector unionists (both female) led the Saskatchewan Federation of Labour. The only major unions outside the "house of labour" have been the provincial teachers' union, and the provincial nurses' union. The latter, however, joined the Federation of Labour in the late 1990s, one of the first nurses' unions in the country to end its unaffiliated status.

There are stresses within the Saskatchewan labour movement. As in other provinces, the public-private split is always evident. Yet the sheer dominance of the public sector unions somehow renders the duality less volatile. Indeed, the private sector unions seem to have more than their share of influence in the federation. This may be due to another potential line of cleavage — political. A major factor in Saskatchewan's labour politics is the relative weakness of the Canadian Auto Workers' Union (CAW), which in larger and more industrial provinces has formed a left-wing bloc with the Canadian Union of Public Employees (CUPE) and several smaller unions. While CUPE is large in Saskatchewan, the relative absence of the CAW makes such a bloc less viable. The inherent conservatism of the government employees' union (partly due to its large proportion of members in correctional facilities) also tends to keep the left at bay. The absence of a strong left has given the private sector unions ideological, if not numerical clout. This may also explain, in general, the weakness of left-wing opposition to the rightward turn in the NDP.

More will be said below about the role of employers in Saskatchewan industrial relations. While there is no dominant employers' association, the provincial and local Chambers of Commerce, the Federation of Independent Business, and some industry associations (particularly in construction, food and beverage, and tourism) have considerable influence on the government's labour policy under the Conservatives and the NDP.

As for labour law and policy itself, the years since Tommy Douglas's first government have seen a gradual "normalization." Other jurisdictions have long caught up with what used to be progressive and innovative laws and policies. And successive Saskatchewan governments themselves have muted the forward thrust. For instance, the Devine Conservative government's repeal of the right to strike in mid-collective agreement has not been altered by the NDP. Indeed, with the election of the NDP in 1991, labour policy and law remained solidly in the Canadian "mainstream."

Romanow's NDP: Labour Takes a Back Seat

When the 1991 election was called, the NDP was a government in waiting. Despite its attempts to curb public sector spending, the Conservatives had rung up a massive debt through unwise giveaways and aborted projects. Even the business community, at home and outside the province, was weary of the incumbents. This put the NDP in an enviable position; it owed nothing to any interest group, labour or business. Moreover, when it was elected and performed an "opening of the books" show, it declared the treasury cupboard bare — with the largest per capita debt in the country. Citizens were told they were in for years of blood, tears, toil, and sweat, and they responded by drastically lowering their expectations. Claims that the government was exaggerating fell upon deaf ears.

Prior to the election, talks between new leader Roy Romanow's caucus and the labour movement revealed the stark truth to the labour movement.

> It was the SFL, rather than the NDP, which was more desperate to get a deal out of these meetings. In 1991, the SFL felt that it had only one choice: to support the NDP or risk another term of Tories in power. In this situation, organized labour politically aligned itself with the NDP and hoped that the new government would implement at least some of the unions' agenda in return (Kijkowski 1997, 31).

As well as a massive debt, the new government inherited a political and economic development dilemma. During the decade that the NDP was in opposition, neo-liberalism had become the reigning economic and political orthodoxy. Before the recession of the early 1980s, capital was more tolerant of moves toward political and economic democracy. In that more benign climate, NDP administrations of the 1960s and 1970s promised and delivered to capital the four benefits they (as epitomized by the Saskatchewan Blakeney regime) could claim to deliver better than governments of any other political party. These four "competencies" were: astute oversight of capitalist economic development, sound and honest public administration, domestication of the labour and social movements and cautious and incremental amelioration of the welfare state, *in that order of priority*.

In the political climate of the 1990s, business hostility to political and economic democracy had sharpened. As seen by its hostility to the NDP governments in Ontario and British Columbia, capital was especially intolerant of NDP governments. The three NDP governments in office during the 1990s were elected less for their own policy and more from rejection of the hypocrisy (of public restraint and private profligacy) and scandal by their predecessor governments of the right. Once in office, the NDP has attempted to mollify capital by pleading the four competencies. But business was unimpressed. As much as the Ontario and BC governments tried to show that they could pilot economic development, run honest administrations, broker labour and social peace, and hold the line on social programs, business did not cease public denunciation. Indeed, yielding to business pressure has often had the perverse effect of fuelling further attacks on the NDP (Panitch and Swartz 2003).

Yet the Saskatchewan situation was different. Perhaps the corruption of the previous government had been especially egregious. Perhaps the Saskatchewan NDP had fewer obligations to labour and social groups. Perhaps the social democratic tradition in Saskatchewan was just too strong for capital to hope for anything better. Perhaps the NDP under Romanow could be relied upon more than any other party to reduce the public debt. Certainly debt-reduction became the centrepiece of public policy throughout the first Romanow government, affecting all else. Perhaps too, the Saskatchewan NDP was the only one in the country to have more than superficial roots in the business community. Other provincial NDPs made attempts to court the business community, but in Saskatchewan the connection was real. The structure of the business community is also different from most other provinces. Small and medium-sized firms dominate the provincial economy. Only 14 firms have more than 1,000 employees and many of those are owned by some level of government or are cooperatives. Eighteen of the top one hundred companies ranked by gross sales have fewer than one hundred employees. Thus, a critical mass of employers hostile to the NDP is far from assured. Moreover, unlike elsewhere in Canada, Saskatchewan social democrats can be said to be "the party of power" and it is simply not good politics for businesses to attack the NDP too vigorously.

For their part, the powerbrokers in the NDP have seen that grooming a good relationship with business is now more important than currying favour with labour. Business has alternatives; labour has none. At worst, labour can stay home during an election. This helped defeat the government in 1982; but when labour's support faltered somewhat in the 1995 and 1999 elections, the NDP won handily anyway, making it even less beholden to labour.

Saskatchewan views the NDP and the labour movement with two faces: the humanistic and the technocratic. The former reflects a strong residual commitment to consensus-building, free collective bargaining, and community and trade union participation. Thus, the NDP in government is prepared to take modest pro-labour initiatives in collective bargaining, labour standards, occupational health and safety, and workplace equity. Moreover, with a perceived necessity to curtail public spending, some NDP regimes have felt a strong need to bring trade unions and managements into a comprehensive negotiated consensus, which more right-wing governments have not been inclined to do.

But this desire for consensus has revealed the other, less attractive face. Beset by economic and political stress, NDP governments are prone to grow impatient and petulant with the trade union movement for opposing government policy and resisting the government's consensus initiatives. Unlike other parties, which, from the start, see the labour movement as an alien camp, unreliable if not hostile, the NDP often purports *to know better than labour what is in labour's best interests*, even to the point of punishing labour "for its own good."

The labour law reform process highlighted this tendency in the early 1990s. Unlike previous governments dating back to 1944, the new NDP government took a long time putting its agenda together, almost until the end of its first term.

> Once the government decided that consensus was necessary between labour and business before the amendments to the TUA were made, and since it was obvious that business would continue to oppose any significant reform of the TUA, it was clear there would be no significant changes to the TUA. In summary, the requirement for consensus imposed by the NDP as a condition for the reform of the TUA tied the hands of labour and gave business the opportunity to veto any changes it did not agree to (Kijkowski 1997, 80).

As far as labour was concerned, the mountain had laboured to bring forth a mouse. Changes to collective bargaining and employment law reversed some, but by no means all, of the forfeitures of the Devine era. Perhaps more informative than what labour law reform the government did introduce is what it did *not* introduce. The following is a list of initiatives, all launched earlier in other provinces (and by no means all by NDP governments), which the Saskatchewan government might have introduced but did not.

Pay equity. Most provinces have some form of regulation for equal pay for work of equal value. But in Saskatchewan's *Labour Standards Act* "equal pay for similar work" is still the law.

Proactive employment equity. Saskatchewan still has a complaints-based approach where the Human Rights Commission can order an employer to implement an employment equity plan, but only if an employee makes a successful formal complaint of discrimination.

Allowing strikes while a collective agreement is in force. The NDP government had no intention of reversing the Conservative prohibition on mid-term strikes, and the labour movement did not make this issue a priority.

Retroactivity in banning construction employer-union avoidance. Back in power, the NDP restored the prohibition on non-union spin-offs, but failed to make it retroactive, putting the barn door back, but only after the horses had gone. The government did implement a union-friendly tendering policy in Crown corporation construction.

Broad-based bargaining. By the 1990s, the growth of the private service sector and the decline of manufacturing and public services had made it more difficult for unions to grow or even maintain their membership. The ability to accrue and expand a bargaining unit as a union adds new certifications and the extension of union provisions to non-union employees essential tools for unions to keep up with the growth of the service economy. Though legislation was introduced by the NDP governments in British Columbia and Ontario and were in effect in Quebec, no such legislation was forthcoming in Saskatchewan.

Labour standards. When the NDP government first proposed its labour standards changes it appeared to be going much further than any other provincial government in curtailing the use and exploitation of part-time workers. But by the time the dust had settled, little bite was left.

A bold initiative giving part-timers "most available hours" when an employer needed more personnel, passed third reading in the legislature but the government never submitted it to royal assent, thereby killing it. Another provision, mandating prorated benefits for part-timers was enacted, but applied only to larger employers and those who gave full-timers benefits in the first place. Only part-timers working over 15 hours a week were eligible and some employers reduced employee hours to avoid the threshold. The government introduced increased notice periods for dismissal and layoff. But employers' ability to have "rolling layoffs" remained. This meant that some employers could avoid paying any remuneration in lieu by keeping employees in a constant state of notice.

Occupational health and safety. This was one area in which the labour movement looked strongly for succor from the new government. The Devine victory in 1982 had crippled the inspectorate and aborted the career of one of the architects of Canadian health and safety legislation (Robert Sass). Sass's reputation among the province's employers caused the NDP to resist labour pressure to re-hire him. Labour badly wanted all of Saskatchewan's exposure levels to be at least as good as those of the US Occupational Safety and Health Administration (OSHA), but these standards were not met in a number of key areas such as airborne carcinogens and airborne contaminants. Labour applauded some changes such as the ability of inspectors to investigate and mediate complaints of harassment, not only on the grounds prohibited by the Human Rights Code, but on height and weight as well.

"Anti-scab" and essential services legislation. Legislation outlawing replacement workers during strikes has been a feature in Quebec, Ontario (under the NDP), and British Columbia, and the Saskatchewan labour movement lobbied for it. But the Saskatchewan government did not have the stomach for even a watered-down version. Indeed, it warned the labour movement that the price for anti-scab legislation might be restrictions on strikes in "essential services." Most of the labour movement backed off. But events in the next few years would show that the government did not take this "bargain" seriously.

Despite the lack of explicit anti-scab legislation, the Saskatchewan Labour Relations Board ruled in July 1997 that the Saskatoon Pepsi-Cola bottler could not hire strikebreakers during a lockout. The reasoning of the board was that, like a strike, a lockout should impose some hardship on both union and management. The decision was a creative interpretation of the law, but the Saskatchewan LRB has always had considerable autonomy. Previous NDP governments had always refused, as a point of principle, to intervene in board decisions. But the day after the Pepsi case, amid the clamor of outrage from employers, Premier Romanow faced the media and angrily denounced the decision as unacceptable. Three months later, under a new chairperson, the board took the unusual step of reconsidering and overturning the earlier decision.

There was another important outcome of the Pepsi lockout. During the dispute, the union had picketed retail outlets and placed signs at a hotel where replacement workers were lodged. They also picketed outside the homes of some managers. The employer successfully applied for an injunction prohibiting picketing activities at secondary locations. The appeal court upheld the prohibition on picketing private homes, but allowed the other actions. When the case reached the Supreme Court of Canada, nine judges unanimously ruled that peaceful secondary picketing was protected by the freedom of expression provisions of the *Charter of Rights and Freedoms.*

> "We can find no persuasive reason to deprive union members of an expressive right at common law that is available to all members of the public," the judgment said. "In our opinion, a blanket prohibition is too blunt a tool with which to handle such a vital freedom."[3]

Despite its putative promise to the labour movement, the government did not hesitate to pass essential services legislation, twice. In mid-1998 it legislated an end to a dispute between Sask Power and the International Brotherhood of Electrical Workers. Labour and management had earlier negotiated a deal, but the Cabinet vetoed the settlement for exceeding its public sector pay guidelines. Moreover, by refusing to substitute binding arbitration and instead imposing an agreement on the parties, the government engaged in behaviour that even more conservative regimes have eschewed. The Sask Power affair evoked a firestorm of condemnation from labour. When Premier Romanow addressed the Saskatchewan Federation of Labour convention a few weeks' later delegates booed him and followed him out to his car with angry chants of reproach.

> But the most notorious example of government mauling of labour came with a spring 1999 nurses' strike. The NDP government had grown accustomed to the acquiescence of the labour movement and was perhaps overconfident in perceiving its adeptness to "handle" dissent. In so doing, it ignored lessons from across the country, especially with regard to nurses' strikes. The nurses' dispute plumbed deep popular insecurity about the future of the health care system and Medicare. Unlike any other group, nurses have been able successfully to wrestle with governments over stewardship of the public interest (Haiven 1995).

Attempting to continue the public sector compensation guidelines that resulted in the power workers' dispute earlier in the year, several Cabinet ministers let it be known that the government would not hesitate to use draconian back-to-work legislation again. This naturally had a chilling effect on health-care negotiations and especially those involving nurses. A last-minute personal mediation attempt by Premier Romanow failed to dispel, indeed may have worsened, the union's distrust and hostility. Mere hours after the subsequent legal strike began, the government convened the legislature and legislated the nurses back to work and, as with the power workers, imposed collective agreement terms. Armed with the new law, the employers' association sought a contempt ruling in court. Defiant nurses carried on the illegal strike another ten days, and gained substantial public sympathy.

Some militants in the provincial labour federation attempted to distill this outrage into censure of, or withdrawal from, the NDP and even a general strike. At a tumultuous meeting, conservative trade unionists strongly opposed any protest action. Rather than force a split between private and public sector unions, as happened over the social contract in Ontario, the militants backed down. CLC President Bob White gave a rousing speech to a nurses' rally. But except for sporadic public protestations and pledges of money to the nurses, organized labour's voice was largely muted. Moreover, Romanow took the wind out of the militants' sails when he mused publicly that he would not be upset if the link between the party and the labour movement were permanently broken.

Having imposed settlement terms, the government had boxed itself into a corner with the nurses. But the scene shifted to other health-care bargaining areas, where new government money was forthcoming to ensure settlement. Eventually, the nurses themselves settled for a package in excess of the government's original guidelines. The nurses' union was cited for contempt, but a judge imposed a relatively lenient fine of $120,000.

The reckless ending of the nurses' strike cost the NDP dearly in the election three months later. Many NDP voters stayed home, and buoyed by a farm protest vote and the customary Saskatchewan swing to the opposite political pole, the Saskatchewan Party almost won the 1999 provincial election. This amalgam of federal Reform Party supporters, former Tories, and right-wing Liberals captured the majority of the popular vote. Only an uneasy coalition with the three remaining Liberal members kept the NDP in power. Yet the coalition held despite a fractious and demoralized Liberal caucus.

After the election, both labour and management laid out the main points of their public policy agenda. Labour hoped for an anti-scab law similar to the one in Quebec and a "union wage" policy requiring Crown corporations to tender construction on the basis of union wages and conditions. The government responded by making it easier for construction unions to gain back certifications they had lost during the Devine years. Unions pushed for more regular inspections of workplaces by health and safety officers. They urged the government to proclaim the "most available hours" section of the *Labour Standards Act*[4] and to end the "Northern Exemption" in that legislation (an exemption that appears in no other province's legislation). A major bone of contention was the failure of the

government to pass equal pay for work of equal value legislation to surpass the equal pay for equal work law (though the government made comparable worth *de rigueur* in the broader public sector). Finally, labour
proposed a minimum wage hike beyond the middle-of-the-provincial-pack
$6.00 per hour.

Another major labour concern heated up at the beginning of 2000.
Agricultural labourers had long been exempt from coverage by labour
standards law — an attempt to keep the important farmer vote happy. But
the 1990s saw a burgeoning of commercial hog barns (more like small
factories than farms) as Asian markets for pork opened up. Until a union
exposed it publicly, a government agency actually touted this lack of coverage to entice investment into the province. Workers at Bear Hills Pork
(a subsidiary of the Saskatchewan Wheat Pool) joined a union to rectify
the situation, but had to fight to include provisions in their collective
agreement (like overtime pay, statutory holidays, minimum yearly vacation and maximum consecutive days of work) that other, non-union workers had by law. A lockout by their employer raised the public profile of the
issue, thus embarrassing the government. The ensuing dispute dragged
on for three years until the government changed the law.

Saskatchewan employers, variously represented by the Chamber
of Commerce, the Federation of Independent Business, and single-issue
organizations had a very different public policy agenda. They naturally
opposed labour's proposals and, looking to neo-liberal regimes in Alberta
and Ontario, submitted suggestions of their own for the reform of labour
policy. Many of these were raised in the legislature by MLAs from the
Saskatchewan Party. Employers championed measures to make union organizing more difficult, such as including removing "automatic certification" and imposing a compulsory vote. They advocated the freedom of
employers to address captive audiences of their workers during a unionization drive. Perhaps the most provocative suggestion was for the introduction of "right to work" legislation which exists in some American states
and bars union security clauses and prohibits the dues check-off.

The employer offensive came amid a surge in new union organizing, especially in the hotel and services sector. When the Service Employees International Union organized workers at DirectTel in Saskatoon, the
workers received leaflets from a Right to Work Alliance. A spokesperson
from the Right to Work Employee Legal Defense Foundation appeared
on several platforms and conservative open-line shows. At the end of 2001,
the Chamber of Commerce, the Federation of Independent Business, and

the Construction Association formed the Saskatchewan Alliance for Economic Growth, in order to promote that agenda.

A major battlefield emerged after five years of budgetary surpluses and just before the 1999 election. The Romanow government decided to follow Alberta and several other provinces in lowering its provincial personal income taxes. Left-wing critics of the NDP, including many long-time party members were dismayed that the party should consider disbursing its surplus in tax cuts rather than restoring all the services cut to balance the budget. But the premier, the finance minister, and some other party stalwarts argued that Saskatchewan's income taxes were the second highest in the country and that it was impossible to *not* keep taxes close to those in Alberta. Moreover, the largest tax cuts should benefit the highest income groups, to stem a possible exodus of wealthy citizens to Alberta.

The government appointed a committee composed of accountants to investigate the tax system. It was obvious that the consultants' mandate was not "whether" but "how" to lower income taxes. The province's unions joined with other left-wing organizations to oppose the tax cuts. The employers and their allies lined up on the other side. Not surprisingly, the committee recommended a large personal income tax cut, and regressive changes in the tax structure.

The government's own eventual tax cut followed the committee's advice on income tax, but reduced the harshness of the sales tax changes. However, it introduced the sales tax hikes straightaway while postponing the cuts for six months. This, and a healthy budget surplus from high oil and gas prices disguised the impact on the government's treasury. The revenue shortfall would be felt hardest only later, when the provincial economy suffered a downturn.

Romanow Leaves

Romanow left as premier and announced his exit from Canadian politics in September 2000. The NDP's biography of him summarized the major accomplishments in his nine years as premier as: "the Romanow government introduced numerous fiscal, economic and social reforms. These include an expansion of the ground-breaking Action Plan for Children, the introduction of the Building Independence strategy to help move families off social assistance, enhancements to the provincial health care system, the continued development of key economic sectors, and the tabling of Saskatchewan's 6th consecutive balanced budget."

As for health care, government spending as a share of provincial expenditure rose by 15 percent, causing leading government figures to wonder if the province's public health-care system was sustainable. However, this figure is dangerously misleading. Health spending actually declined over the NDP government's term, from 6 percent of provincial GDP to 5.4 percent, a drop of 10 percent. The reason? Provincial *revenues* as a proportion of GDP had declined by 20 percent. Under the NDP, government's share of the economy had plunged even during some of the best economic times in the province's history, putting health care and other important social spending in danger. This too was part of the policy legacy of Romanow's NDP government.

Lorne Calvert, a veteran Cabinet minister, took over from Romanow in February 2001. Calvert almost immediately showed signs of greater union friendliness than his predecessor. He introduced a comparatively benign budget. He made an unprecedented visit to the picket line of hotel workers in Saskatoon who had been on strike for eight months. This one act, which was a striking departure from the Romanow repertoire, earned Calvert long-lasting plaudits from labour. The new premier appointed as labour minister an MLA with trade union roots, and then a half-year later replaced him with one having even stronger trade union connections. In the summer, the government concluded negotiations with its civil servants, agreeing to a more generous package than their union had seen since the NDP government was first elected. A provincewide hospital strike by 12,000 hospital support workers occurred in that summer. Unlike in 1999, the government did not declare the strike illegal, and it was settled quickly. A much longer hospital strike occurred in 2002. Health professionals (excluding nurses and physicians) struck for 29 days. Again the government avoided legislation, and the parties settled. Business and opposition leaders promised to eliminate such strikes in the future.

In May 2002, the government implemented the first stage of its eventual 11 percent hike to the minimum wage. In June 2002, the government finally amended the *Labour Standards Act* to end the exemption of workers (above six in number) working in intensive agricultural operations like hog barns or egg hatcheries, although labour protested that many employers could avoid the provisions of the Act. In the same month, the government improved payouts to workers from the Workers' Compensation Board.

While labour still had plenty on its public policy agenda, trade unionists were considerably more pleased than they had been with

Romanow. But Romanow's indifference and periodic hostility to labour made any improvement look good by comparison. As the NDP government planned for a 2003 election, the last thing it wanted was the open labour hostility that so plagued the 1999 campaign.

Business, on the other hand, was concerned. In March 2002 the provincial director of the Federation of Independent Business outlined a myriad of complaints. The communication stressed its members' "concern about labour laws (highest in Canada)." The Saskatchewan Alliance for Economic Growth said it was "appalled [the] government approved an 11 percent minimum wage increase without any economic impact analysis or other documentation to justify the increase" (SAEG 2002). Employers also voiced concern with the 7 percent increase in government spending and the increase of 570 government employees in the previous budget.

On the whole, the NDP government, at over a decade the most stable New Democrat regime in the country, exercised a cautious, modest, and sometimes punitive labour agenda. Its own public justification for this, the "test of time" excuse, is revealing of not only its relationship with labour but also its political philosophy. Asked in 1993 why the government had taken so long to come out with the new employment legislation and offered labour so little, the labour minister replied that whatever the government introduced had to "stand the test of time." By that, he said, he meant that the government did not want to introduce anything new that would be cast aside by a future government of a different political stripe.

Labour and social justice activists have pointed out that with this attitude, previous NDP and CCF governments would never have introduced any of their innovative and progressive measures — the original *Trade Union Act*, occupational health and safety reform, or nationalization of potash mines. Indeed, the same rationale would have precluded even the introduction of medicare, whose acceptance (as evidenced by the infamous doctor's strike and the opposition's promise to scrap it) was very much in doubt for several years. The Saskatchewan Party is on record as favouring the US-style "back-to-work" legislation. With this group waiting in the wings, with Ralph Klein to the west of them, Mike Harris to the east of them, and the right-to-work state North Dakota to the south of them, what continues to summon whatever loyalty Saskatchewan labour has to the NDP is no longer favour, but rather fear, of the alternative.

CONCLUSION

Early in the twenty-first century the pattern of Saskatchewan industrial relations was established. A continuing tension between the NDP's
reform tradition and the economic reality of a precarious economy dominated by natural resources affected labour relations. Private sector unions
lacked the tradition of militancy found in other resource-based industries. An increasingly vocal business community, primarily composed of
small- and medium-sized firms, resisted any pro-labour measures. Modest swings in the popular vote can bring substantial changes in legislation.
The labour movement, unable to expand its base in the private sector, exercised limited influence on the government of the day. Its opportunities for
political and economic gains were most promising under the combination of
strong markets for resources and a reform-minded NDP government.

NOTES

[1]This invaluable manuscript, written by two veteran labour activists some
time in the late 1970s, was commissioned by the Saskatchewan Federation of
Labour as a history of the Saskatchewan labour movement. It was never published and exists only in typescript. References to it refer to the chapter numbers
and pages within the chapter. Because it is not dated, the date is referred to as
"n.d."

[2]Both quotes from "'Class' Law," *The Leader-Post,* 7 November 1944 as
cited in Kijkowski (1997).

[3]*R.W.D.S.U., Local 558 v. Pepsi-Cola Canada Beverages (West) Ltd.*
Supreme Court of Canada. 2002 SCC 8.File No.: 27060.

[4]This provision enjoined employers to increase the proportion of full-
time workers by assigning any extra work to incumbent part-timers rather than
hiring new part-timers. While the legislature passed this provision along with
other amendments in 1994, the government, bowing to employer pressure, did
not submit this provision for royal assent.

REFERENCES

Abella, I. 1975. *The Canadian Labour Movement, 1902-1960,* Historical Booklet
    No. 28. Ottawa: Canadian Historical Society.
Brown, L. 1995. "The Blakeney Years," *Briarpatch* 24 (1):8-9.
Cotterill, M. and B. Davies. n.d. (circa late 1970s). Manuscript on Saskatchewan
    labour history. Unpublished paper.
Dunn, C. and D. Laycock. 1992. "Innovation and Competition in the Agricul-
    tural Heartland," in *The Provincial State: Politics in Canada's Provinces
    and Territories,* ed. K. Brownsey and M. Howlett. Toronto: Copp Clark
    Pitman.

Gruending, D. 1990. *Promises to Keep: A Political Biography of Allan Blakeney.* Saskatoon: Western Producer Prairie Books.

Haiven, L. 1995. "Industrial Relations in Health Care: Regulation, Conflict and Transition to the 'Wellness Model,'" in *Public Sector Collective Bargaining in Canada: Beginning of the End or End of the Beginning?* ed. G. Swimmer and M. Thompson. Kingston: IRC Press, pp. 236-71.

Harding, J., ed. 1994. *Social Policy and Social Justice: The NDP Government in Saskatchewan during the Blakeney Years.* Waterloo, ON: Wilfrid Laurier University Press.

Kijkowski, M. 1997. "Charles E. Lindblom's Revised Pluralism and the 1994 Reform of Saskatchewan's *Trade Union Act.*" Master's Dissertation, University of Regina.

Laux, J.K. and M.A. Molot. 1981. "The Potash Corporation of Saskatchewan," in *Public Corporations and Public Policy in Canada*, ed. A. Tupper and G.B. Doern. Montreal: The Institute for Research on Public Policy, pp. 189-219.

—— 1988. *State Capitalism: Public Enterprise in Canada.* Ithaca: Cornell University Press.

Lipset, S.M. 1968. *Agrarian Socialism: The Cooperative Commonwealth Federation in Saskatchewan: A Study in Political Sociology.* Garden City, NJ: Doubleday.

Makahonuk, G. 1997. *Class, State and Power: The Struggle for Trade Union Rights in Saskatchewan, 1905-1997.* Saskatoon: Canadian Union of Public Employees, Local 1975.

McQuaig, I., B. Sass and M. Stobbe. 1994. "Labour Pains: The Birth of a New Industrial Relations Order in Saskatchewan, 1982-1990," in *Devine Rule in Saskatchewan: A Decade of Hope and Hardship*, ed. L. Biggs and M. Stobbe. Saskatoon: Fifth House Publishers, pp. 151-75.

Panitch, L. and D. Swartz. 2003. *From Consent to Coercion: The Assault on Trade Union Freedoms.* Toronto: Garamond.

Pitsula, J.M. and K.A. Rasmussen. 1990. *Privatizing a Province: The New Right in Saskatchewan.* Vancouver: New Star Books.

Richards, J. and L. Pratt. 1979. *Prairie Capitalism.* Toronto: McClelland & Stewart.

Rose, J.B. and K. Wetzel. 1986. "Outcomes of Bargaining Structures in the Ontario and Saskatchewan Construction Industries," *Relations industrielles-Industrial Relations* 41 (2):256-80.

Saskatchewan Alliance for Economic Growth (SAEG). 2002. Letter from Marilyn Braun-Pollon, Chair to Labour Minister Deb Higgins. Letter available at <http://www.saskchamber.com/publications.php?category=3>.

Sass, R. 1994. "Labor Policy and Social Democracy: The Case of Saskatchewan, 1971-1982," *International Journal of Health Services* 24 (4):763-91.

Ternowetsky, G. 1994. "Income Inequality, 1971-82: The Saskatchewan Case," in *Social Policy and Social Justice*, ed. Harding, pp. 149-71.

Wetzel, K. 1984. "The Saskatchewan Experience with Construction Industry Accreditation Legislation. A Report to Labour Canada." Unpublished paper.

7 NEWFOUNDLAND AND LABRADOR: SHIFTING TIDES

Andrew A. Luchak

Résumé — L'histoire des relations industrielles à Terre-Neuve-et-Labrador ressemble à celle des relations industrielles dans les autres provinces canadiennes. Ce qui la différencie tient davantage au degré qu'à la nature des caractéristiques et s'explique en grande partie par la dispersion géographique de la population de cette province, la dépendance économique aux ressources naturelles et l'isolement relatif par rapport au reste du Canada.

À l'instar des gouvernements des autres provinces, celui de Terre-Neuve-et-Labrador a joué un rôle actif dans la mise en place de l'infrastructure nécessaire à la croissance de l'industrie. Toutefois, le fait que cette province dépende plus que les autres des ressources naturelles a entraîné une économie moins diversifiée, plus exposée aux influences extérieures et moins en mesure d'assurer des sources de revenu et des perspectives d'emploi. Depuis la fin des années 1990, la situation économique terre-neuvienne s'est cependant améliorée par rapport au reste du pays, et l'expansion économique s'est accompagnée d'un important mouvement d'abandon des emplois traditionnellement liés à la pêche.

La politique du travail terre-neuvienne a également évolué de façon semblable à celle des autres provinces : interdisant d'abord toute négociation collective, elle en est venue à l'appuyer de façon dynamique sous l'impulsion de la Seconde Guerre mondiale, puis le gouvernement lui a apporté des modifications, petit à petit, par la suite. Elle a aussi été modelée par les influences britannique, américaine et canadienne, mais ces influences se sont fait sentir bien plus tard que dans les autres provinces, l'influence anglaise ayant été prépondérante à Terre-Neuve-et-Labrador en raison de l'entrée tardive de cette province dans la Confédération. Dans le même ordre d'idées, le wagnérisme n'a fait son entrée à Terre-Neuve-et-Labrador qu'en 1950, soit six ans après l'adoption du CP 1944–1003 obligeant employeurs et représentants d'employés à négocier de bonne foi.

Aujourd'hui, la régulation du marché du travail à Terre-Neuve-et-Labrador accuse encore un retard par rapport à l'ensemble du pays, probablement en raison de la grande précarité de l'assise économique de cette province et des efforts déployés par son gouvernement pour attirer les investissements des entreprises. Néanmoins, des modèles canadiens de législation du travail y semblent bien établis, et le gouvernement a fait preuve d'une certaine volonté d'améliorer la législation dans ce domaine à la suite de la récente expansion de l'économie provinciale. Comme ailleurs au pays, la négociation dans le secteur public a subi les effets des tribulations économiques du dernier quart du XXᵉ siècle. Cependant, contrairement aux autres provinces, Terre-Neuve-et-Labrador est peut-être à l'aube d'une nouvelle ère de coopération patronale-syndicale dans le secteur public. Cela dépendra probablement de la bonne volonté des parties de poursuivre ce qui a déjà été commencé par la formation récente d'une alliance stratégique entre le gouvernement Grimes, le milieu des affaires et les syndicats.

On voit surgir les mêmes grands modèles de changement de la structure syndicale à Terre-Neuve-et-Labrador que dans le reste du Canada. L'organisation syndicale y a vu le jour plus tard qu'ailleurs, résultat probable de l'industrialisation tardive, des difficultés de transport et de communication avec le monde extérieur (également entre les localités côtières dispersées) et de l'application tardive de la protection juridique de la négociation collective. Toutefois, les partis politiques terre-neuviens appuyés par les travailleurs n'obtiennent pas les mêmes succès électoraux que les tiers partis dans les autres provinces, probablement en raison des orientations plus traditionalistes de la province. Terre-Neuve-et-Labrador a un des taux de syndicalisation les plus élevés du pays, mais ce fait est dû en partie aux différences de structure de son marché du travail. Cette réalité a des conséquences importantes pour le mouvement syndical, car, dans l'avenir, le nombre d'emplois est susceptible de diminuer dans les industries primaires et celles qui lui sont apparentées, de même que dans le secteur public. On peut également expliquer en partie le taux élevé de syndicalisation par une plus grande demande de représentation syndicale, conséquence probable d'une population dispersée géographiquement et, dans une grande mesure, isolée socialement. Les taux élevés de représentation syndicale dans l'ensemble de la collectivité peuvent suppléer le succès électoral mitigé du NPD dans cette province.

Les critiques dont les relations de travail font l'objet sont quelque peu exagérées en ce qui concerne Terre-Neuve-et-Labrador. Dans cette province en effet, la structure industrielle, le taux de syndicalisation élevé et quelques grèves d'envergure expliquent en partie le résultat moyen élevé en matière de grève, tandis que les conventions collectives témoignent de formes de partage des risques plutôt audacieuses et que le processus administratif de ces conventions y semble plus efficace que dans les autres provinces. Il existe des preuves de collaboration patronale-syndicale dans le secteur privé, mais, jusqu'à récemment, il y a eu une absence manifeste d'une telle collaboration dans le secteur public, ce qui peut être l'expression des injustices perçues dans le processus de désignation des travailleurs essentiels, de restriction salariale et de rationalisation au cours des années 1980 et 1990. Bien qu'il soit encore tôt pour en parler, les récents succès du gouvernement libéral dans la formation d'une alliance stratégique entre le gouvernement, le monde des affaires et les syndicats pourraient représenter une transition dans les relations patronales-syndicales de la province. Grâce à l'économie dont le taux de croissance est un des plus élevés au Canada ces dernières années, au mouvement de grève modéré depuis cinq ans et à un mouvement syndical fécond et en plein essor qui a voix au chapitre en ce qui concerne le développement socio-économique de la province, le régime terre-neuvien des relations industrielles semble très solide et prêt à contribuer à une croissance et à une prospérité accrues au cours des prochaines années.

INTRODUCTION

Industrial relations in Newfoundland and Labrador has been shaped by the province's small, geographically dispersed population; economic dependence on natural resources, especially the fishery; social, political, and economic isolation from the rest of North America; government initiatives aimed at encouraging economic development; and its own unique history. These factors have contributed to an industrial relations system that differs from the rest of Canada, not so much in kind, but as a matter of degree. This chapter provides an overview of the external environment, actors, and major processes and outcomes of industrial relations in Newfoundland and Labrador, with primary emphasis on understanding the provincial system and its major sources of difference and similarity with other jurisdictions across Canada. To place the analysis in context, the chapter starts with an historical overview of industrial relations in the province.

A BRIEF HISTORY OF INDUSTRIAL RELATIONS IN THE PROVINCE

Newfoundland and Labrador is Canada's most eastern province. Fish brought Europeans to the province and fish dictated both patterns of settlement and early social structures (for a review, see Inglis 1985). By the 1850s, Newfoundland and Labrador was a self-sufficient colony in the British Empire with a system of responsible government and an economy sustained by exports of dried salt codfish, a highly regarded product on the European market. The population was scattered in numerous settlements around the colony's rugged coastline, ranging in size from a few families to a few hundred families. The capital city of St. John's was the centre for trade, finance and government, while the vast interior of the province remained virtually uninhabited.

Fishing dominated economic activity in the late nineteenth century, accounting for more than 80 percent of employment (Gillespie 1986). Much of the fishery was seasonal, occurring during the summer and early autumn. For the rest of the year, fisher households maintained themselves by growing their own vegetables, cutting their own fuel and lumber, building houses and boats, agriculture, and hunting and trapping. For items fishers could not produce, a truck or barter system was used. In the spring, merchants supplied fishers with necessary gear and supplies in exchange for their production of salt codfish at the end of the season. After a good season, a fisher could clear debt and purchase sufficient supplies for the winter. If the season were poor, fishers relied on credit to obtain winter supplies. By controlling prices for both supplies and fish, merchants profited at both ends of the arrangement, while fishers and their families faced an endless cycle of debt.

Skilled craftsmen such as shipwrights, masons, and coopers formed the earliest labour organizations in Newfoundland and Labrador. The "craft" advantage enabled these early labour organizations to survive in the face of an unfavourable legal environment. The development of a transportation system and resource industries in the late nineteenth and early twentieth century, together with the easing of legal restrictions, led to the emergence of a permanent trade union movement. In the early twentieth century, the first broad-based organization of fishers was established. The Fishermen's Protective Union (FPU) was founded in 1908 by William Coaker to obtain the emancipation of fishers from the truck system by providing credit for them to buy their equipment, supplies, and services and to sell their fish at fair prices for cash. The FPU enjoyed widespread appeal and entered provincial politics. Forming an alliance with the Liberals, they elected eight of the nine candidates they ran in the 1913 election, and 11 of 12 in 1919. After World War I, Coaker became minister of fisheries and attempted to introduce some of the FPU's long hoped-for reforms. The merchant class resisted these initiatives strongly. By the 1920s, the FPU resembled a mercantile undertaking more than a workers' movement, and support from fishers faded. The early twentieth century was also marked by the formation of industrial unions, such as the Newfoundland Industrial Workers Association (NIWA) in 1917, as well as the arrival of international craft unions.

A prolonged recession after World War I, followed by the Great Depression, hit Newfoundland and Labrador particularly hard in the 1920s and 1930s. During this period, union membership predictably declined. In the mid-1930s, however, a "renaissance" in organizing, militancy and political action began, as it occurred elsewhere in North America (Hattenhauer 1970; Kealey 1986). Union membership surged after the establishment of industrial unions in mining and logging. The Newfoundland Trades and Labour Council (NTLC) was established in 1936 and by 1938 it included three-quarters of existing unions for a total membership of 20,000. The NTLC was renamed the Newfoundland Federation of Labour (NFL) in 1939, and later, the Newfoundland and Labrador Federation of Labour (NLFL).

American military spending in Newfoundland and Labrador during World War II brought employment for thousands of workers. Labour shortages enhanced union bargaining power and unions capitalized on the opportunity by organizing workers in increasing numbers. Unfortunately, World War II did not solve the basic structural problems of Newfoundland and Labrador's economy and in 1949, a promise of improved incomes and services available in Canada convinced a small majority of its citizens to vote in favour of Confederation (Inglis 1985). It was Joseph Smallwood who championed the cause for Confederation, a role that subsequently led to an invitation to form an interim government and be sworn in as the province's first premier.

Smallwood was a populist, who actively courted the labour vote in his campaign for Confederation and in his first years as Liberal premier. Working people in the province regarded him as their advocate.

Determined to modernize the province, Smallwood's Liberal government enacted legislation governing labour relations processes, minimum wages, and workers' compensation. Although the new province adopted the broad outlines of Canadian labour legislation, its labour laws were among the most progressive in Canada. The *Labour Relations Act* was modelled in part on the American *Wagner Act* of 1935 and the federal *Industrial Relations and Disputes Investigation Act* of 1948. It marked a shift in labour policy away from English voluntarism and toward the more administrative approach in North America by setting out an orderly method for the establishment and revocation of bargaining rights, creating a duty to bargain, dealing with unfair labour practices, regulating industrial conflict and providing for a Labour Relations Board to administer, enforce, and interpret the Act. The *Trade Union Act* offered unions greater protection than most other provinces in that it continued the tort immunity protections established in the early part of the century (Cohen 1972). These two laws made the province's system of labour laws one of the more progressive for the times (Harris 1996). The *Minimum Wage Act* established a permanent government body responsible for establishing minimum wage rates. It also set the maximum number of hours per week and the minimum wage rate for hours worked in excess of this maximum. The *Workmen's Compensation Act* provided the province with its first comprehensive approach to workers' compensation. The Act followed the Ontario model of a mandatory, employer-financed, no-fault insurance system designed to compensate employees for injuries and diseases arising out of their employment. The system would be administered by an independent Workers' Compensation Commission (Cohen 1972).

Labour relations were tranquil during the 1950s, a likely consequence of the prominent role played by labour in the Smallwood government. This came to an abrupt end on 31 December 1958, when loggers represented by the International Woodworkers of America (IWA) threatened Smallwood's plans for economic development by going on strike against the Anglo-Newfoundland Development Company (AND Co.).

The ensuing dispute between the IWA and the AND Co. was one of the key labour struggles in Canadian labour history. While the AND Co.'s intransigence at the bargaining table and the loggers' uncharacteristic acts of violence and sabotage are noteworthy in their own right, the most remarkable feature of this epic struggle was the role of the Smallwood government in the labour dispute. The Smallwood government intervened, initially, by launching a savage verbal attack on the IWA leadership and international unionism, secondly, by attempting to form a rival, government-led union and thirdly, by using the legislature to destroy the IWA. On 6 March 1959, the *Trade Union (Emergency Provisions) Act* became law, revoking the certifications of the two IWA locals involved in the dispute and prohibiting their re-application for certification without Cabinet approval. On 10 March 1959, a combined force of RCMP and Newfoundland Constabulary officers clashed with demonstrating loggers leading to the death of a constable, and the loss of public support for the strike. While the IWA was struggling with the effects of the constable's death on its membership, Smallwood's Newfoundland Brotherhood of Woodworkers (NBWW) quietly conducted negotiations with AND Co. and reached an agreement granting a first year, five-cent hourly wage increase, precisely what the AND Co. had refused the IWA three months earlier. Premier Smallwood was called a fascist for his repressive legislation decertifying the IWA and denounced by labour organizations nationally and internationally. The International Labour Organization, an agency of the United Nations, pronounced Smallwood's labour laws unjust and undemocratic.

The loggers' strike of 1959 caused the downfall of the federal minister of justice, the resignation of Canada's national RCMP commissioner, and deeply divided the Liberal Party nationally (Ladd 1985). It stands as an important reminder of the power of government and the disastrous consequences of government intervention in a dispute on behalf of one of the participants. The strike also underscores the fragility of union recognition and collective bargaining processes and the ease with which these rights may be dissolved (Morton 1990).

During the 1960s, the economy of Newfoundland and Labrador benefited greatly from federal funding for public works, including development of the Trans-Canada Highway, and the development of hydroelectric power, first, at Bay d'Espoir, and later, at Churchill Falls. Support for the Smallwood government started to erode in the late 1960s in response to its inability to deal with problems in the fishery and the financial difficulties faced by many organizations that were subsidized by economic development policies.

The Smallwood political dynasty ended in 1972. He was succeeded by Frank Moores, the first Progressive Conservative premier of the province. Again, following the Canadian pattern, the 1970s witnessed the extension of collective bargaining rights to fish harvesters and public employees. The *Fishing Industry (Collective Bargaining) Act*, 1971 provided for the right of fish harvesters and processors to whom they sold various species of fish to form their own associations, to engage in collective bargaining, and to cease business dealings (i.e., strike or lock-out) if a collective agreement could not be reached (for a review, see Task Force on Fish/Crab Price Settlement Mechanisms 1998). Collective bargaining rights in the public sector were established through a series of statutes, covering provincial government and health-care workers, elementary and secondary school teachers, police officers, and St. John's firefighters. Later, in 1984, the interns and residents of the province also received access to collective bargaining. With the exception of police and firefighters, all public sector workers had the right to strike, subject to the designation of essential employees.

The 1970s and early 1980s were notable for the large increase in strike activity in Newfoundland and Labrador. The major contributor to the early part of this trend was the mining industry, which saw major struggles between the United Steelworkers of America and mining companies in Labrador City, Buchans, and Wabush almost every year between 1969 and 1975. Many of these strikes were over wage and benefit issues, reflecting the volatile economic conditions of the time (e.g., oil price and trade shocks, unanticipated inflation) to which mining was particularly sensitive. This period also saw many key recognition strikes in the fishery, initially among plant workers in the fishing town of Burgeo in 1971–72, and later, by trawlermen in 1974. Fishery strikes again exploded in 1980 with a 15,000-strong inshore fishers' strike during July and August of that year over the price of fish. The strike activity of the 1980s also included a bitter public sector labour dispute between the Progressive Conservative government of Premier Brian Peckford and the Newfoundland Association of Public and Private Employees (NAPE). In 1986, against a backdrop of restrictive public sector legislation (Bill 59), NAPE led 5,500 highway, snow-clearing, clerical, and administrative employees on strike, ignoring the new provisions requiring the designation of essential services before any work stoppage was allowed to occur. The strike escalated thereafter when it was declared illegal. In the end, the president of NAPE and leader of the provincial NDP were sentenced to jail terms and NAPE were also fined $110,000.

The early 1990s featured significant legislative action restricting labour relations in the public and private sectors. The Liberal government of Premier Clyde Wells turned to the right. It introduced Bill 16 which imposed a one-year wage freeze on public employees, effective 1 April 1991. The Wells government also introduced amendments to the *Labour Relations Act* providing for mandatory representation votes and secret ballot strike votes in the private sector. The negative impact of mandatory representation votes was mitigated by a requirement for the vote to be taken within five days of an application for certification.

Newfoundland and Labrador saw both economic crisis and opportunity in the early 1990s with the declaration of a fishing moratorium on significant groundfish stocks, including the historically important cod, in 1992 and the start of construction on the Hibernia oil production platform, respectively. The moratorium left fishing boats and processing plants in many rural communities idle, unravelling a way of life for approximately 30,000 fish harvesters and processing workers and their families. The start of construction of the Hibernia oil production platform opened a new chapter in the province's economic development involving yet another natural resource. The $5.8 billion price tag included over 31,500 person-years of work. The Hibernia project has been a large contributor to the economy, accounting for $2.7 billion in additional expenditures within the province's economy up to the end of 1997 (Strategic Concepts *et al.* 1999). The successful completion of the Hibernia project

solidified the province's position as a serious contender for future opportunities arising from the development of offshore petroleum resources,
both inside and outside Canada. Following this success, construction of
the floating production, storage and offloading facility for the Terra Nova
oil field commenced. The pre-production capital costs of this facility have
been estimated at $2.8 billion. Oil production commenced in 2002 and is
expected to reach a sustained level of 125,000 barrels of oil per day for
the next 15 to 18 years.

In 1996, Brian Tobin succeeded Clyde Wells as the premier of
the province. Like previous administrations, Tobin's approach to labour
relations was contradictory. For example, despite its stated goal of cooperation and consultation between labour and management, the Tobin
government, unilaterally and without consultation, shifted jurisdiction for
educational support staff from the *Labour Relations Act* to the *Public
Service (Collective Bargaining) Act* in the face of a threatened strike by
school support staff. The change imposed limitations on the right to strike.
The government also created a perception that labour issues had become
a low priority; many of the Department of Labour's functions were re-
assigned and the labour portfolio itself was combined with the environment to form a new Department of Environment and Labour. Moreover,
the government ignored the 1996 Report of the Labour Relations Working Group, a bipartite committee consisting of a neutral chair and 12
experienced union and management representatives. The report was the
most comprehensive labour reform document issued in the province during the previous two decades. Yet, in 1997 the Tobin government amended
the *Labour Relations Act* to accommodate the unique labour relations
considerations of offshore petroleum production only after consulting
interested stakeholders. A similar approach was used in the review of dispute settlement procedures under the *Fishing Industry (Collective Bargaining) Act*. The government also ended an eight-year salary freeze for
many government, health, and education workers by agreeing to modest
wage increases effective 1 April 1998, thus demonstrating a willingness
to share some of the recent good fortunes of the province.

On 3 February 2001, Roger Grimes was elected the new leader
of the Liberal Party, and became the new premier, replacing Brian Tobin,
who went to rejoin federal politics in the fall of 2000. One of Grimes'
first initiatives was to re-establish a stand-alone Department of Labour
and address important deficiencies in labour standards and health and
safety legislation. This provided a clear indication that labour issues were
a high priority. In contrast to previous administrations, Grimes' approach

has been more consultative and cooperative. Perhaps the best indicator of the new approach is the launch of a strategic partnership between the Grimes' government and the business and labour communities. Announced at the start of 2002, this partnership is intended to advance the socio-economic interests of the province through a consensus-building approach involving senior business and labour leaders and government officials. Such tripartite consultation and cooperation could scarcely have been imagined a few years earlier. As might be expected, the new spirit of cooperation appears to be having positive spillover effects, particularly in the public sector, where recently negotiated agreements with the nurses and teachers were reached without work stoppages.

As Newfoundland and Labrador enters the twenty-first century, it does so with a clearer vision than existed 50 years earlier. And while the province has not yet become the industrial giant Joey Smallwood imagined it might become, its economic outlook is very encouraging. While the collapse of significant groundfish stocks continues to prevent a full-scale return of this fishery and way of life for many, the province is expected to experience significant growth due to the continuing development of its other resources, most notably offshore oil and gas, nickel, and hydro-electricity. Economic expansion and contraction have presented the industrial relations actors with numerous challenges. While it is still early to tell how sustainable the new spirit of cooperation and consultation between business, labour, and the Grimes' government will be, initial signs are encouraging and suggest that the province's industrial relations system is very much intact and poised to offer a source of competitive advantage to the province in the years to come.

SOCIAL AND ECONOMIC STRUCTURE

Newfoundland and Labrador has Canada's second smallest population, approximately 512,930 citizens according to the 2001 Census Population Count. Since Confederation in 1949, it has been one of Canada's least wealthy provinces, with per capita gross domestic product (GDP) approximately two-thirds of the Canadian average. Because of a heavy reliance on natural resources, it has a higher proportion of employment in primary resource industries and in allied manufacturing categories such as fish processing and pulp and paper production (Table 1). There is also a significantly higher proportion of provincial employment in public services, a consequence of the wide dispersion of the population, which makes such services more costly to provide (Cohen 1972).

TABLE 1
AVERAGE INDUSTRIAL DISTRIBUTION OF EMPLOYMENT,
1987–2001

	Newfoundland and Labrador (%)	Canada (%)
Goods-producing sector	**24.34**	**26.97**
Agriculture	0.65	3.19
Forestry, fishing, mining, oil and gas	8.02	2.16
Utilities	1.28	0.95
Construction	5.64	5.62
Manufacturing	8.75	15.05
Service-producing sector	**75.66**	**73.03**
Trade	17.53	15.76
Transportation and warehousing	5.28	5.04
Finance, insurance, real estate and leasing	3.77	6.25
Professional, scientific and technical services	2.79	5.17
Management administrative and other support	1.87	2.92
Educational services	8.62	6.68
Health care and social services	13.28	10.07
Information, culture and recreation	3.28	4.18
Accommodation and food services	5.44	6.14
Other services	5.19	4.83
Public administration	8.61	6.00
All industries	**100.00**	**100.00**

Source: Statistics Canada, CANSIM, Matrices 3472 and 3473 and calculations by the author.

Newfoundland and Labrador's historical and current reliance on natural resources has meant that the provincial economy has always been relatively more "open" and influenced by economic activity outside its boundaries (Government of Newfoundland and Labrador 1992). Thus, for example, fluctuations in employment are greater than other provinces. Reliance on primary industries also means the province tends to experience more pronounced seasonality in employment which contributes to lower earnings, higher rates of unemployment, and ultimately, lower levels of personal income compared to the rest of the country (Table 2). Reflecting the higher levels of unemployment, the province relies more heavily on federal income transfer programs such as Employment Insurance (May and Hollett 1995).

As Newfoundland and Labrador enters the twenty-first century, it does so with a social and economic structure very much in transition. With no full-scale return of the cod fishery in sight, and other fisheries much less labour intensive, income-earning and employment opportunities from this sector will be dramatically reduced. The decline in opportunities is reflected in the drop in the province's population by 55,544 (or 10.8 percent of the current population) between the 1991 and 2001 Census Population Counts. In the midst of this adversity, however, the provincial economy has enjoyed buoyant growth in recent years due largely to expansion of the offshore oil and gas sector. Further economic growth is expected in response to continuing developments in this sector, the potential for large, open-pit mining at Voisey's Bay nickel mine in Labrador and corresponding processing plant at Argentia, expansion of the hydro-electric development at Churchill Falls, and more recently, diversification into previously unexploited fisheries such as crab and shrimp, and other value-added initiatives in this sector. This will improve Newfoundland and Labrador's ability to provide sustainable income and employment opportunities.

PATTERNS OF POLITICAL BEHAVIOUR

In 1949, Newfoundland and Labrador was the last Canadian province to join Confederation. Previously, the province had its own system of responsible government, except for the period 1934–49 when a non-elected Commission of Government assumed control in the face of an impending financial crisis.

Since Confederation, the provincial House of Assembly has been dominated by the Liberal Party, which first governed the province under Joseph Smallwood from 1949 to 1972. The Progressive Conservative Party then controlled the government for the next 17 years; first under the leadership of Frank Moores (1972–79) and later, Brian Peckford (1979–89). The Liberal Party then reclaimed majority support under Clyde Wells (1989–96) who would later be succeeded by Brian Tobin (1996–2000). In February 2001, Roger Grimes became premier.

TABLE 2
EMPLOYMENT, UNEMPLOYMENT AND WAGES AND SALARIES, 1976–2001

Year	Newfoundland and Labrador				Canada			
	Total Employment ('000)	Annual Change (%)	Unemployment Rate (%)	Average Wage and Salary ($)	Total Employment ('000)	Annual Change (%)	Unemployment Rate (%)	Average Wage and Salary ($)
1976	159.3		13.3	781.40	9,776		7.0	873.52
1977	161.1	1.13	15.4	859.29	9,915	1.42	8.0	951.08
1978	166.0	3.04	15.9	879.54	10,212	3.00	8.3	1,000.76
1979	177.5	6.93	14.7	944.77	10,658	4.36	7.5	1,078.73
1980	183.4	3.32	13.1	995.77	10,970	2.93	7.5	1,188.09
1981	186.3	1.58	13.3	1,189.28	11,297	2.98	7.6	1,325.11
1982	180.6	-3.06	16.2	1,311.79	10,947	-3.10	11.0	1,458.59
1983	180.8	0.11	18.0	1,365.85	11,027	0.73	11.9	1,512.03
1984	179.1	-0.94	20.1	1,450.83	11,300	2.48	11.3	1,587.65
1985	182.0	1.62	20.8	1,482.92	11,617	2.81	10.7	1,662.96
1986	186.5	2.47	18.9	1,512.56	11,979	3.11	9.6	1,720.67
1987	189.3	1.50	18.1	1,635.24	12,321	2.85	8.8	1,817.78
1988	199.0	5.12	16.2	1,637.67	12,710	3.16	7.8	1,933.08
1989	206.2	3.62	15.5	1,752.95	12,986	2.17	7.5	2,045.19
1990	207.4	0.58	16.9	1,835.83	13,084	0.75	8.1	2,123.84
1991	204.6	-1.35	18.0	1,895.83	12,851	-1.78	10.3	2,195.24
1992	193.5	-5.43	20.2	1,967.98	12,760	-0.71	11.2	2,240.52
1993	191.9	-0.83	20.4	2,007.98	12,858	0.76	11.4	2,250.54
1994	192.2	0.16	20.2	2,067.57	13,112	1.98	10.4	2,262.14
1995	194.3	1.09	18.1	2,081.63	13,357	1.87	9.4	2,285.90
1996	187.0	-3.76	19.3	2,091.99	13,463	0.79	9.6	2,325.71
1997	189.3	1.23	18.6	2,045.67	13,774	2.32	9.1	2,408.08
1998	194.2	2.59	18.0	2,055.93	14,140	2.66	8.3	2,470.41
1999	204.9	5.51	16.9	2,054.89	14,531	2.76	7.6	2,554.18
2000	204.6	-0.15	16.7	2,208.10	14,910	2.60	6.8	2,704.36
2001	211.6	3.42	16.1	2,222.58	15,077	1.12	7.2	2,792.25
Average	188.9	1.10	17.3	1,630.99	12,370.4	1.69	9.0	1,875.71

Note: Average Wage and Salary represents total wages and salaries divided by total employment.
Source: Statistics Canada, CANSIM, Matrices 3472, 3473, 6611, 6612, 10555. 10556 and calculations by the author.

By contrast, the New Democratic Party (NDP) has never been a significant political force in provincial politics. However, labour has been consistently politically active (Kealey 1986). Labour-sponsored political parties such as the FPU enjoyed some electoral success in the second decade of the twentieth century. The labour movement in St. John's was also active in provincial politics at this time, as was the St. John's District Labour Party in municipal politics. After these encouraging developments, however, the labour movement did not figure prominently in provincial politics until 1959 when the Newfoundland Democratic Party was founded by the NLFL in the aftermath of the loggers' strike of that same year. The absence of a labour party presence between the emergence of the FPU and 1959 likely reflected the initial pro-labour leanings of the Smallwood government in the post-Confederation period, and limited opportunities for involvement in the political affairs of the province under the non-elected Commission of Government during the colonial era. After 1962, the Newfoundland Democratic Party adopted the national New Democratic Party name and maintained a constant, albeit minor, presence in provincial politics thereafter. Organized labour also made its presence felt in politics through active lobbying.

The marginal success of left-wing political action in Newfoundland and Labrador may be explained by the absence of influences and conditions within the province, which would enhance its development. Unlike other provinces, Newfoundland and Labrador experienced industrialization without the influence of radical British and European immigrants, due to the late beginning of the modern economy (Inglis 1985). Moreover, the traditionalist orientations of Newfoundlanders and Labradoreans have served to maintain a two-party system and undercut third parties seeking to challenge the Liberals and the Tories (Adamson and Stewart 1991). Party loyalties in the province "run deep," as entire families remain either Liberal or Conservative for generations. The Liberals and Progressive Conservatives have been and continue to be the only serious contenders for political office in Newfoundland and Labrador.

STRUCTURE OF THE PARTIES

Unions

The pattern of union growth from the 1930s to the present in Newfoundland and Labrador is shown in Figure 1. The figure shows the rapid growth of the movement from the mid-1930s to the end of the

FIGURE 1

UNION MEMBERSHIP IN NEWFOUNDLAND AND LABRADOR

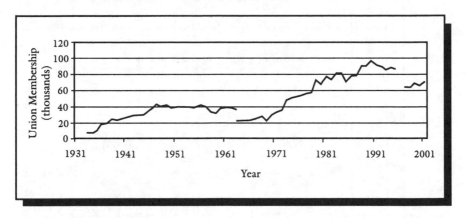

Sources: 1933 to 1969 based on Kealey (1986); 1970 to 1995 based on CALURA; 1997 to 2001 based on Akyeampong (1997, 1999, 2001).

1940s due to the organizational efforts of the NLFL, economic boom brought on by World War II, and favourable legislation which helped establish collective bargaining rights during and after World War II. Union growth stagnated through the 1950s, and declined somewhat in the aftermath of the loggers' strike of 1959. The 1970s marked the beginning of a second growth spurt for the labour movement, initiated by the organization of the fisheries, and the extension of collective bargaining rights to the fish-harvesting sector of the economy and the public sector, most notably the civil service and teachers. As in the rest of Canada, these legal developments contributed to union growth. Unlike the rest of Canada, however, Newfoundland and Labrador's growth was fuelled as much by developments in the private sector as by the public sector. Since the late 1970s, aggregate membership continued to grow but with significant year-to-year variation.

As indicated in Table 3, Newfoundland and Labrador is one of the most highly organized of the Canadian provinces. In 2001, union membership stood at 33.6 percent of total employment compared to 25.1 percent for the rest of Canada. The later emergence of union organization was due to the combined effects of later industrialization (Hattenhauer 1970), barriers to transportation and communication with the outside world and among scattered coastal communities, and the later emergence

TABLE 3

UNION MEMBERSHIP AND DENSITY, 1976–2001

	Newfoundland and Labrador				Canada			
Year	Total Members ('000)	As % of Employment (%)	As % of Labour Force (%)	Percentage Female (%)	Total Members ('000)	As % of Employment (%)	As % of Labour Force (%)	Percentage Female (%)
1976	54.0	33.9	29.4	18.5	2,773.4	28.4	26.4	27.0
1977	56.8	35.3	29.8	4.0	2,816.7	28.4	26.1	12.5
1978	57.8	34.8	29.3	18.9	2,901.1	28.4	26.0	28.7
1979	73.5	41.4	35.3	n/a	3,029.0	28.4	26.3	n/a
1980	67.7	36.9	32.1	22.2	3,085.6	28.1	26.0	30.2
1981	77.0	41.3	35.8	21.4	3,153.5	27.9	25.8	31.0
1982	73.9	40.9	34.3	23.0	3,048.1	27.8	24.8	32.2
1983	81.7	45.2	37.1	26.2	3,383.4	30.7	27.0	34.8
1984	81.2	45.3	36.2	27.1	3,431.6	30.4	26.9	35.4
1985	71.1	39.1	31.0	29.3	3,484.9	30.0	26.8	36.2
1986	78.0	41.8	33.9	32.6	3,595.4	30.0	27.1	36.3
1987	78.4	41.4	33.9	32.9	3,662.1	29.7	27.1	37.2
1988	90.6	45.5	38.1	29.0	3,772.8	29.7	27.4	37.5
1989	91.4	44.3	37.5	35.2	3,873.1	29.8	27.6	39.1
1990	97.8	47.2	39.2	37.6	3,887.6	29.7	27.3	39.9
1991	92.1	45.0	36.9	34.9	3,888.2	30.3	27.1	40.6
1992	89.8	46.4	37.0	35.3	3,854.8	30.2	26.8	41.2
1993	86.3	45.0	35.8	35.6	3,824.0	29.7	26.4	42.0
1994	88.9	46.3	36.9	36.4	3,842.6	29.3	26.3	42.3
1995	87.3	44.9	36.8	37.7	3,906.5	29.2	26.5	42.7
1997	64.0	33.8	27.5	n/a	3,547.0	25.8	23.4	45.1
1998	64.0	33.0	27.0	45.3	3,608.0	25.5	23.4	45.9
1999	69.0	33.7	28.0	46.4	3,594.0	24.7	22.9	46.6
2000	67.0	32.7	27.3	46.3	3,740.0	25.1	23.4	46.9
2001	71.0	33.6	28.2	n/a	3,788.0	25.1	23.3	47.4

Source: Statistics Canada, CANSIM Matrices 3530, 3516, 3472 and 3473; Akyeampong (1997, 1999, 2001); and calculations by author.

of legal protection for collective bargaining in two of the most dominant industries in the province: public services and fish harvesting.

The higher union density in Newfoundland and Labrador compared to other Canadian provinces is an interesting labour market outcome, especially given the numerous obstacles to union organization already mentioned. Several factors, including methods of calculating union density, labour market structure, and other factors help explain this outcome. First, the use of employment in calculating union density exaggerates the extent of union presence in the labour market in a province such as Newfoundland and Labrador with a high rate of unemployed union members. This is evident from Table 3, which shows that whereas union membership per employed in Newfoundland and Labrador exceeds the Canadian average by 34 percent in 2001, this figure is 21 percent where union membership per labour force member is used in the calculation.

Second, a relatively high proportion of the labour force in Newfoundland and Labrador is employed in mining, construction, transportation and communications, community services, and public administration, all of which are more heavily unionized (Martinello and Meng 1992; Ng 1992).

Third, unions in Newfoundland and Labrador may enjoy stronger forms of union security than are found in other jurisdictions. For instance, the *Labour Relations Act* has provided for compulsory dues check-off since 1985, which has been found to be associated with a higher probability of union coverage (Martinello and Meng 1992). As will be shown later, unions in the province have also been much more successful in negotiating union shop provisions.

Fourth, there may be a stronger sense of collectivism in certain segments of the province. This may be particularly the case in industries such as mining and the fishery which are more likely situated in communities characterized by slow rates of population growth, geographic isolation, and a lack of economic diversification. Collective action may be more likely to emerge in such communities because people see it as the only realistic way of advancing their shared economic and social interests, particularly where work is dangerous or the employer dominates the community (Krahn and Lowe 1992). Indeed, an examination of rates of unionization by industry generally shows that the mining and fishing industries in Newfoundland and Labrador have significantly higher rates of unionization compared to other jurisdictions (Statistics Canada 1994). This stronger sense of collectivism may also help explain the recent organizing successes of the Communication, Energy and Paperworkers

Union (CEP) among employees working on offshore oil and gas platforms. Despite considerable employer resistance and a special legislative exception requiring an all-encompassing bargaining unit, the CEP was certified in 2001 to represent all employees working on the Hibernia production platform. This is the first group of offshore workers ever to be organized in Canada. At the time of writing, the CEP had filed an application for certification for the Terra Nova platform, claiming to represent two-thirds of the employees in the bargaining unit.

It is also apparent from Table 3 that the percentage of female union membership in the province, as in the rest of Canada, has been steadily rising since the 1970s. The growth in public sector unionism in the 1970s, particularly in health services and education, clearly contributed to this development as it outpaced union membership gains in the fisheries, notably fish harvesting, which is predominantly a male-dominated occupation.

The largest unions in the province are in the public sector and include the Newfoundland Association of Public and Private Employees (NAPE), Newfoundland and Labrador Teachers' Association (NLTA), Newfoundland and Labrador Nurses' Union (NLNU), and the Canadian Union of Public Employees (CUPE). The largest private sector union is the Fish, Food and Allied Workers/Canadian Auto Workers Union (FFAW/CAW). This union represents nearly all of the fishery, incorporating into one union offshore and inshore fishers, and fish plant workers.

Prior to Confederation the vast majority of workers in Newfoundland and Labrador belonged to independent unions. After Confederation, many of the independents were affiliated with international unions (Kealey 1986). Since then time, however, the international presence has declined substantially, with such unions representing approximately one-fifth of all union members in the province in 1992 (Statistics Canada 1994). This shift has largely been due to the relatively stronger growth of national unions, particularly in the public sector (e.g., NAPE, CUPE), and to some significant splits from parent US unions, the most notable and largest in this province being the 1987 split from the United Food and Commercial Workers Union (UFCW) by the Newfoundland Fish, Food and Allied Workers' Union (NFFAW) and its subsequent affiliation with the Canadian Auto Workers' Union (CAW) to form the FFAW/CAW.

Most unions and labour federations in Newfoundland and Labrador are affiliated with the Canadian Labour Congress (CLC). The CLC's provincial affiliate is the Newfoundland and Labrador Federation of Labour (NLFL), which is the largest provincial labour federation in the province representing some 50,000 members. Like its counterparts in other

provinces, the main objectives of the NLFL are to promote trade unionism and represent worker interests at the provincial government level.
Unlike many of its provincial counterparts, the federation steered away
from left-wing politics until the 1959 loggers' strike after which it formed
the Newfoundland Democratic Party which eventually was subsumed by
the New Democratic Party of Canada. Also affiliated to the CLC are six
Local Labour Councils operating at the municipal level.

Large independent unions such as the NLTA and NLNU do their
own political lobbying, as do larger CLC affiliates such as the FFAW/
CAW. Since the 1970s, the FFAW/CAW has represented the collective
voices of fishers in fishing industry policy and regulation, helping focus
attention on important issues such as industry restructuring, quality assurance, conservation, and the marketing of fish products. A more recent
and visible example is the FFAW/CAW's effective lobbying for adjustment assistance in response to the 1992 fishing moratorium, first under
the Northern Cod Adjustment and Recovery Program (NCARP) in 1992,
and later, the Atlantic Groundfish Adjustment Strategy (TAGS) in 1994
and its successor program in 1998 (Government of Newfoundland and
Labrador 1998).

Management Organization

While most bargaining takes place at the plant level, some employer organizations have been formed for the purposes of representing
members in collective bargaining. Such employer organizations are most
common in construction (Construction Labour Relations Association of
Newfoundland and Labrador; Hibernia Employers' Association), the fishery (Fisheries Association of Newfoundland and Labrador), education
(Newfoundland and Labrador School Trustees' Association), and health
care (Newfoundland and Labrador Health Board Association, formerly
the Newfoundland and Labrador Hospital and Nursing Home Association). For the most part, such employer associations are a response to a
strong union presence across the specific industries in which they exist
(Hattenhauer 1970).

The Newfoundland and Labrador Employers' Council (NLEC)
is the largest political lobby group for employer interests, and includes
union and non-union members. Established in 1982, its purpose is to
represent employers in industrial relations matters, provide counselling
services to employers, and promote research and education on employment-
related topics.

Government Agencies and Consultative Bodies

The first Department of Labour in Newfoundland and Labrador was established in 1949 to administer the labour legislation of the province. Until the mid-1990s, the minister of labour was responsible for the supervision, control and direction of labour relations, employment standards, human rights, and occupational health and safety. In 1996, the labour portfolio was combined with environment to form a new Department of Environment and Labour. That move diluted the department's scope by shifting the Human Rights Commission to the Department of Justice and merging much of its Occupational Health and Safety Division with the Workers' Compensation Commission to form a new Workers' Health, Safety and Compensation Commission in 1998. The diminished status of the labour portfolio combined with other government initiatives to reduce the regulatory burden on business in the 1990s, signalled a clear preference for economic over social development. This contributed to a further cooling of relations between the government and the labour-management community.

In February 2001, however, the Grimes' government helped allay stakeholder concerns by re-establishing a separate Department of Labour. The new department now has four divisions. The Labour Standards Division primarily promotes and enforces the *Labour Standards Act*, the Labour Relations Division provides conciliation and mediation services, appoints arbitrators or nominees to boards of arbitration as requested, and administers the province's Preventive Mediation Program, and the Occupational Health and Safety Division retains responsibility for workplace health and safety policy and inspections. The fourth division is the independent, quasi-judicial Labour Relations Board, which adjudicates disputes under a variety of labour relations statutes. While those divisions removed in the 1998 realignment have not been returned, the creation of a department has important symbolic value. It indicates a commitment by government to renewing its partnership with business and labour, and balancing the province's social and economic development goals.

Consultations among business, labour, and government do not have a strong tradition in Newfoundland and Labrador. Suspicion and mistrust between previous governments and the labour movement may have contributed to this lack of cooperation. As a result, bipartite structures between labour and management have been more common. One of the oldest bipartite structures in the province is the Labour Management Cooperation Committee (LMCC), comprising employer and union representatives and founded in the late 1960s under the leadership of Rolf

Hattenhauer. While initially intended to have a much broader mandate, its main function is the selection, training, and evaluation of grievance arbitrators in the province. After successfully completing training, including the preparation of several mock awards, the LMCC will recommend the person as an approved labour arbitrator in the province. More recently, bipartism was followed in the previously discussed Labour Relations Working Group. The working group was initiated by Premier Clyde Wells who made a commitment not to interfere with its process and to seriously consider its recommendations for reforming collective bargaining laws in the province. In November 1996, after an extensive effort to consult and achieve consensus across the province, the working group's final report was filed with the provincial government (Labour Relations Working Group 1996), but fell on deaf ears.[1]

While it is still too early to tell, a new tradition of tripartite consultation may be emerging in response to the formation of a strategic alliance between the Grimes' government and the business and labour communities. The seriousness and potentially positive impact of this development is underscored by the participation of several of the province's major stakeholder groups, including the Newfoundland and Labrador Federation of Labour, Newfoundland and Labrador Employer's Council, St. John's Board of Trade, Newfoundland and Labrador Chamber of Commerce, and the Ministries of Industry, Trade and Rural Development, and Labour.

LABOUR LEGISLATION AND POLICY

From the progressive milieu of the 1950s, successive governments have engaged in incremental changes to collective bargaining and general employment laws. Like other provinces, Newfoundland and Labrador has frequently adopted provisions from other jurisdictions, most notably Ontario. In recent years, the province has demonstrated a willingness to experiment with new labour relations processes, particularly dispute-resolution mechanisms, as reflected in amendments to the *Labour Relations Act* for offshore oil and gas production platforms and those to the *Fishing Industry Collective Bargaining Act* for setting fish prices.

Collective Bargaining Law

As in other jurisdictions, the *Labour Relations Act* states that every employee has the right to belong to a trade union and to participate in its

activities. Certification is the primary mechanism for establishing bargaining rights. In 1994, Newfoundland and Labrador joined the growing
number of provinces that require representation votes to determine
majority support in applications for certification. As in some other
Canadian jurisdictions, representation votes are expedited, with the vote
occurring within five days of the application for certification. In 1997,
the legislature placed constraints on the Labour Relations Board's power
to fashion bargaining units in the offshore petroleum industry. The legislature mandated bargaining units encompassing all employees on offshore
production platforms (excluding construction and start-up personnel). It
also required the board to consider the impact on productivity and stability of an application for certification by a council of trade unions (see, for
a review, Cooper 1997).

The *Labour Relations Act* is similar to collective bargaining legislation in other provinces insofar as it specifies numerous unfair labour
practices. The Act regulates various aspects of the bargaining process,
such as, the duty to bargain in good faith and make reasonable efforts to
conclude a collective agreement, and requires that collective agreements
provide for the final and binding settlement of disputes, without stoppage of work by arbitration or otherwise. Further, where a certified bargaining agent and employer have failed to conclude a first collective agreement, either party may request the minister of labour to inquire into the
dispute, and if advisable, direct the Labour Relations Board to inquire
into the dispute, and where the board considers it advisable, to settle the
terms and conditions of a first collective agreement. However, the board has
fewer powers than other jurisdictions, for example, the power to grant interim orders and/or relief, to regulate or prohibit picketing, to determine
the legality of strikes or to grant automatic certification where the employer
has interfered with the certification process.

Like most jurisdictions in Canada, the *Labour Relations Act* requires conciliation before strikes or lockouts may occur. Perhaps one of
the more interesting provisions of the Act governing industrial conflict is
that requiring conventional arbitration and prohibiting strikes and lockouts for first-agreement disputes on offshore oil production platforms.

The *Fishing Industry Collective Bargaining Act* also establishes
interest arbitration as the dispute-resolution mechanism for determination of fish prices. Under this regime, the parties may choose between
conventional and final-offer selection arbitration. Interestingly, since its
inception as a pilot project in 1998, the parties have consistently chosen
final-offer selection. This labour relations regime was enshrined in the

legislation in July 2000. In the public sector, government has recently provided binding interest arbitration to the Royal Newfoundland Constabulary, the province's only police force. This move is in response to a strong lobby by the police for binding arbitration in the wake of the government's rejection of a recommended wage increase made through an advisory arbitration process in the late 1990s.

In addition to supporting these recent innovations, the government recently commissioned a review of the effectiveness of current labour relations legislation as it applies to the offshore oil and gas fabrication and construction sector (see Cooper 2000). The review largely arose out of a concern for the lack of stable labour relations during the fabrication and construction of the production vessel to be used in the Terra Nova oil development. The ensuing report led to legislative amendments in 2001 aimed at encouraging the parties to work together to identify and resolve joint problems and should prove useful in future major fabrication and construction projects, such as in the development of the production facility to be used in the Whiterose oil field.

General Employment Law

Employment law in Newfoundland and Labrador today resembles other Canadian provinces, but substantive protections have typically lagged those found elsewhere, as might be expected in a province with a relatively low per capita GDP. The gap, however, has recently been narrowed with the economic growth experienced in the province over the past several years. Thus, prior to amendments in 2001, the *Labour Standards Act* (R.S.N. 1990, c. L-2) provided one of the lowest entitlements to termination pay (one to two weeks) of any Canadian jurisdiction. Before granting a $0.25 increase in May 2002, the province's minimum wage was also one of the lowest in Canada at $5.50 per hour. While the high risk of accidents in primary industries such as fishing, mining, and forestry places Newfoundland near the top of the Canadian provinces for workplace accidents, the *Occupational Health and Safety Act* (R.S.N. 1990, c. O-3) goes no further than most other provinces and lags in certain other respects. For example, prior to an amendment in 2001 making health and safety committees mandatory in organizations with ten or more employees, Newfoundland and Labrador was relatively unique in making such committees subject to the minister's discretion. Also, this law still places a slightly higher onus on employees' refusing unsafe work by requiring that an "imminent" danger exist. Despite a recent increase in wage loss benefits from 75 percent to 80 percent of net income in the later 1990s, the province's system of workers' compensation also continues to provide one of the lowest replacement rates for injured workers across the country (Alcock 1997). Finally, private sector pensions only came under provincial regulation in 1983 under the *Pension Benefits Act* (R.S.N. 1990, c. P-4), almost 20 years after Ontario first introduced such laws and a decade behind most other provinces. Moreover, this province's law seriously lagged behind others in important areas such as the minimum vesting requirements, which were only changed from age 45 and ten years of service to two years of service in 1996, despite many other jurisdictions having changed to a maximum vesting period of two years of service in the late 1980s. Many public sector pension plans in the province also have very serious unfunded liabilities.

DISPUTE PATTERNS

A time series of Newfoundland and Labrador's strike record since the 1930s is provided in Figure 2. Like Canada generally, there are peaks of strike activity and periods of relative quiescence. The first notable peak occurred in 1948 when, as in the rest of Canada, worker militancy rose in anticipation of acquiring collective bargaining rights and protecting real

FIGURE 2
PERSON-DAYS LOST DUE TO STRIKES IN NEWFOUNDLAND
AND LABRADOR

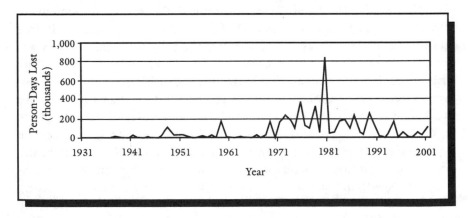

Source: 1933 to 1948 based on Kealey (1986); 1949 to 2001 based on data supplied by the Workplace Information Directorate, HRDC.

incomes due to rapidly rising prices in the immediate postwar period. The first ten years of Confederation exhibited relative labour quiescence, a likely result of the prominent role labour played in the pro-labour Smallwood government. The next peak occurred in 1959, due almost entirely to the first contract struggle by the IWA against the logging companies. Union militancy remained low for the next decade, a likely reaction to the perceived high costs and uncertainty of striking while the Smallwood government remained in power, after having destroyed the IWA. An explosive period of strike activity began in 1969, peaked in 1980 and declined slowly through to the end of the century. The major contributor to the early part of this trend was the mining industry, which, as an export-driven industry, was susceptible to the volatile economic conditions of the time (e.g., oil price and trade shocks and unanticipated inflation). The 1980s and 1990s also produced a rash of large fishery and public sector strikes. Strikes in the fishery must be viewed against the backdrop of declining fish stocks and fluctuating prices for fish in the commodity markets in which much of it was sold. Strikes in the public sector must be viewed in the context of selective income restraints, privatization, contracting-out, lack of consultation and highly politicized bargaining processes. In the first quarter of 2002, strike activity reached a five-year low, a likely consequence of the new spirit of labour-management cooperation permeating the labour relations community generally, and the fishery and public sector, in particular.

During the 1990s, Newfoundland and Labrador was generally regarded as one of the more strike-prone of the Canadian provinces. This led some to question the labour climate in the province (Labour Relations Working Group 1996). A variety of standardized measures of strike activity for this province and Canada as a whole are shown in Table 4. The table shows that Newfoundland and Labrador has a higher volume of strike activity that appears to be caused by a higher frequency of strikes that are smaller in size but longer in duration.

Two major factors appear to explain the above-average level of strike activity. First, Newfoundland and Labrador has a higher level of union density than other provinces making the threat of strikes more pervasive. The effects of controlling for union density are shown in Table 4 by comparing person-days lost due to strikes by employment and union membership for Newfoundland and Labrador and Canada as a whole. Whereas days lost by employment for Newfoundland and Labrador is 85 percent higher than the Canadian average, it is only 29.8 percent higher when examined relative to total union membership. Thus, higher union

TABLE 4

AVERAGE ANNUAL STRIKE STATISTICS, 1976–2001

	Newfoundland	Canada	Percentage Difference (%)
Strike frequency			
Frequency (annual average)	20.04	622.42	
Frequency per thousand employed	0.11	0.05	110.8
Frequency per thousand union members	0.26	0.18	47.9
Strike size			
Workers involved (annual average)	7,161.65	331,748.31	
Workers involved per strike	357.40	532.99	−32.9
Person-days lost per strike	6,233.59	7,100.34	−12.2
Strike duration			
Person-days lost (annual average)	124,911.54	4,419,414.04	
Person-days lost per thousand employed	661.10	357.26	85.0
Person-days lost per thousand union members	1,635.32	1,259.67	29.8
Person-days lost per thousand workers involved	17,441.72	13,321.59	30.9
Excluding five largest Newfoundland strikes			
Person-days lost (annual average)	85,597.69	4,380,100.19	
Person-days lost per thousand employed	453.03	354.08	27.9
Person-days lost per thousand union members	1,120.63	1,248.46	−10.2
Person-days lost per thousand workers involved	14,738.38	13,257.18	11.2

Source: Calculations by author based on data supplied by the Workplace Information Directorate, HRDC.

density explains some but not all of the provinces higher strike activity. Second, strike statistics are inflated by a very small number of large strikes. For example, of the 521 strikes that occurred between 1976 and 2001 in Newfoundland and Labrador, the top 1 percent (or five strikes) represented approximately 19 percent of all workers involved and 32 percent of total person-days lost during the entire period. When the strike statistics are re-estimated without these outlying values, the differences between the provincial and national strike records actually reverses with average person-days lost per union member now being 10.2 percent lower in Newfoundland and Labrador compared to Canada as a whole.

After controlling for these factors, however, the re-estimated statistics also reveal that the average worker involved in a strike in Newfoundland and Labrador loses approximately 11.2 percent more person-days than the average Canadian worker. One likely reason for this is the higher concentration of employment in strike-prone industries found in the province. Primary industries may be more strike prone because their susceptibility to the business cycle contributes to informational problems and divergent offers and demands in the bargaining process. These factors, combined with the lack of alternative labour market opportunities, reduced social mobility, and the isolation of many communities in Newfoundland and Labrador may leave little alternative but the use of the strike as a method of dispute resolution (Krahn and Lowe 1984). In effect, a higher number of small, protracted disputes may be used to reconcile divergent expectations or elicit private information about ability to pay. Newfoundland and Labrador also has a higher proportion of employment in public services where strike volumes rose in the 1980s and 1990s. Combined with this, public sector employees in Newfoundland and Labrador have also had more opportunity to strike than in other jurisdictions, given that some Canadian jurisdictions have denied their public sector workers the right to strike since granting them collective bargaining rights in the 1970s.

Combined, these factors suggest that the higher average level of strike activity in this province, relative to Canada, may have less to do with a poor labour climate than with the province's higher union density, a few very large strikes, and a higher concentration of strike-sensitive industries. This conclusion is consistent with empirical work on strike activity in Canada between 1971–83, which shows fishing, mining, and wood-related industries to be among the most strike prone of Canadian industries (Gunderson, Kervin and Reid 1986). More telling, these results showed little evidence of regional variation in the labour climate across Canada, as might be expected to show up, all else being equal, in variables controlling for provincial location. Nevertheless, it is clear that certain decisions within the ambit of the parties' control can have an impact on the level of strike activity in the province. In particular, the recent decision to adopt a system of final-offer selection in fishery bargaining can be expected to have a noticeable impact on strike activity in this sector. Also, the new strategic alliance between business, government, and labour should help establish an improved context for public sector bargaining. These two developments may help explain the drop in strike activity experienced in the province in the first quarter of 2002.

INDUSTRIAL RELATIONS PROCESSES AND OUTCOMES

The 1990s was a period of economic restraint in the public sector, as public debt had risen substantially. Limits were imposed on public sector bargaining. In 1992, the Northern Cod Moratorium brought the province's groundfish fishery and fish-processing sector to a standstill. The economic environment of the 1990s also presented some opportunities, most notable of which was the growth experienced in the highly competitive offshore oil and gas sector. These challenges and opportunities have been forcing labour and management to adopt more efficient practices.

Innovations in the Bargaining Process

With no full-scale return of a groundfish fishery in sight and the winding down of income support under federal assistance programs, income and employment security have become critical issues in the fishery. These circumstances may have prompted the FFAW/CAW and FANL to agree to a two-year pilot project in 1998 using interest-based bargaining facilitated by a third-party neutral and final-offer selection to settle bargaining impasses over the price of fish sold to local processing plants across the province (Task Force on Fish/Crab Disputes 1998). This approach sought to avoid job action that prevents the industry from selling during peak demand periods when fish prices, and therefore, income and employment opportunities in the fishery, would be at their highest.

Use of final-offer selection is rare in interest arbitration; rarer still in private sector negotiations. While the parties may choose conventional interest arbitration, their consistent use of final-offer selection may be indicative of a commitment to reasonable approaches to the negotiation of fish prices. Whatever their reason, the use of interest arbitration is a ground-breaking approach to fish price negotiations in North America. In July 2000, this process left the pilot project stage and became enshrined in the *Fishing Industry Collective Bargaining Act.* Incentives for cooperation in the fishery may be expected to grow as the fishery of the future is expected to be substantially less labour-intensive.

Mid-Contract Dispute-Resolution Mechanisms

There is some evidence to suggest that mid-contract dispute mechanisms operate somewhat more efficiently in Newfoundland and Labrador compared to other jurisdictions in Canada. A review of published research articles on sources of delay in grievance arbitration in separate Canadian jurisdictions, for example, shows much lower pre- and post-hearing sources of delay in Newfoundland and Labrador (Thornicroft 2001). More recent estimates of delay in reported arbitration awards in this province indicate a sizeable reduction in pre-hearing delay from 250 to 150 days between 1992 and 1994, respectively (Labour Relations Working Group 1996). Finally, a recent evaluation of the province's grievance mediation program[2] concluded that users perceived grievance mediation to be faster than arbitration and facilitated the internal settlement of disputes (McDonald Human Resources 1996).

Care must be exercised in drawing conclusions from the foregoing. Published studies of delay in grievance arbitration are not strictly comparable due to a myriad of differences, not least of which are the time periods and issues in dispute under study. Survey information from users of grievance mediation provides no information on outcomes that may have occurred in the absence of the intervention, a caution underscored by an Ontario study showing an important half-life effect in relations-by-objectives programs (Hebdon and Mazerolle 1995). Nevertheless, lower average levels of pre-hearing delay may be indicative of maturation in the parties' approach to collective agreement administration. While lower average levels of post-hearing delay may be directly linked to changes in arbitrator behaviours, one cannot ignore the potential impact of the parties' changing expectations on the behaviour of persons they choose to serve as arbitrators.

Emerging Practices

Emerging practices witnessed recently in the high-growth segments of the private sector have emphasized a number of trade-offs between flexibility and employment security, and between industrial stability, income security, and union recognition. An example of the first may be found in the fabrication yard agreement negotiated between PCL Industrial Constructors Inc. (PCL) and the Newfoundland and Labrador International Building Trades Petroleum Development Association (PDA) for the fabrication of topsides modules to be installed on the floating production vessel to be used in the Terra Nova oil development. This agreement emphasized flexibility in work assignments and the elimination of disputes over work jurisdiction (Cooper 1997) in an effort to secure the fabrication yard's future in the burgeoning offshore oil development industry. The effectiveness of this agreement has since been called into question, however, as conflict over work assignments led to the need to add a jurisdictional dispute-resolution mechanism to the project collective agreement. These disputes, and their effect on future investment of this type in the province, provided much of the impetus for the government introducing legislation in 2001 to enhance stability and productivity on major offshore oil and gas fabrication and construction projects (see Cooper 2000).

An example of the trade-off between industrial stability, income security, and union recognition is the agreement negotiated between FFAW/CAW and Cancrew concerning future employees on the shuttle tankers to transport oil from Hibernia to the transhipment facility. The parties recently negotiated a 25-year collective agreement providing for the indexing of wages and the submission of bargaining impasses for resolution through interest arbitration (Cooper 1997).

The extent to which these practices are representative of other labour-management relationships is not fully known. Some insight into this point may be obtained by examining collective agreement provisions from Human Resources Development Canada's major collective-agreement data-bank (Table 5). These data must be treated cautiously, however, as they are based on bargaining units of more than 500 employees, effectively excluding over 50 percent of union membership in Newfoundland and Labrador, particularly those in smaller bargaining units.

The data indicate a proportionately higher level of risk-sharing in this province, relative to the rest of Canada, in terms of income and employment security, due process guarantees, and union security. For example, 13.6 percent of employees have some element of variable compensation in Newfoundland and Labrador compared to 10.2 percent across Canada. Possibly in exchange for this risk, unions have been able to negotiate stronger forms of union security, seniority protection, and better

TABLE 5

EMPLOYEES COVERED BY COLLECTIVE-AGREEMENT PROVISIONS, 1996 AND 1998

	Newfoundland (%)		Canada (%)	
	1996	1998	1996	1998
Union-management relationship				
Union shop	28.9	21.7	13.8	16.7
Modified union shop	25.3	26.7	24.2	20.3
Check-off	98.8	100.0	93.1	87.2
Labour-management committee	94.6	90.1	73.5	79.7
Wage-effort bargain				
Cost-of-living allowance	3.7	4.2	36.4	29.8
Wage incentive plans	12.7	13.6	7.2	10.2
Equal pay for work of equal value	35.7	48.7	20.2	22.6
Control of jobs				
Supervisors and non-bargaining unit members	60.0	55.6	27.7	31.9
Restrictions on contracting-out	41.4	65.8	53.1	62.9
Seniority in cases of				
Promotion	66.1	63.9	47.5	49.9
Transfer	49.9	41.2	44.1	52.3
Layoff	98.8	100.0	67.0	67.8
Recall	96.4	98.6	65.8	65.7
Bumping	81.4	75.1	47.2	51.6
Job Posting	96.4	97.6	59.5	59.3
Notice of layoff	72.7	71.2	55.3	58.9
Job sharing	23.7	25.8	10.5	16.5
Severance pay	86.7	79.8	52.8	53.7
Technological change				
Advance notice	67.7	61.0	58.3	50.0
Right to retraining	55.1	46.7	25.8	22.4
Joint committee	9.2	12.7	27.9	21.0
Relocation allowance	5.3	4.2	7.2	5.7
Employment guarantee	52.7	43.5	12.4	9.3
Income guarantee	60.0	51.3	19.4	16.0
Control of work behaviour and environment				
Probationary period after hiring	96.6	100.0	63.6	66.2
Clearing of employees' record of discipline	87.5	88.7	60.4	55.7
Sexual harassment	64.8	86.7	48.0	53.9
Day care facilities	14.4	37.6	6.5	5.8
Counselling services	26.4	32.8	13.4	19.4
Alcohol/drug addiction program	41.8	46.4	24.6	28.2
Training (on-the-job)	45.5	35.3	48.1	54.1
Training (outside courses)	7.4	8.0	34.0	40.4
Health and safety – right to know and refuse unsafe work	10.7	7.2	25.1	35.1
Health and safety – powers of committee	22.6	27.4	24.7	30.2

Source: Bureau of Labour Information, Collective agreement databank covering 500 or more employees.

consultative rights through joint labour-management committees. For example, 48.4 percent of union members in the province are covered by union shop or modified union shop provisions, compared to 37 percent across Canada; seniority is much more extensively used in job assignment cases such as promotion (63.9 percent versus 49.9 percent), layoff (100 percent versus 67.8 percent) and job posting (97.6 percent versus 59.3 percent); and labour-management committees cover 90.1 percent of union members in Newfoundland and Labrador compared to 79.7 percent for the country overall. Again, this evidence of somewhat more efficient trade-offs between labour and management would not be possible in a poisoned environment and is suggestive of the artifactual character of Newfoundland and Labrador's reputation as a strike-prone province.

DISTINCTIVE AND COMMON FEATURES OF INDUSTRIAL RELATIONS

Industrial relations in Newfoundland and Labrador resembles other jurisdictions, with the differences more a matter of degree than of kind. Where differences exist, they largely reflect the province's geographically dispersed population; economic dependence on natural resources; and relative isolation from the rest of Canada.

Like the rest of Canada, the Government of Newfoundland and Labrador played an active role in the development of infrastructure necessary to promote industry (Sack and Lee 1989). The province, however, was more reliant on natural resources than other jurisdictions, which led to a less diversified economy which is more open to outside influences and less able to sustain income earning and employment opportunities. Since the late 1990s, the economic position of the province has improved relative to the rest of the country. Economic expansion has produced a substantial shift in employment away from jobs traditionally supported by the fishery.

The evolution of provincial labour policy has also been similar to other jurisdictions, starting with an early period of outright prohibition against collective bargaining, to active support by World War II, and piecemeal change thereafter. Labour policy has also been shaped by British, American, and other Canadian influences; however, their timing has been very different with English influence playing a more prominent role in Newfoundland and Labrador due to the province's later entry into Confederation. Thus, for example, the province enacted compulsory conciliation in 1938, but the rest of Canada followed the lead of the *Industrial*

Disputes Investigation Act of 1907. Similarly, Wagnerism arrived in New-foundland and Labrador in 1950, six years after most of the country experienced PC 1003 in 1944. Today, labour market regulation continues to lag the rest of the country, a possible consequence of the more precarious economic base and government efforts to attract business investment. Nevertheless, Canadian models of labour and employment law appear well entrenched and the government has shown some willingness to improve the law with the provincial economy's most recent expansion. As in the rest of the country, public sector bargaining suffered from growing pains over the last quarter of the twentieth century (Swimmer and Thompson 1995). Unlike the rest of the country, however, Newfoundland and Labrador may be on the verge of a new era of labour-management cooperation in the public sector, a result that will likely depend on the continued goodwill between the parties.

The same broad patterns of change in trade union structure appear in Newfoundland and Labrador as in the rest of Canada. Labour-sponsored political parties, however, have not enjoyed the same electoral successes as third parties in other provinces, possibly a result of more traditionalist orientations found in the province. While Newfoundland and Labrador has one of the highest levels of union density in the country, part of this reflects differences in the structure of its labour market. This has important implications for the labour movement given that primary and allied industries, as well as the public sector, will likely sustain lower employment levels in the future. Part of the province's higher union density, however, may reflect a greater demand for union representation, a potential result of a population that is geographically dispersed and to a large extent, socially isolated. This greater sense of collectivism may help explain the recent organizing successes on offshore oil and gas platforms despite considerable employer opposition and a legal requirement to organize an all-employee unit. High levels of union representation in the community at large may substitute for the limited electoral success of the NDP in this province.

Criticisms of labour relations are somewhat overstated for Newfoundland and Labrador. Industrial structure, higher union density and a few large strikes help explain its higher average strike record, while collective agreements evidence somewhat stronger forms of risk-sharing and the collective-agreement administration process appears to run more efficiently than in other provinces. Although there is evidence of labour-management cooperation in the private sector, until recently, there has been a discernible absence of such cooperation in the public sector, perhaps a reflection of perceived inequities in the process of designating essential workers, wage restraint, and downsizing over the 1980s and 1990s. While it is still too early to tell, the recent success of the liberal government in forging a strategic alliance with the business and labour communities may represent a turning point in labour-management relations in the province. With the provincial economy having one of the strongest rates of growth across Canada in recent years, strike activity at a five-year low, and a vibrant and growing labour movement with a stronger voice in the province's social and economic development, the provincial system of industrial relations seems very much intact and poised to contribute to further growth and prosperity in the years ahead.

NOTES

I would like to thank Randy Hollahan and Jacqueline Power for capable research assistance and the Centre for Newfoundland Studies for their cooperation. Without implicating them for any of the contents of this manuscript, I would also like to acknowledge helpful comments from David Alcock, Lorne Bennett, Peter Boswell, Morgan Cooper, Anthony Cuomo, Alex Faseruk, Dennis Hogan, Greg Kealey, Elaine Price, Joe Rose, Anthony Smith, John Staple, Mark Thompson and Marilyn Tucker. Financial assistance from the Government of Canada's funded project on Regional Aspects of Employment Relations Policy in Canada is gratefully acknowledged.

[1]One factor that contributed to the government's lack of action was the group's recommendation that its report be accepted *in toto*, an unlikely outcome in light of some contentious recommendations. For example, the group recommended board-supervised presentations of positions prior to certification votes; compulsory training and interest arbitration in cases of first collective agreements; and the establishment of an independent, arm's-length agency to handle all of the government's labour relations and collective bargaining functions.

[2]Grievance mediation is actually one component of the province's Preventive Mediation Program, which also includes mediator consultations; first-agreement orientation; labour-management committees; supervisor-steward joint training; and relationship by objectives. Of these components, the vast majority of interventions have been for grievance mediation.

REFERENCES

Adams, G. 1995. *Canadian Labour Law*. Aurora, ON: Canada Law Book.

Adamson, A. and I. Stewart. 1991. "Party Politics in Atlantic Canada: Still the Mysterious East?" in *Party Politics in Canada*, 6th ed., ed. H. Thorburn. Scarborough: Prentice Hall.

Akyeampong, E.B. 1997. "A Statistical Portrait of the Trade Union Movement," *Perspectives on Labour and Income* 9 (4):45-54.

—— 1999. "Unionization: An Update," *Perspectives on Labour and Income* 11 (3):45-65.

—— 2001. "Fact-Sheet on Unionization," *Perspectives on Labour and Income* 13 (3):46-54.

Alcock, D. 1997. *Time to Refocus: Report of the 1996-97 Statutory Review Committee on the Workers' Compensation Act.* St. John's: The Committee.

Cohen, M. 1972. *Report of the Royal Commission on Labour Legislation in Newfoundland and Labrador.* St. John's: The Commission.

Cooper, M.C. 1997. *Labour Relations Processes on Offshore Oil Production Platforms.* St. John's: Labour Relations Board.

—— 2000. *Labour Relations Processes on Offshore Oil and Gas Fabrication and Construction Projects.* St. John's: Labour Relations Board.

Gillespie, W. 1986. *A Class Act.* St. John's: Newfoundland and Labrador Federation of Labour.

Government of Newfoundland and Labrador. 1992. *Change and Challenge: A Strategic Economic Plan for Newfoundland and Labrador.* St. John's: Government of Newfoundland and Labrador.

—— 1998. *The Atlantic Groundfish Strategy: An Analysis of the Program on a Regional Basis.* St. John's: Government of Newfoundland and Labrador.

—— n.d. *Exploring Options for Improved Labour Relations: A Paper Relating to Issues of Importance for Employers, Unions and Workers.* St. John's: Government of Newfoundland and Labrador.

Gunderson, M., J. Kervin and F. Reid. 1986. "Logit Estimates of Strike Incidence from Canadian Contract Data," *Journal of Labour Economics* 4 (2):257-76.

Harris, J. 1996. "Newfoundland Labour Law History." Paper presented to Canadian Industrial Relations Association (Newfoundland Chapter), St. John's, Newfoundland.

Hattenhauer, R. 1970. *A Brief Labour History of Newfoundland.* St. John's: Royal Commission on Labour Legislation in Newfoundland and Labrador.

Hebdon, R. and M. Mazerolle. 1995. "Mending Fences, Building Bridges: The Effect of Relationship by Objectives on Conflict," *Relations industrielles-Industrial Relations* 50 (1):164-85.

Inglis, G. 1985. *More than Just a Union: The Story of the NFFAWU.* St. John's: Jesperson Press.

Kealey, G.S. 1986. *The History and Structure of the Newfoundland Labour Movement.* St. John's: Royal Commission on Employment and Unemployment.

Krahn, H. and G.S. Lowe. 1984. "Community Influences on Attitudes Towards Unions," *Relations industrielles-Industrial Relations* 39 (1):93-113.

Labour Relations Working Group. 1996. *New Century – New Realities: Creating a Framework Together. Final Report of the Labour Relations Working Group.* St. John's: Government of Newfoundland and Labrador.

Ladd, H.L. 1985. "The Newfoundland Loggers' Strike of 1959," in *Lectures in Canadian Labour and Working-Class History,* ed. W.J.C. Cherwinski and G.S. Kealey. St. John's: Committee on Canadian Labour History and New Hogtown Press.

Martinello, F. and R. Meng. 1992. "Effects of Labour Legislation and Industry Characteristics on Union Coverage in Canada," *Industrial and Labor Relations Review* 46 (1):176-90.

May, D. and A. Hollett. 1986. *The Causes of Unemployment in Newfoundland*. Background Report for the Royal Commission on Employment and Unemployment. St.John's: Government of Newfoundland and Labrador.

—— 1995. *The Rock in a Hard Place: Atlantic Canada and the UI Trap*. Toronto: C.D. Howe Institute.

McDonald Human Resources. 1996. *Evaluation of the Preventive Mediation Program*. St. John's, Newfoundland.

Morton, D. 1990. *Working People*, 3d ed. Toronto: Summerhill Press.

NG, I. 1992. "The Probability of Union Membership in the Private Sector," *Relations industrielles-Industrial Relations* 47 (1):43-56.

Sack, J. and T. Lee. 1989. "The Role of the State in Canadian Labour Relations," *Relations industrielles-Industrial Relations* 44 (1):195-221.

Statistics Canada. 1994. *Corporations and Labour Unions Returns Act*. Ottawa: Supply and Services Canada.

Strategic Concepts Inc., Wade Locke and Community Resource Services. 1999. *Harnessing the Potential – Atlantic Canada's Oil and Gas Industry*. St. John's: Strategic Concepts Inc.

Swimmer, G. and M. Thompson. 1995. "Collective Bargaining in the Public Sector: An Introduction," in *Public Sector Collective Bargaining*, ed. G. Swimmer and M. Thompson. Kingston: IRC Press, Queen's University.

Task Force on Fish/Crab Price Settlement Mechanisms. 1998. *New Beginnings: Bringing Stability and Structure to Price Determination in the Fishing Industry*. Report of the Task Force on Fish/Crab Price Settlement Mechanisms in the Fishing Industry Collective Bargaining Act, St. John's: The Commission.

Thornicroft, K. 2001. "The Grievance Arbitration Process: Theory and Practice," in *Union-Management Relations in Canada*, 4th ed., ed. M. Gunderson, A. Ponak and D.G. Taras. Toronto: Addison-Wesley Longman.

8 NOVA SCOTIA: TAKING CARE OF BUSINESS?

Terry H. Wagar

Résumé — Comme dans les autres provinces de l'Atlantique, les relations industrielles en Nouvelle-Écosse ont été fortement influencées par les initiatives gouvernementales visant à protéger les emplois et à encourager les investissements. La Nouvelle-Écosse fut la première province à adopter la législation du travail inspirée de la Wagner Act. Pourtant, la tension a été constante entre les droits des travailleurs et le désir des gouvernements libéraux et conservateurs qui se sont succédé d'adopter des politiques et des programmes favorisant le développement économique.

Il y a 943 000 habitants en Nouvelle-Écosse. Environ 100 000 sont membres d'un syndicat (le taux de syndicalisation est légèrement supérieur à 28 %), et le taux de chômage tourne autour de 10 %. Dans cette province, l'organisation des travailleurs a pris naissance dans les mines de charbon du Cap-Breton et, encore aujourd'hui, les observateurs parlent de deux mouvements ouvriers distincts : celui de l'île du Cap-Breton et celui de la partie continentale de la Nouvelle-Écosse, le premier étant perçu comme plus favorable à la syndicalisation que ne l'est l'autre. Contrairement à certaines provinces canadiennes, il n'y a eu que deux partis qui ont gouverné en Nouvelle-Écosse depuis les années 1930, soit les partis libéral et conservateur qui, à tour de rôle, ont exercé le pouvoir.

Au cours du dernier siècle, des changements importants ont marqué les relations industrielles en Nouvelle-Écosse. Dès la fin des années 1800, ces relations dans l'industrie du charbon avaient mûri au point où les parties concluaient des contrats sur des questions telles que la sécurité d'emploi, la rémunération et l'ancienneté. Dans les années subséquentes, on a de plus en plus régulé la négociation collective et, en 1937, la Nouvelle-Écosse devint un leader dans l'élaboration de la législation du travail avancée en promulguant la *Trade Union Act*. Cependant, cette position a été de courte durée, puisque, deux décennies plus tard, le gouvernement néo-écossais réglementait de plus en plus les relations de travail, l'attitude envers les syndicats devenait inamicale et une escalade des conflits patronaux-syndicaux se manifestait.

Dans les années 1960, la notion voulant que travailleurs et employeurs pouvaient et devaient coopérer était consacrée par la mise sur pied du Joint Labour-Management Study Committee (comité d'étude patronal-syndical).

La politique du gouvernement néo-écossais durant la dernière moitié du XXᵉ siècle a contribué à attirer l'investissement des entreprises afin d'encourager le développement économique, mais également servi à diminuer l'influence du syndicalisme. Dans les années 1970, deux modifications législatives majeures ont affaibli le pouvoir des syndicats, brisé les relations entre les travailleurs et le gouvernement, provoqué le démantèlement du Joint Labour-Management Study Committee et différencié le droit syndical de la Nouvelle-Écosse de celui des autres provinces canadiennes.

La première a permis au gouvernement de commencer à obliger la tenue d'un vote pour toute demande d'accréditation syndicale. Ce changement a représenté une dérogation importante par rapport à ce qui se faisait dans les autres provinces (où les syndicats pouvaient être accrédités sur présentation d'un certain nombre de cartes de membres) et rendu la syndicalisation plus difficile. Il faut souligner que, ces dernières années, les autres provinces ont suivi l'exemple de la Nouvelle-Écosse et que plusieurs exigent maintenant la tenue d'un vote pour accorder l'accréditation syndicale.

La deuxième a eu lieu en 1979 par l'adoption du fameux projet de loi Michelin en plein durant une campagne de recrutement syndical dans une des usines de fabrication de pneus Michelin de la province. Ce projet de loi modifiant la *Trade Union Act* prévoyait qu'un employeur dans le domaine de la fabrication pouvait demander à la Commission des relations de travail de la Nouvelle-Écosse que tous ses établissements « autonomes » soient considérés comme une seule unité de négociation aux fins de la négociation collective. Rétroactive, cette modification a entraîné l'annulation d'un vote d'accréditation à l'usine Michelin visé par le syndicat. Plusieurs tentatives subséquentes de syndicalisation des travailleurs des trois usines Michelin en Nouvelle-Écosse (la dernière par les TCA) ont échoué.

Le projet de loi Michelin a prouvé l'importance d'attirer des entreprises et des investissements dans la province. Les gouvernements conservateurs et libéraux subséquents ont agi dans ce sens, assurant la prépondérance des intérêts en affaires et en finances sur les droits des travailleurs. L'échec de l'application de normes de sécurité à la mine Westray, la suppression du droit de négociation collective dans le secteur public tant par le gouvernement conservateur que libéral des années 1990 et l'adoption récente du projet de loi 68 qui enlève le droit de grève aux travailleurs de la santé, tout indique une stratégie favorisant les intérêts en affaires aux dépens de ceux des travailleurs.

INTRODUCTION

Like the other Atlantic provinces, Nova Scotia's labour relations and industrial policy have, in recent decades, been heavily influenced by government initiatives aimed at protecting jobs and encouraging investment in the province. Although Nova Scotia was the first province to introduce labour legislation based on the *Wagner Act* model, there has been a constant tension between worker rights and the desire of successive Liberal and Conservative governments to introduce policies and programs aimed at enhancing economic development.

The labour movement in Nova Scotia is small, highly determined, and somewhat militant. It has continued to survive in a province that gives a high priority to business interests. For most of the past two decades, Nova Scotia was the only province to require a vote in certification elections, regardless of the percentage of bargaining unit members that had signed membership cards. Although it appeared that labour relations in the province were improving since the removal of wage rollback legislation in November 1997, the election of John Hamm's Conservative government has produced new concerns over government restraint programs and the removal of collective bargaining rights.

This chapter provides a brief historical overview of important industrial relations developments, summarizes some of the key features of labour legislation in the province, examines dispute-resolution procedures, and investigates the nature of the relationship between labour and management.

ECONOMIC STRUCTURE

Nova Scotia has 943,000 inhabitants, and approximately 470,000 Nova Scotians are members of the labour force. As of July 2002, the unemployment rate was about 10 percent and exceeded the Canadian rate (7.5 percent) by a considerable margin. However, unemployment is lower in Nova Scotia than the other three Atlantic provinces — New Brunswick's unemployment rate is 10.5 percent and the rates for Prince Edward Island and Newfoundland are approximately 12.4 percent and 15 percent, respectively (Statistics Canada 2002). The seasonally adjusted labour force participation rate is about 62 percent, which is somewhat lower than the Canadian average of 66.8 percent (Statistics Canada 2002). The participation rate is about 68 percent for men and 57 percent for women.

The Nova Scotia economy is service-based with approximately 80 percent of employees working in the service and not-for-profit sectors. The major industries include community, business and personal services, trade, public administration, manufacturing and processing, and construction (see Table 1). The largest employers in manufacturing include Trenton Works Ltd., I.M.P. Group Ltd., and Michelin N.A. (Canada) Ltd. The largest non-governmental employers in the service sector are Maritime Life Assurance Company, Atlantic Wholesalers, Sobey's Inc., Maritime Telegraph and Telephone Co. Ltd., Royal Bank of Canada, Bank of Nova Scotia, and Nova Scotia Power Incorporated.

TABLE 1
EMPLOYMENT BY INDUSTRY SECTOR, 2001

Sector	Employment ('000s)	% of Employed Workforce (%)
Agriculture	6.9	1.7
Other primary industries	15.0	3.7
Manufacturing	45.0	11.0
Construction	21.8	5.3
Transportation/communication	21.0	5.1
Utilities	2.1	0.5
Trade	70.7	17.3
Financial services	23.0	5.6
Community/business/personal services	177.6	43.5
Public administration	25.6	6.3

Source: Canada. HRDC.

Although the province's origins were in the resource-based industries of mining, fishing, and forestry, the economy has diversified and the important industries include high technology manufacturing, aerospace, ocean research, the film industry, information technology, and tourism. Nova Scotia is witnessing the growing development of offshore mining (of oil and gas)[1] and Halifax seeks to become a superport.

The average annual personal income of Nova Scotians (2001) is slightly under $24,500 and average weekly earnings are approximately $560. However, there are important interindustry differences. Employees in mining, public administration and transportation, communication and other utilities earn well above the average, while the lowest paying jobs are in the trade and service industries. In addition, of the more than 32,000 businesses in Nova Scotia, almost three-quarters employ less than five people (NS. Department of Finance 2001).

The gross domestic product (GDP) for the province is about $25 billion and tourists spend more than $1.2 billion in the province annually. In terms of foreign exports, about 75 percent are to the United States. The major exports include fish and fish preparations, paper and paperboard, transportation equipment, non-metallic minerals and mineral fuels, and wood pulp and similar pulp.

Just fewer than 18 percent of Nova Scotians live on Cape Breton Island. The Island has faced considerable adversity over the years; in 2002 the unemployment rate for Cape Breton stood at around 16 percent, which is considerably higher than in other parts of the province. The economy of the region suffered as a result of the sale of the provincially owned Sydney Steel Company (SYSCO) and the closure of the Cape Breton Development Corporation's (DEVCO) last mine.

The historical roots of organized labour in Nova Scotia began in the coal mines of Cape Breton. Labour relations in the mining industry were characterized by "bitterness, hostility and outright violence" (Antoff 1981). Indeed, observers often speak of two labour movements within the province — Cape Breton Island and mainland Nova Scotia. Cape Breton Island is perceived as being more pro-union than mainland Nova Scotia (Gilson, Spencer and Granville 1989). Gilson and Wagar (1995) found that the likelihood of a union being certified was greater if the organizing drive was held in Cape Breton. Moreover, labour disputes in Cape Breton attract considerable attention. For instance, there was extensive media coverage when unionized construction workers set fire to a partially constructed apartment complex in Sydney (which was being built by non-union labour) and also torched a pickup truck and construction trailer (MacIntyre 1997). However, some recent studies have found that Cape Breton's reputation for union militancy is somewhat overstated (MacGillivray 1997).

PATTERNS OF POLITICAL BEHAVIOUR

Unlike some other Canadian provinces, which have experienced considerable change in public policy as different political parties formed the government, Nova Scotia has had only two parties come to power since the 1930s. From the early 1930s to 1956, the Liberal Party was in power (Table 2). For the next 14 years, the Progressive Conservatives governed the province. Over the next three decades, the two parties alternated in forming the government: there was a Liberal government between 1970 and 1978, the Progressive Conservatives ruled until 1993, the Liberals held power until 1999, and the Progressive Conservatives were elected in 1999.

In 1937, Nova Scotia became the first Canadian province to introduce trade union legislation modelled on the US *Wagner Act*. Over the next five decades, changes to the labour law were aimed at reducing

TABLE 2
NOVA SCOTIA PREMIERS AND GOVERNING PARTIES
(1933 TO THE PRESENT)

Time Period	Premier	Governing Party
1933–1940	Angus L. Macdonald	Liberal
1940–1945	A.S. MacMillan	Liberal
1945–1954	Angus L. Macdonald	Liberal
1954	Harold Connolly	Liberal
1954–1956	Henry D. Hicks	Liberal
1956–1967	Robert L. Stanfield	Progressive Conservative
1967–1970	G.I. Smith	Progressive Conservative
1970–1978	Gerald A. Regan	Liberal
1978–1990	John M. Buchanan	Progressive Conservative
1990–1991	Roger S. Bacon	Progressive Conservative
1991–1993	Donald W. Cameron	Progressive Conservative
1993–1997	John Savage	Liberal
1997–1999	Russell M. MacLellan	Liberal
1999–Present	John Hamm	Progressive Conservative

the power of trade unions and encouraging businesses to locate in the province (Earle and McKay 1989). Both Liberal and Progressive Conservative governments shared these goals.

From the perspective of the labour movement, a very dark moment in Nova Scotia industrial relations history came with the 1979 passage of the "Michelin Bill" (currently section 26 of the *Trade Union Act*, described below) by the Conservative government of John Buchanan. Although the direct impact of the Michelin Bill was limited to protecting the Michelin plants from unionization, it sent a clear message to labour that the government favoured attracting industry to the province over progressive labour legislation.[2]

In the wake of the Michelin Bill, the relationship between labour and the government remained relatively cool during the 1980s. It deteriorated even further with the introduction of public sector wage restraint and rollback legislation of the 1990s. In 1991, the Conservative government of Donald Cameron introduced the *Public Sector Compensation Restraint Act,* which, in effect, froze the wages of "public employees" (very broadly defined). In May 1993, Nova Scotians elected the Liberal government of John Savage. Shortly after, the Liberals enacted the *Public Sector Unpaid Leave Act*, which required public employees (again, very broadly defined) to take unpaid leaves of approximately five days. Despite public criticism, the Savage government, in March 1994, introduced the *Public Sector Compensation (1994–1997) Act*, which froze all compensation plans until 1 November 1997 and reduced all pay rates by 3 percent (save for employees earning less than $25,000).[3] Whereas Nova Scotia unions and public employees felt betrayed, Premier Savage stated that the fiscal pressures made collective bargaining untenable.

> We made the decision that collective bargaining, which is important to us, is a sham if you have nothing to offer. We literally have nothing to offer for the next couple of years. The decision to go with the three percent cut is made, and that is non-negotiable. We are finding it difficult to get across to people that if we don't take measures to cut back public expenditures, we may have, for instance, only six hospitals in this province ... purely and simply, we don't have the resources to continue to provide the service we have got (Madill 1994).

A 1995 ruling from the International Labour Organization (ILO) stated that freezing and cutting wages of employees directly or indirectly working for the government constituted a severe restriction on the right of collective bargaining. The ILO did not accept the argument of the Nova Scotia government that the fiscal situation of the province demanded legislative intervention into the collective bargaining process. The committee of the ILO reported that

> the committee deplores that the government did not give priority to collective bargaining as a means of determining wages of workers in the public sector, but that it felt compelled to adopt these legislative measures. The committee insists that the government refrain from taking such measures in the future (ILO 1995).

Although the ILO ruling represented a moral victory for the union movement, Premier Savage maintained that the province's fiscal situation justified its actions. As the premier noted, "we anticipated the ruling and it will not give us any change" (Shaw 1995).

When the wage rollback legislation expired in November 1997, Russell MacLellan's minority Liberal government was in power. Although interviews with union leaders suggested that the industrial relations climate in the province was improving, collective bargaining was strained in the 1998–99 period. The expiration of the rollback legislation resulted in a flurry of contract negotiations and, while agreements in most major sectors were settled, the period was also marked by considerable labour unrest and uncertainty. For example, there were bitter labour disputes at a number of nursing homes, the federal government announced that it was ending subsidies to DEVCO, and Volvo closed its auto plant in Halifax after 35 years of operation (MacDonald 1998). Although Premier MacLellan indicated that his government would try to ensure that workers were treated properly, many Nova Scotians felt betrayed by Volvo's decision to withdraw from the province. The Volvo plant in Halifax was very productive and there was a trust between Volvo and the community. Volvo's claim that the plant was too small (production capacity was about 8,000 cars annually) troubled Nova Scotians when it was revealed that the company was planning to start manufacturing automobiles in Mexico (Taylor 1998).

In July 1999, Nova Scotians elected a majority Conservative government, led by Dr. John Hamm. Shortly after the election, the government revealed that the budget surpluses announced by Liberal governments over the previous three years were a sham. High-cost items such as health and school board deficits had been left off the balance sheet, leaving a large deficit of $384 million (Cox 1999*b*).

The bad news about the state of provincial finances was accompanied by an announcement that the government would conduct an internal review of all government programs to identify areas for reducing expenditures (Jackson 1999). Government employees, who experienced wage freezes and rollbacks for most of the 1990s, naturally were concerned about job cuts and a proposal to establish a four-day work week (with a resulting cut in pay). They bitterly concluded that the Hamm government had already set its agenda and was not prepared to consult with their union (ibid.).

The Hamm government's approach to labour relations produced worker unrest. For example, early in its term, the government experienced a bitter labour dispute with paramedics in the province. Ultimately, the government eliminated the paramedics' right to strike, replacing it with binding arbitration (Smith and Jackson 1999).

Another heated labour dispute between the Hamm government and health-care workers occurred in the summer of 2001. Hundreds of nurses voted to sign letters of resignation in response to Bill 68, which removed their right to strike. Premier Hamm stated that his government was considering imposing fines of up to $2,000 per person per day if employees did not return to work (Tutton 2001). Public opinion polls indicated that a large majority of Nova Scotians sympathized with the nurses' pay demands over the provincial government position (Lightstone 2001).

Initially, the Hamm government refused to consider interest arbitration to resolve the health-care disputes, arguing that it could not let an outside party make decisions that affected the financial stability of the province. After considerable pressure by health-care workers, the government and the two unions involved in the dispute agreed to interest arbitration on 5 July 2001. The arbitrator accepted the nurses' position, but found in favour of the government's position with respect to the other group of health-care workers (e.g., licensed practical nurses and lab technicians). The headline in the Halifax *Mail Star* aptly summarized the result: "Government 1, Health Unions 1."

The degree of public sector unrest is also evident when one examines strike data for 2000 and 2001. In 2000, Nova Scotia had five strikes, four of which involved the private sector. However, of 11 strikes in 2001, eight involved the public sector.

A BRIEF OVERVIEW OF LABOUR HISTORY

While some industrial relations scholars point to PC1003 and the *Industrial Relations and Disputes Investigation Act* of 1948 as important breakthroughs for organized labour, Earle and McKay (1989) argue that the so-called industrial relations "innovations" emerging in the 1940s had been tried previously in the Nova Scotia coal fields. In 1885, the Cumberland Railway and Coal Company and the Pioneer Lodge of the Provincial Workmen's Association (PWA) signed what may have been the first collective agreement in the Nova Scotia coal industry (ibid.). The agreement contained provisions covering employment security, seniority rights, and compensation. Three years later, Canada's first compulsory arbitration legislation, the *Nova Scotia Mines Arbitration Act* of 1888, received union support and in 1920, the United Mine Workers traded off the right to strike during the collective agreement for a more favourable wage settlement. Without the legal right to strike, workers with grievances during the term of the contract had to rely on an unsatisfactory internal grievance procedure (McKay 1983). According to Earle and McKay:

> It was thanks to the coal miners — who were unusual in the Canadian context in having organized a large, militant, industrial union — that Nova Scotia could justifiably claim, in both the 1880s and 1930s, that

its labour legislation and collective bargaining mechanisms were far more sophisticated and "advanced" than those of other provinces (1989, 12).

In 1937, the *Trade Union Act*[4] was passed. Incorporating aspects of the US *Wagner Act*, the legislation provided for dues check-off and gave employees the right to join a union and bargain collectively with the employer. While industrial unionism blossomed in the 1940s, unions in Nova Scotia did not experience the growth that other Canadian unions enjoyed. Although the *Trade Union Act* placed Nova Scotia at the forefront in terms of progressive labour legislation, rapid changes in key industries such as shipbuilding, reduced militancy among union leaders, and industrial decline in primary resource industries and manufacturing led to a decline in the strength of the labour movement. Furthermore, the role of government has been characterized by Earle and McKay as a "conscious effort (especially since 1947) to weaken labour's position in the province as part of a strategy of economic development" (1989, 17). Although one may debate this point, both the Liberal and Conservative governments over the past half-century have placed considerable emphasis on developing the Nova Scotian economy.

In 1947, the *Trade Union Act* incorporated many of the features of PC1003, including the prohibition on strikes during the life of the collective agreement and compulsory conciliation. During the 1950s, while the labour movement was growing in other provinces, unions in Nova Scotia experienced difficulty recruiting new members. A number of union leaders believed that a system of collective bargaining, which enshrined worker rights and demanded accommodation on the part of both labour and employers would contribute to higher labour productivity, reduce labour unrest, and hence be supported by the government. Instead, the government's efforts to attract major investors to the province suggested it was reluctant to support organized labour actively. For example, in the 1957–58 Windsor Gypsum strike, which lasted 13 months, the company refused to grant dues check-off.

The Joint Labour-Management Study Committee (JLMSC)

Following the strike at Windsor Gypsum, union leaders sought legislation guaranteeing union security. In response, the government appointed Judge Alexander A. McKinnon in 1960 to examine existing labour legislation and to evaluate whether it promoted industrial peace (McKinnon 1962). Employers and unions were divided over the issue of union security. The McKinnon Report, which was made public in 1962, concluded, "the compulsory union shop should not be made a legislative provision because it is one of the most important issues which should be decided by mutual agreement resulting from collective bargaining" (ibid., 51).

As an alternative, McKinnon proposed a joint union-management board to develop greater understanding and trust between the parties. The Joint Labour-Management Study Committee (JLMSC) was established in 1962. Leaders of the Nova Scotia Federation of Labour believed that the JLMSC would usher in a new era of cooperation between employers and unions. The committee could reduce the adversarial relations between the parties, provide labour with a "voice" in promoting progressive labour legislation, and give labour equal representation with employers and the government on boards and committees affecting workers.

Cooperation was particularly attractive because, as Gilson and Wadden (1989) observed, union membership was declining, the province's economy was faltering, the Windsor Gypsum strike suggested industrial action was ineffective, and union leaders accepted the government's plan to attract outside investment to revive the economy.

The JLMSC had seven members each from both management and labour and two representatives from the Institute of Public Affairs at Dalhousie University (including the chair, Guy Henson). The parties met monthly and sponsored an annual study conference for representatives from both sides along with observers.

The development of legislative proposals typically followed a four-step procedure: (i) identification of problem areas to be studied by a subcommittee; (ii) presentation of the changes to the annual study conference for discussion; (iii) communication of accepted proposals to labour and management groups throughout the province represented by the JLMSC; and (iv) final discussion by a special legislative committee of the JLMSC (where the minister of labour was invited to attend as an observer) and the development of a written brief (Henson 1969).

However, by the early 1970s, the Liberal government of Gerald Regan was dissatisfied with the efforts of the JLMSC. According to former Federation of Labour President Ed Johnstone, the Regan government favoured the demands of multinational corporations who were unwilling to subscribe to the cooperative approach of the JLMSC (Gilson and Wadden 1989). In 1972, the *Trade Union Act*[5] was amended; in addition to adopting the unfair labour practice provisions contained in the Canada Labour Code and permitting the use of a single arbitrator to resolve

disputes arising out of collective agreements,[6] the government moved toward the American model by requiring certification votes. More specifically, the board was required to order a certification vote if the union had
the support of between 40 and 60 percent of bargaining unit members
(Adams 1997).[7] This change, although ultimately approved by the JLMSC,
was followed by other amendments initiated without JLMSC authoriza-
tion, indicating that unilateral lobbying for changes in labour legislation
had occurred.

In 1973, the International Union of Operating Engineers applied
to the NSLRB for certification of a group of stationary engineers at
Michelin's Granton plant. A few days prior to the hearing, the Governor-
in-Council enacted new regulations to the *Trade Union Act* (which became known as the Michelin Regulations) that effectively barred the certification of *craft* units in manufacturing facilities (Langille 1981).

The government also became dissatisfied with the time it took
the JLMSC to make recommendations. As a result, ministers, often responding to pressure from individual employers not directly participating
in the JLMSC, bypassed the process. The JLMSC was perceived as restricting the government's freedom to make decisions, particularly once
the province began using pro-employer labour legislation to attract investment from multinational firms (Antoff 1981). While the JLMSC continued until the passing of the "Michelin Bill" in 1979, its power and
influence had declined markedly.

In 1977, additional amendments to the *Trade Union Act* made
certification more difficult for unions. While the requirement that at least
60 percent of bargaining unit members participate in the certification
vote was dropped, the NSLRB was required to hold a pre-hearing vote
(what became known as the "quickee vote"). For many years, Nova Scotia
was the only province requiring mandatory representation votes; in other
jurisdictions, unions could be automatically certified based on signed
membership cards.

THE MICHELIN BILL

A defining moment in Nova Scotia labour relations came in 1979
with the passage of the Michelin Bill. While the details of this amendment
to the *Trade Union Act* is discussed below, the thrust of the amendment
was that an employer in manufacturing with more than one location could
apply to the NSLRB for a determination that the appropriate bargaining

unit was all plant locations. This made union certification much more difficult because labour organizers could no longer target one plant or facility. Instead, they had to treat workers in separate facilities or plants as a single bargaining unit. In enticing Michelin to locate in Nova Scotia, the government was supporting a multinational company with a world-wide policy of remaining union-free.

The Michelin Bill was passed during an organizing drive at a single Michelin plant and effectively destroyed any chance of union certification at the facility.[8] Organized labour was outraged at the Conservative government of John Buchanan and union members of the JLMSC subsequently resigned from the committee.

To understand the anger of organized labour with the Michelin Bill it is necessary to briefly trace the developments prior to the passage of the legislation. After the election of the Buchanan government in 1978, the labour minister maintained the practice of regular meetings with the JLMSC, and indicated that he would consult with the JLMSC prior to proposing amendments to the *Trade Union Act*, as his predecessors had. In April 1979, the minister informed the JLMSC that he would introduce an amendment to the *Trade Union Act* to prevent the United Rubber Workers from organizing Michelin. When the executive of the JLMSC expressed grave misgivings about the proposed legislation, the minister let the JLMSC know that the bill would not be introduced in the spring sitting of the legislature. The JLMSC studied the bill further. In September 1979, the JLMSC stated that it would be inappropriate to amend the *Trade Union Act* as a means of attracting investment into the province (Antoff 1981).

On Friday, 30 November 1979, a new draft of the bill was sent to the JLMSC, advising that it would be introduced during a special session of the legislature in December. Despite a flurry of activity, labour and management representatives within the JLMSC were unable to agree over whether to actively oppose the bill. The labour members of the JLMSC then resigned and the Michelin Bill became law (ibid.).

The passage of the Michelin Bill severely strained relations between the government and the Nova Scotia Federation of Labour. The federation marched on Province House and withdrew its representation from most government committees and boards (one notable exception was the NSLRB). Organized labour felt the Michelin Bill was part of the government's "anti-union" strategy to cater to the demands of anti-union, multinational corporations in order to create jobs and reduce unemployment.[9] While the enactment of the Michelin Bill was preceded by a radio and television campaign against the amendment, large crowds protesting at

Province House, strong attacks from the New Democratic Party, and intense public debate, there was little discussion of the industrial relations merits or deficiencies of the legislation (Langille 1981). However, the government reminded the Liberal opposition of the Michelin regulations it passed in 1973.

GOVERNMENT WAGE RESTRAINTS

In the summer of 1982, the federal government introduced the *Public Sector Compensation Restraint Act* (the "6 and 5" program) as part of its inflation-fighting program. Despite protests from the Nova Scotia Government Employees Union (using the campaign slogan "Negotiate–Don't Legislate"), the Conservative government of John Buchanan (and most other provinces) followed the lead of the federal government by adopting wage-restraint legislation.

Provincial government involvement in the collective-bargaining process increased during the 1990s. As noted previously, the *Public Sector Compensation Restraint Act* (1991) and the *Public Sector Compensation (1994–1997) Act* effectively suspended collective bargaining over compensation for public sector employees. In addition, major restructuring and amalgamation in municipal government, education and health care substantially altered labour-management relationships and, in a number of cases, pitted unions against each other for representation rights of amalgamated bargaining units.

THE WESTRAY MINE EXPLOSION

The Westray mine, located in Pictou County (the riding of then Premier Donald Cameron), commenced operations in September of 1991. Nine months earlier, the Department of Labour issued its first safety order — the mine had conducted underground blasting in the absence of qualified people. As Glasbeek and Tucker (1995) note, this was the first of a number of orders in which no charges were laid, and work continued without corrections being made.

In their review of safety problems at Westray, Glasbeek and Tucker (ibid.) provide numerous examples of questionable safety practices during 1991 and 1992 (including rock falls, a cave-in, and high methane levels). On 29 April 1992 (just ten days prior to the explosion), the Department of Labour issued formal orders requiring Westray to comply with safety standards. However, government inspectors did not determine if Westray had complied with the orders.

On 9 May 1992, a violent explosion at the Westray mine instantly killed 26 miners, provoking a public inquiry conducted by Justice K. Peter Richard. In his report, Justice Richard described the disaster at Westray as a "complex mosaic of actions, omissions, mistakes, incompetence, apathy, cynicism, stupidity and neglect." He noted that several persons and entities had defaulted in their legislative, business, statutory, and management responsibilities. He found that Westray management failed in their primary responsibility of operating the Westray mine in a safe manner. However, he also blamed the Nova Scotia Department of Labour (in particular, the mine inspectorate) for its failure to demand strict compliance with the *Coal Mines Regulation Act* and the *Occupational Health and Safety Act* (Richard 1997).

In June 1999, Justice Minister Robbie Harrison agreed that a stay of proceedings against two mine managers should not be lifted, thus ending the attempt by the Nova Scotia prosecution service to seek convictions on manslaughter and criminal negligence charges. Conflicting expert evidence concerning the cause of the explosion indicated that the probability of convicting the two managers was uncertain (Cox 1999*a*).

The Westray mine disaster reveals what can happen when one mixes an employer who consistently refuses to address safety issues, employees with relatively little voice in the workplace, and government safety inspectors who fail to ensure that safety standards are being met and orders are being complied with. Neglect of safety standards was seen as a tragic example of the government's desire to encourage investment at the expense of labour.

STRUCTURE OF THE PARTIES

Nova Scotia Unions

In Nova Scotia, the major coordinating body is the Nova Scotia Federation of Labour. It has three major functions: legislative lobbying at the provincial level, providing research on a variety of labour relations issues, and education (such as providing courses on union organizing). In addition, there are several district labour councils in the province.

The number of unions in Nova Scotia declined from 99 unions in 1991 to 78 unions in 1997 (Labour Organizations in Nova Scotia 1991 and 1997). There appear to be several reasons for the decline. First, several small unions ceased to exist. Second, massive public sector restructuring resulted in some unions being defeated in run-off elections (e.g., in health care and police services). Third, there were several union mergers (i.e., the Communications, Energy and Paperworkers Union of Canada).

Union membership declined in this period, albeit modestly.[10] The industrial distribution of union membership reveals that 37 percent of union members were in community, business, and personal service industries, 23 percent were in public administration and defence, 12 percent were in manufacturing, 11 percent were in construction, and 17 percent were in a variety of other industries (NS. Department of Labour 1994).[11]

In mid-2002, union membership in the province exceeded 100,000, a number that had been stable for two decades (see Table 3). While the level of unionization (28.4 percent in 2001) is somewhat lower than the Canadian average, it is comparable to union density rates in the other provinces in Atlantic Canada except for Newfoundland. The three largest unions in the province (based on membership) are the Nova Scotia Government Employees Union, the Canadian Union of Public Employees, and the Nova Scotia Teachers' Union. The two largest private sector unions are the Canadian Auto Workers and the United Steelworkers of America (NS. Department of Labour 1997).

TABLE 3
UNION MEMBERSHIP

Year	Total Membership	% of Non-Agricultural Paid Workforce (%)
1985	103,560	35.0
1989	106,326	31.9
1993	102,852	33.0
1997	102,353	32.5
2001	102,400	28.4

Source: Statistics Canada. Note that care must be exercised in the interpretation of the union density figures because of changes over the years in the calculation of such numbers.

Government Agencies

While industrial relations touches on several government agencies and departments, the Department of Environment and Labour is particularly important. Although several divisions within the department (e.g., Labour Standards, Occupational Health and Safety, and Research) play important roles in industrial relations, the Labour Relations Board and the Industrial Relations division are most relevant. The Industrial Relations division is charged with the administration of the *Trade Union Act* and its duties include the appointment of conciliation and mediation officers and the delivery of several preventive mediation programs (NS. Department of Labour 1987–88 to 1998–99). The Nova Scotia Labour Relations Board is tripartite with all part-time members.

Employers

For the most part, employers bargain on an individual basis with local unions. The primary exception is the construction industry, where an accredited employers' organization is the bargaining agent for construction firms.

Although most bargaining is done by individual employers, there are several important employer groups outside the realm of collective bargaining, including the Chamber of Commerce, the Human Resources Association of Nova Scotia, the Nova Scotia Association of Health Organizations, the Information Technology Association of Nova Scotia, and the Canadian Federation of Independent Business. In addition, there are a variety of agencies concerned with economic development, including the Greater Halifax Partnership, Enterprise Cape Breton, and the Waterfront Development Corporation.

Voluntary Planning's Labour-Management Forum

In 1992, Voluntary Planning established the Labour-Management Forum to increase partnership activities between labour and management.[12] The role of the Labour-Management Forum is to "be an ongoing mechanism to promote increased harmony in the workplace and in the economy between labour and management" (Voluntary Planning 1998, 9). The Labour-Management Forum, which in some ways parallels the structure of the Joint Labour-Management Study Committee established in the 1960s, is co-chaired by a representative from labour and management and both parties have equal representation on the forum. Employer and labour members include individuals drawn from both the public and private sectors who are active in labour relations.

The Labour-Management Forum seeks to bring labour and management together to discuss important issues and to improve labour legislation and enforcement (Voluntary Planning 1998). It sponsored a joint labour-management conference addressing major labour relations issues, including: labour legislation and regulations; casual, part-time and contract employment; a greater advocacy role for the forum in the area of labour standards; and promoting the use of voluntary "non-binding" arbitration (ibid.).

LABOUR LEGISLATION AND POLICY

With the enactment of the *Trade Union Act* in 1937, Nova Scotia became the first Canadian province to introduce labour legislation requiring employers to bargain with trade unions. From this initial display of progressive labour legislation, provincial governments in Nova Scotia (particularly over the past 25 years) have moved toward a more "employer-oriented" approach with the aim of attracting multinational investment and, more recently, reducing the provincial deficit.

While the *Trade Union Act* covers most employees in the province, the *Teachers' Collective Bargaining Act* covers teachers. In addition, provincial government employees are covered under the *Civil Service Collective Bargaining Act* that bars strikes.

Basic Features

Similar to the legislation in other jurisdictions, the *Trade Union Act* provides "employees" with the right to join a trade union and participate in its activities. It also requires parties to bargain in good faith,[13] and establishes employer and union unfair labour practices.[14] However, unlike some provinces, there is no statutory duty of fair representation.

Organizing a Union

Nova Scotia was the first province to adopt a mandatory expedited certification vote procedure. A union seeking to organize a group of employees may apply to the Labour Relations Board to be certified if it has the support (signed cards) of at least 40 percent of the employees in a unit appropriate for collective bargaining. This procedure, which differs from the traditional card-based approach, was subsequently adopted in several Canadian jurisdictions.

Unlike the American approach, which normally results in protracted organizing campaigns, the Nova Scotia approach is sometimes referred to as a "quickee vote." In most certification applications, the NSLRB will conduct the vote within eight working days of receipt of the certification application. While conducting a vote in every application makes unionization more difficult, the quickee vote avoids drawn-out campaigns and minimizes the likelihood of unfair labour practices. In order to be certified, the union must obtain the support of the majority of employees voting in the election.[15]

Union Certification Results

What has been the success of Nova Scotia unions under the mandatory certification votes? Although the union success rate in certification applications before the Labour Relations Board varies over the 12-year period beginning in 1987, the overall success rate was just over 68 percent or 65 percent if withdrawn or lapsed applications are included in the analysis. In order to explore whether certification success rates changed over time, the data were grouped into two six-year periods (from 1987–88 to 1992–93 and from 1993–94 to 1998–99). The union's success rate (68 percent) was the same in both periods.[16]

Although the Nova Scotia mandatory vote procedure resembles the US model, unions in Nova Scotia have been more successful than American unions; in the United States, unions are certified in about 50 percent of the organizing campaigns (Reed 1989; Peterson, Lee and Finnegan 1992). However, certification drives in Nova Scotia were somewhat less successful when compared with Quebec and Ontario where 81 percent of organizing drives resulted in certification (Thomason and Pozzebon 1998).[17]

What factors are associated with successful union organizing drives? Gilson and Wagar (1995) found that national unions had greater success than international unions. Furthermore, organizing success was higher among smaller bargaining units and units located in Cape Breton (a traditional union stronghold). However, lower success rates were achieved in wholesale and retail trade, and in services.

Related Labour Legislation

Similar to other jurisdictions, Nova Scotia has legislation addressing human rights, occupational health and safety, and labour standards.[18]

Over the past two decades, Nova Scotia has followed the lead of other provinces and occupies a mainstream position.

There were major amendments to the *Human Rights Act* in the early 1990s and the prohibited grounds of discrimination are in most instances similar to those found across the country (Commerce Clearing House 1998). However, there is no legislative protection against discrimination on the grounds of criminal conviction. Moreover, while sexual harassment is a prohibited category, Nova Scotia has not followed the lead of other jurisdictions and introduced legislation banning "harassment" in general. Note, as well, the *Human Rights Act* specifically prohibits discrimination on the ground of an *irrational* fear of contracting an illness or disease.

Nova Scotia's new *Occupational Health and Safety Act* came into force in 1997. The legislation followed an extensive review by labour and management representatives. The Westray mining disaster, the movement in the early 1990s toward the establishment of programs to foster greater labour-management cooperation, and a recognition of the importance of labour input and support for the legislation motivated the government to adopt a consultative approach.

It should be noted that as a result of the Westray Mine Public Inquiry, the Department of Labour developed responses to the 74 recommendations (which included a variety of issues such as the development of job descriptions for mine positions, training programs within the mine, and the need for a number of legislative amendments).

As in other jurisdictions, the Labour Standards Code addresses a number of employment standards (e.g., minimum wages, vacation pay, hours of work, and termination). However, unlike most other provinces, there is an unjust dismissal procedure that permits the reinstatement of *non-union* employees with more than ten years service in cases of wrongful dismissal.[19] In addition, Nova Scotia requires that an employee quitting his or her job provide the employer with notice.

DISPUTE PATTERNS

Conciliation

Similar to provisions found in other jurisdictions, the *Trade Union Act* requires conciliation to assist in resolving bargaining impasses. Either party may apply to the minister of labour for conciliation. In the event that an agreement is not reached, the conciliation officer has 14 days to file a report with the minister of labour outlining the issues the parties have and have not agreed upon and any other relevant matters. A legal work stoppage may take place 14 days after the conciliation officer files a report with the department.[20] Although infrequently used, the *Trade Union Act* also provides for conciliation boards or industrial inquiry commissions.

Is conciliation effective? In examining the resolution of cases referred to conciliation (using data obtained from the Department of Labour *Annual Reports*) two trends merit attention. First, the use of conciliation has declined dramatically. Between 1987 and 1991, the number of applications for conciliation ranged from 115 to 173 annually; in the 1994 to 1999 period, there were between 56 and 67 cases annually. Second, conciliation officers have, for the most part, been very successful in assisting the parties in labour disputes; in a number of the years, more than 90 percent of cases proceeding to conciliation were settled by the conciliation officer.

Grievance Arbitration

Although the study is somewhat dated, Gilson and Gillis (1987) content-analyzed grievance arbitration activity for the 1980 to 1986 period. Overall, about 31 percent of cases dealt with financial issues (such as wages, benefits, and overtime pay), 34 percent involved punitive issues (such as discipline and discharge), 10 percent focused on bargaining unit issues (such as contracting-out and work stoppages), just over 20 percent dealt with job-property rights (such as seniority, transfers, job posting, and layoff and recall rights), and 5 percent addressed other issues.

About two-thirds of the cases involved the private sector, 40 percent addressed group grievances and single arbitrators were involved in two-thirds of the cases. In examining outcomes, the authors found unions won 56 percent of the cases, but their success varied by issue — union win rates were 71 percent for bargaining unit issues, 61 percent for punitive issues, 55 percent for financial issues, and 45 percent for issues relating to job-property rights. Looking specifically at discipline and discharge cases, Gilson and Gillis (1987) found that union grievances were allowed or partly allowed in 65 percent of the discharge cases and 59 percent of the discipline decisions.

Strikes

Between 1946 and 2001, Nova Scotia had 1,206 work stoppages (accounting for 4.3 percent of the work stoppages across the country)

(Table 4). Nearly 348,000 workers were involved in such disputes (2.4 percent of the Canadian total) and 3,454,484 person days were lost (1.7 percent of the Canadian total) (Table 5).

The incidence of work stoppages in the province (as a proportion of the national total) was relatively high between 1946 and 1971, but declined in subsequent years. Between 1976 and 2001, Nova Scotia accounted for less than 2 percent of workers involved in work stoppages and person-days lost. Considering that Nova Scotians account for about 2.5 percent of total union membership in Canada, the work stoppages record is in line with membership representation. However, the data also indicate that strikes in Nova Scotia tend to be smaller on average and of shorter duration.

A notable feature of Nova Scotia labour disputes is the relatively high incidence of illegal strikes. Nova Scotia had 529 such strikes (10.6 percent of the Canadian total) involving 204,518 workers (5.4 percent of the Canadian total) and 563,392 person-days lost (5 percent of the Canadian total). Although the number of illegal strikes declined in the mid-1970s and early 1980s, there was a sharp increase in illegal strikes between 1986 and 1995. Illegal strikes are generally short and concentrated in the construction industry.

Several observations can be made about strike activity in Nova Scotia. First, the average size of strikes reflects the predominance of very small bargaining units. Second, there is considerable variation in annual person-days lost to strikes — one major strike can have a dramatic effect on the number of person-days lost. Third, although Nova Scotia government employees are not permitted to strike, recent government restructuring has brought numerous employees under the *Trade Union Act* (rather than the *Civil Service Collective Bargaining Act*), and given them the right to strike. Finally, the wage rollback legislation imposed by the Savage government in 1997 led to increased conflict. Not only was there a pent-up demand for wage catch-up, but collective bargaining activity increased.

Improving the Relationship Between Labour and Management

In the early 1990s, the Department of Labour established a number of preventive mediation programs.[21] These voluntary programs included grievance mediation, joint supervisor-steward training, labour-management committees, and Relationship By Objectives (RBO). As mentioned earlier, Voluntary Planning also plays a role in the resolution of labour relations issues.

TABLE 4
WORK STOPPAGES, 1946–2000
(NOVA SCOTIA AS PERCENTAGE OF CANADA IN PARENTHESES)

Period	Number of Work Stoppages (%)	Workers Involved (%)	Person-Days Lost (%)
Work Stoppages			
1946–1950	73 (8.0)	38,935 (7.4)	225,425 (2.2)
1951–1955	68 (6.9)	36,458 (9.5)	256,386 (3.1)
1956–1960	100 (8.2)	51,302 (12.1)	231,947 (2.8)
1961–1965	85 (4.8)	30,686 (5.8)	114,441 (1.5)
1966–1970	225 (7.9)	71,040 (4.9)	485,790 (1.7)
1971–1975	211 (4.9)	57,752 (2.4)	768,120 (2.1)
1976–1980	134 (2.7)	20,182 (0.6)	548,390 (1.4)
1981–1985	112 (2.9)	16,308 (1.1)	479,130 (1.8)
1986–1990	86 (2.7)	10,712 (0.5)	177,310 (0.7)
1991–1995	59 (3.0)	7,464 (1.0)	50,085 (0.5)
1996–2000	53 (3.0)	6,963 (0.5)	117,460 (0.9)
Totals	1,206 (4.3)	347,802 (2.4)	3,454,484 (1.7)
Illegal Strikes			
1946–1950	42 (15.8)	20,946 (19.4)	43,525 (11.8)
1951–1955	38 (15.4)	25,480 (27.0)	65,356 (18.3)
1956–1960	70 (19.9)	46,523 (41.0)	98,521 (25.1)
1961–1965	40 (8.8)	22,273 (19.6)	37,810 (11.8)
1966–1970	128 (17.6)	47,747 (16.1)	151,170 (15.5)
1971–1975	96 (8.3)	23,285 (3.4)	74,880 (2.4)
1976–1980	40 (4.1)	3,779 (0.3)	8,260 (0.3)
1981–1985	17 (3.9)	6,593 (1.1)	71,310 (3.3)
1986–1990	29 (10.6)	3,295 (1.4)	5,730 (0.6)
1991–1995	29 (27.4)	4,597 (4.1)	6,830 (2.3)
Totals	529 (10.6)	204,518 (5.4)	563,392 (5.0)

Source: Workplace Information Directorate, Human Resources Development Canada.

TABLE 5

MEAN NUMBER OF WORK STOPPAGES, WORKERS INVOLVED
AND DAYS LOST

Period	Number of Work Stoppages (mean)	Workers Involved (mean)	Person-Days Lost (mean)
Work Stoppages			
1946–1950	14.6	533.4	3,088.0
1951–1955	13.6	536.1	3,770.4
1956–1960	20.0	513.0	2,319.5
1961–1965	17.0	361.0	1,346.4
1966–1970	45.0	315.7	2,159.1
1971–1975	42.2	273.7	3,640.0
1976–1980	26.8	162.8	4,092.5
1981–1985	22.4	145.6	4,278.0
1986–1990	17.2	124.6	2,061.7
1991–1995	11.8	126.5	848.9
1996–2000	10.6	131.4	2.216.2
Totals	21.9	288.4	2,864.4
Illegal Work Stoppages			
1946–1950	8.4	498.7	1,036.3
1951–1955	7.6	670.5	1,719.9
1956–1960	14.0	664.6	1,407.4
1961–1965	8.0	556.8	945.2
1966–1970	25.6	373.0	1,181.0
1971–1975	19.2	242.6	780.0
1976–1980	8.0	94.5	206.5
1981–1985	3.4	387.8	4,194.7
1986–1990	5.8	113.6	197.6
1991–1995	5.8	158.5	235.5
Totals	10.6	386.6	1,065.0

Source: Workplace Information Directorate, Human Resources Development
Canada.

Grievance Mediation

Grievance mediation was established to assist labour and management resolve grievances. In light of the high costs and time delays associated with arbitration, as well as the negative impact on the labour-management relationship (Wagar 1996/1997), a number of employers and unions looked to grievance mediation as an alternative dispute-resolution mechanism. If mediation is unsuccessful, the dispute may be referred to arbitration.

The demand for grievance mediation was strong in 1993–94 and 1994–95, but declined in subsequent years (see Table 6).

Joint Supervisor-Steward Training

Joint supervisor-steward training provides management and union representatives with the skills and knowledge to deal effectively with labour-management problems. The program attempts to give each side an appreciation of the other's point of view, improve problem-solving and communication skills, and to recognize the rights and responsibilities of one's counterpart. The Department of Environment and Labour conducts one to three training sessions annually. While mediator assistance is also available to par-

TABLE 6
GRIEVANCE MEDIATION

Year	Grievances Settled	Grievances Referred to Arbitration	Grievances Withdrawn
1992–1993	32	7	0
1993–1994	75	16	1
1994–1995	122	21	1
1995–1996	56	12	17
1996–1997	32	12	0
1997–1998	42	6	0
1998–1999	27	8	0

Note: For reporting purposes, the Nova Scotia Department of Labour uses the period from 1 April of one year to 31 March of the next year. Cases pending at the end of the relevant time period are not included in that year's analysis.
Source: Nova Scotia Department of Labour. *Annual Reports.*

ties wishing to establish joint labour-management committees or relationships by objectives, the demand for these services has been modest.

Labour-Management Forum's Voluntary, Non-binding Arbitration Process

An innovative program established in late 1994 by Voluntary Planning's Labour Management Forum was the "Voluntary Preventative Process to Avoid the Necessity of Compulsory Arbitration." For a nominal fee, parties with a grievance can appear before a panel comprised of one labour and one management representative selected from a rotation list. In early 2002, the program was turned over to the Department of Environment and Labour.

The process involves the parties presenting their arguments at an informal hearing (which runs about two hours) and the panel provides the parties with their assessment of how the case would be decided if it proceeded to arbitration. The parties are not bound by the decision of the panel and are not precluded from taking the case to arbitration. Statistics from the Labour-Management Forum indicate the program has been successful. As of 31 March 1998, 65 applications were submitted to the Labour-Management Forum Panel Process and only three cases heard by panel members were subsequently taken to arbitration (Voluntary Planning 1998).

RESULTS OF INDUSTRIAL RELATIONS PROCESSES

Labour-Management Relations

Survey results based on responses from 160 unionized employers and 280 local union officials provide insight into labour-management relations in the province (Wagar 1994a, b). One question asked the parties to describe the labour-management relationship (using a six-point scale with one being a very adversarial relationship and six being a very cooperative relationship). Employers perceived the relationship as more cooperative (mean of 4.48) than union respondents (mean of 3.61). In addition, while more than 18 percent of employer respondents viewed the relationship as very cooperative (score of six), only about 7 percent of union participants held this view.

Using a scale adapted from Dastmalchian, Blyton and Adamson (1991), the respondents were asked about the labour-management climate. There are major differences in management and union perceptions of fairness issues and labour-management consultation — in short, local union officials held far less positive assessments of the labour-management climate.[22]

In light of the growing interest in workplace transformation and high-performance work practices,[23] employer and union participants were asked a series of questions about incentive and job design programs, and the presence of joint labour-management committees. With reference to incentive programs, well under 10 percent of respondents reported having profit-sharing or a productivity-sharing plan. However, there was somewhat stronger support for group or team incentives. About one in five respondents reported having a job-sharing or job enlargement/enrichment program and about one-quarter of the participants indicated a total quality management program was in place. Labour and management were most likely to have committees addressing safety (required by law in many workplaces) and general problem-solving and training, and least likely to have quality circles.

Human resource policies are well developed in unionized workplaces. Almost 90 percent of union officials reported having a pension plan and about two-thirds reported having a sexual harassment policy. Other common practices were a formal performance appraisal system, an orientation program for new hires and an employee assistance program. Just over half of the respondents indicated that the employer had a human resource management or industrial relations department. However, less than one-fifth of respondents reported that the employer conducted employee attitude surveys and only 5 percent indicated that there was a drug testing policy.

Collective Agreement Provisions in Major Contracts

A limited database on collective agreement provisions in Nova Scotia covering 500 or more employees indicates a number of features common in Canadian industrial relations. The closed shop is more common in Nova Scotia, however. Nineteen percent of agreements provided for a closed shop, 32 percent had a union shop or modified union shop, 45 percent had a Rand formula (dues check-off) and 3 percent had no provision. Compared with Canada-wide figures, a higher percentage of agreements in Nova Scotia had a closed shop provision, but a smaller percentage had a union or modified union shop clause. One factor which may help explain these differences is the industrial structure of the province (in particular, the presence of closed shop provisions in construction and the longshore industry). In addition, there is no mandatory Rand formula provision under Nova Scotia legislation — union security provisions are the subject of negotiation. Just under half of the agreements placed restrictions on contracting-out (which is in line with the rest of the country) and 55 percent contained provisions for labour-management committees (lower than the 65 percent figure for Canada).

Employee protection was well developed. Sixty-one percent of agreements contained a sunset clause (a provision clearing an employee's discipline record), 23 percent provided for job-sharing, and 32 percent had a sexual harassment clause. About 45 percent of the contracts contained no provision for technological change and just over one-quarter contained no provision on the application of seniority to promotion, transfer, layoff and recall, bumping or job-posting. Another one-third of the agreements failed to provide for severance pay.

Wage Levels

Over the past five years, the average total personal income of Nova Scotians has been between $19,900 and $22,200. In addition, total personal income increased in each of the past five years (Nova Scotia. Department of Finance 2001). Average weekly earnings rose between 1998 and 2001 from $548 to $570. However, average weekly earnings in Nova Scotia are below the national average (i.e., about 85 percent of the Canadian average). There are significant interindustry differences in average weekly earnings in the province. For example, in 2000, average weekly earnings were $239 in the accommodation and food sector, $390 in retail services, $682 in public administration, and $681 in manufacturing.

CONCLUSION

Over the past century or so, labour relations in Nova Scotia have changed significantly. By the late 1800s, industrial relations in the coal industry were maturing to the stage where the parties had contractually addressed such issues as employment security, compensation, and seniority. In subsequent years there was increasing regulation of collective bargaining and, in 1937, Nova Scotia became a leader in the development of progressive labour legislation when it enacted the *Trade Union Act*. However, its position was short lived. Over the next two decades, increasing regulation of labour relations in the province made it more difficult for unions to attract new members and labour unrest escalated.

The notion that labour and management could and should cooperate was enshrined in the establishment of the Joint Labour-

Management Study Committee in the 1960s. While Nova Scotia government policy over the past half-century has stressed attracting business
investment to spur economic development, this policy has also been used
to weaken the position of organized labour in Nova Scotia (Earle and
McKay 1989).

Two major legislative changes in the 1970s weakened the power
of organized labour in the province, destroyed the relationship between
labour and the government, resulted in the death of the Joint Labour-
Management Study Committee, and distinguished the Nova Scotia trade
union law from the rest of the country.

First, the government requires votes in all certification applications. This change represented a substantial departure from practice in
other parts of the country and made it more difficult to unionize in Nova
Scotia. It should be noted that in recent years, other provinces have fallen
in line with Nova Scotia and require certification votes.[24]

Second, in 1979 the government introduced the infamous
Michelin Bill in the midst of an organizing drive on one of the Michelin
Tire facilities in the province. The amendment to the *Trade Union Act*
provided that an employer in manufacturing could apply to the Nova Scotia
Labour Relations Board to have all "interdependent" locations considered as a single bargaining unit for collective-bargaining purposes. The
amendment was made retroactive and thus nullified a certification vote at
the Michelin facility being targeted by the union. Several subsequent attempts to unionize the three Michelin plants in Nova Scotia (most recently by the Canadian Auto Workers) have failed.

The Michelin Bill demonstrated the importance of attracting business and investment to the province. Subsequent Conservative and Liberal governments have done likewise, thereby indicating that business and
financial interests take precedence over worker rights in the province. By
way of example, the explosion at the Westray mine, the removal of collective bargaining rights for public sector workers by both the Conservative
Cameron government and the Liberal Savage government, and the introduction of Bill 68 (which removed the right of health-care workers to
strike) by the Hamm government all point to a strategy of favouring business interests over labour interests.

Despite the demise of the Joint Labour-Management Study Committee, Nova Scotia continued to experiment with mechanisms to reduce
conflict. These warrant further analysis. First, recent programs such as
grievance mediation, joint labour-management steward training, and facilitating the establishment of labour-management committees represent

an attempt to foster greater labour-management cooperation. Second, Voluntary Planning's Labour-Management Forum represents an interesting initiative on the part of labour and management to work together in developing partnership activities.

In short, labour relations in Nova Scotia continue to evolve. In some ways, the province has been a testing ground for a number of controversial labour law reforms. While there has been an attempt by labour and management to cooperate on some aspects of industrial relations, government policy continues to emphasize attracting business investment to the province.

NOTES

Funding for this project was provided, in part, by the Social Sciences and Humanities Research Council of Canada. As well, I would like to acknowledge the very gracious assistance of the staff at the Nova Scotia Department of Environment and Labour. Note that the Nova Scotia Department of Environment and Labour agreed to provide me with preliminary data for the *Annual Report* years of 1999–2000, 2000–2001 and 2001–2002.

[1]The Sable Offshore project is a $3 billion gas and pipeline development. As a result of the project, the construction phase will have resulted in the creation of more than 4,000 jobs and the 25-year project will require about 250 permanent jobs.

[2]In March 1999, the Nova Scotia Labour Relations Board dismissed an application for certification of Michelin employees by the Canadian Auto Workers. It was the fifth unsuccessful organizing attempt by CAW at Michelin.

[3]Obviously, the restraint and rollback legislation was much more detailed than presented here. For a more complete discussion of restructuring in the Nova Scotia government, see Wagar (2000).

[4]S.N.S. 1937, c. 6.

[5]S.N.S. 1972, c. 19.

[6]Previously, the parties had to use a three-person board to settle an arbitration case.

[7]Note that the board retained the right to automatically certify a union if the union had majority support among bargaining unit members and the board believed that a vote would serve no real purpose.

[8]At the time, Michelin had two plants in the province. It now has three plants (at Bridgewater, Granton, and Waterville).

[9]For a review of the Michelin Bill, see Langille (1981).

[10]The restructuring and privatization activities of the Nova Scotia government in the mid-1990s resulted in a dramatic drop in civil service membership of the Nova Scotia Government Employees Union (from 9,289 members in December 1995 to 5,772 members in April 1997). In effect, several former government workers were moved out of the civil service and into the private sector (under the *Trade Union Act*).

[11]Comparing union density on the basis of industry sector is problematic. The restructuring of the 1990s resulted in a large number of employees originally covered under the *Civil Service Collective Bargaining Act* now coming under the private sector *Trade Union Act*. This trend is examined in more detail by Wagar (2000).

[12]Voluntary Planning is a voluntary association of non-government individuals and groups that is funded by the Nova Scotia government, but operates at arm's length from the government with the goal of improving the social and economic well-being of all Nova Scotians (Voluntary Planning 2002).

[13]A review of the Nova Scotia Department of Environment and Labour *Annual Reports* for the past 15 years indicates that the Labour Relations Board receives about five to fifteen complaints a year in regard to good-faith bargaining. Issuing an order to bargain is quite rare — in some cases, the board either finds that the duty to bargain in good faith was not violated or (more commonly), the complaint is withdrawn.

[14]In reviewing the Department of Environment and Labour *Annual Reports* over the past ten years, the number of unfair labour practice complaints has ranged from between 4 and 25 (with an average of just under 14 complaints a year). The Labour Relations Board found a violation in just under 10 percent of the complaints filed. In almost 75 percent of the cases, the complaint was ultimately withdrawn by one of the parties.

[15]See Weiler (1983) for a review of the automatic certification by cards versus mandatory vote debate.

[16]I recently obtained preliminary data from the Department of Environment and Labour for the last three years beginning 1999–2000. The union win rate for that period was just under 64 percent.

[17]Note that when the Thomason and Pozzebon study was conducted, both the Ontario and Quebec legislation permitted certification based on card evidence. Ontario now requires a mandatory vote to determine whether to certify the union.

[18]See, for example, the *Nova Scotia Human Rights Act*, the *Nova Scotia Occupational Health and Safety Act*, and the Labour Standards Code.

[19]The federal jurisdiction and Quebec are the only other jurisdictions with an unjust dismissal provision. Obviously, the legislation in each of the jurisdictions varies considerably. For example, in Nova Scotia, the legislation is only applicable to employees with ten years of service; in Quebec, it applies to five-year employees; and in the federal jurisdiction, the legislation applies to employees with a minimum of one year of service. For a practical discussion of the Nova Scotia law, see Nova Scotia. Department of Labour (1998).

[20]There are additional procedural requirements relating to conciliation boards and industrial inquiries.

[21]For more information, see Nova Scotia. Department of Environment and Labour (2002*a, b*).

[22]The pattern of results relating to labour climate is similar to that found in other Canadian jurisdictions (Wagar 1996*a, b*).

[23]There is now a huge body of research on this issue. See, for instance, Becker and Gerhart (1996), Pfeffer and Veiga (1999), and Wood (1999).

[24]The legislation in Nova Scotia and some of the other provinces allows the board to certify a union if it determines that employer actions have been such that a representation vote does not reflect the true wishes of the employees in the bargaining unit.

REFERENCES

Adams, G. 1997. *Canadian Labour Law,* 2d ed. Aurora, ON: Canada Law Book.

Antoff, K. 1981. "Harnessing Confrontation: A Review of the Nova Scotia Joint-Labour-Management Study Committee, 1962-1979," in *Labour in Atlantic Canada,* Social Science Series, Vol. 4. Saint John, NB: University of New Brunswick, pp. 103-16.

Becker, B. and B. Gerhart. 1996. "The Impact of Human Resource Management on Organizational Performance," *Academy of Management Journal* 39:779-801.

Canada. Human Resources Development Canada (HRDC). 1999. *Labour Market Summary: February 1999.* Ottawa: HRDC.

—— Human Resources Development Canada. Bureau of Labour Information. 1996. *Provisions in Collective Agreements.* Ottawa: HRDC.

Commerce Clearing House Canadian (CCH). 1998. *Canadian Master Labour Guide: A Guide to Canadian Labour Law.* Don Mills, ON: CCH.

Cox, K. 1999a. "Westray Proceedings Formally Terminated," *The Globe and Mail,* 30 June.

—— 1999b. "Last Three Liberal Budget Surpluses Were Bogus, Nova Scotia Tory Says," *The Globe and Mail,* 29 September.

Dastmalchian, A., P. Blyton and R. Adamson. 1991. *The Climate of Workplace Relations.* London: Routledge.

Earle, M. and I. McKay. 1989. "Introduction: Industrial Legality in Nova Scotia," in *Workers and the State in 20th Century Nova Scotia,* ed. M. Earle. Fredericton, NB: Acadiensis Press, pp. 9-23.

Gilson, C. 1987. *Strikes: Industrial Relations in Nova Scotia 1957-1987.* Hansport, NS: Lancelot Press.

Gilson, C. and A. Wadden. 1989. "The Windsor Gypsum Strike and the Formation of the Joint Labour-Management Study Committee: Conflict and Accommodation in the Nova Scotia Labour Movement, 1957-1979," in *Workers and the State in 20th Century Nova Scotia,* ed. M. Earle. Fredericton, NB: Acadiensis Press, pp. 191-215.

Gilson C. and L. Gillis. 1987. "Grievance Arbitration in Nova Scotia," *Relations industrielles-Industrial Relations* 42:256-71.

Gilson, C. and T. Wagar. 1995. "The US/Canada Convergence Thesis: Contrary Evidence from Nova Scotia," *Relations industrielles-Industrial Relations* 50:66-84.

Gilson, C., I. Spenser and S. Granville. 1989. "The Impact of a Strike on the Attitudes of a Rural Community," *Relations industrielles-Industrial Relations* 44:785-804.

Glasbeek, H. and E. Tucker. 1995. "Death by Consensus: The Westray Mine Story," in *Labour and Working-Class History in Atlantic Canada: A*

Reader, ed. D. Frank and G. Kealey. St. John's: Institute of Social and Economic Research, Memorial University, pp. 399-439.

Henson, G. 1969. "The Nova Scotia Labour-Management Agreements," *Relations industrielles-Industrial Relations* 24:87-128.

International Labour Office (ILO). 1995. *Case No. 1802 – Complaint Against the Government of Canada (Nova Scotia).*

Jackson, D. 1999. "Smaller Government Planned," *The Mail Star* (Halifax), 15 October.

Jackson, D. and S. LeBlanc. 2001. "Government 1, Health Unions 1," *The Mail Star* (Halifax), 14 August.

Langille, B. 1981. "Michelin Amendment in Context," *Dalhousie Law Journal* 6:523-52.

Lightstone, M. 2001. "Union Buoyed by Poll Results," *The Mail Star* (Halifax), 27 June.

MacDonald, A. 1998. "Workers Sit-in for Benefits," *The Daily News* (Halifax), 22 October.

MacGillivray, D. 1997. "Workers in Cape Breton not really Hot-heads," *The Catholic New Times,* 30 March.

MacIntyre, M. 1997. "Unionists Torch Building, Mob Blocks Firefighters, Manhandles Workers," *The Chronicle Herald (Halifax),* 27 February.

Madill, J. 1994. "Cash Crunch Makes Bargaining a Sham," *The Mail Star* (Halifax), 7 May.

McKay, I. 1983. "Industry, Work and Community in the Cumberland Coalfields, 1848-1927." PhD thesis, Dalhousie University.

McKinnon, A. 1962. *Report of Fact-Finding Body re Labour Legislation* (McKinnon Report). Halifax: Government Printers.

Nova Scotia. Department of Environment and Labour. 2002*a. Grievance Mediation: An Alternative.* Halifax: Department of Environment and Labour.

—— 2002*b. Preventive Mediation.* Halifax: Department of Environment and Labour.

Nova Scotia. Department of Finance. 1995. *Nova Scotia Statistical Review 1995.* Halifax: Department of Finance.

—— 1998. *Common Statistics.* Halifax: Department of Finance.

—— 2001. *Nova Scotia Statistical Review 2001.* Halifax: Department of Finance.

Nova Scotia. Department of Labour. 1991. *Labour Organizations in Nova Scotia.* Halifax: Department of Labour.

—— 1994. *Labour Organizations in Nova Scotia.* Halifax: Department of Labour.

—— 1997. *Labour Organizations in Nova Scotia.* Halifax: Department of Labour.

—— Department of Labour. Occupational Health and Safety Division. 1997. *Your Rights, Responsibilities, and the Nova Scotia Occupational Health and Safety Act.* Halifax: Department of Labour.

Nova Scotia. Department of Labour and Manpower (Research Division). 1984. *History of Nova Scotia Labour Legislation 1932-1984.* Halifax: Department of Labour and Manpower.

—— 1998. *Guide to the Labour Codes of Nova Scotia.* Halifax: Department of Labour and Manpower.

—— 1988 to 1999. *Annual Reports* (1987–88 to 1998–99). Halifax: Department of Labour and Manpower.

Peterson, R., T. Lee and B. Finnegan. 1992. "Strategies and Tactics in Union Organizing Campaigns," *Industrial Relations* 31:370-81.

Pfeffer, J. and J. Veiga. 1999. "Putting People First for Organizational Success," *Academy of Management Executive* 13:37-48.

Reed, T. 1989. "Do Union Organizers Matter?: Individual Differences, Campaign Practices, and Representative Election Outcomes," *Industrial and Labor Relations Review* 43:103-19.

Richard, K.P. 1997. *The Westray Story: A Predictable Path to Disaster.* Report of the Westray Mine Public Inquiry. Halifax: The Inquiry.

Shaw, C. 1995. "UN Sides with Labor on Wage Rollbacks," *The Mail Star* (Halifax), 6 July.

Smith, A. and D. Jackson. 1999. "Paramedics Back on Job," *The Mail Star* (Halifax), 30 October.

Statistics Canada. 2002. *Employment, Earnings and Hours*, Cat. No. 72-002. Ottawa: Supply and Services Canada.

Taylor, R. 1998. "Volvo Coy About Mexican Production Plans," *The Mail Star* (Halifax), 6 October.

Thomason, T. and S. Pozzebon. 1998."Managerial Opposition to Union Certification in Quebec and Ontario," *Relations industrielles-Industrial Relations* 53:750-71.

Tutton, M. 2001. "N.S. Nurses Threaten to Resign," *National Post*, 29 June.

Voluntary Planning. 1998. "Labour-Management Forum," *Voluntary Planning Annual Report*. Halifax: Voluntary Planning.

—— 2002. *Voluntary Planning Annual Report 2000-2001.* Halifax: Voluntary Planning.

Wagar, T. 1994a. *Human Resource Management Practices and Organizational Performance: Evidence from Atlantic Canada.* Kingston, ON: Industrial Relations Centre (IRC) Press, Queen's University.

—— 1994b. "Labour-Management Relations in Nova Scotia: A Survey of Union Officials." Unpublished Report. Halifax, NS: Saint Mary's University.

—— 1996a. *Labour Management Relations in Canada: A Survey of Union Officials.* Kingston, ON: Industrial Relations Centre (IRC) Press, Queen's University.

—— 1996b. *Employee Involvement, Strategic Management and Human Resources: Exploring the Linkages.* Kingston, ON: Industrial Relations Centre (IRC) Press, Queen's University.

—— 1996/1997. "The Arbitration Process: Employer and Union Views," *Labour Arbitration Yearbook*. Toronto: Lancaster House, pp. 3-11.

—— 2000. "Provincial Government Restructuring in Nova Scotia: The Freezing and Thawing of Labour Relations," in *Public Sector Labour Relations in an Era of Restraint and Restructuring*, ed. G. Swimmer. Toronto: Oxford University Press, pp. 36-65.

Weiler, P. 1983. "Promises to Keep: Securing Workers' Rights to Self-Organization under the NLRA," *Harvard Law Review* 96:1769-816.

Wood, S. 1999. "Human Resource Management and Performance," *International Journal of Management Reviews* 1:367-413.

9 ALBERTA: INDUSTRIAL RELATIONS IN A CONSERVATIVE CLIMATE

Allen Ponak
Yonatan Reshef
Daphne G. Taras

Résumé — Pour la plupart des Canadiens, le conservatisme albertain est une question de foi. Tout compte fait, cette perception est juste. Toujours élu avec une majorité appréciable, le Parti conservateur de la province gouverne sans interruption depuis 1972. Il a succédé au Crédit social, parti politique plus à droite qui a commercé à gouverner avant la Deuxième Guerre mondiale jusqu'à l'élection des Conservateurs.

L'industrie pétrolière et gazière, dont la culture est imprégnée d'un individualisme acharné et d'une idéologie de laissez-faire, a considérablement contribué à modeler la province. Cette industrie constitue une immense source de richesse en Alberta. Le gouvernement en tirait plus de 80 % de ses revenus à la fin des années 1970, de 25 % à 33 % dans les années 1990 et 38 % en 2000–2001. L'influence de cette industrie est partout présente et se fait sentir bien au-delà de l'aspect économique, puisque la richesse de la province en dépend. Les compagnies pétrolières sont paternalistes, non favorables aux syndicats en général et rémunèrent généreusement leurs employés. Les plus grandes allient des pratiques novatrices de gestion des ressources humaines avec une forte préférence pour l'absence de syndicalisation. Une petite fraction de leur main-d'œuvre est syndiquée, et certaines ont des plans de représentation non syndicale complexes des travailleurs. En conséquence, à l'opposé d'autres provinces, tel l'Ontario avec ses travailleurs de l'industrie automobile syndiqués ou la Colombie-Britannique avec son secteur forestier syndiqué, l'Alberta présente un paradigme de non-syndicalisation en raison de la prédominance des employeurs du secteur privé.

Les modèles de relations industrielles reflètent la présence de ces forces. L'Alberta a le taux de syndicalisation le plus faible au Canada; la liste d'exclusions de son code du travail est plus longue que celle de toutes les autres provinces; peu d'employés de sa fonction publique jouissent du droit de grève; elle exige la tenue d'un vote pour toute demande d'accréditation syndicale; elle a privatisé des secteurs du ministère du Travail dans les années 1990; elle est classée au dernier rang des provinces canadiennes en ce qui a trait aux protections offertes aux travailleurs par les normes d'emploi; en 1995, elle a sérieusement remis en question la loi du droit au travail. Malgré cela, la politique albertaine du travail contient toujours la plupart des éléments importants du droit canadien du travail. Un comité tripartite a refusé unanimement de remettre en question le droit au travail; les présidents qui se sont succédé à la tête de la Commission des relations de travail ont été choisis en fonction du mérite plutôt que des tendances partisanes; l'antisyndicalisme manifeste n'est pas encore socialement accepté.

Le conservatisme albertain, aux racines historiques profondes, favorise les politiciens dont le programme table sur la responsabilisation financière et la réduction de l'intervention de l'État. La révolution Klein des années 1990 a fait ressortir toutes les forces en présence qui influent sur les relations industrielles albertaines. La puissance du conservatisme et le mandat politique confié à Klein et à son parti par la plus grande partie de la population ont permis de restructurer radicalement les finances de la province.

Les syndicats ont subi les effets des politiques gouvernementales conçues d'abord et avant tout pour atteindre des budgets équilibrés et éliminer la dette provinciale. Ne disposant d'aucun moyen de résistance efficace, ils ont dû se soumettre aux pertes d'emploi massives et accepter des réductions salariales dont les effets ont continué de se faire sentir une fois la crise économique passée et la province redevenue prospère. L'absence d'une forte opposition de la part du NPD, et même du Parti libéral, a provoqué la marginalisation politique des syndicats qui, par conséquent, ont dû se servir de la négociation collective comme principale occasion de sensibiliser la population à la cause des travailleurs. Même durant une récente reprise économique, les rondes de négociation collective successives sont demeurées ardues et la marge budgétaire, petite. Les syndiqués eux-mêmes n'appuient pas forcément les objectifs de leur syndicat. Bref, les dirigeants syndicaux albertains ont un rôle non enviable.

INTRODUCTION

Most Canadians accept Alberta's conservatism as a matter of faith. By and large this perception is correct. The provincial Conservative Party has governed uninterrupted, with sizable majorities, since 1972, succeeding Social Credit, a political party even further to the right, which had held power continuously since before World War II. Neither the Cooperative Commonwealth Federation (CCF) nor the New Democratic Party (NDP) has ever been a force, and in 2002 the NDP had but two elected representatives in the provincial legislature.[1] It is no surprise that the most right-of-centre of current federal political parties, the Canadian Alliance Party (and its predecessor, the Reform Party), originated in Alberta. The province has the lowest minimum wage and per capita social services expenditures outside the Maritimes and takes fierce pride in having the lowest taxes in the country, particularly the absence of a provincial sales tax (Flanagan 1997). In 1997, the government set a target for per capita government expenditures of 5 percent below the average expenditures of the other nine provinces (Alberta 1997).[2] In 2003, a flat income tax system is being introduced and Alberta is an aggressive advocate of more private health-care spending.

The oil and gas industry, with its culture of rugged individualism and *laissez-faire* ideology and roots in Oklahoma and Texas (Harrison and Laxer 1995), has played an important role is shaping the province. While oil and gas exploration in Alberta date to the early 1900s, it was the 1947 discovery of Leduc No. 1, a huge oilfield just outside Edmonton that changed the economic landscape of the province irrevocably. The energy bonanza has not abated. Fifty years after Leduc, new mega-projects are underway to exploit northern tar sands oil deposits that rival those of Saudi Arabia.

The industry, based in Calgary, is an enormous source of provincial wealth, contributing up to 80 percent of all government revenues in the late 1970s, one-quarter to one-third in the 1990s (McMillan and Warrack 1995; *Calgary Herald*, 13 February 1997), and 38 percent in 2000–2001 (Alberta Resource Development 2001). With the fortunes of the province tied closely to those of the industry, its influence is pervasive and extends well beyond economics. Petroleum companies are paternalistic, predominantly non-union, and compensate their employees generously. The larger firms combine innovative human resource practices with a strong preference to remain union free. Only a fraction of their workforce is unionized and some of the larger firms have sophisticated non-union representation plans (Taras and Ponak 1999; Taras and Copping 1998; Taras 2000). Thus, in contrast to other provinces such as Ontario with its unionized auto industry or British Columbia with its unionized forestry sector, in Alberta the dominant private employers set a non-union paradigm.

Patterns of industrial relations reflect these forces. Union density is the lowest in Canada (Statistics Canada 2002*a*), Alberta has one of the most extensive lists of exclusions from its labour code; few public employees have the right to strike; the province requires votes in all certification applications; parts of the labour ministry have been privatized; Alberta employment standards protections to workers were the lowest in Canada (Block and Roberts 1998), and right-to-work legislation was actively considered in 1995. Despite these features, Alberta labour policy still contains most of the significant elements of Canadian labour law. Right-to-work was rejected unanimously by a tripartite committee (Alberta Economic Development Authority 1995), successful labour board chairs have been chosen on merit rather than partisan leanings, and overt union busting is still not socially acceptable.[3] The province is hardly a low-wage backwater; average weekly earnings are the third highest in Canada (Statistics Canada 2002b) and Albertans report significantly higher satisfaction levels with their quality of life than residents of any other province (Angus Reid poll commissioned by Royal Bank, in Avram 1997).

The purpose of this chapter is to examine the industrial relations system in Alberta and the forces shaping it. The economic, political, and social context is analyzed, the main elements of Alberta labour-management relations are detailed, current problems and prospects of the labour move-

TABLE 1

ALBERTA GROSS DOMESTIC PRODUCT AT FACTOR COST

	Gross Domestic Product (millions of dollars)						
Year	Current Dollars (millions)	Adjusted to 1997 Dollars (millions)	% Change (adjusted dollars) (%)	Year	Current Dollars (millions)	Adjusted to 1997 Dollars (millions)	% Change (adjusted dollars) (%)
1971	7,393	34,605		1986	54,286	64,829	1.05
1972	8,450	37,905	9.54	1987	56,022	65,836	1.55
1973	10,541	42,280	11.54	1988	59,168	70,546	7.15
1974	14,006	40,434	−4.37	1989	61,455	70,946	0.57
1975	16,978	41,223	1.95	1990	66,548	72,272	1.87
1976	19,817	43,814	6.29	1991	66,596	74,319	2.83
1977	22,915	46,908	7.06	1992	68,370	76,245	2.59
1978	27,031	50,019	6.63	1993	73,450	80,589	5.70
1979	33,850	55,749	11.46	1994	79,556	86,079	6.81
1980	41,011	57,486	3.12	1995	83,625	88,908	3.29
1981	48,214	62,171	8.15	1996	89,733	90,612	1.92
1982	51,248	59,874	−3.69	1997	99,020	99,020	9.28
1983	54,075	58,671	−2.01	1998	98,597	100,284	1.28
1984	57,629	60,468	3.06	1999	106,589	102,652	2.36
1985	61,172	64,157	6.10	2000	132,770	107,602	4.82

Source: Government of Alberta (2001).

ment are discussed, and the distinctive features of Alberta industrial relations are highlighted.

ECONOMICS AND THE LABOUR MARKET

Alberta's economy has experienced booms and busts, largely mirroring the fortunes of the energy sector. Table 1 provides annual provincial gross domestic product (GDP) growth from 1971; Table 2 shows unemployment rates in the same period; and Table 3 tracks average negotiated wage increases for the private and public sectors since 1978. These tables show periods of very strong growth, with high wage increases and falling unemployment, followed by abrupt transitions to periods of no (or negative) growth accompanied by wage decline and layoffs.

TABLE 2
ALBERTA UNEMPLOYMENT RATE

Year	Unemployment Rate (%)	Year	Unemployment Rate (%)
1970	5.2	1986	9.9
1971	5.7	1987	9.7
1972	5.7	1988	8.1
1973	5.3	1989	7.3
1974	3.5	1990	7.1
1975	4.2	1991	8.3
1976	4.0	1992	9.5
1977	4.5	1993	9.7
1978	4.7	1994	8.6
1979	3.9	1995	7.8
1980	3.8	1996	6.9
1981	3.9	1997	5.8
1982	7.7	1998	5.6
1983	10.7	1999	5.7
1984	11.1	2000	5.0
1985	10.1	2001	4.6

Source: Statistics Canada. CANSIM II Database, Table 384-0013. Selected Economic Indicators, 1902, Provincial Economic Accounts.

TABLE 3

ANNUAL AVERAGE NEGOTIATED WAGE INCREASES

Year	Public Sector Effective Wage Increase in Base Rates (%)	Private Sector Effective Wage Increases in Base Rates (%)
1978	7.6	8.1
1979	8.2	9.5
1980	10.8	11.9
1981	14.3	14.1
1982	12.8	12.8
1983	6.8	2.7
1984	0.7	3.0
1985	2.2	−1.5
1986	3.3	0.9
1987	2.1	2.2
1988	2.9	4.1
1989	4.3	5.1
1990	5.6	4.5
1991	5.0	4.7
1992	3.5	3.5
1993	0.7	0.0
1994	−1.4	−0.6
1995	−0.4	0.8
1996	1.1	2.2
1997	2.0	2.2
1998	2.7	2.6
1999	3.3	4.5
2000	4.0	4.4
2001	4.4	4.0

Source: Statistics Canada, CANSIM II Database, Table 278-0008, Major Wage Settlements by Region, 7504 – Labour Canada.

A good example of this pattern is found in the early 1980s. Soaring oil prices produced a sustained boom in the mid- to late-1970s. A significant decline in oil prices in the 1980s, combined with the federal government's National Energy Program led to a sudden reversal of provincial fortunes. Gross domestic product, which had risen by over 8 percent in 1981, *fell* by

3.5 percent in 1982 and a further 2 percent in 1983. Unemployment doubled in one year, exceeding 10 percent by 1983 (Table 2). Housing foreclosures in Calgary went from 150 in 1981 to 4,000 in 1984 (Ponak 1985).

The precipitous change in the economic environment had dramatic consequences for industrial relations. Negotiated wage increases dropped from 13 percent in 1982 to 1 percent in 1984 (Table 3), with half of all employees receiving no wage increase (ibid.). Unionized construction in particular was decimated as building activity collapsed and industry unemployment exceeded 30 percent. Contractors, in the face of union refusal to renegotiate long-term collective agreements signed during the boom, used a variety of methods to terminate collective agreements and thereafter to hire workers at greatly reduced wages. Union density in construction fell from 85 percent to 10 percent between 1982 and 1986 (Fisher and Kushner 1986).

A similar pattern occurred in the mid-1990s. Sharp declines in natural resource per capita revenue after 1988 resulted in budget deficits, accumulating debt, and increasing debt-service costs (McMillan and Warrack 1995). The government delayed any dramatic action at first, but in the absence of an upturn in energy revenue, took draconian steps to reduce and restructure public services. The University of Calgary, for example, had its provincial grant reduced by 21 percent over three years beginning in 1994. Major hospitals were closed in Calgary and Edmonton and tuition for kindergarten was imposed.

Again the consequences for industrial relations were dramatic. Almost all public employers negotiated 5 percent wage cuts that lasted up to three years. Large-scale public sector layoffs led to intense scrutiny of previously untested collective-agreement layoff provisions, especially in the area of bumping rights, resulting in numerous arbitrations. Job security became the predominant bargaining issue. For reasons that are explored later in the chapter, unions could not resist either public sector restructuring or wage reductions. Alberta's experience in the 1990s was not unique. Deficit reduction became a mantra for governments across Canada during this period (Swimmer 2001). However, until Ontario, and much later British Columbia, decided to emulate the Alberta approach, nowhere else were the changes as abrupt or as far reaching.

While the effects of an economic collapse are visible and dramatic, robust economies also have posed special industrial relations problems. A rebounding economy, spurred by resurgent oil and gas prices, led to 20 percent wage and fee increases for nurses and doctors in the late 1990s. When the economy slowed, health-care support workers struck illegally and teachers launched a provincewide strike in efforts to win similar wage increases. More subtly, human resource professionals commented that boom periods have led to rapid escalations of benefits, particularly in the energy sector, that employers elsewhere in the economy cannot match. As examples, one labour relations manager in the public sector described health-club memberships, dental plans far more generous than those offered elsewhere, and "golden" Fridays (i.e., every third Friday off). Furthermore, benefits granted during good times were not easy to eliminate during bad times, especially for unionized employers.

While most media attention was directed to the public sector, private sector employees experienced successive waves of wrenching layoffs following the energy bust of the early 1980s. Over a ten-year period, the major integrated oil and gas companies such as Imperial Oil and Petro-Canada cut their employment by more than half, with the deepest cuts made to head office employees (Taras and Ponak 1999). These events revealed an implicit trade-off in the industry: premium wages and benefits are accompanied by a high risk of job loss.

In short, Alberta industrial relations has been greatly affected by the impact of energy price fluctuations on the provincial economy. High prices create boom conditions leading to tight labour markets and upward wage and benefit pressures. Declining prices, especially if abrupt, can destroy the viability of collective agreements and necessitate unprecedented restructuring that includes wage cuts, benefit reductions, and layoffs. This creates a difficult environment for unions. The leading employers, offering the best compensation and conditions, tend to be non-union; when collective agreements start to catch up, economic forces frequently intervene to undermine such efforts. This is one of the reasons that union density, as will be seen in the next section, is the lowest in Canada.

PATTERNS OF UNIONIZATION

Despite the province's conservatism, radicalism was a feature of Alberta's early labour movement. The One Big Union, whose leaders were in the forefront of the Winnipeg General Strike, was founded in Calgary in 1919 on a platform that advocated Marxist-syndicalist labour organization and expressed solidarity with the new Bolshevik regime in Moscow (Bercuson 1975). The Western Federation of Miners, which shared radical roots with the Wobblies (Industrial Workers of the World, IWW) was active in early twentieth-century Alberta (Caragata 1984; Logan 1948). The IWW itself organized and led strikes among workers building the railroads. Indeed, the early militancy of Alberta unions was an important factor in the development of Canadian labour law. Coal and railroad strikes in the Crow's Nest Pass (southwestern corner of Alberta) and Lethbridge helped provide the impetus for the McKenzie King-led Royal Commission on Industrial Disputes and then, in 1907, the *Industrial Disputes Investigation Act* (Caragata 1984).

Through World War I, Alberta unionism developed in the mining, rail, and construction industries. As elsewhere in western Canada, both radical and more conservative unions affiliated with the Trades and Labour Congress competed for worker allegiance. The high-water mark for western Canadian radical unionism was the Winnipeg General Strike of May 1919 that spawned short-lived sympathy strikes in Calgary, Lethbridge, and Edmonton (and elsewhere throughout the country). The crushing of the strike took much of the wind out of radical sails (Bercuson 1975), except for some flirtation with communist-led unions in the 1930s (Caragata 1984).

The decline of radical unions helped pave the way for the ascendancy of labour organizations closely linked to the United States and the business unionism philosophy of Samuel Gompers. The American-based unions dominated the Alberta labour scene until public sector unions supplanted them in the 1970s. In this sense, the development of the labour movement in Alberta followed a familiar western Canadian pattern — an early period of radicalism, especially in the resource sector, followed by a period dominated by international unions, first craft then industrial, which in turn gave way to mass public sector unionism.

What makes Alberta different is its low level of union density, which in 2001 stood at 22.5 percent. No other province comes close (Statistics Canada 2002*a*). One possible explanation for Alberta's low union density, the impact of the boom and bust economy, has been outlined in a previous section. A second explanation is the impact of the dominant energy industry, which has been largely non-union from its inception and remains largely non-union today. The energy sector provides a powerful demonstration of a non-union model (this model is discussed in a later section of the chapter).

It is beyond the scope of this chapter to explore fully other factors which might account for Alberta's low union density. Suffice to say that research has indicated that industrial mix, especially the early absence of a strong manufacturing base, the proportion of white-collar workers, government ideology, and the strength or weakness of a labour party all play a role in determining the extent of unionization (see, e.g., Murray

TABLE 4
UNION MEMBERSHIP AND UNION DENSITY IN ALBERTA

Year	Total Number of Employed Members ('000s)	Union Density (%)	Year	Total Number of Employed Members ('000s)	Union Density (%)
1974	157.5		1988	270.8	27.1
1975	167.3		1989	280.3	26.8
1976	180.2		1990	286.0	27.3
1977	179.4		1991	287.3	27.3
1978	186.6		1992	281.4	27.4
1979	195.8		1993	270.7	25.4
1980	211.8		1994	258.8	23.9
1981	230.1		1995	249.3	22.8
1982	229.7		1996	245.9	21.8
1983	264.1		1997	252.1	21.2
1984	263.5		1998	261.8	22.0
1985	253.2	26.7	1999	279.7	23.0
1986	260.4	26.3	2000	270.1	21.1
1987	255.4	25.7	2001	300.4	22.5

Sources: Statistics Canada. *Corporations and Labour Unions Returns Act*, 1974–1984.
Statistics Canada. Labour Force Survey, 1985–1998.
Statistics Canada. *Perspectives on Labour*, 1997, 1999 and 2001.

1995; Farber and Krueger 1993; and Beaumont and Harris 1995). In Alberta each one of these factors point in the direction of low union density.[4]

Whatever the explanation, both union membership and union density declined in Alberta throughout the 1990s. Table 4 shows that the number of union members in 2000 was less than the number of union members in the 1990.[5] Only in 2001 did total union membership actually surpass earlier totals. The same pattern emerged with respect to union density, which, according to Table 4, dropped from 27 percent in 1990 to 21 percent in 2000. Since then it has increased slightly (Statistics Canada 2002a) but it is too early to predict if this signals a new trend.

TABLE 5

UNION DENSITY BY ALBERTA INDUSTRIAL SECTOR

Sector	1983 (%)	2001 (%)
Agriculture and other primary	4.3	8.3
Manufacturing	34.3	18.7
Construction	70.8	19.9
Utilities	n/a	42.9
Transportation and warehousing[1]	48.5	36.9
Trade	9.0	11.6
Finance	0.0	4.3
Education	n/a	62.7
Health and social assistance	n/a	51.6
Accommodation, food and other services	n/a	3.5
Public administration	79.3	60.9
Public sector[2]		64.8
Private sector[2]		11.7

Notes: [1]Includes Utilities for 1983.
[2]Public and private sector union density for 2001 was provided by Marc Levesque, Statistics Canada Labour Force Survey.
Sources: 1983: *Membership in Labour Organizations in Alberta,* 1983. Alberta Labour, Planning and Research Branch.
2001: Statistics Canada, Labour Force Survey.

Tables 5 and 6 provide respectively, for 1983 and 2001, a break-down of union density by industrial sector and the membership totals of the largest unions. These tables highlight the weakness of private sector unionism and the relative strength of public sector unionism in Alberta. In 2001 public sector union density stood at 64.8 percent compared to 11.7 percent for the private sector (Table 5). Four of the five largest labour organizations represent employees in the public sector. Of the major private sector unions, only the United Food and Commercial Workers has shown substantial membership increases since 1983. Public sector unions have grown over the same period. The rate of Alberta public sector unionism is 91 percent of the national average (71 percent nationally according to Statistics Canada 2002*a*).

TABLE 6

TEN LARGEST ALBERTA LABOUR ORGANIZATIONS, 2001

Organizations	2001	1983
Alberta Union of Provincial Employees	51,834	48,011
Canadian Union of Public Employees	33,224	21,017
Alberta Teachers Association	32,182	37,402[1]
United Food and Commercial Workers	24,140	14,338
United Nurses of Alberta	21,345	10,731
International Brotherhood of Electrical Workers	13,074	16,475
Health Sciences Association of Alberta	10,314	3,550
Communication, Energy and Paperworkers Union	9,477	4,099[2]
Teamsters Union	9,123	7,290
Christian Labour Association of Canada	7,545	556

Notes: [1]The membership figures of the Alberta Teachers Association should be treated with great caution due to definitional changes in the way membership is reported from year to year.
[2]This total was derived from summing the total Alberta membership of the Communications Workers, Energy and Chemical Workers, and Paperworkers unions.
Sources: 1983: *Membership in Labour Organizations in Alberta*, 1984. Alberta Labour, Planning and Research Branch, January 1985.
2001: Government of Alberta, Data Development and Evaluation, provided by Nancy King.

　　　　　Alberta private sector union density is only 65 percent of the national average (18.1 percent nationally according to Statistics Canada 2002*a*) and is in decline (Table 5). Construction unions have never recovered from the turbulence of the early 1980s and now represent less than 20 percent of the workforce, two-thirds the national rate for their industry (Statistics Canada 2002*a*). In 1983, these unions had organized almost three-quarters of construction workers. The decline in union density in manufacturing is also significant, falling to under 20 percent in 2002 compared to 34 percent in 1983. The national rate of union density in manufacturing is 30 percent (ibid.).

　　　　　An analysis of certification application rates (Table 7) show that applications peaked in the late 1970s at more than 300 per year and then declined to a low of less than 200 annually in the early 1990s.[6] Since then

TABLE 7
APPLICATIONS FOR CERTIFICATION IN ALBERTA

Year[1]	Average Annual Number of Applications
1956–60	198
1961–65	233
1966–70	242
1971–75/76	304
1975/76 – 1980/81	324
1981/82 – 1985/86[2]	249
1986/87 – 1990/91	225
1991/92 – 1996/97	199
1997/98 – 2001/02	238

Notes: [1]Data collected from 1 April to 31 March annually.
[2]1983–84 excluded because reissuance of certificates render data non-comparable.
Source: Records of the Alberta Labour Relations Board, provided through assistance of ALRB analyst, Bob Poburan.

application rates have risen to 238 applications per year (in the five-year period ending in 2001–02), but are still substantially less than earlier levels.

Because of significant changes in reporting methods in the 1980s, it was not possible to develop an historical time series on the number of actual certifications per year or the proportion of certifications granted to number of applications.[7] Up until 1981, it appears that slightly more than two-thirds of applications resulted in certifications. In 1988, Alberta switched from a card-based certification system to a mandatory election-based system. In 1997, the Alberta Labour Relations Board reported that unions had won 70 percent of certification votes in the previous five-year period, a pattern that according to the board "shows a relatively static level of success ... since ... votes were introduced in 1988" (ALRB *Annual Report* 1997, 11). Between 1997 and 2002, this pattern held, with unions winning 73 percent of certification votes.[8] Thus, at first glance, certification rates under the election model appear to be at least as high as the certification rates under the card-based system. However, many applications do not reach a vote for a variety of reasons, including inappropriate bargaining unit or failure to achieve the threshold of 40 percent support necessary to hold a vote. Thus, the number of certifications granted to the number of applications for certifications was in the 40 to 50 percent range (ALRB *Annual Reports* various years). On this measure, certification rates would appear to be declining.

Certainly there is a perception among union leaders that it is difficult to organize in Alberta. We were told by a senior officer of one of Canada's larger private sector unions that his union had made a decision to stop new organizing drives in Alberta because the union perceived its chances as negligible. Another explanation for the dismissal of large numbers of applications is the growing practice, particularly in construction and maintenance applications, but also in health care, of filing multiple applications in the hopes of achieving a single success.[9]

Because the more recent data on certification rates are simply not comparable to the earlier data, no firm conclusions can be drawn as to whether actual union success rate in organizing has declined. It is clear that the number of applications has declined since the 1980s. Therefore, even if the rate of certifications as a proportion of applications can be interpreted to have remained constant (based on union certification election victories), the annual certification rate must have declined as well. This pattern is consistent with the overall decline in union density.

As might be expected given the low level of unionism and significant public sector strike prohibitions, work stoppages in Alberta have been well below the Canadian average. Table 8 provides a comparison of proportional time lost in Alberta to that in Canada since 1975. Consistent with overall Canadian trends there has been a decline in time lost (as a proportion of the workforce) due to strikes and lockouts in more recent years (Gunderson, Hyatt and Ponak 2001).

TABLE 8
DAYS LOST PER PAID WORKER DUE TO WORK STOPPAGES

Time Period	Alberta (rank among provinces)	Canada
1975–79	0.29 (9th)	0.94
1980–89	0.18 (8th)	0.46
1990–98	0.08 (8th)	0.19

Sources: 1975–79: Anderson and Gunderson (1992, Table 3, 227).
1980–98: Gunderson, Ponak and Taras (2001, Table 11.3, 325).

Since 1980, Alberta has ranked eighth among the provinces in terms of per capita time lost due to work stoppages, but the amount of strike activity of Alberta workers relative to Canadian workers has increased slightly. Between 1975 and 1979, work stoppage time lost in Alberta was 31 percent of the Canadian average. Between 1980 and 1989 it rose to 39 percent of the Canadian average and in the 1990s, it was 42 percent of the national average. From the strike data it is difficult to draw definitive conclusions about the militancy of the Alberta labour movement. We would expect that the lower rate of union density and the high proportion of workers prohibited from striking would explain a significant amount of the lower Alberta strike rate. Unfortunately, we do not have data available to determine, after controlling for union density and proportion of workers with the right to strike, whether Alberta strike activity is still well below the Canadian average. Certainly some Alberta unions have engaged in highly visible strikes with great impact. The United Nurses of Alberta struck provincewide three times in the 1980s and used their aggressive reputation to advantage in subsequent rounds of bargaining. In 1997 the United Food and Commercial Workers struck Canada Safeway for ten weeks, involving 10,000 employees at 75 stores. Though the stores remained open with replacement workers (and 20 percent of bargaining unit employees), customers largely stayed away and sales revenue fell by more than half (Nikiforuk 1997). In 2000, hospital workers belonging to the Alberta Union of Provincial Employees struck illegally across the province. The union was heavily fined, but made sizable gains in the next round of bargaining with the government.

In summary, Alberta has the lowest level of union density in Canada. Both union density and the absolute number of union members declined in the 1990s, especially in the private sector. Alberta unionization rates in the private sector now more closely resemble United States patterns than Canadian ones. It is no surprise that a serious effort to introduce right-to-work legislation took place in 1995 and that a survey of 1,240 Albertans showed that almost 70 percent would not join a union if one existed in their workplace (Fong, Kinzel and Odynak 1995). Time lost due to work stoppages remains well below the national average, though significant and highly visible strikes still occur from time to time.

PATTERNS OF NON-UNION REPRESENTATION

A distinctive feature of Alberta's industrial relations landscape, especially in the energy sector, has been the existence of well-established non-union representation plans designed for employees who might otherwise become unionized (Taras and Copping 1998; Taras and Ponak 1999; Taras 2000). These plans were popular in the United States in the 1920s, but outlawed by the 1935 US *Wagner Act* and rapidly disbanded. Due to deliberate differences in the crafting of labour law, non-union employee representation remained legal and continued to exist in some parts of Canada (Taras 1997*a*).

The most influential of the plans, the Joint Industrial Council (JIC), was the creation of William Lyon McKenzie King, who devised the scheme of worker representation while he was employed as a consultant to the Rockefeller companies in the mid-1910s (Gitelman 1988). Under the JIC plan, an equal number of appointed managers and elected employees meet frequently to discuss the terms and conditions of employment, as well as any matters of interest that arise within the company (Taras and Copping 1998). The plan was introduced in Canada in 1918 through Imperial Oil, a Rockefeller-owned company. Within Alberta, non-union representation dates to the first major oil field development in the province in the 1920s, located in Turner Valley, 50 kilometres south of Calgary.

Imperial Oil has 80 years of uninterrupted practice with JICs, and this non-union plan is the firm's prevalent mode of industrial relations. Other energy companies practise similar forms of non-union employee representation, for example, Petro-Canada's employee-management advisory committees (Taras and Ponak 1999). About one-third of all hourly workers employed in oil and gas fields, refineries, and plants belong to some type of structured non-union plan, one-third are unionized, and one-third have no formal representation (ibid.). While non-union representation plans are found mainly in Alberta's energy industry, they also exist in telecommunications (e.g., Northern Telecom), the public sector (the Town of Banff), retail grocery (IGA) and meat processing (XL Foods). Due to the lack of systematic data about these non-union practices throughout Canada, we cannot say with certainty that Alberta companies currently practise non-union representation in industries other than the energy sector with more frequency than is the case in other provinces.

The contemporary effects of these non-union plans within the energy sector are instructive. The companies, which practise non-union forms of representation carefully, monitor wage rates and benefits to ensure that they do not fall below those negotiated in unionized firms. As a result, there is virtually no variability in compensation for hourly workers in the same position who work for different companies, union or non-union.[10] Thus, there is no economic incentive for petroleum workers in Alberta to join unions. When these workers do unionize, the motivators tend to be non-economic: overly autocratic management style, worker desire for greater input into decision-making, and so on.

The industrial relations practices of the energy industry have promoted the development of mechanisms for information-sharing between union and non-union firms. One such mechanism is the Red Deer Group. Twice a year, the industrial relations or human resource managers representing approximately 25 large and mid-sized employers share information in meetings at Red Deer, a small city equidistant between Calgary and Edmonton (Taras 1997c, 190-92). This group started in the early 1950s in response to management concerns about whipsawing after the first wave of concerted union organizing. The initial criterion for membership to this group was that companies had to be bargaining with the primary union in the energy sector (OCAW in the 1960s to 1970s, then ECWU until 1994, now CEP). Over the years, even union-free firms became members. Through the exchange of information about bargaining intentions and expected wage settlements, petroleum firms act in a coordinated fashion to remove wages from competition among firms, and as a result, the industry has tightly clustered wage contours.[11] The critical point here is that industrial relations in the province's most significant private sector industry involves a dynamic interaction between unionized and non-unionized employers. A large part of the province's most influential industry is non-union by design rather than happenstance, and management works hard to maintain its non-union status.

LABOUR LEGISLATION

Industrial relations in Alberta is governed by two main statutes, the Alberta Labour Relations Code (Labour Code) and the *Public Service Employee Relations Act* (PSERA). The Labour Code, consistent with the approach across the country, covers virtually all private sector employees falling under provincial jurisdiction as well as certain public sector employees such as municipal workers and hospital workers (Ponak and Thompson 2001, 426).

PSERA primarily regulates the provincial public service, but also covers employees of government boards and agencies (e.g., Alberta Cancer Board, Banff Centre) and support staff at Alberta technical institutes, colleges, and universities. In addition to the Labour Code and PSERA, several other statutes apply to labour relations in specific sectors: the *Police Officers Collective Bargaining Act* for municipal police forces; the *Technical Institutes Act, Colleges Act,* and the *Universities Act* for faculty members of these institutions; and the *School Act* for specified aspects of labour relations relevant to school teachers, especially dismissal procedures.

Bringing some cohesion to the proliferation of legislative regimes is the authority given to the Labour Relations Board, established under the Labour Code, to regulate matters that may arise under PSERA, including police and schoolteachers. The board is tripartite in composition, with approximately 25 part-time members drawn from major employers and unions, two full-time vice-chairs, two part-time vice-chairs and a chair appointed by Cabinet for a five-year term.

Given the centrality of the Labour Relations Board to industrial relations matters in the province, recent governments have generally avoided the partisan turnover of LRB chairs which has characterized Ontario and British Columbia. Alberta Labour Board chairs have been appointed on merit and acceptability to the parties rather than political ideology. The sudden firing of the LRB chair in 1999, therefore, was a departure from previous practice and raised concerns about whether the board would remain a neutral agency. The new chair, however, was well regarded by all parties, suggesting that the Alberta board will retain its non-partisan reputation.

By and large Alberta labour law follows prevailing Canadian models. The Labour Code is based on *Wagner Act* principles and PSERA resembles other provincial statutes directed primarily at civil servants (e.g., it statutorily sets bargaining units and restricts the scope of bargaining). Unionization and collective bargaining are protected and the usual array of unfair labour practices apply to both labour and management.

Within this general framework, Alberta labour law is more employer friendly than is true in other provinces. The preamble of the Labour Code sets this tone by emphasizing the "competitive world-wide market economy" and the "common interest in the success of the employing organization" on the part of employees and employers. The preamble never refers to unions or labour organizations, only to employees, and provides a tepid endorsement of collective bargaining as "*an* appropriate mechanism" for establishing terms and conditions of employment. (This is in contrast to other labour statutes that speak of collective bargaining as "*the* appropriate mechanism" or as a desirable process.) Fewer of the "extra" protections that unions want, such as first contract arbitration or access to an employee mailing list during organizing, are found in Alberta law, and more of the provisions favoured by employers, such as ensuring management freedom of expression during organizing and last-offer contract votes, are present.

Consistent with this over-all direction, the Labour Code contains a more comprehensive list of exclusions than is true in other provinces or in the federal jurisdiction. Excluded from coverage are doctors, lawyers, dentists, architects, and engineers (section 1(l)(ii)), ranch and farm workers involved in primary production (section 4(e)), and domestic employees such as nannies (section 4(f)). All of these exclusions were commonplace across Canada at one time, but many provinces have gradually eliminated such restrictions (Rayner 1995, 8-12 – 8-15). This is not true in Alberta.

There are more restrictions on the right to strike in Alberta than in other jurisdictions. Provincial civil servants, college and university employees, police, fire fighters, and health-care workers are prohibited from striking and must submit interest disputes to arbitration. Aside from the usual criticisms of compulsory arbitration (see Ponak and Falkenberg 1989) arbitral criteria have proved contentious over the years. At one time, arbitrators were required to consider the fiscal policies of the provincial Treasurer (Mason 1984); currently, wages and conditions in non-union workplaces are a mandatory element in the criteria (section 99 of the Labour Code; section 55 of PSERA).

Unions further complain that, unlike provisions of PSERA, where the LRB appoints arbitrators in the event that the parties cannot agree, the Labour Code disadvantages unions in a right-wing province by having the elected minister of labour make such appointments. This affects hospital unions in particular, the largest potential "consumers" of interest arbitration under the Labour Code, and gives rise to union concerns about possible manipulation.[12] In the 1997–98 round of bargaining in health care, several short-term illegal strikes occurred.

In 1988, Alberta became the third province (the others were Nova Scotia and British Columbia) to require a vote for new certifications.[13] Even if the union applying for certification can demonstrate significant majority support through signed membership cards, a vote must still be held. Union representatives claim that the mandatory vote requirement makes organizing more difficult, although there is little systematic data to support that claim. (For discussion of the pros and cons of cards versus votes, see Sims, Blouin and Knopf 1995; Weiler 1983.) As indicated earlier in the chapter, unions have been successful in 70 percent of certification elections since the introduction of the election system, a success rate that the board views as consistent with certification rates under the card system prior to 1988. This rate of union success may be due partially to the board's approach of ensuring that certification votes occur quickly to avoid the type of US-style election campaign that has proven destructive to union organizing. In 2001–2002, more than 70 percent of certification applications were completed within 30 calendar days and the average duration in 2001–02 was 43 days (ALRB 2002).

Other aspects of Alberta labour law that reflect employer preferences, in contrast to most other Canadian jurisdictions, include: the absence of board remedial power to impose certification in the face of substantial illegal employer interference with union organizing; the absence of a requirement to include a Rand formula in the collective agreement upon union request (Taras 1997*b*); weaker protection for striking workers (Budd 1996); and the absence of a reverse onus in respect of alleged employer unfair labour practices.[14]

The province's legislature has contained a significant core of elected representatives holding a fundamentalist Christian ethic, and this has had an impact on the province's employment relations. The effect is best illuminated by the Supreme Court's 1998 Vriend decision (*Vriend v. Alberta* 1998). Alberta never wrote protections for sexual orientation into any of its human rights or employment statutes, and over the years government legislators have staunchly resisted any initiatives for reform.[15] Some collective agreements, by consent of the parties, protect sexual orientation in their non-discrimination clauses (e.g., the United Nurses of Alberta). But where there was no protection proffered by the employer and union, gay and lesbian Albertans could not turn to the human rights laws of the province.

The landmark case involved a homosexual man, Delwin Vriend, who was fired in 1991 allegedly for his sexual orientation by a private Christian college in Edmonton. Because Alberta's *Individual Rights Protection Act* (now called the *Citizenship and Multiculturalism Act*, and in other provinces called human rights acts) was silent on sexual orientation as a protection against discrimination, he could not have his dismissal reviewed by the Alberta Human Rights Commission. The Canadian Supreme Court ruled that Alberta's failure to include sexual orientation protections in its various statutes violated the federal *Charter of Rights and Freedoms*. The seven-to-one decision had the effect of inserting the words "sexual orientation" into Alberta's laws prohibiting discrimination.[16] The government came under intense pressure from elements of the public and from powerful Cabinet ministers to reject the decision by invoking the "notwithstanding clause" of the Charter.[17] Ultimately, however, the government reluctantly accepted the Court's decision.

In short, while labour policy trends in Canada from the Second World War through the early 1990s were in the direction of providing more encouragement to union activity and more protection in general to employees, Alberta lagged other jurisdictions. Though the main elements of the *Wagner Act* model and human rights law are well established, innovations introduced elsewhere arrived later in Alberta or, in some cases, not at all. The province has chosen a labour law niche as the province most likely to defer to employer predilections.

RIGHT-TO-WORK (RTW)

One of the most contentious issues that arose in Alberta's 1990s labour relations policy arena involved a movement to adopt American-style right-to-work legislation. In the United States, 21 states have exercised their limited labour jurisdictional powers (given to them by the 1947 Taft-Hartley amendments to the 1935 *Wagner Act*) to pass legislation which prohibits unions and management from negotiating and concluding collective agreements that enforce universal union membership or compulsory dues deductions.

Canada never adopted the American treatment of union security issues. Today, most Canadian jurisdictions make an agency shop (commonly known in Canada as the Rand formula) mandatory. Over 90 percent of Canadian collective agreements contain mandatory dues deductions, and at a minimum the Rand formula or even stronger union protection (union shop or closed shop) is the norm. Alberta law is silent on union security, leaving this issue to be determined by the parties during collective bargaining. In practice, the Rand formula is less common in Alberta than in the rest of the country.

While there have been other initiatives to introduce RTW in Canada (e.g., Weiler 1980, 140), Alberta gave RTW more serious consideration than any other province, largely due to the intensive lobbying efforts of the Alberta arm of the National Citizens' Coalition (NCC),[18] headed by Rob Anders (who subsequently was elected as a Canadian Alliance member of Parliament). The NCC decided to promote RTW in Alberta because Alberta had the most "friendly government" and the most "sensible" labour laws according to NCC national director.[19] In 1995 the sustained lobbying paid off when a private member's bill to initiate a study of RTW narrowly passed. The minister of labour, Stockwell Day (who did not vote for the motion), took the position that there was no need for any significant change in labour law. Premier Klein was not an active participant in the debate that ensued.

The Alberta Economic Development Authority Committee was asked to review RTW with special consideration of its economic effect in Alberta.[20] Elaine McCoy, a former Alberta minister of labour, headed the committee, which also included representatives of business, government, and labour.

Unexpectedly, the majority of large Alberta employers or employer groups who responded to the call for submissions were *opposed* to RTW. Such major employers as Syncrude, Canada Safeway, and Westfair Foods wrote that RTW was neither necessary nor desirable for the operation of their businesses. A representative of Safeway pointed out that: "Due to the fact that we operate in other Provinces, we know that the current legislation in Alberta is already more advantageous to Employers than in other areas. We see no point in drawing attention to legislation that is working." The vice-president of Westfair Foods (a wholesale and retail food and general merchandise company operating Real Canadian Superstore and a number of other outlets) agreed and added that RTW would favour the entry of low-wage American competitors to the detriment of existing unionized grocery chains.

Construction employers associations, including Construction Labour Relations and the Construction Owners Association of Alberta, urged the government to recognize that the introduction of RTW would destroy labour relations stability in the industry, and reverse the many positive union-management achievements of the previous decade. Both the Calgary and Edmonton Chambers of Commerce feared that RTW would unnecessarily instigate labour unrest. The Human Resources Institute of Alberta, an umbrella organization representing diverse professional groups throughout the province, felt that there existed neither the rationale nor evident economic benefit for RTW. Many large, and potentially influential non-union employers, such as Northern Telecom and integrated energy companies, made no submissions because the issue simply was not relevant to them.

The committee's final report unanimously rejected RTW, concluding that there were few economic benefits and the possibility of labour relations instability (Alberta Economic Development Authority 1995). The RTW issue remains close to the surface, however. The current Alberta minister of human resources and employment (the successor to Alberta Labour) has warned that any moves to amend the Labour Code would likely re-open the RTW debate.

THE KLEIN REVOLUTION

Ralph Klein was elected leader of the Alberta Conservative Party in 1992. The election called shortly thereafter was fought over which political party would most reduce public spending. The Conservatives won the election with a substantial majority and were re-elected easily in 1997 and 2001. Upon election in 1993, Premier Klein and his party embarked on a plan, popularly known as the "Klein Revolution," to eliminate the provincial deficit within four years without increasing taxes. To meet this objective, program expenditures were reduced by 20 percent on average (Lisac 1995). At the time "no one was prepared for the fast, furious, and severe assault on the public sector that transpired" (Taylor 1995, 313). Union leaders were no exception. Most failed to anticipate that the government had both the resolve and the electoral mandate to make fundamental and rapid changes, and the determination to "not blink" in imposing this agenda onto organized labour.

There were several cornerstones to the government's approach. Beginning in 1993 the government introduced sharp reductions in program expenditures over a four-year period. Reductions ranged from 5.6 percent in basic education to 15.3 percent in higher education and 17.7 percent in health care. Government departments took average budget cuts of 20 percent. Social service providers and social workers were particularly hard hit, with some agencies suffering 30 percent cuts. Government agencies were expected to move toward a business planning approach: not only would programs become more accountable, but a review would be made of what services could be divested to other (usually private) service deliverers, and remaining core activities would be developed through the "Delegated Administrative Organizations" approach (Alberta Labour 1994).

The experience of Alberta Labour, the department responsible for public safety, occupational health and safety, labour relations and workplace standards, is instructive. Until 1991, Alberta Labour was a traditional bureaucracy, consisting of seven layers of management run in a centralized fashion. In 1991 a decision was made to respond to major political forces for change in Alberta, including an awareness of deficit and debt problems and a sense of over-governance (Bowerman and Ford 1994). Alberta Labour adopted a "Quality Service Through Partnerships" approach, requiring significant restructuring, identification of key competencies, new leadership, teamwork, and the use of business plans (ibid.). With the election of the Klein government, the pace of reform accelerated, and the Alberta Labour approach to business planning became a central part of the Klein government strategy. Alberta Labour's use of this approach reduced its draw on tax dollars by 54 percent from 1991 to 1995, and eliminated many layers of middle management (Ford 1995; Alberta Labour 1996). The actual number of manager-supervisor positions was reduced from about 150 to 50 (Farquhar 1995).

The *Balanced Budget and Debt Retirement Act*, enacted in 1995, essentially banned budget deficits and directed that surpluses be used for debt reduction. Major restructuring was introduced in health care, education, and the civil service (Hughes, Lowe and McKinnon 1996; Reshef and Lam 1999). For example, the number of school boards was reduced from 146 to 62 and 17 regional health authorities replaced some 200 hospital boards and numerous community health facilities. Further savings were achieved by a privatization wave that included retail sales of beer, wine, and spirits, provincial campgrounds, and labour mediation. The budget cuts and restructuring produced substantial layoffs. Between 1993 and 1995, the health-care workforce declined by 21 percent (Alberta Health 1995), by early 1997 there were 1,500 fewer teachers (Johnsrude 1997), and the number of government employees fell 23.5 percent from 1994 to 1997 (Alberta. Personnel Administration Office 1995–97).

In industrial relations terms the most pervasive element of the government strategy was its insistence that all members of the broad public sector accept a 5 percent reduction in compensation during the 1994–97 period. These reductions were imposed on non-union employees (e.g., hospital managers, senior civil servants, provincial court judges) and achieved through collective bargaining for unionized employees. Because the reductions were negotiated in the unionized sector, the contours of these reductions varied by sector and bargaining agent. University of Calgary faculty, for example, negotiated an outright wage reduction of 2 percent in 1994 plus seven unpaid days off, the total of which amounted to a 5 percent reduction. There were no wage increases or decreases in 1995, 1996, or 1997 and the unpaid days were eliminated gradually in that period. Registered nurses working in hospitals, on the other hand, took a one-time, 5 percent wage reduction in 1994 and received no further salary adjustment (up or down) until 1997. One way or another, most public employees "contributed" 5 percent of their compensation to the Klein Revolution. These reductions were realized with almost no strikes and a minimal amount of other forms of overt conflict.

Why did unions in Alberta acquiesce with so little apparent struggle? The Ontario labour movement, in contrast, organized general strikes and mass demonstrations at Queen's Park. Ontario teachers struck for two weeks against the changes being introduced by their Conservative government. At the outset, Alberta union leaders were optimistic that they could unite workers across the province against the Klein deficit elimination policies and "the government would cave in and the labour movement would rise as a major political force in Alberta" (Feschuk and Mitchell 1994). The newly elected president of the Alberta Union of Provincial Employees, the province's largest union, declared, "you are headed for one of the biggest labour battles that you've ever seen in this province" (Coulter 1993). This rhetoric proved to be empty.

One explanation for the inability of unions to mobilize their membership was that employees throughout the province had witnessed deep private sector layoffs and as a result were fearful of their own job security. They were prepared to take whatever steps might be necessary to save their jobs. In some cases, as union leaders were deliberating whether or not to negotiate pay concessions, their own members lobbied them for pay cuts in the hope of saving jobs. One union leader whom we interviewed stated that at the end of 1993 "many members started [saying] that it was okay to accept the five percent; by spring/summer 1994 it was ... almost 'we demand that you accept the five percent regression to save jobs.'" Another labour official added, "I don't think anyone wants to advocate rolling back, but when the membership is saying 'we're desperate, we're afraid, do it,' you don't have a choice."[21]

A second explanation for the relative ease with which the wage concessions and other elements of the government's program were achieved was the high level of public support enjoyed by Premier Klein. Even though many concerns were raised about the impact of government policies on education and especially health care, Albertans seemed willing to separate Klein from his policies. Opinion polls consistently showed that whereas respondents believed that the budget cuts reduced education and health-care quality, the majority supported the premier and his deficit elimination policies (Hughes, Lowe and McKinnon 1996). Klein's voter satisfaction index numbers in 1996 were higher than any other first minister's (Wilson-Smith 1996). Undoubtedly, many union members voted for Klein. Even when oil and gas royalties unexpectedly buoyed Alberta coffers in 1996, leading to a substantial budget surplus, Albertans maintained their faith in fiscal caution, and expressed a preference toward paying down the debt rather than restoring the public sector. When the federal government announced an expected surplus in the 1997–98 budget, most Canadians hoped that tax cuts would be the first outcome, but Albertans (and British Columbians) ranked deficit reduction as the bigger priority (Mulawka 1997).

Third, in a province renowned for its boom and bust cycles and rugged entrepreneurial machismo, there was little sympathy for union goals of job security and high wages. Private sector workers, who had only a few years earlier suffered massive job losses, viewed public sector unions as whining and the public sector generally as bloated and sluggish. Klein was given high marks by many voters for his courage in tackling public sector cuts and forcing government workers to confront the ostensible realities of the modern business age: to become lean, responsive, and accountable. In a late 1996 *Maclean's*/CBC public opinion poll, respondents across Canada were asked about corporate responsibility (Wells 1996). Was it acceptable that profitable corporations pursue worker layoffs? "No," said 58 percent of Canadians, with highs of 66 percent in Atlantic Canada and 64 percent in Quebec. By contrast, 51 percent of Albertans said "Yes." On the outsourcing issue, respondents were asked whether corporations should close in-house departments and buy from outside suppliers. While the Canadian average was 54 percent in favour of outsourcing (with a low of 46 percent in Ontario), Albertans, at 67 percent, were most supportive.

Fourth, the government did a good job of popularizing its programs through public consultation, undercutting organized labour's ability to offer alternatives. Major government vehicles were roundtables and an economic summit, which, on their face, engaged the public in a series of open discussions on government policies and the province's future. Through participation in these forums, representatives of the public were expected to advise the government on where and how much to cut, and eventually, on reinvestment. The result was to persuade Albertans that the new socio-economic policies came from the people (Lisac 1995). Whenever union leaders tried to challenge this voice, they were labelled as special interest groups and marginalized.

A fifth factor in the inability of unions to mount any kind of effective challenge to the government program was the decision of union leadership to use regular collective bargaining, rather than political or social protest, to address the wage concessions demanded by public employers. In some ways this may have been a pragmatic decision — union officials were unanimous in their belief that they had no choice but to negotiate the pay cuts. In an interview, a union president elaborated:

> I don't think in this day and age there's too many union leaders that honestly believe they have the power to suddenly say "OK boys, throw the tools down. We're out on the street!" and everybody will follow it. I don't think much of that happens anymore ... We don't seem to be a province that marches and demonstrates.

Some observers believe that one of the main unions affected, AUPE, was financially crippled at this point by reduced dues income, and union officials even feared foreclosure of their building. The finances for mounting an elaborate campaign against the Klein government were absent.

Whether planned or not the Klein government was savvy in offering unions the option to negotiate over wage concessions. In a decentralized public sector collective-bargaining system, local unions directed their energies to negotiating with their respective employers, shifting their focus away from the government and its policies. A former union officer stated:

> What it did was put the battle at the bargaining table. The battle was not the fight that probably should have been against the provincial legislators. It went down to the bargaining table, and it was a scrap between the union and the employer.

The end result was that without effective political protest or the development of alternatives, public employees made the wage concessions willingly.

While a limp and exhausted labour movement was unable to forestall the Klein Revolution, a challenge emerged from a surprising source. In November 1995, 120 Calgary hospital laundry workers went on a wildcat strike to protest the outsourcing of their jobs (McGrath and Neu 1996). Two years earlier, they had accepted pay cuts of 28 percent in order to help their employer, the Calgary Regional Health Authority, meet its budget and preserve their jobs. With the announcement that the laundry function was to be privatized and sent to a non-union firm in Edmonton, they struck and were soon joined by other hospital support staff. Laundry workers received considerable support from doctors, nurses, and most importantly, the general public. The courage of the lowest paid workers in the health-care system galvanized the province. The "David-and-Goliath" nature of their struggle had strong appeal for Albertans. The traditional reticence about organized labour was largely absent from the public response to these particular workers (ibid.). Seventy-two percent of Calgarians supported the strike. Eventually, more than 2,500 workers from 15 health-care facilities walked off the job, and many more who remained at work launched work-to-rule campaigns in support of the strikers.

In the end, the striking laundry workers won a longer notice period and severance, but the strike achieved a larger purpose. It caused the first major reversal in the Klein government's "no blink" policy (*Maclean's* 1995*b*). The strike drew attention to health care and in its aftermath, 75 percent of Albertans polled believed that health-care cuts were too fast and too deep (McGrath and Neu 1996). In unprompted questions about important issues facing Albertans, another poll found that the principal concern of the majority of Albertans, 53 percent, was the deterioration in health care and hospitals (*Western Report* 1996). Within a few days of the strike, the government announced that it was cancelling a scheduled $53 million cut in health care, and Klein conceded that "We're taking a bit of a detour," and that his government had underestimated the "human factor." Public support for the government was restored, and Klein maintained his image as a tough but populist leader.

AFTERMATH OF THE KLEIN REVOLUTION

In 1997, the economy began to perform well beyond original predictions, but unions found it extraordinarily difficult to achieve restitution for their earlier sacrifices.[22] Oil royalty windfalls created a $2.2 billion surplus in the 1997 budget, and the government began a cautious program of reinvestment in health care, education, and social services. New money, however, did not flow unrestricted back into the budgets of employers. Rather it was earmarked for specific purposes. Yet employee expectations were raised.

When a crisis atmosphere about the deficit had prevailed earlier, union members responded by accepting wage reductions in order to assist Klein to get his economic house in order. With the budget surplus announcements, expectations ran high that wage gains would follow shortly. Instead, unions had to wait until the expiry of collective agreements and then bargain hard to restore the 5 percent cut rather than achieve significant new gains in tandem with the rising economic fortunes of the province.

While private sector wages, particularly in the oil patch, began soaring again, public sector workers remained locked in a battle merely to bargain back what was once theirs. Rounds of negotiations were particularly difficult because employers frequently lacked the budgetary resources to acquiesce to union demands. The Calgary Public School negotiations through 1996 and 1997 were typical: both the employer and the union essentially were on the same side of the bargaining table, pressuring the government for more money with little effect. The result for Alberta's labour relations was a significant suppression of wages for many years beyond the immediate deficit crisis. Hard bargaining prevailed, and unions were preoccupied with restoration of wages rather than putting themselves in a position to use the economic buoyancy to launch aggressive wage initiatives. Unions learned that once concessions were given, they were not easily recovered, regardless of economic prosperity.

Two strikes are illustrative. On 24 May 2000, more than 10,000 licensed practical nurses, nursing attendants, and support staff at 159 hospitals and long-term care facilities represented by the Alberta Union of Provincial Employees commenced an illegal strike (hospital workers in Alberta do not have the right to strike and must submit disputes to arbitration). The strike was synchronized across several bargaining units by the union, part of a strategy to enhance its bargaining power. Wages were at the heart of the dispute. Management offered the workers 12.2 percent over three years; the union asked for 15 to 23 percent over two years.

The strike lasted three days. Based on a mediator's recommendation all employees received a 4 percent increase on 1 April 2000 and a further 4 percent increase the next year. As well, licensed practical nurses (LPN) and nursing attendants received additional market adjustments in August 2000 and 2001; the LPNs received 4 percent each year and the nursing attendants received 3 percent, bringing their wage increase to 16 and 14 percent respectively over two years.

Shortly after the strike ended, the union was found guilty of civil contempt of court and was fined $400,000, but on appeal the fine was reduced to $200,000.[23] The lower court judge said that he would have considered jailing the AUPE president but decided against it because the Provincial Health Authorities of Alberta, which had sought the contempt ruling, did not ask for a jail sentence (Thomas 2000). In April 2001, the Alberta Labour Relations Board ruled that the province's health authorities could stop collecting dues on behalf of the union for two months.[24] This decision (currently under appeal) could cost the union up to $500,000 if all members who participated in the strike declined to voluntarily submit their dues to the union.

An aspect of the strike that deserves some attention is the role of Premier Ralph Klein who seemed willing to use his political clout to give the striking workers a substantial raise. The premier publicly stated that the AUPE president, Dan McLennan, and the people he represented were good people who had earned a raise (McFaul 2000), a stark contrast to his rhetoric and actions during the heyday of the Klein Revolution. The enthusiasm of Klein for the AUPE leader did not stop there. In early 2001, the Canadian Labour Congress expelled the AUPE, and the Alberta Federation of Labour charged that it "raided" members from the Canadian Union of Public Employees (CUPE). Once again, the premier did not hesitate to throw his weight behind MacLennan: "I sort of agree with Dan on this whole point. He's a different sort of union organizer, to say the least ... Dan's the man" (*Edmonton Sun* 2000).

Two years later, it was the teachers' turn. On 4 February 2002 the Alberta Teachers' Association coordinated an unprecedented series of strikes across 19 of Alberta's 62 school districts, immediately affecting almost half of the province's students. Two weeks later teachers in three more school districts struck; at that point, the strike included the two largest bargaining units, Calgary (5,944 public teachers and 99,528 students) and Edmonton (4,780 public teachers and 81,863 students) and almost two-thirds of the province's students.[25] The strike ultimately lasted 13 working days and was ended by back-to-work legislation with which the union complied (though teachers declined to perform extracurricular activities for a period of time).

The roots of the 2002 strike can be partially traced to changes in school funding introduced in 1994 as part of the government's deficit-cutting campaign. The *School Amendment Act* removed local school board taxation powers, centralizing all school financing at the provincial level, greatly limiting the discretion of local school boards to raise and spend money (Reshef 2001). Thus, while bargaining ostensibly occurred on a local basis, in practice the provincial government's budget decisions drove the process. In early 2001, doctors and then registered nurses negotiated 22 percent and 17 percent fee and wage increases respectively over two years, greatly raising teacher expectations. These expectations were heightened when Premier Klein stated "there is no doubt Alberta teachers were part of the (economic) solution a few years ago. We'll make sure that our teachers and instructors and professors are fairly compensated and given as good a work environment as they can have so that they know how much they are appreciated" (Thomson 2001).

The government then proceeded to provide school boards with salary funding far below what would be needed to match doctors and nurses.[26] In most districts, the parties quickly arrived at a bargaining impasse, as local school boards simply did not have the financial means necessary to satisfy the ATA demands. Strike votes were held around the province and it became clear that the only way to avoid a series of coordinated strikes was for the government to allocate more money to the school boards for pay increases. The government refused.

The ensuing strike was ended by legislation that imposed binding arbitration and banned work stoppages until September 2003. The legislation ending the strike and the terms of arbitration themselves became the subject of litigation and direct negotiation between the premier and the president of the ATA. In July 2002, the first arbitration awards, which covered both Calgary and Edmonton, were released. They provided salary increases of 14 percent over two years, although the increase was staggered to reduce school board costs. The school boards immediately appealed to the provincial government to fund the arbitration settlements, pleas that fell on deaf ears.

Two lessons can be drawn from the "post-Klein Revolution" developments. First, budget and legislative changes introduced during the Klein Revolution have centralized revenue collection and allocation decisions in the provincial government at the expense of local authority. Public sector agencies, be they school boards or health-care providers, lack real decision-making power in negotiations. Unions are aware of this fact and increasingly direct their efforts at the provincial level, notwithstanding that negotiations actually occur locally.

Second, Premier Klein became more personally involved in public sector disputes. The cases of AUPE and the teachers illustrate this point. In the first case, he was instrumental in getting the AUPE members a settlement they approved; in the second case, his direct intervention overcame the intransigence within his own caucus. Public sector workers who find themselves at loggerheads with their employer may conclude that the path to a decent settlement runs through the premier's office.

CONCLUSIONS

While each province has unique elements, all, including Alberta, have adopted the basic principles of Wagnerism. Where Alberta is distinctive is its resistance to creating a public policy framework that goes further than merely accepting collective bargaining. The industry mix, particularly the predominant role of the energy sector, has led to low union density. The low levels of private sector unionism are especially noteworthy.

Unions are an anathema to the provincial ethos of entrepreneurship and individuality, and it is not surprising that over time there have been a number of initiatives to undermine unions. There is a strong reluctance to foster collective bargaining. On the other hand, there is no great outcry for reform of labour policy in whole cloth, and occasionally and unpredictably the Alberta public rouses itself to defend unions and employees who are believed to have been treated inequitably.

The inherent conservatism of the province has enhanced the appeal of politicians whose agenda highlights fiscal responsibility and reducing "over-government." Unions have taken the fallout of government policies that are designed first and foremost to promote balanced budgets and eliminate the provincial debt. Without a strong opposition voice through the NDP or even the Liberals, unions have been politically marginalized and have had to use collective bargaining as their principal opportunity for achieving greater public awareness. But successive rounds of collective bargaining have been hard, with little budgetary slack, and union members themselves do not necessarily support union objectives. Alberta union leaders have an unenviable role.

The Klein Revolution highlighted all the inherent forces that characterize Alberta's industrial relations. The strength of conservatism and the huge political mandate delivered to Klein and his party colleagues (called "Ralph's Team" during election campaigns) made it possible to aggressively restructure the province's finances. Lacking any available weapons for effective resistance, unions had to endure massive job losses and a wage cut whose effects did not dissipate once the economic crisis was over and the province had returned to prosperity. For labour, Alberta is likely to remain the province most likely to have periodic assaults on union legitimacy.

In evaluating the Alberta experience, it is instructive also to examine the right-to-work campaign, the laundry workers strike, the Vriend decision, and the teachers' dispute. Klein's brand of fiscal conservatism does not necessarily extend to embracing the same spectrum espoused by his right-wing colleagues and supporters. While in industrial relations terms the impact of the Klein Revolution on the labour movement has been devastating, Klein himself has no record of any sympathy for union busting or gay bashing. However, the job of managing his caucus cannot be an easy one in a province with a bedrock of support for the Canadian Alliance Party and ultra-conservative positions. The right-wing *Alberta Report* commented, "The thing about Ralph Klein that most people forget is that he is a liberal, not a conservative. He never was a conservative.

He doesn't like conservatives, and he detests their issues. But because he heads a conservative party, he must constantly fear and disperse any formation of conservative strength" (Byfield 1998). In Alberta, the most difficult political challenges come from the right, not the left.

NOTES

The authors would like to thank Robert Bourne and Kelly Williams for their research assistance and the Industrial Relations Research Group, University of Calgary for its financial support. We appreciate the feedback on earlier drafts from William Armstrong, Robert Blair, Claude Dupuis, Ron Franklin, David Harrigan, Hugh McPhail and Ronald Neuman.

[1]The New Democratic Party in Alberta actually calls itself the "New Democrats" (NDs) but for the sake of common nomenclature, will be referred to as the NDP. As of January 2003, there were two New Democrats, seven Liberals, and 73 Conservatives in the provincial legislature.

[2]We estimate that Alberta has fallen short of this target; its per capita government expenditures are only 1 percent less than the Canadian average.

[3]In 1986, public pronouncements by the owner of a Gainers meat-packing plant that he intended to permanently replace his striking employees was condemned by the provincial government and resulted in Labour Code amendments protecting striking employees.

[4]In the absence of systematic research on the question of low Alberta union density, our explanations must be treated cautiously.

[5]There are several different data series on union membership in Alberta (e.g., Akyeompong 1999). They tend to show different union membership totals and union density, though in most cases the differences are not large. They are all consistent in terms of the trend line, which is in the direction of declining membership and density.

[6]These raw data must be viewed with some caution because they include the construction industry, which has a certification pattern quite different than other industries.

[7]Until the early 1980s the Alberta Labour Relations Board had a specific category for "applications granted"; after that time, the board began reporting certification applications as either "concluded" or "outstanding," making it difficult to determine how many of the concluded applications had been granted and how many had been rejected. It should be noted that this information may very well be available in the board archives, but an investigation of these archives is beyond the scope of this chapter.

[8]Unpublished data provided by the Alberta Labour Relations Board.

[9]Our appreciation to Robert Blair, former chair of the Alberta Labour Relations Board, for this insight.

[10]For over three decades, 1960s to the 1980s, wages were taken out of competition among firms in this industry. In the 1990s, however, companies began introducing variable compensation plans (e.g., gain-sharing, profit-sharing, value-sharing, and bonus schemes) which introduced some instability in the

industry's previously tight wage contour, but early indications are that companies are moving quickly to match their competitors' initiatives and restore parity from firm to firm.

[11]The exchange of information by employers for the purpose of coordinating wage and benefits rates across the industry is legal according to the *Canadian Competition Act*. By contrast, collusion to fix the price of products is illegal.

[12]As a matter of actual practice, appointments of arbitrators by the minister of labour have been from among the ranks of the most acceptable and experienced arbitrators.

[13]Since that time, Manitoba and Ontario have introduced similar legislation. Manitoba repealed its legislation in 2000. British Columbia subsequently repealed, and then reintroduced the mandatory vote system.

[14]There has been some debate as to whether Alberta's conservatism has influenced the likelihood of reinstatement for discharged employees. Studies of arbitration initially found that Alberta reinstatement rates were similar to those of other provinces, at about 45 to 50 percent; more recent data show a steep decline in Alberta reinstatements. In the late 1990s, only 37 percent of Alberta's dismissed grievors were reinstated (Williams and Taras 2000). National data are required to determine whether this is a trend shared throughout the country or unique to Alberta.

[15]Albertans tend to resist employment equity initiatives more than other Canadians. In a *Maclean's*/CTV poll, which asked Canadians "You are qualified for a promotion at work, but are informed that you are ineligible because the job has to go to a member of a minority group. What do you do [accept, protest, quit, etc]?" Across Canada, 58 percent of respondents said they would make a formal protest or quit, but in Alberta and British Columbia the number was 63 percent. The lowest was New Brunswick with 46 percent.

On a different question, asking respondents whether they might cheat on an exam, the national average was 21 percent who said they would cheat, with Alberta scoring the lowest at 10 percent and Quebec the highest at 38 percent (*Maclean's* 1995a).

[16]The Supreme Court's decision involved Vriend's right to have his case heard by the Alberta Human Rights Commission. The Court was not asked to determine whether the discrimination which occurred in his particular case was defensible or not. The question of whether sexual orientation might form a *bona fide* occupational qualification for a Christian college remains unsettled.

[17]In September 1997, Premier Klein announced that the government would abide by the Court's decision even if it favoured Vriend's arguments (Friesen 1997), but elements within his party caucus strongly disagreed. When the Court's decision was announced in 1998 a newly formed Canada Family Action Coalition denounced the decision and urged the provincial government to invoke the "notwithstanding clause" to repel the incursion of "non-elected Ottawa judges" into Alberta's law-making. The phone and fax campaign that ensued was unsuccessful in altering Klein's position.

[18]The National Citizens' Coalition in Canada was formed in 1975. Information about the NCC can be found in various submissions to the Alberta Economic Development Authority report on RTW.

Because of its wealthy benefactors, the NCC is described as a "Millionaire's Club" even by the right-wing weekly magazine *Alberta Report*. NCC in the mid-1980s sponsored the Lavigne case to the Canadian Supreme Court, and then the Norma Janzen case in British Columbia in the early 1990s. The current leader of the Canadian Alliance Party headed the NCC for several years.

[19]Submission by Guy Smith for the Alberta Union of Provincial Employees, Edmonton, August 1995, p. 1, to the Alberta Economic Development Authority. The NCC has a Webpage which describes its positions on unionism and other issues (www.citizenscoalition.org).

[20]The Alberta Economic Development Authority is a consultative body first established by the Klein government, and is co-chaired by the premier and a private sector business leader. It gathers prominent Albertans together into various committees to comment on important matters of the day.

[21]Quotes without attribution in this section were taken from interviews conducted by Reshef as part of a larger research project on union response to the Klein government's agenda in Alberta.

[22]This discussion is set within the context of the public sector, but the lessons apply equally to private sector workers who accepted significant rollbacks when their employers faced hard times. Particularly instructive was the UFCW/Safeway strike of spring 1997 (Nikiforuk 1997). Neither the union nor the company anticipated the enormous public refusal to cross picket lines. The UFCW achieved public support by stressing the fairness theme and tapping into the populism of many Albertans: workers who had sacrificed so much when the company was hurting in the early 1990s should not be betrayed after the company restored profitability. Safeway revenues fell by as much as 70 percent during the 75-day strike.

[23]*Continuing Care Employers' Bargaining Association, Capital Health Authority, Alberta Mental Health Board, Provincial Health Authorities of Alberta v. Alberta Union of Provincial Employees and Dan MacLennan*, Alberta Court of Appeal, 10 June 2002.

[24]*Re Provincial Health Authorities of Alberta and Alberta Union of Provincial Authorities* [2001] Alta. L.R.B.R. 187.

[25]All the figures are taken from the ATA Web site at <http://www.teachers. ab.ca/what/Strike_Information/Strike_update.htm>.

[26]There is some debate over exactly how much was provided for salaries because the allocated money was divided into several different budget items. At the low end, it was estimated that 6 percent was set aside for two years; at the high end it was estimated that 12 percent was set aside.

REFERENCES

Akyeampong, E. 1997. *A Statistical Portrait of the Trade Union Movement*, Cat. No. 75-001-XPE. Ottawa: Statistics Canada.

—— 1999. *Unionization – An Update*, Cat. No. 75-001-XPE. Ottawa: Statistics Canada.

Alberta. 1997. *Measuring Up - Third Annual Report on the Performance of the Government of Alberta*. Edmonton: Government of Alberta.

—— 2001. *Economic Accounts 2000*. Edmonton: Government of Alberta.

Alberta. Economic Development Authority. 1995. *Final Report of the Joint Review Committee, Right-to-Work Study*. Edmonton: The Authority.

Alberta. Labour Relations Board (ALRB). 1997. *Annual Report, 1996/97*. At <http://www.gov.ab.ca/ALRB/>.

—— 2002. Unpublished data supplied at request of authors.

Alberta. Ministry of Health. 1995. *Health Workforce in Alberta, 1994 & 1995*. Edmonton: Queen's Printer.

Alberta. Personnel Administration Office. 1995, 1996, 1997. *Public Service Commissioner's Annual Report: Profile of the Alberta Public Service*. Edmonton: Government of Alberta.

Alberta Labour. 1993. "Impact of 'Right-to-Work' Legislation." Edmonton: Issues Management.

—— 1994. "Delegated Administrative Organizations: A 'Third Option,'" Discussion Paper on a New Way of Delivering Programs and Services. Edmonton: Alberta Labour.

—— 1996. "Alberta Labour Business Plan 1996-97 to 1998-99," issued 28 February.

Alberta Resource Development. 2001. *Annual Report, 2000-2001*. At <http://www.energy.gov.ab.ca/its/docs/AR2001.pdf>.

Anderson, J. and M. Gunderson, eds. 1982. *Union-Management Relations in Canada*. Don Mills, ON: Addison-Welsey Publications.

Avram, J. 1997. "Happiness is ... Alberta," *Alberta Report* 24 (6):35.

Beaumont, P. and R. Harris. 1995 "Union De-Recognition and Declining Union Density in Britain," *Industrial and Labor Relations Review* 48 (3):389-402.

Bercuson, D. 1975. "The Winnipeg General Strike," in *On Strike*, ed. I. Abella. Toronto: James Lorimer & Company.

Block, R. and K. Roberts. 1998. "An Analysis of Labor Standards in the United States and Canada." Paper presented to annual conference of the Industrial Relations Research Association, Chicago.

Bowerman, J. and R. Ford. 1994. "A New Vision for Government: Learning in the Public Service: Alberta Labour," in *Creating the Learning Organization*, ed. J.J. Phillips, K.E. Watkins and V.J. Marsick. Alexandria, VA: American Society for Training and Development, pp. 211-20.

Budd, J. 1996. "Canadian Strike Replacement Legislation and Collective Bargaining: Lessons for the United States," *Industrial Relations* 35 (2):245-60.

Byfield, L. 1998. "Apart from Gambling and Balanced Budget, What Exactly Does Ralph Klein Believe in?" *Alberta Report*, 23 March. At <www.familyaction.org/Research/Homosexuality/Kleinbackstab.html>.

Caragata, W. 1984. "The Labour Movement in Alberta: An Untold Story," in *Essays on the Political Economy of Alberta*, ed. D. Leadbeater. Toronto: New Hogtown Press.

Coulter, D. 1993. "Worst Labour Strife Ever Seen in Cuts," *The Edmonton Journal*, 25 November, p. A6.

Edmonton Sun. 2000. "Klein Backs 'Dan's the Man:' Supports Alberta Union Leader's Fight with National Body," 29 March.

Farber, H. and A. Krueger. 1993. "Union Membership in the United States: The Decline Continues," in *Employee Representation*, ed. B. Kaufman and M. Kleiner. Madison, WI: Industrial Relations Research Association.

Farquhar, C.R. 1995. "Business and Organizational Planning Case Study Series: Department of Alberta Labour." Prepared for the Centre for Leadership, the Cabinet Office, by the Conference Board of Canada.

Feschuk, S. and A. Mitchell. 1994. "Klein Juggernaut Has Unions Quacking," *The Globe and Mail*, 2 November, p. A13.

Fisher, E.G. and S. Kushner. 1986. "Alberta's Construction Labour Relations During the Recent Downturn," *Relations industrielles-Industrial Relations* 41 (4):778-801.

Flanagan, G. 1997. "Alberta: Rich Province Poor Services?" Presentation to the Parkland Institute Conference, 7 November.

Fong, D., C. Kinzel and D. Odynak. 1995. *The Alberta Survey (A): Sampling Report.* Edmonton: Population Research Laboratory. Department of Sociology, University of Alberta.

Ford, R. 1995. "The Third Option." Presentation to the Workshop on Civil Service Reform for Private Sector Development: Vision and Strategies, 16 and 17 September, Cairo, Egypt.

Friesen, L. 1997. "Ralph's new Vriend: Premier Klein Says He'll Cave-in on Gay Rights Rather than Opt Out," *Alberta Report* 24 (39):13.

Fryer, J. 1995. "Provincial Public Sector Labour Relations," in *Public Sector Collective Bargaining in Canada*, ed. G. Swimmer and M. Thompson. Kingston, ON: IRC Press, Queen's University.

Gitelman, H.M. 1988. *Legacy of the Ludlow Massacre.* Philadelphia: University of Pennsylvania Press.

Gunderson, M., D. Hyatt and A. Ponak. 2001. "Strikes and Dispute Resolution," in *Union-Management Relations in Canada*, ed. Gunderson, Ponak and Taras.

Gunderson, M., A. Ponak and D.G. Taras, eds. 2001. *Union-Management Relations in Canada*, 4th ed. Toronto: Addison Wesley.

Harrison, T. and G. Laxer, eds. 1995. *The Trojan Horse: Alberta and the Future of Canada.* Montreal: Black Rose Books.

Harrison, T. and G. Laxer. 1995. "Introduction," in *The Trojan Horse*, ed. Harrison and Laxer.

Hughes, K., G. Lowe and A. McKinnon. 1996. "Public Attitudes Toward Budget Cuts in Alberta: Biting the Bullet or Feeling the Pain?" *Canadian Public Policy/Analyse de Politiques* 22 (3):268-84.

Jacoby, S. 1997. *Modern Manors: Welfare Capitalism Since the New Deal.* Princeton, NJ: Princeton University Press.

Johnsrude, L. 1997. *The Edmonton Journal*, 2 February.

Lisac, M. 1995. *The Klein Revolution.* Edmonton: NeWest.

Logan, H.A. 1948. *Trade Unions in Canada.* Toronto: MacMillan.

Maclean's. 1995a. "Looking Inward: The Maclean's/CTV Poll," 2 January, pp. 10-12, 14.

—— 1995b. "Ralph Klein Blinks: Faced with Labour Strife, Alberta Backs Off Health Cuts," 4 December, p. 41.

Mason, D.B. 1985. "Bill 44: What for and What Next," in *Proceedings of the 2nd Annual University of Calgary Labour Arbitration Conference*, ed. A. Ponak and C.L. Rigg. Calgary: Industrial Relations Research Group.

McFaul, B. 2000. "Give Him Glasses," *Calgary Herald*, 8 June.

McGrath, A. and D. Neu. 1996. "Washing our Blues Away: The Laundry Workers Strike Alberta," *Our Times* 15 (1):25-36.

McMillan, M. and A. Warrack. 1995. "One Track (Thinking) Towards Deficit Reduction," in *The Trojan Horse*, ed. Harrison and Laxer.

Meadows, J. 1977. "A Look at the Right-to-Work Question," *Labour Research Bulletin*. British Columbia, Ministry of Labour, Research and Planning. Victoria, BC, 16-22 March.

Mulawka, B. 1997. "Impress the Pollster Effect," in *B.C. Report*, 24 November, p. 8.

Murray, G. 2001. "Unions: Membership, Structures, and Action," in *Union-Management Relations in Canada*, ed. Gunderson, Ponak and Taras.

Nikiforuk, A. 1997. "Why Safeway Struck Out," *Canadian Business*, September. pp. 27-31.

Ponak, A. 1985. "When Boom Goes Bust - Lessons from Alberta," *New Directions in Industrial Relations*, Proceedings of the 33rd Annual Conference, McGill University Industrial Relations Centre.

Ponak, A. and L. Falkenberg. 1989. "Resolution of Interest Disputes," *Collective Bargaining in Canada*, ed. A. Sethi. Toronto: Nelson.

Ponak, A. and M. Thompson. 2001. "Public Sector Collective Bargaining," in *Union-Management Relations in Canada*, ed. Gunderson, Ponak and Taras.

Rayner, W.B. 1995. *The Law of Collective Bargaining*. Scarborough, ON: Carswell.

Reshef, Y. 2001. "The Logic of Labor Quiescence," *Journal of Labor Research* 22:636-52

Reshef, Y. and H. Lam. 1999. "Union Responses to Quality Improvement Initiatives: Factors Shaping Support and Resistance," *Journal of Labour Research* 20:111-31.

Sims, A., R. Blouin and P. Knopf. 1995. *Seeking a Balance: Review of Part I of the Canada Labour Code*. Ottawa: Government of Canada.

Statistics Canada. 2002a. "Fact Sheet on Unionization," *Perspectives on Labour and Income*, Cat. No. 75-001-XPE. Ottawa: Statistics Canada.

—— 2000b. *The Daily*, 26 April 2002. At <www.statscan.ca/english/dai-quo/>.

Swimmer, G., ed. 2001. *Public-Sector Labour Relations in an Era of Restraint and Restructuring*. Don Mills, ON: Oxford University Press.

Taras, D.G. 1997a. "Why Nonunion Representation is Legal in Canada?" *Relations industrielles-Industrial Relations* 52 (4):763-86.

—— 1997b. "Collective Bargaining Regulation in Canada and the United States: Divergent Cultures, Divergent Outcomes," in *Government Regulation of the Employment Relationship*, ed. B. Kaufman. Madison, WI: IRRA.

—— 1997c. "Managerial Intentions and Wage Determination in the Canadian Petroleum Industry," *Industrial Relations* 36 (2):178-205.

—— 2000. Contemporary Experience with the Rockefeller Plan: Imperial Oil's Joint Industrial Council," in *Nonunion Employee Representation*, ed. B.E. Kaufman and D.G. Taras. Armonk, NY: M.E. Sharpe.

Taras, D.G. and A. Ponak. 1999. "Petro-Canada: A Model of Union Acceptance within the Canadian Petroleum Industry," in *Contract and Commitment,* ed. A. Verma and R. Chaykowski. Kingston, ON: IRC Press, Queen's University.

—— 2002. "Mandatory Agency Shop Laws as an Explanation for Canada-US Union Density Divergence," in *The Future of Private Sector Unionism in the United States,* ed. J. Bennett and B. Kaufman. Armonk, NY: M.E. Sharpe.

Taras, D.G. and J. Copping. 1998. "Formal Nonunion Employee Representation and the Unionization Process: A Contemporary Case," *Industrial and Labor Relations Review* 52 (1):22-44.

Taylor, J. 1995. "Labour in the Klein Revolution." in *The Trojan Horse,* ed. Harrison and Laxer.

Thomas, D. 2000. "Union to Pay $400,000 Fine on Thursday," *Edmonton Journal,* 21 June.

Thomson, G. 2001. "Klein Hints at Hefty Pay Hikes for Teachers," *Edmonton Journal,* 6 April.

Vriend v. Alberta. 1998. 156 D.L.R. (4th) 385 S.C.C.

Weiler, P. 1980. *Reconcilable Differences.* Toronto: Carswell Co. Ltd.

—— 1983. "Promises to Keep: Securing Workers' Rights to Self-Organizing under the NLRA," *Harvard Law Review* 96 (8):1769-827.

Wells, J. 1996. "Haves and Have-nots: Canadians Look for Corporate Conscience," *Maclean's,* 30 December, pp. 26, 37.

Western Report. 1996. "Alberta Reopens the Big Spending Tap: In the End There Was a Real Long-Term Cut of About 15% in Healthcare, but Demand is Rising on all Sides to Undo the Whole Ralph Revolution," 30 December, pp. 9-10.

Williams, K. and D. Taras. 2000. "Reinstatement in Arbitration: The Grievors' Perspective," *Relations industrielles-Industrial Relations,* 55 (2):227-49.

Wilson-Smith, A. 1996. "Life after the Budget Cuts," *Maclean's,* 30 December, p. 21.

10 REGIONAL DIFFERENCES IN CANADIAN INDUSTRIAL RELATIONS: IS THERE A "CANADIAN" SYSTEM

Mark Thompson
Joseph B. Rose

Résumé — Comme le démontrent les chapitres de ce livre, il existe des différences notables dans le régime des relations industrielles des diverses provinces canadiennes. Deux explications de ce fait ressortent de la comparaison établie entre ces régimes : la manière dont le mouvement syndical s'est développé dans une province et l'institutionnalisation des relations industrielles dans cette province.

Il est prouvé à l'échelle internationale que l'existence d'un parti politique favorable aux travailleurs contribue à renforcer le mouvement syndical. Au Canada, le Nouveau Parti Démocratique (NPD) remplit ce rôle, sauf au Québec où c'est le Parti québécois (PQ). Le NPD est important en Ontario, au Manitoba, en Saskatchewan et en Colombie-Britannique, et le PQ a déjà gouverné au Québec. Dans trois des provinces de l'Atlantique et en Alberta, le NPD n'a jamais été une force politique importante.

La seconde explication est liée à l'histoire. Lorsque le mouvement syndical jouissait d'une situation prépondérante en matière de représentation des travailleurs dans les industries primaires et manufacturières essentielles au moment de la constitution des syndicats en personnes morales ou lorsque les institutions fondamentales des relations industrielles ont été établies dans une province, les syndicats ont gagné la reconnaissance des élites des affaires ou des gouvernements. Ceux qui étaient forts avaient alors un nombre de membres suffisant qu'ils pouvaient mobiliser tant au plan économique que politique.

Les provinces ayant un régime de relations industrielles reconnu (le Québec, l'Ontario, le Manitoba et la Colombie-Britannique) avaient une voix politique et une force économique au moment de la constitution des syndicats en personnes morales. Dans ces provinces, le mouvement syndical et les institutions de négociation collective sont intégrés dans la vie économique et politique provinciale, et ils sont capables de résister aux pressions exercées par des gouvernements et des employeurs conservateurs. Au cours des premières phases de leur développement, ces provinces avaient un large secteur manufacturier et de ressources naturelles. Les travailleurs étaient réunis en syndicats militant énergiquement pour la défense de leurs intérêts et se sont mobilisés au moment de la constitution des syndicats en personnes morales, c'est-à-dire soit dans les années 1930 soit dans les années 1940, selon les provinces. Les syndicats ont délaissé la philosophie du syndicalisme d'affaires conservateur des anciens syndicats de métier et se sont engagés dans l'action politique. Grâce à leur habitude de lutte, ils ont été capables de mobiliser leurs membres au besoin. Toutefois, cette habitude ne signifie pas forcément des grèves plus nombreuses. Quand le syndicalisme a gagné le secteur public, le mouvement syndical a été capable d'absorber les nouveaux membres, et de nombreux syndicats nouvellement formés ont adopté la tradition de lutte de leurs prédécesseurs du secteur privé. Les provinces ayant un régime de relations industrielles reconnu ont un taux de syndicalisation supérieur à la moyenne nationale, sauf l'Ontario, et sont plus urbanisées que la moyenne, sauf le Manitoba.

Terre-Neuve-et-Labrador, la Nouvelle-Écosse, la Saskatchewan et l'Alberta ont un régime de relations industrielles subordonné. C'est aussi le cas du Nouveau-Brunswick d'après les données restreintes dont nous disposons. Dans un régime subordonné, il existe des syndicats et un réseau de négociation collective, mais ils sont incapables de résister aux efforts déployés par les employeurs ou le gouvernement pour miner les droits et les intérêts des travailleurs. Durant leur période d'établissement, la Saskatchewan, l'Alberta et la Nouvelle-Écosse ne disposaient pas d'une base économique solide dans le domaine des ressources naturelles et aucune n'avait développé un secteur manufacturier important. Lorsque les syndicats ont été constitués en personnes morales dans les années 1940, ils n'étaient pas suffisamment forts pour faire progresser le respect de leurs intérêts. À Terre-Neuve-et-Labrador, ils ont une assise importante dans le secteur des ressources naturelles et le taux de syndicalisation est élevé dans cette province, mais il manque un parti politique qui défendrait les intérêts des travailleurs. Par ailleurs, le NPD gouverne généralement en Saskatchewan, mais le mouvement syndical n'a pas d'assise solide dans l'industrie. En Alberta, le mouvement syndical n'a jamais joui d'un fort appui dans l'industrie primaire, et le gouvernement est dominé par l'industrie pétrolière qui a un parti pris antisyndical.

Dans les provinces ayant un régime de relations industrielles subordonné, le taux de syndicalisation varie du plus élevé (Terre-Neuve-et-Labrador) au plus bas (Alberta). Une analyse minutieuse du taux de syndicalisation révèle que des provinces telles que Terre-Neuve-et-Labrador ont un haut pourcentage de leurs syndiqués dans le secteur public. Les syndicats de ce secteur sont moins capables que ceux du secteur privé d'exercer des pressions sur le gouvernement et les employeurs pour préserver les institutions concernant les relations industrielles. Lorsque le régime des relations industrielles est subordonné, les conflits de travail sont plus nombreux, y compris les grèves illégales.

Les huit provinces étudiées dans ce volume traduisent les principales tendances en matière de relations industrielles canadiennes. Il y a relativement peu de différences dans leur droit du travail. La procédure d'accréditation syndicale et l'intervention gouvernementale en cas de grève demeurent des questions litigieuses. Le Québec a innové à cet égard, mais les modifications qu'il a effectuées ne se sont pas répercutées dans les autres provinces. Les interventions gouvernementales les plus extrêmes (le démantèlement d'un syndicat à Terre-Neuve en 1959; le projet de loi Michelin en Nouvelle-Écosse qui a empêché la syndicalisation des travailleurs d'une usine; les techniques interventionnistes adoptées par le gouvernement de la Colombie-Britannique en 1987) n'ont pas été imitées par d'autres provinces. La négociation collective est une institution établie partout au Canada qui a résisté aux efforts déployés par des employeurs pour l'éliminer. Les syndicats n'ont pas réussi à syndiquer le secteur privé des services. Il n'y a qu'au Québec et en Colombie-Britannique que les employeurs ont formé des associations pour les représenter. Les grèves provinciales types expriment ordinairement les tendances nationales.

Ce volume démontre que le Canada possède un régime de relations industrielles, mais qu'il existe aussi dans les provinces qui le constituent des régimes distincts. Par exemple, personne ne pourrait assimiler les relations industrielles du Québec avec celles de l'Ontario. C'est la même chose en ce qui concerne la Colombie-Britannique et l'Alberta. Ces différences sont peut-être indicatrices de ce que seront les relations industrielles canadiennes dans l'avenir. D'autres provinces conservatrices reproduiront-elles le modèle albertain caractérisé par des syndicats peu puissants et une faible protection des travailleurs offerte par le gouvernement? Les changements survenus dans les relations industrielles d'une province seront-ils adoptés par d'autres provinces?

Les provinces sont importantes dans le régime canadien des relations industrielles, et pas seulement au plan géographique. Une province ne se réduit pas en effet à l'aspect spatial : elle a des dimensions historiques, politiques et économiques.

The chapters in this book display considerable variation in the character of industrial relations in the provinces examined. Although the differences are not enough to discard the notion of a "Canadian industrial relations system," they highlight differences among the provinces. No longer is it necessary to group provinces geographically to compare their industrial relations. In many ways, Quebec and British Columbia have more in common than Alberta and British Columbia, for instance. The role of labour in Saskatchewan and Manitoba can easily be distinguished. Newfoundland and Labrador, despite its high levels of union density, is similar to Nova Scotia and New Brunswick, where unionism is less well established. The central issue raised by the eight provincial studies is how to explain these differences.

SOURCES OF REGIONAL DIFFERENCES

Two theoretical propositions go to the root of the provincial differences: the pattern of union growth and the institutionalization of industrial relations. Both are drawn from studies of comparative industrial relations at the national level.

Among developed market economies, three conditions favour union growth: the existence of a viable and active labour party, centralized labour market structures and the administration of unemployment insurance plans (Western 1997). The third condition does not exist in Canada, where the federal government administers unemployment insurance without substantial influence from either employers or unions.

The first two conditions vary among provinces, however, and the existence of an effective labour party is a significant source of regional difference in industrial relations. The New Democratic Party (NDP) is a substantial political force in four provinces (British Columbia, Saskatchewan, Manitoba, and Ontario) where it has governed, at least briefly, and where it has been the official opposition to other more conservative governments. In Quebec, the Parti Québécois has strong social democratic tendencies and has acted as a labour party for most of its history. The NDP has never approached that status in either Alberta or the Atlantic provinces, where right-of-centre parties have governed continuously, often with long periods of a single party controlling the provincial government.

Canadian labour market structures are highly decentralized by international standards. However, some variation does exist among provinces. British Columbia and Quebec have long been known for their centralized bargaining institutions, and Ontario has had a strong pattern of bargaining in manufacturing and resource industries. Overall, the link to union growth is not great, as the theoretical impact of centralized bargaining structures is that labour's importance in bargaining gives it influence in other economic and social decisions through corporatist systems of interest representation. Apart from Quebec, this tradition is weak in Canada.

The second theoretical explanation for regional differences is historical. Evidence from the development of national labour movements points to the importance of the position of labour at the time of its "incorporation" into the social, legal, and political life of a jurisdiction. Where labour has been powerful, the institutional arrangements of labour law, government intervention, collective bargaining and employer policies reflect its relative strength (Berquist 1986, 1996). Mass unionization developed in Canada first in the resource sector, followed by manufacturing. The concentration of workers in these industries provided labour with the critical mass to mobilize both industrially and politically. By contrast, light industry, services, and construction were typically more fragmented than primary industries and manufacturing. In addition, primary and secondary industries were significant to the Canadian (and provincial) economy. These industries were the engines of growth for the nation as a whole, and when labour was powerful in them, other political and economic actors treated it accordingly.

Labour became entrenched in resource and manufacturing sectors early in the twentieth century and mobilized during the 1930s and especially in World War II. The process of incorporation took place in the provinces, except for Quebec, in the post-World War II period. Where labour had demonstrated the ability to conduct effective industrial action and had a parliamentary political voice, incorporation recognized it as a significant element when the outlines of labour legislation, government intervention, bargaining structures and the like were established. By contrast, other sectors, where labour tended to be weak, did not generate the organizational strength for the labour movement, even when labour was strongly organized, as in construction.

This theoretical framework is much less reliant on industrial structure as an explanatory variable for variation in industrial relations than previous treatments of regionalism and industrial relations discussed in Chapter 1. Of the eight provinces under review, only Alberta, dominated by the petroleum industry, was heavily influenced by industrial structure. The other seven jurisdictions have various proportions of resources and manufacturing as engines of their economies, with growing service sectors. Since the provinces have the power to regulate employment, political issues are more important than in regions without separate political structures, as in American cities, Australia, and British regions described in Chapter 1.

Industrial structure is important, but so are political and social forces. Virtually all provincial economies began with the exploitation of natural resources. The Canadian economy continued to rely heavily on primary industries through the beginning of the twenty-first century. Several provinces, Quebec, Ontario, and Manitoba, in particular, developed large manufacturing sectors. Yet dependence on primary and secondary industries did not produce homogeneity in industrial relations. Newfoundland and Labrador continued to have a large resource sector, but developed a distinctive pattern of industrial relations, for example.

REGIONAL DIFFERENCES: CONFIRMED INDUSTRIAL RELATIONS SYSTEMS

It is always difficult to group social units under a single heading. Inevitably, differences will be concealed and disagreements over the categories will emerge. The use of typologies, however, is an established technique in the social sciences, although not one commonly found in the study of industrial relations.

The eight provinces under analysis in this study fall comfortably into two groups, which we have entitled the "confirmed industrial relations systems" and the "dependent industrial relations systems."

A confirmed industrial relations system is one in which the institutions of collective bargaining and union representation are firmly embedded in the economic, political, and social life of the province. Even when provincial politics shift to the right, the business community and government respect the legitimacy of the industrial relations system, especially in the private sector. When centrist governments rule, union representatives exercise leadership beyond the confines of industrial relations or the workplace. Until the 1990s, even right-wing governments and employers respected and consulted informally with organized labour. With the election of the Harris government in Ontario, that pattern may be breaking down.

The confirmed industrial relations systems are found in Quebec, Ontario, Manitoba, and British Columbia. The four jurisdictions share a number of common characteristics. In the early stages of economic development, all had substantial resource or manufacturing components in their economies. In fact, except for Manitoba, the development of these economies began with the exploitation of natural resources, principally minerals and forest products. These commodities were crucial to the early development of the Canadian economy. Workers in these industries formed militant unions that would defend their interests energetically. In turn, their unions embraced left-wing or social unionism at some point in their development. In the cases of Ontario, Manitoba, and British Columbia, this tradition began early in the twentieth century. Quebec unions went beyond this philosophy after the Quiet Revolution in the 1950s, when Marxism-Leninism was influential. As the relative importance of resources diminished, manufacturing became the focus of the labour movement, and the patterns of representation continued.

Evidence from the development of national labour movements points to the importance of the position of labour at the time of its incorporation into the social, legal, and political life of a jurisdiction. Where labour has been powerful, the institutional arrangements of labour law, government intervention, collective bargaining, and employer policies reflect its relative strength (Berquist 1986, 1996).

The Canadian provincial experience confirms the institutionalization theory. Labour in the four provinces was highly mobilized relative to other jurisdictions at the time of its incorporation. "Mobilization" had both a political and an industrial dimension. A parliamentary party represented the labour movement politically, and unions had demonstrated their ability to mount significant bargaining campaigns, despite employer resistance. When these conditions existed, even the right-of-centre parties which have normally controlled provincial governments had to recognize the strategic place of labour in their polities.

In all four cases, the degree and militancy of unionization formed the basis of the labour movement in its formative years. Labour organizations avoided the conservative business unionism promoted by international unions and favoured by unions in the construction and transportation industries. In the anglophone provinces, labour supported successful efforts to establish the Cooperative Commonwealth Federation and later the NDP. In Quebec, labour was a strong supporter of the Liberal Party when the Quiet Revolution began and later, the Parti Québécois. In all cases, labour had a relatively reliable parliamentary voice which promoted favourable labour legislation, pressured more conservative governments to adopt employment and welfare policies that assisted the working class. Although the NDP only held power for more than one term on three occasions — 1969–77 and 1981–88 in Manitoba and 1991–99 in British Columbia — their presence as a significant voice in the provincial legislature, often the official opposition, has moderated employer efforts to undermine labour policies during periods of conservative governments. The alliance between labour and the Parti Québécois in Quebec is based on nationalist as well as class ties, but the effects are the same.

A tradition of struggle within the labour movement exists in these provinces. In Quebec, labour was a leading actor in the Quiet Revolution, and labour militancy was the highest in the country in the 1970s and early 1980s. Strikes in Ontario during the 1940s were a major factor in the reluctant decision of the federal government to proclaim PC 1003 in 1944. Major strikes in the automobile, steel, and mining industries in the 1960s and 1970s were among the most notable labour disputes in Canadian history. British Columbia experienced major disputes in forest products and construction, and in 1983 labour pushed the province to the brink of a general strike in protest against a government legislative program. The pattern is somewhat less clear in Manitoba. Certainly, the Winnipeg General Strike was a defining event in the history of labour not only in the province, but also throughout western Canada. Although the defeat of the strikers cast a pall on the labour movement for years after the event, Goddard reports that a strong working-class culture remains, especially in Winnipeg. Labour disputes have been unevenly distributed, but disproportionately high under Conservative administrations.

The tradition of struggle does not necessarily translate into frequency of strikes. Between 1970 and 2001, British Columbia, Ontario and Quebec had the highest average number of strikers (Manitoba ranked sixth). The highest strike rates, as shown in Table 1, defined as number of strikes per 10,000 employees, were in Newfoundland, Nova Scotia, and Quebec. British Columbia was in fourth place, followed by Saskatchewan and Ontario. Manitoba and Alberta experienced the lowest strike rate.

TABLE 1
NUMBER OF STRIKES PER 10,000 UNION MEMBERS, 1970–2001

Jurisdiction	Rate
Quebec	2.4
Ontario	1.7
Manitoba	1.1
British Columbia	1.7
Newfoundland and Labrador	3.3
Nova Scotia	2.5
Saskatchewan[1]	2.1
Alberta	0.9

Note: [1]Saskatchewan data for 1971–2001.
Source: Canada. HRDC (2002).

Similarly, the confirmed industrial relations systems produce fewer illegal strikes. Data on illegal strikes are available for the period 1970–95, shown in Table 2. For the 26 years in question, Manitoba, Quebec, and Ontario had the lowest percentage of illegal strikes, ranging from 5.9 to 8.8 percent. Only British Columbia and Alberta were outliers, with 24.7 percent of all strikes being illegal in the former and 5.9 percent in the

TABLE 2
ILLEGAL STRIKES, BY JURISDICTION, 1970–1995

Jurisdiction	Percentage Illegal Strikes (%)	Percentage Person-Days Lost (%)
Canada	19.5	7.9
Quebec	8.0	9.8
Ontario	8.8	2.2
Manitoba	6.0	0.5
British Columbia	24.7	7.8
Newfoundland and Labrador	30.0	9.8
Nova Scotia	34.9	8.3
New Brunswick	38.6	17.8
Saskatchewan	18.4	10.1
Alberta	5.9	4.8

Source: Canada. HRDC (2002)

latter. By contrast, Newfoundland and Labrador, Nova Scotia, and New Brunswick all had illegal strike activity above the national average. Saskatchewan's experience was almost identical to the national average.

In the 1960s, labour strength shifted to the public sector. The confirmed industrial relations systems adapted to the new entrants into the collective bargaining and the labour movement. In all four cases, the largest unions were in the public sector. However, the traditions and continuing strength of private sector labour organizations have continued to be important. In 2001, public sector union membership as a percentage of all union members was below the national average of 52.6 percent in three of the four provinces and ranged from a low of 49 percent in Ontario to 61 percent in Manitoba (Canada. HRDC 2002). These levels are lower than the other provinces discussed below.

In three of the four provinces, Ontario being the exception, union density is above average, ranging from 37 percent in Quebec to 26.6 percent in Ontario, as shown in Table 3 (Canada. HRDC 2002; Statistics Canada 2002). It should be noted that union density is not the sole or even dominant indicator for the "confirmed" provinces. Almost invariably,

TABLE 3

UNION MEMBERSHIP BY PROVINCE, 2001 (PUBLIC AND PRIVATE SECTORS)

Jurisdiction	Union Members	Density	Percent Public Sector (%)
Canada	3,831.3	30.0	52.6
Quebec	1,105.4	38.6	49.8
Ontario	1,328.0	26.1	49.2
Manitoba	166.0	35.0	61.0
British Columbia	534.5	33.8	51.5
Newfoundland and Labrador	72.2	38.8	63.8
Nova Scotia	102.4	27.8	63.6
New Brunswick	80.4	27.3	67.9
Saskatchewan	128.1	34.6	65.2
Alberta	297.8	22.1	57.3

Source: Canada. HRDC (2002).

Newfoundland and Labrador has the highest union density of any province, for instance. Luchak and Cooper explain the high levels of union density in that province by the industrial structure, weighted more heavily toward resources and public administration, high unemployment levels (unemployed union members count in union membership, but not in the labour force) and the prevalence of union security provisions in collective agreements.

Except for Manitoba, the confirmed provinces are also the most heavily urbanized provinces in the nation. According to the 2001 census, the Canadian average for urbanization was 79.7 percent, with Ontario and BC being the most urbanized, followed by Alberta and Quebec. Manitoba occupied fifth place at 71.9 percent.[1] Union membership and propensity to collective action are often associated with urbanization, and the dominance of large cities — Toronto, Montreal, Winnipeg, and Vancouver — are a factor in labour's political and economic strength.

REGIONAL DIFFERENCES: DEPENDENT INDUSTRIAL RELATIONS SYSTEMS

The other four provinces in the sample, Newfoundland, Nova Scotia, Saskatchewan, and Alberta, can be described as "dependent" industrial relations systems. The limited information available on New Brunswick in the Rose "Précis" (see Appendix to book) indicates clearly that the province has a dependent industrial relations system. In provinces with dependent systems, the labour movement and components of a collective-bargaining system continue to exist, but are unable to resist efforts by employers or the government to undermine their rights and entitlements.

The theoretical model outlined above is valid to explain the dependent systems. Their roots lie first in their formative periods. Three provinces — Nova Scotia, Saskatchewan, and Alberta — lacked a strong economic base in natural resources and none developed a substantial manufacturing sector. Labour organizations in these provinces were never sufficiently strong to become a major economic or political force in the province. (Were it treated as a separate region, Cape Breton Island probably would be an exception to these generalizations.) When labour was incorporated into these provinces, generally in the 1940s, labour lacked the organizational strength to assert its interests with much effect. The Nova Scotia case is instructive. The province's first labour legislation was passed in 1937, apparently as a reaction to labour unrest on Cape Breton Island. As the importance of the coal and steel industries there diminished, a succession of governments, first Liberals and then Conservatives, passed legislation with the general objective of maintaining a weak labour movement. The Michelin Bill helped forestall unionization in manufacturing as the provincial government had intended. Despite labour's protests, the bill was enacted, and the government was re-elected with an increased majority (Dyck 1996).

Newfoundland is a special case. Relative to its size, it has always had a large resource sector. In addition, it had an early working-class party. Incorporation really occurred shortly after the province entered Confederation. Initially, labour benefited from the pro-labour policies of the province's first premier, Joey Smallwood, and was content to rely on the Liberal Party to protect its interests. The situation reversed sharply in 1959, when the Smallwood government broke a strike by the International Woodworkers of America. In one of the most repressive actions by any government since the 1930s, Smallwood not only ended the strike, he formed a new union beholden to the government and physically expelled IWA officers from the province. Labour had no significant allies to which it could turn, and Smallwood continued to govern the province for another 13 years. Labour never attained a significant parliamentary voice.

Saskatchewan is the only province in the dependent category with a significant NDP. Indeed the NDP has consistently received 40 percent of the popular vote in provincial elections and provided four different premiers since Tommy Douglas was elected in 1944. However, as Haiven explains, the New Democrats in Saskatchewan are essentially an agrarian party, with strong support from farmers and small business. Although the Saskatchewan New Democrats have been leaders in social policy and occasionally were innovators in labour policy (notably their granting of full bargaining rights to public employees in 1944), the party could never forget its agricultural base of support. As the number of farmers declined, the New Democrats relied increasingly on small business and the urban middle-class for their electoral support.

Alberta's economy has been dominated by the oil industry, with a long (and international) tradition of using generous and paternalistic human resource policies to remain non-union. When agrarian protest movements emerged, they lacked any substantial labour base and evolved into a very conservative Social Credit Party, leaving labour numerically small and without any significant political support. The Ponak, Taras and Reshef chapter outlines a social contract among the actors in the Alberta industrial relations system. Government protections for labour are among the most limited in Canada, a function of labour's political weakness and a wealthy, paternalistic petroleum industry that dominates the province. Driven by that industry, the private sector in Alberta offers workers benefits that are not available in most other jurisdictions.

The four provinces with dependent systems contain the widest possible variation in union density, from Newfoundland with the highest level, slightly over 40 percent, to Alberta, which has unionization of a little more than 20 percent. The significant element of union density in all of these provinces is the dominance of the public sector, as Table 3 shows. The highest proportion of public sector union membership is in Saskatchewan, at 65 percent. Newfoundland and Nova Scotia are only slightly lower at 64 percent, followed by Alberta at 57 percent (Canada. HRDC 2002).

Union density is a traditional way of measuring the strength of a national or regional labour movement. However, examining these provinces leads to a more complex analysis. In the Atlantic provinces, New-foundland and Labrador in particular, federal public service unions are numerically important in the labour movement. Apart from their lack of any strong tradition of militancy, their political voice is obviously directed toward Ottawa. Provincial government employees, teachers, and nurses are often constrained in economic action by restrictions on the right to strike or essential services legislation. Politically, they must deal with their employers, either directly or through surrogates, and they risk becoming embroiled in confrontations with governments. The history of such con-frontations in these provinces is that governments accept them and al-most universally emerge victorious. In 1993, for instance, Premier Clyde Wells based his re-election campaign on confrontation with the Newfound-land and Labrador Teachers' Federation and was returned to office, al-though with a reduced majority (Dyck 1996). Alberta public sector workers accepted wage cuts triggered by Premier Ralph Klein's policies of elimi-nating the budget deficit without protest. After the deficit had disap-peared, they were unable to make up those reductions in their first multi-year contracts. In 1998–99, the NDP government of Roy Romanow im-posed back-to-work legislation twice, once on employees of the provin-cial electric monopoly before they went on strike and again on the nurses' union, who defied the law, one of the few defeats that governments in these provinces had experienced.

The dependent industrial relations systems are not without con-flict. In fact, Newfoundland and Nova Scotia have the highest strike rates except for Quebec. Only Alberta and Saskatchewan fall below the na-tional average. A more compelling statistic is the proportion of illegal strikes. The highest incidence of illegal strikes is in Nova Scotia and New-foundland, each with over 30 percent. By contrast, Ontario and Quebec are below 9 percent.

COMMON CHARACTERISTICS ACROSS REGIONS

The eight provincial chapters in this volume capture central ten-dencies in Canadian industrial relations, as well as regional distinctions. A number of common features can be stated to establish the basis for dis-cussion of regional differences. The similarities reinforce some of what has been written about the Canadian industrial relations system in gen-eral, although never before with the support of such a rich body of data.

Given the constitutional autonomy of the provinces in Canadian labour law, the lack of variation among them is in many ways notable. In all eight provinces, labour legislation reflects the philosophy of PC 1003 in 1944 and many of the recommendations of the Woods Task Force in 1968. The administrative arrangements in Quebec are somewhat different from the other jurisdictions, but these distinctions are more form than substance. A traditional argument for federalism in social policy is the freedom of subordinate units to experiment with legislation. All in all, the degree of experimentation in Canadian labour law has been slight. All provincial statutes protect the freedom to organize, require bargaining in good faith, bar strikes during the term of a collective agreement, and provide for a separate administrative agency to administer labour legislation (known as a labour relations board in every province but Quebec).

The number of exceptions to this generalization are modest. In general, the most innovative jurisdiction has been Quebec, but not all of these provisions have spread to other provinces. In the 1930s, Quebec introduced the decree system to extend the provisions of collective agreements to unorganized employers in industries with many small firms. The system has not been used elsewhere, although some construction legislation approaches decrees and is diminishing in importance in Quebec. The federal government, Quebec, and Nova Scotia included statutory appeals mechanisms for cases of unjust dismissal, perhaps not even a labour relations issue. Little information about the operation of these provisions is available, and neither of the authors of the Quebec and Nova Scotia chapters thought they were sufficiently important to warrant more than a passing reference. Quebec was also the first province to introduce legislation banning replacement workers (known as "anti-scab" laws in labour circles). Similar provisions were later adopted in Ontario, British Columbia, and in federal law, although the Ontario provision was repealed and the British Columbia version is under attack from employers.

Despite this lack of experimentation, virtually every province has experienced controversy generated by changes in labour legislation. Two topics generate the most significant debate: certification procedures and government intervention in individual labour disputes (either specific disputes or dispute-settlement procedures) (Thompson 1996). Three of the more extreme examples of government action in these areas, the destruction of the IWA in Newfoundland in 1959; the so-called Michelin Bill in Nova Scotia, passed to forestall an organizing campaign at one plant; and an array of government intervention techniques enacted in 1987 in British Columbia, have not been emulated. No other province has enacted legislation based on the Michelin Bill, and the 1987 BC legislation was repealed and quickly forgotten after a change in government. Smallwood's actions are virtually forgotten. The most recent controversies in labour legislation arose from the changes passed by the stridently pro-business Harris government in Ontario and they focused primarily on the public sector. Changes in private sector legislation substituted mandatory representation votes for card checks for certification, removed the ban on replacement workers, and weakened successor rights. Although these changes were one-sided and imposed on an angry labour movement, they did not remove Ontario from its traditional place in the mainstream of Canadian labour law.

While union density varies considerably among provinces, collective bargaining is an established institution in Canada. Although governments have intervened in labour disputes, sometimes very harshly, none has attempted to eliminate the institution completely. The possible exception to this generalization is the construction industry, where employers effectively dismantled bargaining arrangements in several provinces during the recession of the early 1980s. Although most authors did not discuss construction specifically, their neglect of this industry may indicate that the unionized sector has not recovered from the damage it suffered.

Perhaps the relative conservatism of Canadian labour law explains the failure of unions to organize the private service sector. Despite varying legal and political climates, including circumstances where the labour movement is otherwise very powerful, no provincial labour movement has made substantial inroads into this rapidly growing segment of the economy.

Outside Quebec and British Columbia, employers have no peak associations to represent them in labour matters. Even associations for bargaining are rare outside the construction and hospital industries. The Canadian experience mirrors that of employers elsewhere — businesses join for bargaining or other purposes principally when strong unions or corporatist political structures confront them. While Canadian collective bargaining is quite decentralized, the frame of reference for bargaining normally is provincial, so that employers might have organized formally to consult at that level. In general, social democratic parties favour corporatist political arrangements as a means of involving their labour allies in political and economic decisions. Over time, NDP governments might foster such structures, but the only province where the party has governed more than briefly is Saskatchewan. Because of the agrarian roots of the NDP in that province, labour has seldom been an influential actor politically.

Employers are organized for political purposes in all jurisdictions, and in most provinces the local branch of the Canadian Federation of Independent Business (CFIB) has become a vocal representative of small employer interests in the 1990s. It is not clear whether this activism is a national strategy of the CFIB, but the message is clear and consistent: oppose any extension of union rights or improvement of employment standards in the province.

By and large, authors reported that strike patterns in their provinces followed national trends, except for British Columbia, where strikes are especially large. Because of its size and industrial importance, this conclusion is almost inevitable for Ontario. Overall, this finding would support economic, not political, explanations for variations in work stoppages, since macroeconomic forces (inflation, unemployment) differ less than political factors. During the period beginning in 1981, when strike activity declined in Canada, the three provinces with the highest levels of time lost due to strikes — Newfoundland, Quebec, and British Columbia — experienced the greatest declines, bringing them close to the average of the other provinces.

The purpose of this project was not to reiterate the central tendencies in Canadian industrial relations. It was to discover differences among regions and provinces. Substantial differences do exist among provincial industrial relations systems, not exclusively on traditional regional lines.

CONCLUSIONS

The definition of a national industrial relations system, quoted in the introductory chapter, the "institutional arrangements shaped by legislative frameworks, historical traditions, accumulated vested interests and learned patterns of behaviour" (Hyman 1994), applies to Canada. Canada has a national industrial relations system, but distinct subnational systems also exist. Although several authors, all in small provinces classified as dependent systems, had difficulty in distinguishing industrial relations practices from the rest of Canada, elements of a subnational system clearly exist in the larger and more industrialized provinces. To take the most obvious extremes, one would not confuse industrial relations in Quebec and neighbouring Ontario any more than one could combine industrial relations in the adjacent provinces of Alberta and British Columbia.

The regional analysis may be instructive in projecting the future of Canadian industrial relations in Canada. In the 1970s and 1980s, Quebec was in many ways a major change agent among the provinces. The transformation of Quebec industrial relations that Grant analyzes may not be possible in other jurisdictions. Depending on the political climate in other provinces, the Alberta model may be instructive. The minimal role for the state in Alberta industrial relations outlined in the Ponak, Taras and Reshef chapter has great appeal to the right of centre in other provinces. As the Alberta economy expands relative to the rest of Canada, its model of industrial relations, or at least a truncated version of it, may be imitated in other jurisdictions. An example of this development is the southern region of the United States. In the 1950s, the aggressive anti-union, employer-government strategy in the region was considered an exception to national patterns that would disappear as the South industrialized. In fact, the opposite has occurred. The growing influence of the South in US politics and economic life has been accompanied by the spread of anti-unionism into other regions of the country. No province in Canada matches Alberta's natural wealth, but the temptation to imitate its social policies may be strong.

This collection invites further research. All authors received extensive data on collective agreements in their provinces, but only the Nova Scotia and Newfoundland and Labrador chapters incorporated any extensive analysis of the outcomes of bargaining. An obvious question is whether the status of industrial relations in a province has any impact on terms and conditions of employment independent of industrial structure. Certainly, the data on illegal strikes were counter-intuitive. It would be valuable to investigate the circumstances that lead to such stoppages in greater detail.

Clearly, region matters, although not on purely geographical terms. In an era dominated by globalization, multinational corporations and international financial transactions, smaller units of analysis are important, perhaps more so than ever. As geographers noted, "region" is not merely spatial. It is historical and psychological. Economics matter, but so do history and political institutions. The variations across provinces revealed in this book confirm those generalizations for industrial relations.

NOTE

[1]See www.statisticscanada.ca/census01.

REFERENCES

Berquist, C. 1986. *Labor in Latin America: Comparative Essays on Chile, Argentina, Venezuela and Columbia.* Stanford: Stanford University Press.

—— 1996. "Postscript: Comparative Research and the 'New World Order,'" *Labour/Le Travail* 38/*Labour History* 71 (Joint Issue):278-88.

Dyck, R. 1996. *Provincial Politics in Canada: Towards the Turn of the Century,* 3d ed. Scarborough: Prentice-Hall Canada Inc.

Canada. Human Resources Development (HRDC). 2002. Union membership data, unpublished.

Hyman, R. 1994. *New Frontiers in European Industrial Relations.* Oxford: Blackwell.

Statistics Canada. 2002. "Unionization," *Perspectives on Labour and Income,* Cat. No. 75-001-XPE. Ottawa: Statistics Canada, pp. 73-80.

Thompson, M. 1996. "Labor Law Reform in Western Canada: Rhetoric and Reality," in *Proceedings of the Forty-Eighth Annual Meeting of the Industrial Relations Research Association,* ed. P. Voos. Madison, WI: IRRA, pp. 201-08.

Western, B. 1997. *Between Class and Market: Postwar Unionization in the Capitalist Democracies.* Princeton: Princeton University Press.

APPENDIX

INDUSTRIAL RELATIONS IN NEW BRUNSWICK: A PRÉCIS

Joseph B. Rose

The untimely death of Tony Smith precluded the completion of a chapter on New Brunswick. However, his preliminary work offers some insights into industrial relations in the province.

The province has 730,000 inhabitants or 2.4 percent of Canada's population.[1] Geographically, the province can be divided into the predominantly Acadian and less prosperous north and the anglophone and more prosperous south. The province has the closest English-French balance in Canada and is officially bilingual. While the province does have an economic base in natural resources (forestry, mining, and fishing), it never developed a substantial manufacturing base. The postwar period was dominated by two right-of-centre parties — the Conservatives and the Liberals — who governed continuously. Few ideological differences divide the two parties. Organized labour has not been a strong political force and the New Democratic Party (NDP) has never figured prominently in provincial elections (averaging between 7 and 8 percent of the vote since 1970) (Dyck 1996). The economy has been heavily influenced by two families: the Irvings (forestry, oil refining, gas stations, and a media empire: newspapers, radio and television) and the McCains (the potato industry and other food processing). The families have a slightly paternalistic approach to their labour forces, but their vast resources enable them to defeat a union when they wish. Despite the dominance of these two families, there has not been a strong ideological orientation to New Brunswick politics.

> The lack of such a more ideological cleavage can be explained in part by the Irving media monopoly which maximizes the family's political influence while minimizing critical coverage of the empire. The continued exploitation of potato farmers is also due to their apparent "ingrained individualism," which inhibits collective organization, and to their division by language, distance and size (Dyck 1996, 172).

Like other Atlantic provinces, New Brunswick's economy has been underdeveloped and suffers from high unemployment. As a result, successive governments have relied on federal assistance to spur economic development.

Although the province has strived to strike a balance between business and labour interests, efforts to attract business investment have taken precedence. Nevertheless, and in ways similar to Ontario, successive governments adopted a conservative and pragmatic approach in their pursuit of economic and social development (e.g., bilingualism). They consulted business and labour in the search for consensus on labour policy. Labour reforms have borrowed generously from developments in other jurisdictions, notably the *Ontario Labour Relations Act* for the private sector and the *Public Service Staff Relations Act* for the public sector. However, consistent with its generally conservative approach to labour policy, the province has retained its relatively stable labour-management balance over the past 20 years or so rather than adopt labour reforms initiated elsewhere.

The labour movement is numerically small and not very militant. In 2001, union membership was 80,400 members and the union density rate was 27.3 percent, the third lowest in Canada. Strike activity in the province has been moderate; a number of standardized strike measures were below the Canadian average. However, the province accounted for a disproportionate share of illegal strikes (13 percent of the total between 1946 and 1995). As in other parts of Canada, government-restraint measures in the 1990s led to confrontations with public sector unions. For the most part, the unions failed to alter government policy.

NOTE

[1]See www.statscan.ca/census01.

REFERENCE

Dyck, R. 1996. *Provincial Politics in Canada: Towards the Turn of the Century*, 3d ed. Scarborough: Prentice-Hall Canada Inc.

CONTRIBUTORS

Brian Bemmels is the William M. Hamilton Professor of Industrial Relations in the Faculty of Commerce, University of British Columbia. His research interests include the process of grievance initiation, decision-making in grievance procedures, and justice in grievance procedures. He has published widely in Canadian and American journals. He is Associate Dean, Academic Programs, and holds a PhD from the University of Minnesota.

John Godard is a professor in the Faculty of Management at the University of Manitoba, an editor of the *British Journal of Industrial Relations*, and the author of *Industrial Relations, the Economy, and Society* (Captus, 2000). His work focuses on how institutional environments shape employer practices and ultimately worker and union outcomes. He has published widely in *Industrial and Labor Relations Review*, *Industrial Relations*, and other leading academic journals. He has a PhD from Cornell.

Michel Grant is a professor of industrial relations at the Département des sciences administratives of the University of Québec at Montréal. Previously, he was a senior officer with the Canadian Union of Public Employees (1968–78) and the Québec Federation of Labour (1978–81); during that period, he acted as a negotiator for several major labour disputes, particularly in the public sector where he was the chief negotiator. His most recent book was written with professors Bernard Adell and Allen Ponak, *Strikes in Essential Services*, IRC Press, Queen's University, Kingston, 2001.

Larry Haiven is an associate professor in the Department of Management, Faculty of Commerce, Saint Mary's University. From 1989 he was a faculty member at the University of Saskatchewan's College of Commerce. His professional interests are in industrial conflict, public sector collective bargaining (especially health care), and professionalism. He is co-author with Judy Haiven of *The Right to Strike and the Provision of Emergency Services in Canadian Health Care*. Prior to his academic career, Larry was a union organizer, and union consultant. He has extensive experience in industrial relations, mainly in the public sector. He holds a PhD from the University of Warwick.

Andrew Luchak began this chapter while he was an associate professor at the Faculty of Business Administration, Memorial University of Newfoundland. In 2001, he joined the Department of Strategic Management and Organization at the Faculty of Business, University of Alberta where he teaches human resource management and labour relations. His research interests are in pension plans and industrial relations. He holds a PhD from the University of Toronto.

Allen Ponak is a professor of industrial relations, Haskayne School of Business, University of Calgary. He has held faculty positions at the University of British Columbia and McGill University and has been a visiting scholar in Australia and Israel. Professor Ponak's work has been widely published in leading academic and professional journals with his recent work focusing on dispute resolution, grievance arbitration, and Canada-US labour policy differences. He is a co-author of *Strikes in Essential Services*, published in 2001 by Queen's IRC Press, and *Union-Management Relations in Canada*, the leading textbook in the field. He is chair of the editorial board of *Relations industrielles-Industrial Relations*, is a former president of the Canadian Industrial Relations Association, and is on the Board of Governors of the National Academy of Arbitrators. He holds a PhD from Wisconsin.

Yonatan Reshef is the Eric Geddes Professor of Business, School of Business, University of Alberta. A graduate of the University of Illinois, he was the president of the Canadian Industrial Relations Association in 2000–2001. He has written extensively about union responses to neo-conservative policies. His book, co-authored with Sandra Rastin, *Unions in the Time of Revolution: Government Restructuring in Alberta and Ontario*, is scheduled to appear in early 2004 (University of Toronto Press).

Joseph B. Rose is a professor of industrial relations at the DeGroote School of Business at McMaster University. His research interests include construction labour relations, comparisons of trade unionism in Canada and the United States, public sector collective bargaining and dispute settlement procedures. He acts as an arbitrator in rights and interest disputes.

Daphne G. Taras is a professor of industrial relations and Associate Dean (Research), Haskayne School of Business, University of Calgary. Within industrial relations, her principal research interest is formal non-union forms of employee representation. She has examined industrial relations and human resources issues in a number of major petroleum firms, including Imperial Oil and Petro-Canada. Dr. Taras has published numerous articles and book chapters and has co-edited six journal symposia. She has co-edited *Nonunion Employee Representation* and the leading text *Union-Management Relations in Canada*. She was her faculty's Outstanding New Scholar in 1997 and the recipient of the Dean's Research Excellence award in 2000.

Mark Thompson was a professor of industrial relations in the Faculty of Commerce and Business Administration, University of British Columbia until his retirement in 2002. He received a PhD from Cornell and taught at McMaster University prior to coming to UBC. He is the co-editor of two volumes on industrial relations in the public sector and wrote numerous articles on Canadian and comparative industrial relations. He was president of the Canadian Industrial Relations Association in 1986–87 and is a member of the National Academy of Arbitrators.

Terry H. Wagar is a professor of Human Resource Management and Industrial Relations, Faculty of Commerce at Saint Mary's University in Halifax. Dr. Wagar's research has been published in North America, Europe, Asia, Australia, and New Zealand. He was recognized by the *National Post* with the Leader in Management Education Award (2000), he received the Association of Atlantic Universities Distinguished Teacher Award (2000), and the Industrial Relations Research Association's Excellence in Education Award (2003).

Queen's Policy Studies
Recent Publications

The Queen's Policy Studies Series is dedicated to the exploration of major policy issues that confront governments in Canada and other western nations. McGill-Queen's University Press is the exclusive world representative and distributor of books in the series.

School of Policy Studies

The Nonprofit Sector in Interesting Times: Case Studies in a Changing Sector,
Kathy L. Brock and Keith G. Banting (eds.), 2003
Paper ISBN 0-88911-941-4 Cloth ISBN 0-88911-943-0

Clusters Old and New: The Transition to a Knowledge Economy in Canada's Regions,
David A. Wolfe (ed.), 2003   Paper ISBN 0-88911-959-7 Cloth ISBN 0-88911-961-9

Knowledge, Clusters and Regional Innovation: Economic Development in Canada, J. Adam
Holbrook and David A. Wolfe (eds.), 2002
Paper ISBN 0-88911-919-8 Cloth ISBN 0-88911-917-1

Lessons of Everyday Law/Le droit du quotidien, Roderick Alexander Macdonald, 2002
Paper ISBN 0-88911-915-5 Cloth ISBN 0-88911-913-9

Improving Connections Between Governments and Nonprofit and Voluntary Organizations:
Public Policy and the Third Sector, Kathy L. Brock (ed.), 2002
Paper ISBN 0-88911-899-X Cloth ISBN 0-88911-907-4

Governing Food: Science, Safety and Trade, Peter W.B. Phillips and Robert Wolfe (eds.),
2001   Paper ISBN 0-88911-897-3 Cloth ISBN 0-88911-903-1

The Nonprofit Sector and Government in a New Century, Kathy L. Brock and Keith G.
Banting (eds.), 2001   Paper ISBN 0-88911-901-5 Cloth ISBN 0-88911-905-8

The Dynamics of Decentralization: Canadian Federalism and British Devolution, Trevor C.
Salmon and Michael Keating (eds.), 2001   ISBN 0-88911-895-7

Institute of Intergovernmental Relations

Canada: The State of the Federation 2001, vol. 15, *Canadian Political Culture(s) in*
Transition, Hamish Telford and Harvey Lazar (eds.), 2002
Paper ISBN 0-88911-863-9 Cloth ISBN 0-88911-851-5

Federalism, Democracy and Disability Policy in Canada, Alan Puttee (ed.), 2002
Paper ISBN 0-88911-855-8 Cloth ISBN 1-55339-001-6, ISBN 0-88911-845-0 (set)

Comparaison des régimes fédéraux, 2ᵉ éd., Ronald L. Watts, 2002
ISBN 1-55339-005-9

Health Policy and Federalism: A Comparative Perspective on Multi-Level Governance,
Keith G. Banting and Stan Corbett (eds.), 2001
Paper ISBN 0-88911-859-0 Cloth ISBN 1-55339-000-8, ISBN 0-88911-845-0 (set)

Disability and Federalism: Comparing Different Approaches to Full Participation,
David Cameron and Fraser Valentine (eds.), 2001
Paper ISBN 0-88911-857-4 Cloth ISBN 0-88911-867-1, ISBN 0-88911-845-0 (set)

Federalism, Democracy and Health Policy in Canada, Duane Adams (ed.), 2001
Paper ISBN 0-88911-853-1 Cloth ISBN 0-88911-865-5, ISBN 0-88911-845-0 (set)

John Deutsch Institute for the Study of Economic Policy

Framing Financial Structure in an Information Environment, Thomas J. Courchene and
Edwin H. Neave (eds.), Policy Forum Series no. 38, 2003
Paper ISBN 0-88911-950-3 Cloth ISBN 0-88922-948-1

*Towards Evidence-Based Policy for Canadian Education/Vers des politiques canadiennes
d'éducation fondées sur la recherche,* Patrice de Broucker and/et Arthur Sweetman (eds./dirs.),
2002 Paper ISBN 0-88911-946-5 Cloth ISBN 0-88911-944-9

*Money, Markets and Mobility: Celebrating the Ideas of Robert A. Mundell, Nobel Laureate
in Economic Sciences,* Thomas J. Courchene (ed.), 2002
Paper ISBN 0-88911-820-5 Cloth ISBN 0-88911-818-3

The State of Economics in Canada: Festschrift in Honour of David Slater,
Patrick Grady and Andrew Sharpe (eds.), 2001
Paper ISBN 0-88911-942-2 Cloth ISBN 0-88911-940-6

The 2000 Federal Budget: Retrospect and Prospect, Paul A.R. Hobson and
Thomas A. Wilson (eds.), Policy Forum Series no. 37, 2001
Paper ISBN 0-88911-816-7 Cloth ISBN 0-88911-814-0

Available from: McGill-Queen's University Press
c/o Georgetown Terminal Warehouses
34 Armstrong Avenue
Georgetown, Ontario L7G 4R9
Tel: (877) 864-8477
Fax: (877) 864-4272
E-mail: orders@gtwcanada.com